STRESS AND EMOTION

THE SERIES IN STRESS AND EMOTION:
ANXIETY, ANGER, AND CURIOSITY
(Formerly part of the Series in Clinical and Community Psychology)

CONSULTING EDITORS
Charles D. Spielberger and Irwin G. Sarason

STRESS AND EMOTION
Anxiety, Anger, and Curiosity

Volume 16

Edited by
Charles D. Spielberger
University of South Florida, Tampa, USA

Irwin G. Sarason
University of Washington, Seattle, USA

Guest Editors
John M. T. Brebner
University of Adelaide, South Australia

Esther Greenglass
York University, Toronto, Canada

Pittu Laungani
South Bank University, London, England

Ann M. O'Roark
Management and Leadership Development,
St. Petersburg, Florida, USA

Taylor & Francis
Publishers since 1798

USA	Publishing Office:	Taylor & Francis 1101 Vermont Avenue, N.W., Suite 200 Washington, DC 20005-3521 Tel: (202) 289-2174 Fax: (202) 289-3665
	Distribution Center:	Taylor & Francis 1900 Frost Road, Suite 101 Bristol, PA 19007-1598 Tel: (215) 785-5800 Fax: (215) 785-5515
UK		Taylor & Francis Ltd. 1 Gunpowder Square London EC4A 3DE Tel: 0171 583 0490 Fax: 0171 583 0581

STRESS AND EMOTION: Anxiety, Anger, and Curiosity, Volume 16

1 2 3 4 5 6 7 8 9 0   BRBR   9 8 7 6

This book was set in Times Roman by Harlowe Typography, Inc. The editors were Catherine Simon and Heather Jefferson. Cover design by Michelle M. Fleitz. Printing and binding by Braun-Brumfield, Inc.

A CIP catalog record for this book is available from the British Library.

⊗ The paper in this publication meets the requirements of the ANSI Standard Z39.48-1984 (Permanence of Paper)

Library of Congress Cataloging-in-Publication Data
Advanced Study Institute on Stress and Anxiety in Modern Life,
Murnau, Ger., 1973.

Stress and anxiety: [proceedings]/edited by Charles D. Spielberger,
Irwin G. Sarason. Washington: Hemisphere Publ. Corp.
   v. :ill.: 24 cm. (v. 1–2: The series in clinical psychology
   v. 3–5: The series in clinical and community psychology)
   Includes bibliographies and indexes.
   1. Stress, (Psychology)—Congresses. 2. Anxiety—Congresses.
I. Sarason, Irwin G., ed.   II. Spielberger, Charles Donald, date, ed.
III. North Atlantic Treaty Organization. Division of Scientific Affairs.
IV. Title. [DNLM: 1. Anxiety. 2. Stress, Psychological. WM 172 S755a]
BF575.S75A38   1973   616.8'522   74-28292
                          MARC

ISBN 1-56032-449-X
ISSN 1053-2161

Contents

I
ASSESSING STRESS, EMOTION, AND COPING IN DAILY LIFE

1 Social Support: Current Status, Current Issues   **3**
*Irwin G. Sarason, Barbara R. Sarason, Douglas M. Brock, and
Gregory R. Pierce*

2 Stress and Passionate Love   **29**
Elaine Hatfield and Richard L. Rapson

II
STRESS AND EMOTION IN THE WORKPLACE

III
STRESS AND EMOTION IN THE SCHOOLS

Contributors

JEFFREY R. BEDELL, Mt. Sinai Medical School, Elmhurst, New York, USA

Y. K. BHUSHAN, Narsee Monjee Institute of Management Studies, Bombay, India

JOHN M. T. BREBNER, University of Adelaide, South Australia, Australia

DOUGLAS M. BROCK, University of Washington, Seattle, Washington, USA

JOHN G. CARLSON, University of Hawaii, Honolulu, Hawaii, USA

JAIME L. CARR, Kent State University, Kent, Ohio, USA

FRANCES M. CULBERTSON, Madison Medical Center, Madison, Wisconsin, USA

DEBORAH DRAVING, Cambridge Hospital, Harvard School of Medicine, Boston, Massachusetts, USA

ROBERT GERVEY, Cambridge Hospital, Harvard School of Medicine, Boston, Massachusetts, USA

JOHN R. GRAHAM, Kent State University, Kent, Ohio, USA

ESTHER R. GREENGLASS, York University, Toronto, Ontario, Canada

PETRA HANK, University of Trier, Germany

KJELL J. HÅSETH, Institute of Psychology, University of Oslo, Oslo, Norway

ELAINE HATFIELD, University of Hawaii, Honolulu, Hawaii, USA

JUHANI JULKUNEN, Rehabilitation Foundation, Helsinki, Finland

SANDHYA KARPE, Narsee Monjee Institute of Management Studies, Bombay, India

ARCHNA KRISHNA, Himachal Pradesh University, Shimla, India

PITTU LAUNGANI, South Bank University, London, England

ANNA B. LEONOVA, Moscow State Lomonosov-University, Moscow, Russia

SHANKER MENON, University of South Florida, Tampa, Florida, USA

LAKSHMI NARAYANAN, University of South Florida, Tampa, Florida, USA

ANN M. O'ROARK, Management and Leadership Development, St. Petersburg, Florida, USA

GREGORY R. PIERCE, Hamilton College, Clifton, New York, USA

LOUIS H. PRIMAVERA, St. John's University, New York, New York, USA

RICHARD L. RAPSON, University of Hawaii, Honolulu, Hawaii, USA

BARBARA R. SARASON, University of Washington, Seattle, Washington, USA

IRWIN G. SARASON, University of Washington, Seattle, Washington, USA

PETER SCHWENKMEZGER, University of Trier, Germany
SAGAR SHARMA, Himachal Pradesh University, Shimla, India
CATHERINE Q. E. SIM, Tilburg University, The Netherlands
PAUL E. SPECTOR, University of South Florida, Tampa, Florida, USA
CHARLES D. SPIELBERGER, University of South Florida, Tampa,
    Florida, USA
NORBERT K. TANZER, Karl-Franzens-University, Graz, Austria
MARY E. WESTERBACK, Long Island University, New York, New York,
    USA

Foreword

Volume 16 of the series *Stress and Emotion* (formerly *Stress and Anxiety*) continues the remarkable chain of scientific publications on a topic of wide psychological interest and growing public concern. The majority of the chapters that appear in this volume are based on papers first presented to a critical scientific audience in symposia at the 23rd International Congress of Applied Psychology (ICAP) held in Madrid in July 1994.

The ICAP Congresses allow the International Association of Applied Psychology (IAAP) to unite several thousand psychologists from all over the world to advance the Association's mission of stimulating worldwide contact of applied psychologists with each other. As the sponsor of these quadrennial Congresses, the IAAP offers a unique opportunity to demonstrate the societal significance of applied psychological research. We take pride in helping to disseminate to an even wider audience the papers that make up this volume, which are conceptually and methodologically at the cutting edge of scientific inquiry, and come from a wide variety of social contexts. The volume thus fulfills a double function: It further promotes the scientific study of phenomena related to stress and emotion, and it also documents the major congress activities of the IAAP.

The gamut of the content of the papers assembled in this volume is broad, indeed. By inter-meshing studies of stress and emotion in different social settings (work, culture, professions, family, education) with studies on the impact of stress and emotion on health using a variety of instrumental assessment approaches, the editors have succeeded in highlighting a research field that will, no doubt, continue to merit growing attention from contributors to research in applied psychology.

The senior editor for Volumes 15 and 16 of this series, Charles D. Spielberger, deserves an accolade for placing, with lasting salience, the topics of the series onto the agenda of both basic and applied psychological discourse. Professor Spielberger will take over the presidency of our association on the occasion of the 24th ICAP Congress, which will be held in San Francisco, August 9–14, 1998, linked closely in time and space with the 106th Annual Convention of the American Psychological Association, which is contributing to the organization of the Congress. One may, therefore, justifiably expect that the beneficial synergies of IAAP Congresses and subsequent publication activities will continue well into the future.

Bernhard Wilpert, President, 1994–1998
International Association of Applied Psychology

Preface

Volume 16 of *Stress and Emotion: Anxiety, Anger, and Curiosity* reports theoretical formulations and empirical findings of investigators from three continents and nine countries. In keeping with previous volumes of this continuing series, most of the chapters in Volumes 15 and 16 are based on papers presented in four stress-related symposia at the 23rd International Congress of Applied Psychology convened in Madrid in July 1994. We are indebted to Drs. John M. T. Brebner, Esther Greenglass, Pittu Laungani, and Ann M. O'Roark for organizing these symposia and for their effective work in editing the papers given in their symposia, for publication in these volumes.

The four parts of Volume 16 focus on different aspects of the stress process, which involves the effects of stressful environmental events and personality dispositions on emotional reactions in a variety of life situations, and on coping, maladaptive behaviors, and stress-related disorders. Individual chapters examine the experience, expression, and control of emotions in different countries; the impact of stress on achievement, productivity, and adjustment in the workplace and in school settings; and the effects of stress, emotions, and coping on elevated blood pressure, cardiovascular disorders, posttraumatic stress reactions, and other adverse health consequences.

The chapters in Part I examine efforts to assess the interactive effects of stress and emotion in daily life. In the first chapter, Sarason and his colleagues provide a comprehensive analysis of the concept of social support and its impact on positive and negative emotions, self-concept, and social relationships. Hatfield and Rapson, in Chapter 2, report findings from their pioneering research on passionate love and describe procedures for measuring passionate love and romantic feelings. In Chapters 3, 4, and 5, current research on the assessment of the experience, expression, and control of anger in Singapore, the United States, and Norway is reported by Tanzer and his colleagues, Carr and Graham, and Håseth.

The effects of stress and emotion in the workplace are examined in Part II. The influence of occupational stress resulting from prolonged work in a demanding environment on job performance and the development of stress-related symptoms are reported in Chapter 6 by Leonova, who followed operator managers of a complex automated system for more than 6 years. Time urgency in health care professionals and the impact of family stress on working women are examined by Menon et al. and by Bhushan and Karpe in Chapters 7 and 8. In Chapter 9, Bedell and his colleagues demonstrate that teaching work skills and providing psychological support for persons with severe mental disorders can reduce occupational stress, enhance performance, and improve relationships with family and friends.

The effects of stress and emotion on academic performance, and on depression and blood pressure, are examined for high school and college students in Part III. Four of the five chapters in Part IV report findings from investigations in Canada, Finland, Germany, and India on the effects of the experience, expression, and control of anger and hostility on elevated blood pressure, hypertension, and cardiovascular disorders. From these studies, it is apparent that the expression and control of anger and hostility contribute in complex ways to elevated blood pressure and the progression of atherosclerosis. In the final chapter of Part IV, Carlson reviews procedures for assessing posttraumatic stress disorder and describes interventions that have proved effective in the treatment of PTSD.

This volume will be of interest to investigators who conduct research on stress, emotions, and health and to counselors, psychologists, and behavioral and medical scientists who are concerned with the assessment and treatment of stress-related disorders. The book's unique features include linking stress to research on passionate love and romantic relationships, and demonstrating important relations between emotional reactions to stress and the substantial body of research on social support and self-esteem. With expansion of the knowledge base for understanding how stress, emotions, and coping contribute to behavioral and medical problems, it will be possible to develop and implement more effective treatment and intervention programs for ameliorating and preventing stress-related disorders.

For their contributions to Volumes 15 and 16 of this continuing series, we would like to express our appreciation to the Guest Editors, and to Harry C. Triandis and Bernhard Wilpert, Presidents of the International Association of Applied Psychology in 1990–94 and 1994–98, respectively, for writing the Forewords to these volumes. We also thank Virginia Berch, Diane Gregg, Karen Giel, Eric Reheiser, and Karen Unger of the Center for Research in Behavioral Medicine and Health Psychology at the University of South Florida for their assistance in reviewing the manuscripts and preparing this volume for publication.

Charles D. Spielberger
Irwin G. Sarason

I

ASSESSING STRESS, EMOTION, AND COPING IN DAILY LIFE

1

Social Support:
Current Status, Current Issues

**Irwin G. Sarason, Barbara R. Sarason, and
Douglas M. Brock**
University of Washington, Seattle, USA

Gregory R. Pierce
Hamilton College, Clifton, New York, USA

Abstract *Social support is a concept of interest to researchers in psychology, sociology, and health-related areas. They are studying social support as it relates to clinical and adjustment outcomes, the behavioral and cognitive aspects of social interactions, and, most recently, the contributions to various outcomes of both global and relationship-specific support. This chapter reviews recent work on these topics, and provides an integrative framework for conceptualizing social support and its effects. This framework encompasses situational, interpersonal, and intrapersonal processes that influence various outcome variables. An important aspect of the social support process is the complex set of interacting events, which includes behavioral, cognitive, and affective components. A major piece of empirical evidence is that global perceptions of the forthcomingness of the social environment and relationship-specific perceptions make independent contributions to the prediction of outcomes. The study of social support needs to investigate the roles these two classes of perceptions play in various types of outcomes.*

Social support, either elicited or provided spontaneously, plays an important role in how people deal with challenges and threats. Supportive interactions and the presence of supportive relationships in people's lives have been shown to play a major role in physical health, emotional well-being, and work performance (B. Sarason, Sarason, & Pierce, 1990). Although supportive ties may create dilemmas for both providers and recipients, one's perception of a reliable support system of kin and friends often reduces the risk of disease, enhances recovery from mental and physical illnesses, and reduces the possibility of abuse to self and others.

Social support helps people manage the uncertainties associated with stress, and increases their sense of personal control or efficacy over their environment. When this happens, it facilitates coping with life transitions (e.g., death of family members, divorce, employment changes) and psychological adjustment to catastrophic conditions (e.g., natural disasters, trauma). Equally important, the receipt of support from others frequently moderates the effects of daily hassles and disappointments which can grow into major stressors. This chapter reviews research and theory concerning social support, particularly with regard to preparing for and coping with stress, and considers how supportive interventions promote adaptive coping.

ORIGINS OF SOCIAL SUPPORT RESEARCH

The formal history of research on social support is relatively brief, going back only a little over a decade, although the concept has a much longer history. Durkheim's (1951) development of the idea of anomie, Cooley's (1909) concept of the primary group, Bowlby's (1969) ideas on attachment, Rogers' (1942) conception of the therapeutic process, and Likert's (1961) focus on support as the core of the supervisory process are all examples of important theoretical perspectives that have contributed to present thinking about the role of social support in people's lives.

In addition to the work of these theorists and others, clinical observations, research findings, and political and social changes have provided impetus for work on social support. Clinicians first observed anecdotally, and then through formalized studies, that *support* (defined by the existence of a social network or confidant) prevented illness, reduced birth complications, and speeded recovery (e.g., Gore, 1978; Nuckolls, Cassel, & Kaplan, 1972). Administration of emotional support by health care personnel or others was shown to be beneficial to health in several studies (Auerbach & Kilmann, 1977; Whitcher & Fisher, 1979). Epidemiological research also provided data from large population samples indicating the effect of supportive relationships on mortality (Berkman & Syme, 1979; House, Robbins, & Metzner, 1982).

The common focus of much early work on social support involved the concept of support as a resource that moderated stress. Sociological studies suggested that stressors were more common in certain groups, such as the economically disadvantaged. During the 1960s in the United States, the "War on Poverty" resulted in large-scale intervention attempts focused on prevention, including preschool programs for children at risk, an emphasis on maternal health and well-child programs, community mental health centers, and a proliferation of support groups, many agency-sponsored. In all these areas, effort was directed at providing a variety of types of support—services, practical help, and provision of associations with others—that might help compensate for a deficiency in personal relationships (Pilisuk & Parks, 1986).

As this brief history indicates, many disciplines were interested in social support. As a result of this multidisciplinary interest, however, the definitions of *social support* reflect a variety of viewpoints. Perhaps one of the most urgent exhortations for anyone planning a research project involving social support is to look carefully at the definitions used in prior research efforts, on which the current project is built. In the initial work that sparked interest in the role of social support in health, its presence was often operationalized in simplistic ways—usually as the presence of a spouse or possibly a confidant. Although this definition is appealing because of its ease of measurement, it may be misleading because it lumps together emotionally satisfying and conflictual relationships. Early researchers in the social support field also used other measures of social relationships, including frequency of contacts with friends and relatives, number of such relationships, and membership in and attendance at meetings of organized groups. Like marital status, this information is relatively easy for subjects to report and quantify, although these measures are not as high as marital status in reliability of report. A combined measure that includes these questions is often referred to as a *measure of social integration*. The Social Network Index, developed by Berkman and Syme (1979) for the Alameda County study, represents a formalization of this approach.

A step forward in measuring social support came from attempts to understand the association between the presence of a close relationship to health. A number of theorists in the fields of epidemiology and sociology began to conceptualize social support in terms of the various functions that relationships fulfill (Cobb, 1976; Kaplan, Cassel, & Gore, 1977; Weiss, 1974). More recently, interest in social support as a personality variable has come to fore (Henderson, 1984; B. Sarason, Pierce, & Sarason, 1990; I. Sarason, Sarason, & Shearin, 1986).

THE SOCIAL SUPPORT CONCEPT

Research on social support has focused attention on three topics: (a) the idea that differences in interpersonal connectedness influence how people respond to various types of situations, (b) identification of supportive components of the environment, and (c) the individual's sense of being supported. This research has three aspects. The first concerns assessing social support and relating it to significant clinical and adjustment outcomes; the second concerns the relationship of assessed social support to behavior and cognitions in social interactions; and the third has to do with the relative contributions to a variety of outcomes of both global and relationship-specific support (B. Sarason et al., 1990). Global perceptions of the forthcomingness of the social environment and perceptions of the supportiveness of particular relationships are not the same thing, and they may play distinct and important roles in adjustment and health. Over the years, both types of perceptions have been described by writers, but they have rarely been compared. This chapter provides a thumbnail sketch of current work on conceptualizations and operationalizations of social support, with special attention to how social support functions, the distinction between the perception of social support availability and the actual receipt of support, and the types of interpersonal relationships that provide support.

Social Networks

Definitions of *social support* that emphasize interpersonal connectedness have led to inquiries concerning the structure of individuals' social networks (e.g., their size and correlates). Network analysts often base their studies on the assumption that structural features of a social network (e.g., the density or interconnectedness of network members) influence the impact that social interactions have on network members. This approach calls attention to differences in the patterns of social interaction characterizing different support networks. Measures of network size and availability or adequacy of support have been shown to be only weakly associated (Seeman & Berkman, 1988). This may be because neither the size of the network nor the size of the group of network members to whom the person feels close can indicate how much support he or she actually receives. In general, the evidence of network measures' usefulness in studying the relationship of social support to dependent measures (e.g., health) has not been impressive compared with the more easily administered measures of social support, which simply ask for the number of relationships (House & Kahn, 1985).

The Functions of Support

Researchers who are especially concerned with how social support functions have sought to specify those aspects of social support that are beneficial to individuals in specific types of stressful events. This approach was stimulated by Weiss' (1974) hypothesis that there are six specific provisions of social relationships: attachment, social integration, opportunity for nurturance, reassurance of worth, sense of reliable alliance, and guidance. Cohen and Wills (1985) theorized that the buffering effect of social support, which serves to insulate or partially protect those who are vulnerable to the effects of stress, is a function of the match between the particular need engendered by the stressor and the type of support given. A problem with existing instruments measuring specific functions of support is that the scales representing the different functions tend to be highly correlated. The intercorrelations often are as high as the scale reliabilities. This suggests that the scales are not measuring distinct constructs. For this reason, some researchers have expressed dissatisfaction with the functional approach as it is currently operationalized.

Received and Perceived Support

An important question concerns the relative contributions to adjustment of support received and support perceived to be available. Typically, information on support received from others is gathered from the self-report of the recipient, with the focus on the recipient's account of what he or she regarded as helpful. In using this information, it is important to note that the agreement between givers and recipients on the support given is often only moderate (50%–60%; Antonucci & Israel, 1986; Shulman, 1976). However, it would probably be a mistake to view this finding as an indication of a lack of validity regarding received support measures. Instead, this result underscores the need to consider both the evaluative aspects of social support (i.e., how recipients evaluate supportive efforts) and the objective features of supportive transactions.

The finding that a recipient's evaluation of supportive activity does not necessarily match reports by others suggests that an individual's report of social support reflects at least two elements: objective properties of supportive interactions, and the respondent's interpretation of the interactions. The importance of the subjective side of social support is reflected in the consistent finding that it is the *perception* of social support that is most closely related to adjustment and health outcomes (Antonucci & Israel, 1986; Blazer, 1982; Sandler & Barrera, 1984; Wethington & Kessler, 1986). A focus on perceived social support meshes with and is reinforced by the current emphasis in psychology on cognitive appraisal and the influence of cognitive schemata over behavior. It also fits well with the early conceptualizations of social support by Cobb (1976) and Cassel (1976). Cobb hypothesized that social support's major role is to convey to the individual that others care about and value him or her. Thus, the support emanates not so much from what is done, but from what that indicates to the recipient about the relationship. In a similar vein, Cassel argued that conveying caring and positive regard to the recipient is more responsible for positive outcomes than any specific behavior.

Evidence concerning the importance of perceptions of support suggests the need to consider both the intra- and interpersonal contexts in which supportive provisions become available (I. Sarason, Pierce, & Sarason, 1990). The intrapersonal context emphasizes personal perceptions of social relationships. Internal cognitive representations of self, important others, and the nature of interpersonal relationships influence perceptions of social support. The interpersonal context refers to the transactional quality of relationships (e.g., to what degree they are marked by conflict). Perceived support instruments usually inquire about the adequacy and availability of support. They tend to be only moderately intercorrelated, but the correlations are higher than those for measures based on other definitions, such as those that derive from the network or received support concepts.

The Social Support Questionnaire: A Measure of Perceived Support

Objective research on social support requires psychometrically sound, well-validated, and convenient indices. The Social Support Questionnaire (SSQ; I. Sarason, Levine, Basham, & Sarason, 1983) illustrates the development of instruments designed to assess perceived social support. It is quite reliable, and has considerable construct validity. It consists of 27 items, including: "Who accepts you totally, including your worst and your best points?" and "Whom could you count on to help you if you had just been fired from your job or expelled from school?" Subjects respond to these questions by listing the people who provide pertinent support. The SSQ yields two scores. The first one measures the number of available others individuals feel they can turn to in times of need (Number or Perceived Availability score). The second score measures satisfaction with the support perceived to be available (Satisfaction score). This is indicated on a 6-point Likert scale from *very dissatisfied* to *very satisfied*. The SSQ takes 15–18 minutes to administer, and has good internal consistency and test–retest reliability.

The SSQ was factor analytically derived from a large body of items intended to measure the functions served by social networks. Separate factor analyses of the two SSQ scores showed Number and Satisfaction to be composed of different, unitary dimensions. A large number of data sets have shown only a moderate correlation between the two components, with the correlations typically ranging between .30 and .40. Scores on Number and Satisfaction are negatively related to depression and anxiety, as well as to recollections of anxiety in childhood. The Number score is positively related to extraversion, whereas the Satisfaction score is inversely related to neurotics as measured by the Eysenck Personality Inventory (EPI; Eysenck & Eysenck, 1964). Both scores on the SSQ are negatively correlated with the tendency to experience loneliness, and neither score is significantly correlated with a social desirability response set. When the SSQ has been compared with an extensive structured interview designed to assess socially supportive relationships, the two approaches have yielded comparable results.

Because of the time constraints in many applied settings, a short form of the SSQ has been developed (I. Sarason, Sarason, Shearin, & Pierce, 1987). It consists of the six items that, over several data sets, produced the highest correlations with both the 27-item SSQ scores and the remaining individual SSQ items. The short form has good internal consistency and test–retest reliability, as well as a high degree of correlation with the original instrument. The short form's correlates with personality measures are also similar to those of the full-scale SSQ. It also provides a psychometrically acceptable index that can be obtained in 5 minutes or less.

SOCIAL SUPPORT AND INTERPERSONAL BEHAVIOR

Much research on social support has involved associations among assessed support, clinical outcomes, and field observations. The work described herein, and that of many other researchers, have provided evidence that perceived support is linked positively with physical and mental health indicators, ability to cope with stress, and a variety of self-perceptions. Although the study of social support initially involved assessing features of social networks that might predict these kinds of outcomes, interest has grown concerning both the links between assessed support and interpersonal relationships and the social stimulus value of individuals differing in social support levels.

Perhaps social support arises because an individual has interpersonal skills that attract others into mutual relationships. What is the connection between social support and social skills? With this question in mind, pairs of subjects differing in social support scores were videotaped while they spent 5 minutes getting acquainted and another 5 minutes discussing how to solve a hypothetical problem about a troublesome roommate (B. Sarason, Sarason, Hacker, &

Basham, 1985). Each subject's social skills were rated by the experimenter on the basis of his or her initial contact with the subject, by both the subject and the subject's partner, and finally by raters who viewed the videotape. In addition, the subjects completed a social competence questionnaire and measures of social skills.

Subjects high in self-described social support scored higher than those low in social support on all the social skills measures. The subject's appraisal of his or her own social competence, the appraisals of others, and the subject's knowledge of appropriate behavior in problem situations were correlated. Subjects low in social support appeared to both themselves and others to be less likeable and less effective than other people. Not only did both those high and low in social support elicit different responses from others, but they also seemed to have different cognitions in social situations. Individuals high in social support felt comfortable when interacting with others, whereas those low in social support described themselves as feeling uncomfortable, particularly when looking at others directly, and in getting people to notice them. They lacked confidence in their ability to make friends.

In the study just described, social support was studied as an individual-difference variable, with both cognitive and behavioral components, that plays a role in interpersonal transactions. It can also be approached from the standpoint of how groups differing in this individual-difference variable respond to supportive gestures and environments. In two laboratory studies, the effects of manipulations intended to provide support were investigated (Lindner, Sarason, & Sarason, 1988; I. Sarason & Sarason, 1986). In each study, the experimenter offered help, if needed, to students who were about to work on problem-solving tasks. The experimenter told the subjects that she would be available to them throughout their work, and would answer any questions. Although no subject requested help, those who were low in social support satisfaction, as assessed by the SSQ, performed significantly better after receiving the supportive communication than did those who had not received this communication. The supportive condition did not raise the performance of those high in support satisfaction. Thus, the study showed that supportive behavior may have differential effects depending on the degree to which a person perceives support to be generally available: Support was only helpful to those whose self-evaluated support was low.

More studies are needed to determine the effects of operationally defined supportive interventions on people who differ in their perceptions of support. In addition to their theoretical interest, these studies would have potential applied value by laying the groundwork for supportive interventions in situations for which it is desired to offer help to people experiencing chronic and acute stressors. In addition to obtaining answers to questions concerning whether particular interventions are effective under controlled conditions, it is important to carry out research designed to increase understanding of the process by which a supportive intervention has a positive effect, and to determine the characteristics of people who will experience such effects. What behaviors are intended by the provider to be supportive? Which of the provider's behaviors are used by the recipient in making attributions about the support he or she receives from the provider? What other factors influence the recipient's appraisals of the supportive interaction? What happens when one person tries to help another?

GLOBAL AND RELATIONSHIP-SPECIFIC PERCEPTIONS OF SUPPORT

Research on social support suggests that people have a set of general expectations and attributions about their personal relationships that reflect their ideas about how approachable and forthcoming people within the social environment are likely to be. This aggregate is what measures of perceived social support, like the SSQ, seem to be tapping. They may be assessing people's beliefs about whether others, in general, are likely to provide assistance and emotional support when needed (B. Sarason, Shearin, Pierce, & Sarason, 1987).

Person-specific expectations and attributions are not necessarily just instances of general or global perceptions of available support. In addition to generalized beliefs concerning social support, people also develop expectations and attributions about the availability of support in specific significant relationships. For example, a person who generally sees the social environment as far from benign and forthcoming might still have some specific relationships marked by warmth, caring, and reciprocity. Although general and relationship-specific expectations for social support may be correlated, they reflect different facets of perceived support. Global and relationship-based perceptions of support each play an important and unique role in personal adjustment. Pierce, Sarason, and Sarason (1991) investigated this issue by relating measures of both global and relationship-based expectations to personal adjustment. They found that perceptions of available support from specific relationships added to the prediction of loneliness, after accounting for the contribution made by global perceived available support. They concluded that an independent link exists between relationship-specific perceptions of available support and loneliness (Pierce et al., 1991). More knowledge is needed about this type of linkage. Research needs to explore the processes involved in shaping the distinctiveness of support associated with specific interpersonal relationships, as well as the mechanisms by which both aspects of perceived support (global and relationship-specific) relate to outcomes. Global and relationship-based perceptions of support might impact personal adjustment through quite different pathways. If so, theories of social support need to encompass these pathways.

Other aspects of personal relationships, besides the support they provide, probably play important roles in influencing outcomes. A feature of the Quality of Relationships Inventory (the relationship-specific measure employed by Pierce et al., 1991) is its assessment of perceived conflict, as well as support, in individual relationships. The fact that a relationship is supportive does not mean that it is without conflict. B. Sarason, Pierce, Bannerman, and Sarason (1993) investigated how parents' assessments of their children's positive and negative characteristics are related to each child's global and relationship-specific perceptions of social support. They found that family environments can be conceptualized in terms of specific relationships within the family that differ with regard to support and conflict: Mothers whose children saw their relationships as either conflictual or nonconflictual were equally likely to help their children, whereas fathers with whom children perceived conflict were less likely to be helpful. Generally, parents' descriptions of their children's positive and negative characteristics were more strongly related to their children's perceptions of the supportiveness of their parental relationships than to the children's general perceptions of the supportiveness of the social network of their peers.

AN INTERACTIONAL-COGNITIVE VIEW
OF SOCIAL SUPPORT

The various approaches that have been taken in social support research can seem puzzling. They often focus attention on promising, but different, aspects of the social support equation. Problems can arise when the available findings are lumped together without regard for the methodology employed. When this happens, the literature can appear inconsistent and even contradictory. Differences in the operationalization and assessment strategies associated with each approach limit the generalizability of research findings. For example, as has been seen, an important difference in assessment strategies concerns whether instruments focus on objective events (what actually happened) or subjective evaluations of supportiveness (e.g., perceptions of others' willingness to help).

Although there are many methodological questions that surround social support, its assessment, pertinent interventions, and validation procedures, it is important to focus attention on questions related to the nature of support, factors that pertain to it, and the support process. A model that emphasizes the interactive roles of the situational, intrapersonal, and interpersonal contexts of social transactions has been developed (I. Sarason et al., 1990). The *situational context* encompasses the event to which relationship participants respond. The event could range from minor to major, and from simple to complex (e.g., a bruise from a minor fall, a disappointing academic grade, the break-up of a romantic relationship, the loss of a job, and the death of a loved one are only a few illustrations). Many of these events involve a complex of pertinent considerations. For example, losing a job is likely to involve how much money the person has in the bank account; whether the job loss resulted from poor performance, product phase-out, or company move; and the current state of the job market. The aspect of the situational context that has received most attention concerns whether situations are stressful. However, a broader perspective of situations might be productive.

The *intrapersonal context* refers to the individual's unique, stable patterns of perceiving self, important others, and relational expectations. Bowlby's (1988) attachment theory has influenced studies of the intrapersonal context of social support because of its emphasis on the role of working or cognitive models in the formation of an individual's expectations, appraisals, and responses to the potentially supportive behavior of others, and the provision of support to others (B. Sarason et al., 1990). Working models are cognitive representations of self, important others, and the nature of relationships, which are linked to self-esteem; feelings of self-worth; and perceptions of being loved, valued, and cared for by others. Working models of others and of relationships with them lead to distinctive types of expectations and interpretations of others' behavior, which interact with situational and social processes. Research using the SSQ and other perceived social support measures has shown that attributions and expectations concerning the global availability of social support reflect a stable personality characteristic—the *sense of support* (B. Sarason et al., 1990). The sense of support is linked to an additional feature of personality, the *sense of acceptance*, which grows out of inferences about the self that are related to, but not necessarily implied in, the sense of support (B. Sarason et al., 1990; I. Sarason et al., 1990). The sense of acceptance is people's belief that others love and care for them and that they accept them for who they are, including their best and worst points. It is strengthened when people observe the support that others willingly provide to them, along with their unconditional acceptance. The sense of acceptance may be part of a coherent personality constellation that includes a positive self-image, a favorable view of social relationships, and an expectation that others value them. People who are confident that others will meet their support needs may be able to undertake challenging tasks without excessive preoccupation about failure because they anticipate sufficient support and resources to meet potential demands.

The *interpersonal context* includes the distinctive qualitative and quantitative (e.g., support, conflict, network size, density) features of specific relationships, as well as those of the larger social networks in which these relationships take place. There are several features of relationships that strongly influence the impact of social support on health and well-being. These include interpersonal conflict, the sensitivity with which one participant responds to the support needs of the other participant, and the structure of their interpersonal connections. Cohen and Lichtenstein (1990) showed that the context of a close relationship mediates the impact of specific supportive or nonsupportive behaviors. Accumulating evidence indicates that the impact of social support is influenced (reduced) strongly by the presence of interpersonal conflict (Coyne & DeLongis, 1986; Zavislak, & Sarason, 1991). Support received in the context of conflictual relationships may lead to feelings of indebtedness and ambivalence in the recipient, which increase, rather than decrease, stress (Pierce, Sarason, & Sarason, 1990). Another aspect of the interpersonal context is the extent to which a support provider is aware of and sensitive to the needs of the recipient.

Supportive efforts are successful under certain conditions, but not necessarily others, and these conditions interact with the nature of the relationship between the provider and recipient (Pierce, Sarason, & Sarason, 1996). For example, Dakof and Taylor (1990) found that the effectiveness of a supportive intervention depends on its context, with particular actions being perceived to be helpful from some, but not other, network members. Dakof and Taylor suggested that future investigations of social support might benefit from identifying the source as well as the type of support. Simons, Lorenz, Wu, and Conger (1993) found that spouse support is a more powerful determinant of quality of parenting when social network support is low. Bristol, Gallagher, and Schopler (1988) also found that spousal support plays an important role in quality of parenting. The recipient, the provider, and their relationship need to be studied in an effort to better understand the give and take of social support processes.

The effect of support given to individuals varies as a function of the providers' and recipients' histories of reciprocal supportive relationships. The study by B. Sarason et al. (1993), mentioned earlier, investigated how parents' assessments of their children's positive and negative characteristics are related to each child's general and relationship-specific perceptions of social support and the status of the parent–child relationship. The results of this study were consistent with an interactional view of social support, according to which characteristics of both the recipient and support provider are important determinants of perceptions of social support and outcome measures. The family environment would appear to be a productive setting in which to study the support process. Although general family environmental factors play important roles in perceptions of support availability, specific family relationships make significant contributions (Gurung, Sarason, Keeker, & Sarason, 1992). For some types of questions, relationship-specific measures of social support might be better predictors than measures of general perceived support.

There is great potential in a broadened theoretical perspective of social support that includes life-long units like the family. Such a perspective calls for attention to contemporaneous interactional processes, as well as their origins and development. As Newcomb (1990) pointed out, social support is a personal resource that evolves throughout life. He argued for abandonment of the conception of social support as a unidirectional provision of resources from the external social environment to the individual.

SOCIAL SUPPORT AND COPING

Stress calls forth efforts to reach an acceptable or satisfying resolution to the problem that created the stress. *Coping* refers to how people deal with difficulties in an attempt to overcome them. It is a complex process that involves personality characteristics, personal relationships, and situational parameters. Discussions of coping often start at the time at which a specified event occurs. Lazarus' (1991) model of coping, which emphasizes primary and secondary appraisals, falls into this category. Temporality also plays a role in the buffering hypothesis, according to which social support is beneficial primarily at the time individuals are coping with stress (Cohen & Wills, 1985). However, putting the focus on events when they happen ignores the role that various factors play in whether unwanted life events to which an individual must respond actually occur. Researchers have devoted little attention to the question of why some individuals experience certain types of difficulties while others do not (see Bandura, 1986, for an exception). Both social relationships and personality characteristics play a role in the way individuals construct their environments. Life events are not randomly assigned to individuals, and people—and their social networks—play important roles in how they experience and respond to stressful life events.

Perceived social support influences coping through appraisal of situations and the personal characteristics of the important actors in them. B. Sarason et al. (1991) found that individuals high in perceived social support were more accurate in estimating the personal characteristics of their peers than were others. They also found that high perceived support subjects attributed more positive and less negative attributes to themselves than did other subjects, and that these attributions were positively related to their parents' and peers' perceptions of them. Perceived social support may foster more accurate and positive appraisals of self and others; this, in turn, may enable individuals to develop more effective and realistic coping strategies for dealing with particular situations.

Besides strengthening appraisals of personal resources and exploratory behavior, perceived social support may also enable individuals to confront challenges more effectively because they believe others will help them if the challenge exceeds their personal resources. In one study, subjects high in perceived social support experienced fewer distracting cognitions while completing intellectual tasks and correctly solved more problems than did other subjects (I. Sarason & Sarason, 1986). Other research suggests that individuals who perceive themselves as having good support are more interpersonally effective than others (e.g., they are better able to assume a leadership role and more considerate in their interactions with others; I. Sarason, Sarason, & Shearin, 1986). Thus, perceived social support may serve to promote self-confidence and personal effectiveness which enhance the individual's coping repertoire.

Interactions with others are based, in part, on expectations about how those others will respond. Although high perceived support individuals approach others for support based on their expectation that others are likely to provide help, those low in perceived social support may avoid asking others for assistance because they fear it will not be provided. One reason for this difference may be that high perceived support individuals have higher self-esteem, feel they are valued by others, and therefore are less concerned about how others might perceive them should they need to request assistance. Other evidence supporting this idea comes from an experimental study of social support in which subjects interacted with a confederate trained to provide one of two types of social support to subjects who were preparing to give a speech (Pierce & Contey, 1992). Despite the extensive training given to confederates (who were blind to subjects' level of perceived social support), when randomly assigned to subjects low in perceived social support, confederates provided fewer acts of emotional (e.g., positive feedback) or instrumental (i.e., advice) support than they did to subjects high in perceived social support. People high in perceived social support may provide potential support providers with more opportunities to administer support. Perceived social support influences coping in three ways. It could lead individuals to (a) structure situations so that stressful life events are relatively unlikely to occur, (b) develop effective personal coping skills, and (c) seek and obtain assistance when it is needed.

SUPPORTIVE RELATIONSHIPS

Although people have relatively well-formed expectations and attributions about support in general, they also have specific expectations about the availability of support from particular significant people in their lives. Evidence reported by Pierce et al. (1990) and I. Sarason et al. (1990) suggests that relationship-specific cognitions are not simply the building blocks for general perceptions of available support. Although a person's global and relationship-specific expectations for social support may be related, they reflect different aspects of perceived support, and each may play an important and unique role in coping and well-being. Perceived support grows out of a history of supportive experiences, especially with family members (e.g., parents). The general expectations one has about the forthcomingness of others, in turn, influence whether and how an individual approaches others to form new potentially supportive relationships. Perceived social support, as a working model of relationships, may be especially influential in the formative stages of a relationship before individuals have developed clear ideas about how they would like their relationship partner, as opposed to others in general, to respond in particular situations. As a relationship progresses and relationship-specific expectations develop, each person's global expectations may become less influential in the relationship.

It is also possible for expectations developed within a specific relationship to influence general perceptions of social support. For example, one of the goals of psychotherapy is to provide the client with an interpersonal context in which to revise general working models regarding the nature of personal relationships. By developing a therapeutic alliance, the client and therapist are able to interact to help the client create healthier, more positive views of relationships. This work is often made possible by analysis of the transference relationship, which results in the client's revision of previously established working models of personal relationships.

Support can play a role not only in coping with events once they have occurred, but also in avoiding or preventing the occurrence of stressful events. More attention needs to be paid to preventive coping, which reduces the likelihood of unwanted, undesirable events occurring. Social support can influence coping either by (a) rendering an individual less vulnerable to experiencing a specific life event, or (b) facilitating coping before a situation reaches a maximum point of stressfulness. This could happen as a product of a process that begins with perceptions of support, leads to a problem-solving orientation and willingness to explore the environment, and culminates in an enhanced coping repertoire. This view of social support and coping meshes with Bowlby's (1988) attachment theory—that a secure attachment enhances a child's exploratory behavior and coping skills. These skills, in turn, enhance feelings of personal effectiveness or self-efficacy.

As mentioned earlier, the term *social support* has been an umbrella term that covers a variety of diverse phenomena. A large percentage of research studies on the topic deal with associations between assessed support and particular aspects of life, including health status, illness, recovery from illness, adjustment and psychological functioning, and performance. A review of this research leads to the confident conclusion that social support is a good thing to have. People with satisfying levels of support seem to cope better with stress, are healthier and recover from illness more quickly, are better adjusted, and perform better, especially in the domains of social interaction and interpersonal social skills. Thus, in many ways, perceived social support functions as an individual-difference variable. It remains stable over time, even during periods of developmental transition (I. Sarason et al., 1986).

If it is a good thing to have, and if it inheres within the individual, what is it that is doing the inhering? Perhaps it is a set of working models of oneself, the social forthcomingness of others, and relationships with particular people. These working models lead a person to conclusions about the degree to which he or she is valued—not for surface characteristics, such as mathematics ability, but as someone who is worthy of being loved, valued, and unconditionally accepted. This conclusion influences: (a) development of current relationships with others, (b) acquisition of feelings of self-efficacy that are both generalized and related to specific tasks, (c) perceived availability of social support, and (d) effectiveness in stress coping and the ability to maintain a task focus.

Much research on social support has been directed toward two topics: social support as a stress moderator and the assessment of social support. If the lack of social support is a factor in negative health and adjustment outcomes, more needs to be known about how support is, or can be, provided in an effective manner. Surprisingly, the topic of the *provision of social support* (i.e., how it is provided, by whom, and under what circumstances) has barely been touched on in research. The provision of support has been widely discussed in terms of its role in personal development, clinical processes, and behavior observed in laboratory settings. However, more empirical information is needed about support provision in everyday life. What types of support are most helpful? Do some have negative side effects? Is the outcome of support the same for all people? Should interventions be directed mainly at high-risk groups? More knowledge is also needed about how to help individuals raise their own overall support level, as well as how they might obtain support in particular types of situations.

All of these questions lend themselves to inquiry within the laboratory and in field studies. Supportive interventions exist for a variety of problems, including bereavement in adults and children, divorce, cancer, and unemployment (Gottlieb, 1988). Lehman, Ellard, and Wortman (1986) investigated the impact of friends' supportive comments on bereaved individuals. Gottlieb (1985) studied the effective elements of group interventions on children of divorcing parents, as well as the effects of supportive involvements on both members of adult-child/elderly dependent-parent duos. I. Sarason (1981) found that social support positively influenced subjects' performance in an evaluative situation. Heller and his co-workers (Heller, 1979; Heller & Swindle, 1983; Procidano & Heller, 1983) investigated the effects of the presence of others, either intimates or strangers, on performance in stressful laboratory situations, in which overall support was analyzed as an individual-difference variable.

When the social support concept first became of interest, its preventive, or curative, potentials were recognized. Support can be provided at various levels—ranging from the community, as a stabilizing force in a troubled individual's life, to the empathy a loved one feels and expresses toward someone facing real or imagined difficulties. Rather than sapping self-reliance, strong ties with others—particularly family members—seem to encourage it. Reliance on others and self-reliance are not only compatible, but complementary to one another. Although many examples could be given of social support's role as a buffer against stress, how to communicate support in a way that does not unduly tax the communicator and nurturer needs to be better understood. The Lehman et al. (1986) findings concerning the counterproductive effects of friends' "supportive" utterances to bereaved parents underlines the importance of this need, as do studies in the area of chronic illness. For example, Coyne and DeLongis (1986) found that inappropriate, poorly timed, or over-solicitous support from a spouse may prove quite stressful for chronically ill patients. Revenson and Majerovitz (1990) studied supportive interactions between rheumatoid arthritis patients and their spouses. They found that, although spouses are important sources of support for patients, the amount and quality of extrafamilial support available to the spouses influenced how supportive they were toward the patients.

It is important to analyze the experience or situation that requires an individual to need support. For example, Jacobson (1990) analyzed stress and support in stepfamily formation, and found that a central task in the process is family members' reorganization of their assumptions concerning family interactions and responsibilities. The process of remarriage calls for revision and disassembly of the microculture of the first marriage, and creation of a new social system. From this perspective, support includes information and motivation that enables individuals to undertake a process of cognitive restructuring. Such support offers feedback that alters the way in which a person views and experiences the world, and enables him or her to achieve a better "fit" between the assumptive world and the self or environment. Self-help groups provide contexts in which individuals can reflect on the ideas that shape their behavior, and then begin developing alternative perspectives from which to evaluate and establish the meaning of the circumstances in which they find themselves.

Strong evidence that support can be beneficially provided in real-world settings comes from the areas of health and medical intervention. Kennell, Klaus, McGrath, Robertson, and Hinkley (1991) studied the effects of emotional support given by a companion to a woman during labor and delivery. Compared with no-treatment controls, they found that the presence of a supportive companion (another woman) had a significant positive effect on clinical outcomes. The companion met the study participant for the first time after hospital admission. The companion stayed at her assigned patient's bedside from admission through delivery, soothing and touching the patient and giving encouragement. In addition, she explained to the patient what was occurring during labor and what was likely to happen next. The provision of social support had a number of effects, including fewer Caesarian sections being necessary in the supported group, in contrast with the control group. The supported group also had significantly fewer forceps deliveries than did the control group, and fewer infants born to mothers in the supported group required a prolonged hospital stay.

Relatedly, Bertsch, Nagashima-Whalen, Dykeman, Kennell, and McGrath (1990) found significant differences in clinical outcomes when either male partners of obstetrical patients or female companions (who were strangers) were present. Male partners chose to be present for less time during labor and to be close to the mother less often than the female companions. Further study is needed of the most active ingredients of the supportive process in this type of situation. Answers are needed to such questions as: Does a supportive companion reduce catecholamine levels? Does this happen because maternal anxiety is reduced and uterine contractions and uterine blood flow are facilitated? A companion's constant presence, physical touch, reassurance, explanations, and anticipatory guidance probably all play roles, and may contribute to the laboring woman feeling safer and calmer, and needing less obstetrical intervention for labor to proceed smoothly.

Provided support has been shown to play significant (but not necessarily simple) roles in several medical areas besides obstetrics. Coyne and Smith (1991) found that wives' ability to help their husbands cope with a heart attack depended on several factors: the character of the infarction, the couples' interactions with medical personnel, and the quality of their marital relationship. In a study of recovery from coronary artery surgery, King, Reis, Porter, and Norsen (1993) found that patients' general esteem support was the only type of support that consistently accounted for a unique share of the relationship between social support and surgery outcome. These researchers concluded that the influence of general esteem support on feelings of well-being probably derived from the person feeling valued, loved, and competent.

The evidence concerning the relationship among social support, mental health, physical health, and recovery from illness suggests that, although social support alone may play an important role, it may also interact with other individual-difference and environmental variables, which need to be identified and evaluated.

SOCIAL SUPPORT, ANXIETY, AND ATTENTION

Stress induces high levels of anxiety with its many physiological and psychological concomitants. Studies of the effects of companions on the labor process and obstetrical complications suggest the important role the presence of a caring person can play in bodily processes under stressful situations. Along the same line, Kamarck, Manuck, and Jennings (1990) investigated the effects of a nonevaluative social interaction on cardiovascular responses to psychological challenge. In one condition, a friend accompanied a college student who participated in two laboratory tasks. In the other condition, the subject came to the laboratory unaccompanied. Subjects who were accompanied by a friend showed reduced heart-rate (HR) reactivity to both tasks relative to the alone condition. The results suggest that interpersonal support reduces the likelihood of anxiety and exaggerated cardiovascular responsivity.

Many studies indicate that social support can reduce the anxiety and panic often experienced by disaster victims. Most of the evidence supporting this conclusion comes from naturalistic and correlational studies. However, the evidence from these studies is consistent with controlled research, which has shown that supportive interventions reduce feelings of anxiety and personal insecurity, and increase self-confidence (I. Sarason & Sarason, 1986). Supportive interventions may exert their anxiety-reducing influence by reducing impersonality and diminishing concerns about the unavailability of people on whom the individual can rely. Effective social support interventions reduce perceptions of social isolation (Jones, Hobbs, & Hockenbury, 1982; Peplau & Perlman, 1982).

If providing social support accomplished no more than anxiety reduction and enhanced well-being, its contribution would be substantial. However, support also may play an important role in facilitating attention to important factors in a stressful situation and enabling effective coping efforts. There is considerable evidence that cognitive interference, often in the form of self-preoccupation, reduces the ability to be task-focused under challenging conditions (I. Sarason et al., 1990). This happens because concerns about real/potential threats and self-preoccupations interfere with task-relevant thought. Thoughts about off-task matters and a general wandering of attention from the task function as cognitive intrusions in problem solving. I. Sarason (1981) showed that an opportunity for social association and acceptance by others improves performance and reduces cognitive interference. Lindner et al. (1988) also found that a supportive intervention positively affects cognitive functioning and performance.

THE SENSE OF SUPPORT AND THE SENSE OF ACCEPTANCE

Evidence that perceived availability of support, more than support actually received, influences health and adjustment suggests that critical factors in influencing behavioral and health outcomes might be the *expectations* that people hold concerning the receipt of supportive behaviors and social attributions based on personal cognitive models. Although social support is often communicated through specific behaviors, such as money loans, advice, and willingness to listen uncritically to another's concerns, the offer of these provisions does not constitute social support per se, nor should each of these supportive behaviors be viewed as necessarily distinct categories of support. The most active ingredient of social support might be individuals' beliefs that they have people who value and care about them, and who are willing to help them if they need assistance or other support. With this in mind, Hellstedt (1987) emphasized the importance of coaches' and parents' interest and involvement in athletes' activities.

Although mentors, parents, and friends may differ in their ability to provide specific types of support, knowing that one is loved and that others will do all they can when a problem arises may be the essence of social support. This theoretical perspective does not mean that sampling the availability of particular supportive acts will not provide useful information about social support. Certain behaviors are more likely to convey support than others. To the extent that these behaviors typically reflect the degree to which the individual is cared for, measures of supportive behaviors—either perceived or received—will be measuring social support.

Evidence that the perception of social support's availability is important with regard to health and personal adjustment outcomes is a useful fact. From a theoretical perspective, it may be a potential clue to the processes by which these outcomes are attained. The effects of perceived support might be brought about in several ways. For some people, in certain contexts, perceived support might serve as a stress buffer. Knowing that other people are available to provide help in a particular situation might aid the individual in the coping process. For example, knowing that a coach is available to assist in batting skills may provide the individual with an opportunity to pull out of his or her slump. However, the effect of this specific intervention might not generalize to other performance skills. Perceptions of the willingness of specific and generalized others to help, comfort, and be interested may have generalized as well as specific effects. Viewing support in terms of disaggregated social needs and provisions (e.g., guidance concerning batting skills) may lead to a focus on specific effects (e.g., coping with a particular setback or problem). This focus neglects potential long-term or generalized effects of perceived support, which may be especially important with regard to the role that significant interpersonal relationships play in personality development, generalized ways of relating to others, and cognitive models of reality. In the example discussed earlier, it may be that the coach's communication of respect and confidence concerning the player's efforts to face challenges may be more important in establishing and achieving performance goals than discussing specific skills.

Research has focused on two types of cognitions related to perceived support (I. Sarason et al., 1990). One is the *sense of support*—the belief that there are supportive others who are willing and able to provide support, regardless of what might be required or the sacrifices that might have to be made to provide it. The sense of support may enable an individual to confront a stress-arousing situation that might otherwise seem insurmountable. Many psychological interventions with athletes emphasize the development of individual skills (e.g., particular stress-coping strategies; Greenspan & Feltz, 1989). Although expanding the behavioral repertoire of athletic competitors is clearly valuable, the important role of interpersonal factors should not be neglected.

The second type of cognition, the *sense of acceptance*, stems from inferences about the self that are related to, but not necessarily implied, in the sense of support. People's belief that others accept them for who they are, including their best and worst points, is strengthened when they observe the support others willingly provide to them. When this happens, people conclude that they must have some commendable attributes to elicit such positive responses from others. From this point of view, the sense of acceptance is part of a coherent personality constellation that promotes effective coping with demands and challenges, and fosters the ability to take advantage of opportunities, particularly social ones. It may be especially important in personality development because it initiates a chain of events that contributes to the development of competencies, which stand individuals in good stead in dealing with situations in a task-oriented manner. When this happens, the likelihood of experiencing stress is reduced.

The following salient features have emerged as correlates or consequences of the sense of acceptance: effective interpersonal skills, willingness to explore and take reasonable risks, a sense of self-efficacy leading to effective coping with stressors, low levels of anxiety, positive self-image, expectations of desirable outcomes of social interactions, and a benign view of other people (I. Sarason et al., 1983, 1987). All of these correlates are consistent with the idea that social support is generally a good thing (I. Sarason et al., 1983, 1987). Although meaningful social ties help people meet the challenges of life, people also learn a lot about the social environment and themselves from ordinary life experiences. The models of reality constructed from this learning are often quite stable. When this happens, the models influence all aspects of people's lives. Self-reports concerning the availability of social support and acceptance from others are very stable over many months and even years (I. Sarason et al., 1983).

Evidence is mounting that perceived support is part of an individual's personality. Lakey and Heller (1988) concluded that the generalized appraisal that one is cared for and valued is not necessarily anchored in any specific relationship or particular helping transaction, but rather has become integrated into the personality. Doubtless, a host of factors—including temperament, heredity, and physiological processes—play a role in the perception of social support. Certainly, many questions remain to be answered. How does the sense of having support originate? How does it influence behavior and health? Answers to these questions may be uncovered as the nexus of personality is better understood—shaping interpersonal relationships that influence individuals' assumptions, hopes, and expectations concerning what they and the world are all about. It is interesting that, in sport-related research, successful competitors have been found to be high in self-confidence, loyalty, and conscientiousness, all of which are consistent with characteristics associated with the sense of support and sense of acceptance (Gill, 1986).

Each individual engages in many relationships differing in quality and depth of caring. The essence of a supportive relationship is the communication of acceptance and love. It is the feeling of being loved and valued—the perception that one's well-being is the concern of significant others—that is protective. Yet the primary effect of these communicated feelings is not to protect one from possible harm per se, but to foster the feeling that one is worthwhile, capable, and a valued member of a group of individuals. When this happens, people feel that the resources necessary for the pursuit and achievement of their goals are available to them, either within themselves or through a combination of their own efforts and those of significant others.

CONCLUSIONS

Social support theories need to incorporate the complexity of situational, interpersonal, and intrapersonal processes that shape individuals' perceptions of their social interactions with the significant people in their lives. The study of social support requires a focus not only on general perceptions of social support, but also on the diversity of cognitions, emotions, and behaviors associated with specific personal relationships that shape behavior and well-being under diverse circumstances.

A theoretical perspective that encompasses situational, interpersonal, and intrapersonal processes has implications for the research agenda of the future. What are the cognitive models that lead people to relate to others as they do? Can these models and the behavior that flows from them be influenced, for example, by particular interventions? How do relationships between people and the personal meanings attached to them change over time? The realization that neither social support nor personal relationships are invariant or guaranteed for life has implications for a systems view of the individual. Although the individual is, at any point in time, part of a system that includes situational, interpersonal, and intrapersonal vectors, this multidimensional system undergoes changes over time. Researchers need to improve their ability to describe these processes and their outcomes.

It is now clear that social support is not simply assistance that is exchanged among network members, nor is it solely an appraisal of that assistance, nor it is only one's perceptions of network members. Instead, social support reflects a complex set of interacting events, including behavioral, cognitive, and affective components. Despite this complexity, one finding consistently emerges: Personal relationships are an active, crucial ingredient in the social support equation. An adequate understanding of social support processes must specify the role of personal relationships in the provision, receipt, and appraisal of support.

REFERENCES

Antonucci, T. C., & Israel, B. A. (1986). Veridicality of social support: A comparison of principal and network members' responses. *Journal of Consulting and Clinical Psychology, 54*, 432–437.

Auerbach, S. M., & Kilmann, P. R. (1977). Crisis intervention: A review of outcome research. *Psychological Bulletin, 84*, 1189–1217.

Bandura, A. (1986). *Social foundations of thought and action: A social cognitive theory.* Englewood Cliffs, NJ: Prentice-Hall.

Berkman, L. F., & Syme, S. L. (1979). Social networks, host resistance, and mortality: A nine-year follow-up study of Alameda County residents. *American Journal of Epidemiology, 109,* 186–204.

Bertsch, T. D., Nagashima-Whalen, L., Dykeman, S., Kennell, J.H., & McGrath, S. (1990). Labor support by first-time fathers: Direct observations. *Journal of Psychosomatic Obstetric Gynecology, 11,* 251–260.

Blazer, D. (1982). Social support and mortality in an elderly community population. *American Journal of Epidemiology, 115,* 684–694.

Bowlby, J. (1969). *Attachment and loss: Vol. 1. Attachment.* New York: Basic Books.

Bowlby, J. (1988). Developmental psychiatry comes of age. *American Journal of Psychiatry, 145,* 1–10.

Bristol, M. M., Gallagher, J. J., & Schopler, E. (1988). Mothers and fathers of young developmentally disabled and nondisabled boys: Adaptation and spousal support. *Developmental Psychology, 24,* 441–451.

Cassel, J. (1976). The contribution of the social environment to host resistance. *American Journal of Epidemiology, 104,* 107–123.

Cobb, S. (1976). Social support as a moderator of life stress. *Psychosomatic Medicine, 38,* 300–314.

Cohen, S., & Lichtenstein, E. (1990). Partner behaviors that support quitting smoking. *Journal of Consulting and Clinical Psychology, 58,* 304–309.

Cohen, S., & Wills, T. A. (1985). Stress, social support, and the buffering hypothesis. *Psychological Bulletin, 98,* 310–357.

Cooley, C. H. (1909). *Social organization: A study of the larger mind.* New York: Scribner.

Coyne, J. C., & DeLongis, A. M. (1986). Going beyond social support: The role of social relationships in adaptation. *Journal of Consulting and Clinical Psychology, 54,* 454–460.

Coyne, J. C., & Smith, D. A. F. (1991). Couples coping with a myocardial infarction: A contextual perspective on wives' distress. *Journal of Personality and Social Psychology, 61,* 404–412.

Dakof, G. A., & Taylor, S. E. (1990). Victims' perceptions of social support: What is helpful from whom? *Journal of Personality and Social Psychology, 58,* 80–89.

Durkheim, E. (1951). *Suicide: A study in sociology* (J. A. Spaulding & G. Simpson, Trans.). New York: Free Press.

Eysenck, H. J., & Eysenck, S. B. G. (1964). *Manual of the Eysenck Personality Inventory.* London: University of London Press.

Gill, D. C. (1986). *Psychological dynamics of sport.* Champaign, IL: Human Kinetics Publishers.

Gore, S. (1978). The effects of social support in moderating the health consequences of unemployment. *Journal of Health and Social Behavior, 19,* 157–165.

Gottlieb, B. H. (1985). Social support and the study of personal relationships. *Journal of Social and Personal Relationships, 2,* 351–375.

Gottlieb, B. H. (1988). Marshaling social support: The state of the art in research and practice. In B. H. Gottlieb (Ed.), *Marshaling social support* (pp. 11–51). Newbury Park, CA: Sage.

Greenspan, M. J., & Feltz, D. L. (1989). Psychological interventions with athletes in competitive situations: A review. *The Sport Psychologist, 3,* 219–236.

Gurung, R. A. R., Sarason, B. R., Keeker, K. D., & Sarason, I. G. (1992, August). *Family environments, specific relationships, and general perceptions of adjustment.* Paper presented at the annual meeting of the American Psychological Association, Washington, DC.

Heller, K. (1979). The effects of social support: Prevention and treatment implications. In A. P. Goldstein & F. H. Kanfer (Eds.), *Maximizing treatment gains: Transfer enhancement in psychotherapy* (pp. 253–282). New York: Academic Press.

Heller, K., & Swindle, R. W. (1983). Social networks, perceived social support, and coping with stress. In R. D. Felner, L. A. Jason, J. N. Moritsugu, & S. S. Farber (Eds.), *Preventive psychology: Theory, research and practice* (pp. 87–103). Elmsford, NY: Pergamon.

Hellstedt, J. C. (1987). The coach/parent/athlete relationship. *The Sport Psychologist, 1,* 151–160.

Henderson, S. (1984). Interpreting the evidence on social support. *Social Psychiatry, 19,* 49–52.

House, J. S., & Kahn, R. L. (1985). Measures and concepts of social support. In S. Cohen & S. L. Syme (Eds.), *Social support and health* (pp. 83–108). Orlando, FL: Academic Press.

House, J. S., Robbins, C., & Metzner, H. L. (1982). The association of social relationships and activities with mortality: Prospective evidence from the Tecumseh Community Health Study. *American Journal of Epidemiology, 116,* 123–140.

Jacobson, D. (1990). Stress and support in stepfamily formation: The cultural context of social support. In B. R. Sarason, I. G. Sarason, & G. R. Pierce (Eds.), *Social support: An interactional view* (pp. 199–218). New York: Wiley.

Jones, W. H., Hobbs, S. A., & Hockenbury, D. (1982). Loneliness and social skills deficits. *Journal of Personality and Social Psychology, 42,* 682–689.

Kamarck, T. W., Manuck, S. B., & Jennings, J. R. (1990). Social support reduces cardiovascular reactivity to psychological challenge: A laboratory model. *Psychosomatic Medicine, 52,* 42–58.

Kaplan, B. H., Cassel, J., & Gore, S. (1977). Social support and health. *Medical Care, 15,* 47–58.

Kennell, J., Klaus, M., McGrath, S., Robertson, S., & Hinkley, C. (1991). Continuous emotional support during labor in a U.S. hospital: A randomized controlled trial. *Journal of American Medical Association, 265,* 2197–2201.

King, K. B., Reis, H. T., Porter, L. A., & Norsen, L. H. (1993). Social support and long-term recovery from coronary artery surgery: Effects on patients and spouses. *Health Psychology, 12,* 56–63.

Lakey, B., & Heller, K. (1988). Social support from a friend, perceived support, and social problem solving. *American Journal of Community Psychology, 16,* 811–824.

Lazarus, R. S. (1991). *Emotion and adaptation.* New York: Oxford University Press.

Lehman, D. R., Ellard, J. H., & Wortman, C. B. (1986). Social support for the bereaved: Recipients' and providers' perspectives on what is helpful. *Journal of Personality and Social Psychology, 54,* 438–446.

Likert, R. (1961). *New patterns of management.* New York: McGraw-Hill.

Lindner, K. C., Sarason, I. G., & Sarason, B. R. (1988). Assessed life stress and experimentally provided social support. In C. D. Spielberger, I. G. Sarason, & P. B. Defares (Eds.), *Stress and anxiety* (Vol. 11, pp. 231–240). Washington, DC: Hemisphere.

Newcomb, M. D. (1990). Social support and personal characteristics: A developmental and interactional perspective. *Journal of Social and Clinical Psychology, 9,* 54–68.

Nuckolls, K. G., Cassel, J., & Kaplan, B. H. (1972). Psychosocial assets, life crises, and the prognosis of pregnancy. *American Journal of Epidemiology, 95,* 431–441.

Peplau, K. A., & Perlman, P. (Eds). (1982). *Loneliness: A sourcebook of current theory, research, and therapy.* New York: Wiley.

Pierce, G. R., & Contey, C. (1992). *An experimental study of stress, social support, and coping.* Unpublished manuscript.

Pierce, G. R., Sarason, B. R., & Sarason, I. G. (1990). Integrating social support perspectives: Working models, personal relationships, and situational factors. In S. Duck (Ed.), *Personal relationships and social support* (pp. 173–189). Newbury Park, CA: Sage.

Pierce, G. R., Sarason, I. G., & Sarason, B. R. (1991). General and relationship-based perceptions of social support: Are two constructs better than one? *Journal of Personality and Social Psychology, 61,* 1028–1039.

Pierce, G. R., Sarason, I. G., & Sarason, B. R. (1996). Coping and social support. In M. Zeidner & N. Endler (Eds.), *Handbook of coping* (pp. 434–451). New York: Wiley.

Pilisuk, M., & Parks, S. H. (1986). *The healing web.* Hanover, NH: University Press of New England.

Procidano, M. E., & Heller, K. (1983). Measures of perceived social support from friends and from family: Three validation studies. *American Journal of Community Psychology, 11,* 1–24.

Revenson, T. A., & Majerovitz, D. (1990). Spouses' support provision to chronically ill patients. *Journal of Social and Personal Relationships, 7,* 575–586.

Rogers, C. R. (1942). *Counseling and psychotherapy.* Boston: Houghton-Mifflin.

Sandler, I. N., & Barrera, M., Jr. (1984). Toward a multimethod approach to assessing the effects of social support. *American Journal of Community Psychology, 12,* 37–52.

Sarason, B. R., Pierce, G. R., Bannerman, A., & Sarason, I. G. (1993). Investigating the antecedents of perceived support: Parents' views of and behavior toward their children. *Journal of Personality and Social Psychology, 65,* 1071–1085.

Sarason, B. R., Pierce, G. R., & Sarason, I. G. (1990). Social support: The sense of acceptance and the role of relationships. In B. R. Sarason, I. G. Sarason, & G. R. Pierce (Eds.), *Social support: An interactional view* (pp. 97–128). New York: Wiley.

Sarason, B. R., Pierce, G. R., Shearin, E. N., Sarason, I. G., Waltz, J. A., & Poppe, L. (1991). Perceived social support and working models of self and actual others. *Journal of Personality and Social Psychology, 60,* 273–287.

Sarason, B. R., Sarason, I. G., Hacker, T. A., & Basham, R. B. (1985). Concomitants of social support: Social skills, physical attractiveness and gender. *Journal of Personality and Social Psychology, 49,* 469–480.

Sarason, B. R., Sarason, I. G., & Pierce (Eds.). (1990). *Social support: An interactional view.* New York: Wiley.

Sarason, B. R., Shearin, E. N., Pierce, G. R., & Sarason, I. G. (1987). Interrelationships among social support measures: Theoretical and practical implications. *Journal of Personality and Social Psychology, 52,* 813–832.

Sarason, I. G. (1981). Test anxiety, stress, and social support. *Journal of Personality, 49,* 101–114.

Sarason, I. G., Levine, H. M., Basham, R. B., & Sarason, B. R. (1983). Assessing social support: The Social Support Questionnaire. *Journal of Personality and Social Psychology, 44,* 127–139.

Sarason, I. G., Pierce, G. R., & Sarason, B. R. (1990). Social support and interactional processes: A triadic hypothesis. *Journal of Social and Personal Relationships, 7,* 495–506.

Sarason, I. G., & Sarason, B. R. (1986). Experimentally provided social support. *Journal of Personality and Social Psychology, 50,* 1222–1225.

Sarason, I. G., Sarason, B. R., & Pierce, G. R. (1990). Anxiety, cognitive interference, and performance. *Journal of Social Behavior and Personality, 5,* 1–18.

Sarason, I. G., Sarason, B. R., & Shearin, E. N. (1986). Social support as an individual difference variable: Its stability, origins, and relational aspects. *Journal of Personality and Social Psychology, 50,* 845–855.

Sarason, I. G., Sarason, B. R., Shearin, E. N., & Pierce, G. R. (1987). A brief measure of social support: Practical and theoretical implications. *Journal of Social and Personal Relationships, 4,* 497–510.

Seeman, T. E., & Berkman, L. L. (1988). Structural characteristics of social networks and their relationship with social support in the elderly: Who provides support. *Social Science and Medicine, 26,* 737–749.

Shulman, N. (1976). Network analysis: A new addition to an old bag of tricks. *Acta Sociologica, 23,* 307–323.

Simons, R., Lorenz, F. O., Wu, C.-I., & Conger, R. D. (1993). Social network and marital support as mediators and moderators of the impact of stress and depression on parental behavior. *Developmental Psychology, 29,* 368–381.

Weiss, R. S. (1974). The provisions of social relationships. In Z. Rubin (Ed.), *Doing unto others* (pp. 17–26). Englewood Cliffs, NJ: Prentice-Hall.

Wethington, E., & Kessler, R. C. (1986). Perceived support, received support, and adjustment to stressful life events. *Journal of Health and Social Behavior, 27,* 78–89.

Whitcher, S. J., & Fisher, J. D. (1979). Multidimensional reaction to therapeutic touch in a hospital setting. *Journal of Personality and Social Psychology, 36,* 87–96.

Zavislak, N., & Sarason, B. R. (1991, August). *Predicting parent-child relationships: Influence of marital conflict and family behavior.* Paper presented at the annual meeting of the American Psychological Association, Washington, DC.

2

Stress and Passionate Love

Elaine Hatfield and Richard L. Rapson
University of Hawaii, Honolulu, USA

Abstract *Passionate love is a turbulent emotion, with close links to joy, sadness, fear, anger, and jealousy. Of course, people differ markedly in how pleasurable or stressful their passionate experiences prove to be. Social psychologists have found that secure persons have the most positive experiences in love. For the clingy, skittish, and fickle, passionate love can be stressful and lead to problematic relationships. The consequences of passion also depend, in part, on whether lovers' passionate feelings are reciprocated. When reciprocated, passionate love has been found to be associated with satisfaction and happiness, and to have a beneficial effect on the immune system. Stress resulting from unrequited love seems to be hazardous to mental and physical health. When passionate relationships end, people may experience joy and relief, or guilt, sadness, depression, jealousy, anger, bitterness, or loneliness. As a consequence of this complex of emotions, couples who have broken up are unusually vulnerable to a host of mental and physical illnesses.*

Fischer and his colleagues (Fischer, Shaver, & Carnochan, 1990) defined *emotions* as "organized, meaningful, generally adaptive action systems" (pp. 84–85). They argued that there are five basic emotions: joy, love (which comes in two subtypes—passionate love and companionate love, which they labeled *infatuation* and *fondness*), anger, sadness, and fear. Researchers have found that men and women in a variety of nations, single and married, homosexual and heterosexual, resonate to this distinction (Fehr, 1993). This chapter focuses on *passionate love*. It has been defined this way:

A state of intense longing for union with another. Passionate love is a complex functional whole including appraisals or appreciations, subjective feelings, expressions, patterned physiological processes, action tendencies, and instrumental behaviors. Reciprocated love (union with the other) is associated with fulfillment and ecstasy. Unrequited love (separation) is associated with emptiness, anxiety, or despair. (Hatfield & Rapson, 1993, p. 5)

Almost all of the research cited in the "Evidence" section was derived from the pioneering research of Hazan and Shaver. Our model is simply an attempt to expand their model to include three types of love schemata, which we thought were not recognized in their earlier formulation—the fickle, casual, and uninterested.

Hatfield and Sprecher (1986) developed the Passionate Love scale to tap the cognitive, emotional, and behavioral incidents of this kind of love. (See Appendix 2.1.)

Companionate love is a "cooler" emotion. It combines feelings of deep attachment, commitment, and intimacy. It has been defined in this way: "The affection and tenderness we feel for those with whom our lives are deeply entwined . . ." (Hatfield & Rapson, 1993, p. 9). Psychologists have used a variety of scales to measure companionate love. For example, Sternberg (1988) contended that companionate relationships require both commitment and intimacy. Thus, many researchers have assessed companionate love by measuring commitment and intimacy. Of course, some psychologists (e.g., Fehr, 1993; Hendrick & Hendrick, 1989; Lee, 1973; Rubin, 1970; Sternberg, 1988) have proposed yet other definitions and typologies of love.

THE CROSS-MAGNIFICATION PROCESS

In his 1992 film *Husbands and Wives,* Woody Allen [Gabe Roth] sketched a portrait of Harriet Harmon, the woman he had loved most feverishly. She was "sexually carnivorous." They'd make love in all sorts of combinations and all sorts of places—in the back of cars, in other people's bedrooms, in stalled elevators, in the bushes. Gabe noted:

> *you know me, I was getting a real education and I was, you know, fascinated, I was just absolutely nuts about her and, you know, ultimately she wound up in an institution. . . . (Allen, 1992)*

Gabe said that he had always had a penchant for what he called "kamikaze women." Women who crash their plane into *you,* so you die along with them. Gabe understands the process: It's the challenge—the knowledge that there's no chance of its working out, the knowledge that he is going to confront tremendous obstacles in trying to make the relationship stay afloat—that makes him fall in love with the person. "Of course," he noted ruefully, "it has not worked out well for me. It has not been great."

Woody Allen exaggerated. But for most people, passionate love *is* associated with a variety of emotions, pleasurable and painful. In prototype analyses, social psychologists have found passionate love to be associated with more basic emotions than any other emotion. Hatfield (see Carlson & Hatfield, 1992) argued that, in life, the most intense emotional experiences usually involve blends of emotions. This may not be pure coincidence. Perhaps emotions (especially positive emotions like joy and love) have a better chance to rise to a fever pitch when several emotional units are activated. Love may be more intense than usual when it is kindled by fire and ice—by the impossible paradoxes of ecstasy and insecurity, jealousy and impatience, love and anger. The loss of romantic partners may be especially hard to bear when combined with guilt about the way we treated them. Add grief and anger about the loss to that guilt, and the darkness deepens. There is considerable evidence that mixtures of emotions—good, bad, and neutral—can fuel passion (Hatfield & Rapson, 1993).

THE UNIVERSALITY OF PASSIONATE LOVE

It has been claimed that Americans are preoccupied with love (Murstein, 1986). When Hendrick and Hendrick (1986) asked young people if they had ever been in love, 89% of them said they had been in love at least once. Researchers have found that young men and women from a variety of American ethnic groups—Chinese Americans, European Americans, Japanese Americans, Mexican Americans, and Pacific Islanders (which includes people from the Philippines, Hawaii, Samoa, Guam, Tonga, Tahiti, and Fiji)—were all equally susceptible to falling in love. Almost all had been in love at least once in their lives. Most said they were in love at the present time (Aron & Rodriguez, 1992; Doherty, Hatfield, Thompson, & Choo, 1994; Singelis, Choo, & Hatfield, 1995).

What effect, if any, does cultural background have on how intensely young people fall in love? Hatfield and her students (Doherty et al., 1994; Singelis et al., 1995) asked men and women from Chinese American, European American, Filipino American, Japanese American, and Pacific Island backgrounds to complete the Passionate Love scale and the Companionate Love scale. Students from all of the ethnic groups seemed to love with equal passion (and with equal companionate love). However, researchers have found that some kinds of people, in some kinds of situations, may be more susceptible to passionate love and to have different kinds of love experiences.

LOVE SCHEMATA AND PASSIONATE LOVE

In our clinical practice, we have been struck by the individual differences in what people hope for and expect from love. Recently, social psychologists have become interested in the impact that cognitive schemata have on people's cognitions, emotions, and behaviors. (*Schemata* have been conceptualized as cognitive plans, structures, or programs that serve as guides for interpreting information and guiding action; Fiske & Taylor, 1984.) Theorists have argued that people may possess very different love schemata (i.e., different cognitive models as to what it is appropriate to expect from themselves, those they love, and their love relationships). Hatfield and Rapson (1996) proposed that people's love schemata depend on: (a) how comfortable they are with closeness and/or independence, and (b) how eager they are to be involved in romantic relationships. Those who are interested in romantic relationships fall into one of four types: the secure (who are comfortable with closeness and independence), the clingy (who are comfortable with closeness, but fearful of too much independence), the skittish (who are fearful of too much closeness, but comfortable with independence), and the fickle (who are uneasy with either closeness or independence). Those who are relatively uninterested in relationships fall into one of two categories: the casual (who are interested in relationships only if they are almost problem-free), and the uninterested (who are not at all interested in relationships, problem-free or not).

Hatfield and Rapson (1996) also pointed out that people's love schemata may have multiple determinants. As attachment theorists have proposed, schemata are shaped by children's early experiences and thus are relatively permanent. To some extent, love schemata change as people progress through the various developmental stages. For example, as adolescents mature, they normally become more secure in their ability to integrate closeness and independence (Erikson, 1982). Love schemata also change with experience. Depending on their romantic experiences, people may become better (or less) able to deal with the stresses of love relationships. Finally, of course, people may react differently in different kinds of relationships. For example, the same person may cling to a cool and aloof mate, but become skittish with a smothering one (Napier, 1977).

The Love Schema (LS) scale was designed to identify people who possess various love schemata (Hatfield & Rapson, 1996). For information on the reliability and validity of this scale, see Singelis, et al., 1994. (See Appendix 2.2.)

When Singelis et al. (1994) asked American men and women from a variety of ethnic groups to rate their feelings and experiences, not surprisingly, most (62.2%) reported that they generally felt fairly secure in their romantic relationships. Some admitted that they had been clingy (7.6%), skittish (10.5%), or fickle (12.2%) in their romantic encounters. Only a few said that they had generally been casual (6.7%) or uninterested (.8%) in relationships. Researchers have found that American men and women from a variety of ethnic backgrounds tend to classify themselves in much the same ways on the LS scale (Doherty et al., 1994; Singelis et al., 1994).

Theoretical Background

There is some justification, both theoretical and empirical, for the love schemata typology found to be so useful in a clinical setting. Social psychologists have charted the process by which infants, teenagers, and young adults learn to love and then balance the conflicting desires for closeness and independence. Pioneering scientists such as Ainsworth (1989), Bowlby (1979), Freud (1933/1953), and Hazan and Shaver (1987) charted the way in which infants come to be attached to their caregivers. Erikson (1982) charted the way adolescents and young adults learn to negotiate the delicate balance between independence and interdependence. All assumed that these early experiences have a dramatic impact on what young men and women desire in their love affairs, and how competent they will be at satisfying their desires.

Attachment theory. Social psychologists have argued that passionate love and sexual desire are constructed on the ancient foundations laid down between caregivers and infants. Primatologists such as Rosenblum (1985) and Harlow (1975) pointed out that many primates, such as pigtail macaques, seem to experience a primitive form of passionate love. This attachment is based on the necessity of the caregiver–infant bond, which allows young primates to survive in the wild. Ainsworth (see Ainsworth, Blehar, Waters, & Wall, 1978) and Bowlby (1979), who were well grounded in evolutionary theory, studied the processes of attachment, separation, and loss in human infants. Developmentalists also quickly discovered that infants were capable of forming very different kinds of bonds with their caregivers—they might be classified as *secure, anxious resistant, avoidant,* or *disorganized disoriented* in their patterns of attachment (see Ainsworth et al., 1978; Main & Solomon, 1990). Some social psychologists have argued that these early infantile attachments have a powerful impact on adult passionate attachments (Bowlby, 1979; Hatfield & Rapson, 1993, 1996; Hazan & Shaver, 1987). As Bowlby (1979) observed: "In terms of subjective experience, the formation of a bond is described as falling in love, maintaining a bond as loving someone, and losing a partner as grieving over someone" (p. 69).

There is considerable evidence that childhood and adult patterns of attachment have a powerful impact on adult romantic schemata. (See Bartholomew & Horowitz, 1991; Doherty et al., 1994; Hindy, Schwarz, & Brodsky, 1989; Keelan, Dion, & Dion, 1994; or Shaver & Hazan, 1993, for a review of this research.)

Love and anxiety/stress. Earlier, when discussing the cross-magnification process, it was observed that passion can be fueled by a variety of associated emotions. But given the attachment theoretical perspective, and the special interests of this series (stress and anxiety), the relationship between passionate love and one particular emotion, anxiety, is of particular interest. An array of theorists (Freud, 1933/1953; Reik, 1972) have proposed that it is precisely when people are not at their best—when their self-esteem has been shattered, when they are anxious and afraid, when their lives are turbulent and stressful—that they are especially vulnerable to falling head-over-heels in love. This makes some sense. After all, infants' early attachments (which motivate them to cling tightly to their mother's side when danger threatens and to go their own way when it is all safe) are thought to be the initial prototype of love. Also, passionate love and consuming anxiety are closely related both neuroanatomically and chemically (Hatfield & Rapson, 1993). Several researchers have demonstrated that both children and adults are especially prone to seek romantic ties when they are anxious and under stress. In two studies, Hatfield and her colleagues (Hatfield, Brinton, & Cornelius, 1989; Hatfield, Schmitz, Cornelius, & Rapson, 1988), for example, found that children and teenagers who were either momentarily or habitually anxious were especially vulnerable to passionate love. Young people who varied in age from 12 to 16 years of age, and who were of Chinese-American, European-American, Japanese-American, Korean-American, or mixed ancestry, were asked to complete the Child Anxiety scale (Gillis, 1980) or the State–Trait Anxiety Inventory (STAI) for children (Spielberger, Gorsuch, & Lushene, 1970), which measures both state anxiety (how anxious teenagers happen to feel at the moment) and trait anxiety (how anxious they generally are). Children and adolescents who were high on either trait or state anxiety received the highest scores on the PL scale.

Dutton and Aron (1974) discovered a close link among fear, stress, and sexual attraction. The investigators compared the reactions of young men crossing two bridges in North Vancouver, Canada. The first bridge, the Capilano Canyon suspension bridge, tilts, sways, and wobbles for 450 feet over a 230-foot drop to rocks and shallow rapids. The other bridge, a bit farther upstream, is a solid, safe structure. As each young man crossed the bridge, an attractive college woman approached him, explained that she was conducting a class project on the environment, and asked him to fill out a questionnaire for her. When the man had finished, she offered to explain her project in greater detail, and wrote her telephone number on a small piece of paper so that the man could call her for more information. Which men called? Nine of the 33 men on the suspension bridge called her, but only 2 of the 33 men on the solid bridge called. It appears that passion was intensified by the spillover of feeling from one realm to another. Hence, people's love schemata may be shaped by their early attachments, but their later experiences have been found to play a part as well.

Erikson's stage theory. Developmental theorists have pointed out that, important as infancy is, young people learn even more about passionate love and intimacy in adolescence. Erikson (1982) wrote that: "Anything that grows has a ground plan, and out of this ground plan parts arise, each part having its special time of ascendancy" (p. 92). Stage theorists such as Erikson have pointed out that infancy is only one stage in the life cycle. Throughout their lives, children, adolescents, and adults face a continuing series of developmental tasks. For example, in adolescence, teenagers must confront two tasks: They must develop a relatively stable, independent identity, and they must learn how to participate in a loving, committed, intimate relationship. Erikson (1959) also argued that men and women may differ slightly in how easily they achieve independence and intimacy. He argued that as men mature, they find it easy to achieve an independent identity, whereas they experience more difficulty in learning to be intimate with those they love. In contrast, women have an easy time learning to be close to others, but have more trouble learning how to be independent. Other theorists have agreed (see Gilligan, 1982; Hodgson & Fischer, 1979; White, Speisman, Jackson, Bartis, & Costos, 1986).

Erikson's model, then, suggests that if people are to have a close, loving relationship with others, they must have learned how to be comfortable with both independence and closeness. Until people learn how to negotiate both, they are likely to encounter problems in their love affairs. Researchers provide some evidence in support of Erikson's theorizing (Bellew-Smith & Korn, 1986; Orlofsky & Ginsburg, 1981; Tesch & Whitbourne, 1982).

Other approaches. Neurophysiologists claim that passionate love may also be fueled by pubescent sexual and hormonal changes (Gadpaille, 1975; Money, 1980). Puberty and sexual maturity may bring a new depth to passion (Rabehl, Ridge, & Berscheid, 1992). The love schemata model, then, was designed to integrate the insights of these various theoretical approaches.

The Evidence

Researchers have accumulated considerable evidence that people's love schemata are linked to their thoughts, feelings, and experiences in passionate encounters.

The secure. Men and women who are secure have been found to fall passionately in love fairly often. However, a steady personality does not guarantee smooth sailing in stressful romantic waters. Love is difficult for everyone, and the vast majority of love affairs fail. Nonetheless, the secure do seem to do better than most at negotiating stable, companionate, intimate love relationships. Secure people think of themselves as valuable and worthy of others' affection and concern. They assume their romantic partners are well intentioned, trustworthy, reliable, and available (i.e., they probably would not tolerate romantic partners who were not so well intentioned). They find it easy to get close to others. They feel comfortable relying on others and being relied on by them in return. They rarely worry about being abandoned or smothered by others. They have happier, more positive relationships than do their peers. Their relationships involve more commitment, trust, satisfaction, intimacy, and interdependence than do those of their peers (for evidence in support of these contentions, see Doherty et al., 1994; Hatfield & Rapson, 1996; Hendrick & Hendrick, 1989; and Shaver & Hazan, 1993).

The clingy. Those who are clingy are most vulnerable to "neurotic love." The clingy have low self-esteem. They are ambivalent about their lovers. On the one hand, they idealize them (e.g., the other could give them so much, if only he or she would). On the other hand, they cannot help but resent them for their reluctance to make a commitment, to get as close to them as they would like, and to take care of them in the way they long to be cared for. They are frantic when they think their mate might not really love them. They obsess about the other's feelings. They are so focused on what they long for from an affair that they are sometimes oblivious to the fact that the other might have different feelings and needs. They are addicted and dependent on the relationship. They are on an emotional roller coastal—elated one minute and anxious, frightened, and lonely the next. They have trouble finding a stable, committed, companionate relationship; sometimes their insatiable demands seem to drive others away (Hatfield & Rapson, 1996; Hindy, Schwarz, & Brodsky, 1989; Shaver & Hazan, 1993; Singelis et al., 1994).

The skittish. The skittish seem to fear romantic intimacy. They are pessimistic about love. They are aloof, emotionally distant, and skeptical about relationships. They prefer not to make any serious commitments. They think of their lover as overly eager to hurl precipitously into long-term commitments. They are uncomfortable with a partner who discloses too much too soon. When their lover tries to talk over problems with them, they back away. They avoid emotional confrontations. Rather, they focus their attention on their work, nonsocial activities, or brief, uncommitted, sexual encounters. Not surprisingly, their love relationships rarely go well. Break-ups are not terribly stressful, however. The work of a variety of researchers has led to these gloomy conclusions (Hatfield & Rapson, 1996; Hazan & Shaver, 1987; Hindy et al., 1989; Shaver & Hazan, 1993).

The fickle. As might be expected, the fickle have more problems than do their peers. They are plagued with the problems of both the clingy and the skittish (they desire what they do not have, but flee from what lies just within their grasp). They are clingy when trying to win another's love, but skittish once they are faced with an actual commitment. Thus, although the fickle can fall passionately in love easily enough, especially for someone who is tantalizingly unavailable, they are unlikely to have ever managed an affectionate, committed, intimate relationship. They are wary of commitment. When faced with an impending commitment, they feel trapped—worried that it is too much too soon. The more fickle people are, the less joy and the more anxiety, sadness, anger, and stress they experience in their relationships. Nothing seems to work out for the fickle (Singelis et al., 1994, 1995).

The casual. Researchers have found that men and women who are casual about relationships are less likely than their peers to have experienced either passionate or companionate love. When people are young, it is appropriate to be casual about love. In maturity, most people become interested in settling into committed, permanent relationships. For those who are casual about love in adulthood, love is not a source of joy. They remain detached in the love affairs. They keep their feelings at bay (Hatfield & Rapson, 1996).

The uninterested. Not surprisingly, those who are uninterested in relationships are extremely unlikely to have experienced much passionate or companionate love. The disinterested are simply uninterested in getting committed or even getting involved in an intimate relationship. It is rather an odd question to ask how such love affairs "work out." The uninterested may be barely aware that they are involved in a relationship. Nonetheless, to the extent that the uninterested do pay attention, they may find every reason to stay uninterested. Their affairs bring them little joy and provoke a great deal of sadness and anger (Hatfield & Rapson, 1996).

THE CONSEQUENCES OF PASSIONATE LOVE

As observed earlier, passionate love is a turbulent emotion, with close links to joy, sadness, fear, and anger. Social psychologists have amassed evidence as to the consequences this complex of emotions has for mental and physical health. The sparse existing evidence suggests that the consequences of passion may depend, in part, on whether one's passionate feelings are requited (and thus a source of joy and fulfillment) or unrequited (and thus associated with emptiness, anxiety, and despair).

Requited Love

Satisfaction and happiness. Fehr (1993) asked young men and women in Australia and the United States to list the characteristics they associated with love. People usually listed such positive characteristics as euphoria, excitement, laughing, and contentment. (Similar results were secured by Davis & Todd, 1982; Fitness & Fletcher, 1993; Marston, Hecht, & Robers, 1987.)

Love and the immune system. Smith and Hokland (1988) suspected that love (or at least reciprocated love) is good for people. A famous case in point: The poet Elizabeth Barrett was a frail, sickly invalid. When she fell in love with the impassioned Robert Browning, her health quickly improved. Smith and Hokland interviewed 64 Danish college students. They asked the students several questions: Were they in love? Were their feelings reciprocated? How happy were they? How healthy? When college students were in love and knew they were loved in return, they were at their best. They were self-confident, relaxed, happy, and unusually healthy (e.g., no sore throats or colds). When technicians drew blood samples and assayed natural killer cell (NK cell) activity, they found that lovers' NK cell activity was unusually low. The lovers' immune systems were at full strength. However, when students were suffering from the stresses of unrequited love, they were literally at risk. They reported feeling tense and depressed. They were especially prone to sore throats and colds. Many of them had been drinking alcohol (at least they displayed the tell-tale signs of a hangover). More ominously, their NK cell activity was elevated—a sign that their immune systems were trying to fight off disease.

Unrequited Love

There is also evidence that unrequited love is stressful and unhealthy for the lover, and even worse for the beloved.

Satisfaction and happiness. Recently, Baumeister, Wotman, and Stillwell (1993) asked college students at Case Western Reserve University to think about a time they had broken someone's heart or had their own hearts broken by unrequited love. (Almost everyone could recall these stressful experiences: 95% of men and women had rejected someone who loved them; 93% had felt the slap of such rejection.) The authors asked men and women to tell the story of their doomed love affairs. The would-be lovers and the lovelorn had very different stories to tell.

The rejected. It is painful to be rejected. However, Baumeister et al. found that, for the most "broken-hearted" lovers, the experience of "fatal attraction" remained a surprisingly sweet memory. When they first fell in love, they had been filled with love and hope. They had focused almost entirely on their own needs, wants, and desires. They were convinced that the attraction had been mutual. Later, when things turned sour, they believed they had been led on—that the rejecter had never clearly communicated his or her disinterest. They felt that "all is fair in love and war." They viewed the beloved with incomprehension. How could he or she not love them when they loved so much? They cared little about the beloved's feelings. They were oblivious and indifferent to what the rejecter was going through. Some seemed to enjoy wallowing in the drama of their misery. They blamed the other for not reciprocating their love; they felt angry, annoyed, and resentful at his or her stubbornness. They remembered the infatuation afterward as a bitter-sweet affair, despite the poison of disappointment at the current state of things.

Those who are forced to do the rejecting. Contrary to conventional wisdom, it turned out that the loved were the ones who ended up suffering the most. At first, those who were loved beyond reason were flattered by the would-be lover's adoration. However, they soon found themselves caught up in an impossible situation. Whatever they did was wrong. It seemed cruel to reject someone who cared so much for them. It was even worse to lead someone on. They agonized over how to say "enough" without hurting feelings. But as the would-be lover persisted, guilt turned to annoyance and then rage. Eventually, the rejecters began to feel trapped and persecuted. What can be motivating him? Why won't she go away? Is he crazy? Doesn't she see she's driving me crazy? All in all, it seemed far more pleasant to have loved and lost than to have been loved.

Sometimes, of course, the rejected lover's pursuit of the other turns into harassment. Jason, Reichler, Easton, Neal, and Wilson (1984) defined *harassment* as: "the persistent use of psychological or physical abuse in an attempt to begin or continue dating someone else after they have clearly indicated a desire to terminate a relationship" (p. 261). Rejected lovers' romantic harassment included the following behaviors: repeated calling late at night; ringing the front door bell, running, and watching; repeatedly calling at work; besieging the lover with an avalanche of letters; sending flowers; jumping out of the bushes when the other returned home late at night from a date; insulting or physically attacking; or threatening to kill. The researchers found that a majority of college women (56%) had been romantically harassed at some time or another. (Researchers have not investigated how often men are harassed.) Interestingly enough, when harassers were interviewed, they generally did not think of such activities as harassment. They thought they were merely trying to establish a love relationship.

One might expect that those who suffer from unrequited love would be susceptible to a variety of stress-induced emotional and physical illnesses. As yet, little research has specifically investigated this possibility.

Passionate Relationships That Come to an End

When individuals are in love, they are generally convinced that their passionate feelings will last forever. Yet passion is generally fleeting (Berscheid, 1983; Hatfield & Rapson, 1993). Klinger (1977) warned that: "highs are always transitory. People experience deliriously happy moments that quickly fade and all attempts to hang on to them are doomed to fail" (p. 116).

Solomon (1980) observed that passionate love follows the same pattern as any addiction. At first, passionate love produces giddy euphoria. In time, however, it takes more and more love (or cocaine, alcohol, etc.) to produce even a weak high. Eventually, highs become transitory. If one loses love (or if one goes "cold turkey" on a drug), one must endure the pains of withdrawal (e.g., depression, agitation, fatigue, anger, and loneliness). Marriage and family texts also warn that romantic love is temporary. Passion frequently wanes once the couple moves in together. For example, Reik (1972) warned that, once intensely in love, the best a couple can hope for after several years of living together is a warm "afterglow." There is indeed evidence that passionate love does erode with time (Sternberg, 1988; Traupmann-Pillemer & Hatfield, 1981).

For many couples, the end of passion is the end of the relationship. Recently, Levine and his colleagues (Levine, Sato, Hashimoto, & Verma, 1994) asked American men and women (and men and women in 10 other nations) two questions: *Question 1:* If a man (woman) had all the other qualities you desired, would you marry this person if you were not in love with him (her)? *Question 2:* If love has completely disappeared from a marriage, do you think it is probably best for the couple to make a clean break and start new lives? The sociologists found that, in the United States, only 3.5% of men and women said they would consider marrying someone if there was no "chemistry, provided the person had everything else they wanted." Most young men and women also assumed that romantic love was an important ingredient in determining whether they would stay in a relationship. A full 35.4% of men and women said they would leave if they fell out of love; 29.9% were undecided as to whether they would leave (similar results were secured by Simpson, Campbell, & Berscheid, 1986). Of course, with more experience, young people might find that they were willing to "settle" for less than they assumed they would. In any case, when love ends, dating relationships and perhaps even marriages may come to an end.

People vary in how they react to the end of an affair. Some men and women are happy and relieved. Others care little one way or another. Others are devastated (Sprecher, 1994). One researcher (Stephen, 1987) found that, after a break-up, 52% of men and women reported experiencing little distress, whereas 43% reported a great deal of distress. It is easy to guess the kinds of things that make separation especially painful. People with higher self-esteem have an easier time surviving a break-up. The more satisfied they are with their relationship, the closer they have been, and the longer they have been together, the worse the end will be. Break-ups are also particularly stressful if people fear that they will never find someone else to love, and if they have few friends to provide social support (Berscheid, Snyder, & Omoto, 1989; Frazier & Cook, 1993). It is far less painful to leave someone than to be left. The abandoned are likely to be stunned by the break-up and preoccupied with trying to figure out what went wrong. It takes them far longer to recover and get on with their lives (Frazier & Cook, 1993; Gray & Silver, 1990).

Weiss (1979) observed that, in serious relationships, most men and women experience intense and conflicting emotions after a break-up. They may feel euphoric and relieved while also feeling guilty, anxious, depressed, jealous, and angry. The newly separated feel a whirlpool of emotions, and their feelings shift with such dizzying rapidity that it is difficult for them to deal with the turbulence.

Guilt. Gray and Silver (1990) interviewed newly divorced Canadian men and women. Not surprisingly, they found that those who had decided to divorce often felt guilty.

Sadness and depression. Means (1991) asked college students who had just broken up to comment on their feelings. Many still loved their partners. They wished things could have worked out. Most were sometimes achingly sad. Two months after the break-up, over 40% of the students were clinically depressed, as assessed by the Beck Depression Inventory (BDI; Beck, 1967). The inventory classified 1% of the students as being "minimally depressed," 31% as "mildly to moderately depressed," 10% as "moderately to severely depressed," 2% as "severely" depressed, and 40% as "clinically depressed." Should a love affair or marriage end in death, the bereaved generally grieves for a long time (Beach, Sandeen, & O'Leary, 1990; Solsberry & Krupnick, 1984; Stroebe & Stroebe, 1987).

Jealousy. Berscheid and Fei (1977) studied the factors that ignite jealousy. They found that the more insecure people are, the more dependent they are on their romantic partners and mates. In addition, the more seriously a relationship is threatened, the more fiercely jealous insecure people are. Researchers have found that when men and women are jealous, they tend to react in somewhat different ways. In their review of the existing research on jealousy, Clanton and Smith (1987) found that existing gender roles predispose men and women to react very differently when jealousy strikes. Men generally deny their feelings, while women freely admit to them. Men tend to become upset if they think their partners are having *sexual* activity with other men and they often demand a recital of the intimate details. Women become upset if they think their partner is becoming *emotionally* involved with someone else. Clanton and Smith add:

> Men are more likely to externalize *the cause of the jealousy, more likely to blame the partner, or the third party, or "circumstances." Women often* internalize *the cause of jealousy; they blame themselves. Similarly, a jealous man is more likely to display* competitive *behavior toward the third party while a jealous woman is more likely to display* possessive *behavior. She clings to her partner rather than confronting the third party. (p. 11)*

Finally, Clanton and Smith point out, jealous men are more likely to become enraged and violent than are women.

Israeli psychologists Nadler and Dotan (1992) found that jealous people may respond in two very different ways: (a) Some focus on the threat to their feelings of self-esteem. Their reactions are designed to protect their own egos (e.g., they berate, beat up, leave, or try to get even with their partners). (b) Some focus on the threat to the present relationship. Their reactions are designed to improve their floundering relationship. They may try to make themselves more attractive, talk things out, or learn something from the experience. Hence, the researchers concluded that men and women seem to respond quite differently to jealous provocation. In general, jealous men concentrate on shoring up their sagging self-esteem, whereas jealous women are more likely to do something to strengthen the relationship.

Anger and bitterness. As relationships begin to dissolve, couples often begin to fight. Sometimes when the newly separated think back on their relationship, a volcano of anger erupts. Some have suppressed their own feelings for months or years in the interests of harmony. Now they realize how angry they have been.

Couples may slap, shove, grab, bite, kick, or hit one another with their fists. They may threaten one another with knives or guns, or they may beat one another (Marshall & Rose, 1987). Approximately 22%–40% of dating couples and 38% of engaged couples report that they have had physically violent confrontations with their partners. In this instance, more than half the time (68%), both partners were abusive (Cate, Henton, Koval, Christopher, & Lloyd, 1982; Gryl, Stith, & Bird, 1991).

For example, Gryl et al. (1991) asked 280 first-year college students who were in serious dating relationships how violent their relationships were. They asked students to complete Straus' (1979) Conflict Tactics (CT) scale. This scale asks couples to recall the time in the past year when they and their dates or mates had had a spat or fight. How had they and their partners reacted? The scale then lists 19 tactics couples might have employed during a conflict. The list begins with items from the Reasoning scale, such as "discussed issue calmly." It also includes items from the Verbal Aggression scale, such as "Insulted or swore at the other," and ends with Violence items.

Couples were considered to have had a violent encounter if they admitted to using physical force to get their way (e.g., shoved, slapped, kicked, beaten up, stabbed, or shot their sweethearts during a fight). In this study, men and women were equally likely to inflict and sustain violence (23% of the men and 30% of the women admitted that they had been violent; 39% of the men and 28% of the women reported that they had been the victims of violence). However, most studies have found that men are far more aggressive than women. Men are more likely to punch, kick, choke, beat up, and threaten their lovers with knives or guns than are women. Their violence is also more likely to inflict serious injury on their dating partners—emotionally, sexually, and physically (Makepeace, 1986; Marshall & Rose, 1987).

Researchers have found that homosexual and heterosexual couples are equally likely to try to get their way by resorting to put-downs, throwing things, pushing, and violence (Metz, Rosser, & Strapko, 1994; Waterman, Dawson, & Bologna, 1989). Researchers have also compared rates of violence in couples from African-American, Chinese-American, European-American, Filipino-American, and Japanese-American backgrounds, as well as Hawaiians, part Hawaiians, and Hispanics. Here, too, they find that battering is all too common in these groups (Blanchard & Blanchard, 1982; Cazenave & Straus, 1990; Straus & Smith, 1990).

Loneliness. After a break-up, many men and women suffer from intense loneliness. The lonely hunger for love and, in its absence, may also be angry, anxious, bored, or depressed (de Jong-Gierveld, 1986; Lopata, 1969; Perlman & Peplau, 1981).

Falling ill. Couples who have broken up or divorced are unusually vulnerable to a host of stress-induced mental and physical diseases. They have been found to have unusually high rates of alcoholism, diabetes, heart disease, tuberculosis, and cirrhosis of the liver. They are more likely to die from natural causes, twice as likely to commit suicide, and more likely to be murdered than when they were married (Bloom, White, & Asher, 1979; Stroebe & Stroebe, 1987).

LOVE SCHEMATA AND REACTIONS TO LOSS

People differ in how quickly they recover from the break-up of a love affair. Some mend quickly, whereas others appear to never recover fully. As one might expect, people who endorse different love schemata seem to deal with the stress of loss in quite different ways.

Researchers have discovered that secure people with high self-esteem bounce back better from the loss of love than do others (Frazier & Cook, 1993; Harvey, Agostinelli, & Weber, 1989). When the clingy contemplate breaking up, they may panic. (Of course, their partners, who have been feeling increasingly smothered by their demands, may feel numb relief.) When the skittish break up, they may feel simple relief. In one study of dating couples, Simpson (1990) found that, after a break-up, men who were secure or clingy in their love styles suffered far more than did the skittish. (Their partners may suffer more at abrupt dismissals.) The fickle always want what they do not have. After someone has finally had enough and ended the relationship, the fickle generally realize how much the relationship meant to them and try to persuade the other person to come back. (Not surprisingly, such fickle lovers often are extremely frustrating for their partners. People are naturally enraged at being "jerked around" again and again.) Casual romances end easily, at least so long as everyone involved in the affair understands that the encounter was just for fun. Of course, the uninterested have no interest in a relationship. They would barely notice were their mythical relationship to end. (For evidence in support of these contentions, see Choo, Levine, & Hatfield, in press; Hatfield & Rapson, 1996.)

CONCLUSIONS

This chapter has described passionate love as a bitter-sweet emotion tightly linked to a variety of other emotions. Social psychologists have described the consequences this complex of emotions has for mental and physical health. Reciprocated love has been found to be associated with happiness and satisfaction, and to have a protective effect on the immune system. Unrequited love and the endings of relationships have been found to be associated with joy and relief, or, more commonly, with guilt, sadness, depression, jealousy, anger, bitterness, and loneliness. Couples who have broken up have also been found to be unusually vulnerable to a host of stress-induced mental and physical illnesses.

Generally, passionate love is either viewed as a positive experience or else it is trivialized. However, once one takes a realistic look at love, it is obvious that, for most people, passionate love is a profoundly powerful experience. When unrequited or terminated, passionate love can be extremely stressful, with serious health consequences. These negative consequences, as well as the positive ones, certainly call out for more study.

REFERENCES

Ainsworth, M. D. S. (1989). Attachments beyond infancy. *American Psychologist, 44,* 709–716.

Ainsworth, M. D. S., Blehar, M.C., Waters, E., & Wall, S. (1978). *Patterns of attachment: A psychological study of the strange situation.* Hillsdale, NJ: Lawrence Erlbaum Associates.

Allen, Woody. (1992). *Husbands and wives* [film].

Aron, A., & Rodriguez, G. (1992, July 25). *Scenarios of falling in love among Mexican-, Chinese-, and Anglo-Americans.* Paper presented at the sixth international conference on Personal Relationships, Orono, ME.

Bartholomew, K., & Horowitz, L. M. (1991). Attachment styles among young adults: A test of a four-category model. *Journal of Personality and Social Psychology, 61,* 226–244.

Baumeister, R. F., Wotman, S. R., & Stillwell, A. M. (1993). Unrequited love: On heartbreak, anger, guilt, scriptlessness, and humiliation. *Journal of Personality and Social Psychology, 61,* 377–391.

Beach, S. R. H., Sandeen, E. E., & O'Leary, K. D. (1990). *Depression in marriage.* New York: Guilford.

Beck, A. (1967). *Depression: Clinical, experimental, and theoretical aspects.* New York: Hoeber.

Bellew-Smith, M., & Korn, J. H. (1986). Merger intimacy status in adult women. *Journal of Personality and Social Psychology, 50,* 1186–1191.

Berscheid, E. (1983). Emotion. In H. H. Kelley, E. Berscheid, A. Christensen, J. H. Harvey, T. L. Huston, G. Levinger, E. McClintock, L. A. Peplau, & D. R. Peterson (Eds.), *Close relationships* (pp. 110–168). New York: Freeman.

Berscheid, E., & Fei, J. (1977). Romantic love and sexual jealousy. In G. Clanton & L. G. Smith (Eds.), *Jealousy* (pp. 101–114). Englewood Cliffs, NJ: Prentice-Hall.

Berscheid, E., Snyder, M., & Omoto, A. (1989). The Relationship Closeness Inventory: Assessing the closeness of interpersonal relationships. *Journal of Personality and Social Psychology, 57,* 792–807.

Blanchard, D. C., & Blanchard, R. J. (1982). Hawaii: Violence, a preliminary analysis. In A. P. Goldstein & M. H. Segall (Eds.), *Global perspectives on aggression* (pp. 159–192). New York: Pergamon.

Bloom, B. L., White, S. W., & Asher, S. J. (1979). Marital disruption as a stressful life event. In G. Levinger & O. C. Moles (Eds.), *Divorce and separation* (pp. 184–200). New York: Basic Books.

Bowlby, J. (1979). *The making and breaking of affectional bonds.* London: Tavistock.

Carlson, J. G., & Hatfield, E. (1992). *Psychology of emotion.* Fort Worth, TX: Harcourt, Brace.

Cate, R. M., Henton, J., Koval, J., Christopher, F. S., & Lloyd, S. A. (1982). Premarital abuse: A social psychological perspective. *Journal of Family Issues, 3,* 79–90.

Cazenave, N. A., & Straus, M. A. (1990). Race, class, network embeddedness, and family violence: A search for potent support systems. In M. A. Straus & R. J. Gelles (Eds.), *Physical violence in American families* (pp. 321–339). New Brunswick, NJ: Transaction Publishers.

Choo, P., Levine, T., & Hatfield, E. (in press). *Gender, Love Schemas, and reactions to a romantic break-up. Journal of Social Behavior and Personality.*

Clanton, G., & Smith, L. G. (Eds.). (1987). *Jealousy.* Lantham, MA: University Press of America.

Davis, K. E., & Todd, M. J. (1982). Friendship and love relationships. In K. E. Davis (Ed.), *Advances in descriptive psychology* (Vol. 2, pp. 79–122). Greenwich, CT: JAI.

de Jong-Gierveld, J. (1986). Loneliness and the degree of intimacy in interpersonal relationships. In R. Gilmour & S. Duck (Eds.), *The emerging field of personal relationships* (pp. 241–249). Hillsdale, NJ: Lawrence Erlbaum Associates.

Doherty, R. W., Hatfield, E., Thompson, K., & Choo, P. (1994). Cultural and ethnic influences on love and attachment. *Personal Relationships, 1,* 391–398.

Dutton, D., & Aron, A. (1974). Some evidence for heightened sexual attraction under conditions of high anxiety. *Journal of Personality and Social Psychology, 30,* 510–517.

Erikson, E. H. (1959). Identity and the life cycle. *Psychological Issues, I* (Monograph 1).

Erikson, E. H. (1982). *The life cycle completed: A review.* New York: Norton.

Fehr, B. (1993). How do I love thee? Let me consult my prototype. In S. Duck (Ed.), *Individuals in relationships: Understanding relationship processes series* (Vol. 1, pp. 87–120). Newbury Park, CA: Sage.

Fischer, K. W., Shaver, P. R., & Carnochan, P. (1990). How emotions develop and how they organize development. *Cognition and Emotion, 4,* 81–127.

Fiske, S. T., & Taylor, S. E. (1984). *Social cognition.* Reading, MA: Addison-Wesley.

Fitness, J., & Fletcher, G. J. O. (1993). Love, hate, anger, and jealousy in close relationships: A prototype and cognitive appraisal analysis. *Journal of Personality and Social Psychology, 65,* 942–958.

Frazier, P. A., & Cook, S. W. (1993). Correlates of distress following heterosexual relationship dissolution. *Journal of Social and Personal Relationships, 10,* 55–67.

Freud, S. (1953). Contributions to the psychology of love: A special type of choice of objects made by men. In E. Jones (Ed.), *Collected papers* (Vol. 4, pp. 192–202). London, England: Hogarth. (Original work published in 1933).

Gadpaille, W. (1975). *The cycles of sex.* New York: Scribner's.

Gilligan, C. (1982). *In a different voice.* Cambridge, MA: Harvard University Press.

Gillis, J. S. (1980). *Child anxiety scale.* Champaign, IL: Institute for Personality and Ability Testing.

Gray, J. D., & Silver, R. C. (1990). Opposite sides of the same coin. Former spouses' divergent perspectives in coping with their divorce. *Journal of Personality and Social Psychology, 59,* 1180–1191.

Gryl, F. E., Stith, S. M., & Bird, G. W. (1991). Close dating relationships among college students: Differences by use of violence and by gender. *Journal of Social and Personal Relationships, 8,* 243–264.

Harlow, H. F. (1975). Lust, latency and love: Simian secrets of successful sex. *Journal of Sex Research, 11,* 79–90.

Harvey, J., Agostinelli, G., & Weber, A. (1989). Account-making and the formation of expectations about close relationships. In C. Hendrick (Ed.), *Review of personality and social psychology* (Vol. 10, pp. 39–62). Newbury Park, CA: Sage.

Hatfield, E., Brinton, C., & Cornelius, J. (1989). Passionate love and anxiety in young adolescents. *Motivation and Emotion, 13,* 271–289.

Hatfield, E., & Rapson, R. L. (1993). *Love, sex, and intimacy: Their psychology, biology, and history.* New York: HarperCollins.

Hatfield, E., & Rapson, R. L. (1996). *Love and sex: Cross-cultural perspectives.* New York: Allyn & Bacon.

Hatfield, E., Schmitz, E., Cornelius, J., & Rapson, R. L. (1988). Passionate love: How early does it begin? *Journal of Psychology and Human Sexuality, 1,* 35–52.

Hatfield, E., & Sprecher, S. (1986). Measuring passionate love in intimate relations. *Journal of Adolescence, 9,* 383–410.

Hazan, C., & Shaver, P. (1987). Romantic love conceptualized as an attachment process. *Journal of Personality and Social Psychology, 52,* 511–524.

Hendrick, C., & Hendrick, S. (1986). A theory and method of love. *Journal of Personality and Social Psychology, 50,* 392–402.

Hendrick, C., & Hendrick, S. S. (1989). Research on love: Does it measure up? *Journal of Personality and Social Psychology, 56,* 784–794.

Hindy, C. G., Schwarz, J. C., & Brodsky, A. (1989). *If this is love why do I feel so insecure?* New York: The Atlantic Monthly Press.

Hodgson, J. W., & Fischer, J. L. (1979). Sex differences in identity and intimacy development. *Journal of Youth and Adolescence, 8,* 37–50.

Jason, L. A., Reichler, A., Easton, J., Neal, A., & Wilson, M. (1984). Female harassment after ending a relationship: A preliminary study. *Alternative Lifestyles, 6,* 259–269.

Keelan, J. P., Dion, K. L., & Dion, K. (1994). Attachment style and heterosexual relationships among young adults: A short-term panel study. *Journal of Social and Personal Relationships, 11,* 201–214.

Klinger, E. (1977). *Meaning and void: Inner experience and the incentives in people's lives.* Minneapolis: University of Minnesota Press.

Lee, J. A. (1973). *The colors of love: An exploration of the ways of loving.* Don Mills, Ontario, Canada: New Press.

Levine, R., Sato, S., Hashimoto, T., & Verma, J. (1994). *Love and marriage in eleven cultures.* Unpublished manuscript, California State University, Fresno, CA.

Lopata, H. Z. (1969). Loneliness: Forms and components. *Social Problems, 17,* 248–261.

Main, M., & Solomon, J. (1990). Procedures for identifying infants as disorganized/disoriented during the Ainsworth strange situation. In M. T. Greenberg, D. Cicchetti, & E. M. Cummings (Eds.), *Attachment in the preschool years* (pp. 121–160). Chicago: University of Chicago Press.

Makepeace, J. M. (1986). Gender differences in courtship violence victimization. *Family Relations: Journal of Applied Family and Child Studies, 35,* 383–388.

Marshall, L. L., & Rose, P. (1987). Gender, stress and violence in the adult relationships of a sample of college students. *Journal of Social and Personal Relationships, 4,* 299–316.

Marston, P. J., Hecht, M. L., & Robers, T. (1987). "True love ways": The subjective experience and communication of romantic love. *Journal of Social and Personal Relationships, 4,* 387–407.

Means, J. (1991). Coping with a breakup: Negative mood regulation expectancies and depression following the end of a romantic relationship. *Journal of Personality and Social Psychology, 60,* 327–334.

Metz, M. E., Rosser, B. R. S., & Strapko, N. (1994). Differences in conflict resolution styles between heterosexual, gay, and lesbian couples. *Journal of Sex Research.*

Money, J. (1980). *Love and love sickness.* Baltimore, MD: Johns Hopkins University Press.

Murstein, B. I. (1986). *Paths to marriage.* Beverly Hills, CA: Sage.

Nadler, A., & Dotan, I. (1992). Commitment and rival attractiveness: Their effects on male and female reactions to jealousy arousing situations. *Sex Roles, 26,* 293–310.

Napier, A. Y. (1977). *The rejection-intrusion pattern: A central family dynamic.* Unpublished manuscript, School of Family Resources, University of Wisconsin, Madison.

Orlofsky, J. L., & Ginsburg, S. D. (1981). Intimacy status: Relationship to affect cognition. *Adolescence, 16,* 91–100.

Perlman, D., & Peplau, L. A. (1981). Toward a social psychology of loneliness. In S. Duck & R. Gilmour (Eds.), *Personal relationships: 3. Personal relationships in disorder* (pp. 31–56). London: Academic Press.

Rabehl, S. M., Ridge, R. D., & Berscheid, E. (1992). Love vs. in love. *Journal of Personality and Social Psychology.*

Reik, T. (1972). *A psychologist looks at love.* New York: Holt, Rinehart & Winston.

Rosenblum, L. A. (1985, September 18). *Discussant: Passionate love and the nonhuman primate.* Paper presented at the International Academy of Sex Research meetings, Seattle, WA.

Rubin, Z. (1970). Measurement of romantic love. *Journal of Personality and Social Psychology, 16,* 265–273.

Shaver, P. R., & Hazan, C. (1993). Adult romantic attachment: Theory and empirical evidence. In D. Perlman & W. Jones (Eds.), *Advances in personal relationships* (Vol. 4, pp. 29–70). Greenwich, CT: JAI.

Simpson, J. A. (1990). The influence of attachment styles on romantic relationships. *Journal of Personality and Social Psychology, 59,* 971–980.

Simpson, J. A., Campbell, B., & Berscheid, E. (1986). The association between romantic love and marriage: Kephart (1967) twice revisited. *Personality and Social Psychology Bulletin, 12,* 363–372.

Singelis, T., Choo, P., & Hatfield, E. (1995). Love schemas and romantic love. *Journal of Social Behavior and Personality, 10,* 15–36.

Singelis, T., Levine, T., Hatfield, E., Bachman, G., Muto, K., & Choo, P. (1994). *Love Schemas, preferences in romantic partners, and commitment.* Unpublished manuscript, University of Hawaii, Honolulu, HI.

Smith, D. F., & Hokland, M. (1988). Love and salutogenesis in late adolescence: A preliminary investigation. *Psychology: A Journal of Human Behavior, 25,* 44–49.

Solomon, R. L. (1980). The opponent-process theory of acquired motivation: The costs of pleasure and the benefits of pain. *American Psychologist, 35,* 691–712.

Solsberry, V., & Krupnick, J. (1984). Adults' reactions to bereavement. In M. Osterweis, F. Solomon, & M. Green (Eds.), *Bereavement: Reactions, consequences, and care* (pp. 47–68). Washington, DC: National Academy Press.

Spielberger, C. D., Gorsuch, R. L., & Lushene, R. E. (1970). *STAI manual for the State–Trait Inventory.* Palo Alto, CA: Consulting Psychologists Press.

Sprecher, S. (1994). Two sides to the breakup of dating relationships. *Personal Relationships, 1,* 199–222.

Stephen, T. (1987). Attribution and adjustment to relationship termination. *Journal of Social and Personal Relationships, 4,* 47–61.

Sternberg, R. J. (1988). Triangulating love. In R. J. Sternberg & M. L. Barnes (Eds.), *The psychology of love* (pp. 119–138). New Haven, CT: Yale University Press.

Straus, M. A. (1979). Measuring intrafamily conflict and violence: The Conflicts Tactics (CT) scale. *Journal of Marriage and the Family, 41,* 75–88.

Straus, M. A., & Smith, C. (1990). Violence in Hispanic families in the United States: Incidence rates and structural interpretations. In M. A. Straus & R. J. Gelles (Eds.), *Physical violence in American families* (pp. 341–367). New Brunswick, NJ: Transaction.

Stroebe, W., & Stroebe, M. S. (1987). *Bereavement and health: The psychological and physical consequences of partner loss.* New York: Cambridge University Press.

Tesch, S. A., & Whitbourne, S. K. (1982). Intimacy and identity status in young adults. *Journal of Personality and Social Psychology, 43,* 1041–1051.

Traupmann-Pillemer, J., & Hatfield, E. (1981). Love and its effects on mental and physical health. In R. Fogel, E. Hatfield, S. Kiesler, & E. Shanas (Eds.), *Aging: Stability and change in the family* (pp. 253–274). New York: Academic Press.

Waterman, C. K., Dawson, L. J., & Bologna, M. J. (1989). Sexual coercion in gay male and lesbian relationships: Predictions and implications for support services. *Journal of Sex Research, 26,* 118–124.

Weiss, R. S. (1979). The emotional impact of marital separation. In G. Levinger & O. C. Moles (Eds.), *Divorce and separation* (pp. 201–210). New York: Basic Books.

White, K. M., Speisman, J. C., Jackson, D., Bartis, S., & Costos, D. (1986). Intimacy maturity and its correlates in young married couples. *Journal of Personality and Social Psychology, 50,* 152–162.

APPENDIX 2.1: THE PASSIONATE LOVE SCALE

We would like to know how you feel (or once felt) about the person you love, or have loved, most *passionately*. Some common terms for passionate love are romantic love, infatuation, love sickness, or obsessive love.

Please think of the person whom you love most passionately *right now*. If you are not in love right now, please think of the last person you loved. If you have never been in love, think of the person whom you came closest to caring for in that way. Try to tell us how you felt at the time when your feelings were the most intense.

Who are you thinking of?

○ Someone I love *right now*.
○ Someone I *once* loved.
○ I have never been in love but am describing how I think I *would* feel if I were in love.

Possible answers range from:

(1)	(2)	(3)	(4)	(5)	(6)	(7)	(8)	(9)
Not at all true				Moderately true				Definitely true

1. I would feel deep despair if _____ left me.
2. Sometimes I feel I can't control my thoughts; they are obsessively on _____ .
3. I feel happy when I am doing something to make _____ happy.
4. I would rather be with _____ than anyone else.
5. I'd get jealous if I thought _____ were falling in love with someone else.
6. I yearn to know all about _____ .
7. I want _____—physically, emotionally, mentally.
8. I have an endless appetite for affection from _____ .
9. For me, _____ is the perfect romantic partner.
10. I sense my body responding when _____ touches me.
11. _____ always seems to be on my mind.
12. I want _____ to know me—my thoughts, my fears, and my hopes.
13. I eagerly look for signs indicating _____'s desire for me.
14. I possess a powerful attraction for _____ .
15. I get extremely depressed when things don't go right in my relationship with _____ .

Note. From "Measuring Passionate Love in Intimate Relations," by E. Hatfield and S. Sprecher, 1986, *Journal of Adolescence, 9*, p. 391. Reprinted with permission.

APPENDIX 2.2: ROMANTIC FEELINGS AND EXPERIENCES

People have different experiences in their romantic relationships. Some people prefer to be involved in a romantic relationship, but deep down they know that, if things fall apart, they will be able to manage on their own. Others need to be close to someone; they are miserable when they are forced to be on their own. Still others need a great deal of time on their own. Some people aren't quite sure what they *do* want. (They *think* they want a relationship, but somehow they always seem to fall in love with someone who isn't interested in them.) Finally, some people are just very casual about relationships . . . or uninterested in them.

Please take a moment to think of the times you have been romantically and/ or passionately in love. (It doesn't matter whether or not your feelings were reciprocated.) Please read the following six descriptions, and indicate to what extent each describes *your* feelings and experiences in romantic and passionate love affairs. Please indicate your answers on the following scale:

0%	25%	50%	75%	100%
Never true of me		True of me about **50%** of the time		**Always** true of me

*1. **[Secure]:** *I Am Comfortable With Closeness and/or Independence:* I find it easy to get close to others and am comfortable depending on them and having them depend on me. I don't often worry about being abandoned or about someone getting too close to me.

*2. **[Clingy]:** *I Need a Great Deal of Closeness:* I find that others are reluctant to get as close as I would like. I often worry that my partner doesn't really love me or won't want to stay with me. I want to merge completely with another person, and this desire sometimes scares people away.

*3. **[Skittish]:** *I Need a Great Deal of Independence:* I am somewhat uncomfortable being close to others; I find it difficult to trust them completely, difficult to allow myself to depend on them. I am nervous when anyone gets too close, and often, love partners want me to be more intimate than I feel comfortable being.

4. **[Fickle]:** *I Am Not Quite Sure What I Need:* Sometimes, I don't know *what* I want. When I'm in love, I worry that my partner doesn't really love me or won't want to stay with me. When people get too interested in me, however, I often find that I'm just not interested in them—I end up feeling bored, irritated, or smothered. Either I fall in love and the other person doesn't or the other person falls in love and I don't.

*These three items are based on Hazan & Shaver, 1987, p. 515.

5. **[Casual]:** *I Am Fairly Casual About Relationships:* I like having someone, but I don't want to have to get *too* committed or to have to invest *too* much in a relationship.
6. **[Uninterested]:** *I Am Uninterested in Relationships:* I don't have time for relationships. They are generally not worth the hassle.

Some scientists have also asked men and women to indicate which of the six types sounds most like them:

Love Schemas

In the previous section we described six "love schemas:"

1. I am comfortable with closeness and/or independence.
2. I need a great deal of closeness.
3. I need a great deal of independence
4. I am not quite sure what I need.
5. I am fairly casual about relationships.
6. I am uninterested in relationships.

This time, we are interested in finding out which of the six descriptions sounds *most* like you, which sound somewhat like you, and which sounds *least* like you. Please *rank order* these six descriptions—going from (1) that which sounds most like you and best reflects your experiences in passionate love relationships to (6) that which sounds least like you and least like the experiences you have had. (Just indicate the appropriate number in the circle.)

○ 1. Sounds most like me (the best fitting description).
○ 2. Second best fitting description.
○ 3. Third best fitting description.
○ 4. Fourth best fitting description.
○ 5. Fifth best fitting description.
○ 6. Sounds least like me.

Note. From "Love Schemas and Romantic Love," by T. Singelis, P. Choo, and E. Hatfield, 1995, *Journal of Social Behavior and Personality, 10*, pp. 15–36. Reprinted with permission.

3

Experience, Expression, and Control of Anger in a Chinese Society: The Case of Singapore

Norbert K. Tanzer
Karl-Franzens-University, Graz, Austria

Catherine Q. E. Sim
Tilburg University, The Netherlands

Charles D. Spielberger
University of South Florida, Tampa, USA

Abstract   *The State–Trait Anger Expression Inventory (STAXI) has been used extensively to assess the experience, expression, and control of anger with Anglo-American and European samples, but only limited data are available from non-Western societies. This study investigated the assessment of anger in Singapore, a non-Western, predominantly Chinese society. Although Singaporeans have preserved much of their Eastern culture, they are fluent in English and in Western ways of doing business. The original English form of the STAXI was administered to 273 Singaporean Chinese from different age groups, educational levels, and occupational status. The results in regard to state and trait anger were similar to those in Western countries for both males and females. The factor structure of the STAXI for anger-in, anger-out, and anger control for Singaporean Chinese men was also similar to that found for both men and women in the United States and other Western societies. However, important differences in modes of anger expression were found for the Singaporean Chinese women, for whom the control of anger appears to be an extremely important personality trait.*

The negative impact of anger and hostility on emotional well-being has been demonstrated in numerous studies (e.g., Carmody, Crossen, & Wiens, 1989; Mook, van der Ploeg, & Kleijn, 1990). A growing body of research also provides evidence that anger and hostility play an important role in the pathogenesis of coronary heart disease (CHD) and hypertension (e.g., Harburg, Gleiberman, Russell, & Cooper, 1991; Siegman & Smith, 1994; Smith & Allred, 1989; Spielberger, Johnson, Russell, Crane, & Worden, 1985; Suarez

51

& Williams, 1989; Treiber et al., 1989). Although a cautious interpretation of such findings is recommended (e.g., Colligan & Offord, 1988; Hearn, Murray, & Luepker, 1989; Knight, Paulin, & Waal-Manning, 1987), how individuals experience, express, and cope with anger seems to be a critical factor in the etiology of CHD and hypertension (cf. Dimsdale et al., 1986; Engebretson, Matthews, & Scheier, 1989; Goldstein, Edelberg, Meier, & Davis, 1988; Johnson, 1989; Mills, Schneider, & Dimsdale, 1989; Spielberger et al., 1991).

Despite a large and growing body of research on *anger, hostility,* and *aggression,* the definitions of these constructs are ambiguous, and often confounded and contradictory (Spielberger, Krasner, & Solomon, 1988). The resulting conceptual confusion is reflected in the content and structure of the various scales that have been used to measure anger and hostility in research on CHD and hypertension (cf. Barefoot, Dodge, Peterson, Dahlstrom, & Williams, 1989; Musante, MacDougall, Dembroski, & Costa, 1989). The concepts of *anger* and *hostility* typically refer to feelings and attitudes, whereas *aggression* is most often used to describe punitive and destructive behavior directed toward other persons or objects in the environment.

MEASURING THE EXPERIENCE AND EXPRESSION OF ANGER

Considering the substantial overlap in the definitions of *anger, hostility,* and *aggression,* Spielberger et al. (1985) referred collectively to these constructs as the *AHA! Syndrome.* Most measures of anger and hostility tend to confound the experience of anger with hostility and aggressive behavior, and with the situational determinants of angry reactions. Consequently, it is unclear whether such scales assess transitory emotional states (e.g., angry feelings) or relatively stable individual differences. *Anger,* the simplest and most fundamental component of the AHA! Syndrome, is typically defined as a psychobiological emotional state, consisting of feelings that may vary in intensity from mild annoyance or irritation to intense fury and rage (Spielberger, Jacobs, Russell, & Crane, 1983). *Hostility* is a complex trait that includes angry feelings, attitudes such as resentment and cynicism, and vicious and vindictive behavior.

In developing a conceptual framework for constructing scales to measure the various manifestations of anger, Spielberger (1988) and his colleagues (Spielberger et al., 1983, 1985) emphasized the critical importance of distinguishing between state and trait anger, and defining how anger is expressed. *State anger* (S-Anger) is defined as a psychobiological emotional state or condition, consisting of subjective feelings that may range in intensity from mild irritation or annoyance to intense fury and rage, accompanied by increased muscular tension and arousal of the autonomic nervous system (Spielberger et al., 1983). The intensity of S-Anger varies as a function of perceived injustice, unfair treatment by others, and frustration resulting from barriers to goal-directed behavior.

Trait anger (T-Anger) refers to anger-proneness (i.e., to individual differences in the disposition to perceive a wide range of situations as annoying or frustrating, and to respond to such situations with angry feelings). Persons high in T-Anger are prone to experience S-Anger more often and with greater intensity than individuals low in T-Anger. When anger is experienced, it can be expressed in aggressive behavior directed toward other persons or objects in the environment, held in or suppressed, or consciously or unconsciously controlled.

Consistent with these definitions, Spielberger (1988) constructed the State–Trait Anger Expression Inventory (STAXI) to assess: (a) the intensity of the angry feelings that a person experiences at a particular time, (b) individual differences in anger-proneness as a personality trait, and (c) different modes of anger expression and control. The intensity of the experience of anger as an emotional state is measured by the STAXI S-Anger scale; how often anger is experienced is assessed by the STAXI T-Anger scale. Anger expression is measured by three STAXI scales that assess the frequency that anger is outwardly expressed (AX/Out), held in or suppressed (AX/In), or overtly controlled (AX/Con).

The factor structure of the original English form of the STAXI, which corresponds essentially with the anger constructs defined by the inventory's five scales and two subscales, was confirmed in two recent factor-analytic studies (Forgays, Forgays, & Spielberger, in press; Fuqua, Leonard, Masters, & Smith, 1991). This structure has also been confirmed in factor analyses of the Dutch, German, Italian, and Norwegian adaptations of the inventory (cf. Comunian, 1991; Haseth, 1993; Mook, van der Ploeg, & Kleijn, 1990; Schwenkmezger & Hodapp, 1986, 1989; Schwenkmezger, Hodapp, & Spielberger, 1992; Spielberger & Comunian, 1992; van der Ploeg, 1988). To date, however, there has been relatively little research with the STAXI in non-Western societies (e.g., Yui Miao & Lin, 1990).

ANGER IN EASTERN AND WESTERN CULTURES

Although anger is a universal emotion, how people cope with anger is governed by the norms, customs, and cultural traditions of a particular society (cf. Mesquita & Frijda, 1992). Because the perception of a situation as anger-provoking and the manner in which anger is expressed depend on both the social context (cf. Karniol & Heiman, 1987) and a person's cultural history (cf. Törestad, 1990), the experience, expression, and control of anger may not be the same in Eastern and Western societies. For example, the concept of *face (mian zi)*, the facade that a person presents to the public, is more important in Chinese culture than in Western societies (cf. Bond, 1991).

Traditionally, except for the intimate associates of a Chinese person, only the facade of that person can be seen by strangers, and this limitation often applies even to extended family members. Having been trained from childhood to keep their emotions under control, the Chinese are well known for their inhibition of emotional expression. Indeed, any display of emotion may be considered as a "loss of face," which is equivalent to the loss of one's dignity. Hence, it is of the utmost importance for a Chinese person to present a "good face." Moreover, it is also important to "give face" to other people so as not to embarrass them. Considering the differences between Chinese and Western cultures in customs, traditions, and childrearing styles, it seems plausible that the manner in which anger is experienced and expressed may also differ in these societies.

Although the Singaporean Chinese are quite different in many ways from the Chinese who reside in mainland China, Taiwan, and even Hong Kong, they have retained their language and much of their original Chinese culture. Singapore is not only a great distance from China, but it is also surrounded by Muslim countries and was part of Malaysia before being colonized by Britain. After separation from the British in 1958 and before gaining full independence in 1965, Singapore once again became a state of Malaysia. Although more than 75% of the population is Chinese, Singapore is a multiracial society, as reflected in the fact that all official documents and public signs are in four languages: English, Mandarin, Malay, and Tamil. The influence of these four cultures, which can be observed in Singapore's cuisine and dress code, has contributed to an ongoing acculturation process and the evolution of a particular Chinese subculture known as the *peranakan* (Wu, 1991).

One major consequence of Singaporean acculturation over the many years of British colonial rule was the government's decision to establish English, rather than other local languages, as the medium for school instruction. From the beginning of primary school, English is the language of instruction in all academic subjects. English is also the "unofficial official language" in everyday business life. Consequently, the English comprehension level of younger Singaporeans is essentially equivalent to that of native English speakers.

The primary goal of this study was to assess, examine, and evaluate the experience, expression, and control of anger in a Chinese society. Because it is often difficult to determine whether observed differences between cultures are due to bias arising from the translation and adaptation of test instruments or to genuine cross-cultural factors (cf. Hambleton, 1991; Tanzer, Sim, & Marsh, 1992), an advantage of selecting Singapore for this research was that the original English form of the STAXI could be administered to English-speaking persons in a predominantly Chinese society.

MEASURING ANGER IN SINGAPOREAN CHINESE ADOLESCENTS AND ADULTS

Subjects and Procedure

The English form of the STAXI (Spielberger, 1988) was administered to a heterogeneous sample of 310 Singapore residents (88% Chinese, 5% Malays, 3% Indians, 4% other) who responded anonymously to the inventory on a voluntary basis. To evaluate the experience, expression, and control of anger in a sample with a homogeneous cultural background, only the data for the 273 Chinese participants (58% female, 42% male) were examined. These subjects ranged in age from 12 to 52 years ($M = 24.6$, $SD = 8.9$). Of the Chinese sample, 11% were managers, 49% were self-employed, 27% were employees, and 13% were classified as "other." Approximately half of the participants had either a primary or secondary school education, and half had preuniversity or tertiary education. However, only 44% of the females, as compared with 59% of the males, were in the higher education group.

The STAXI Scales

The STAXI 10-item S-Anger and T-Anger scales were designed to assess the intensity of angry feelings at a particular time (Items S1–S10) and individual differences in the disposition to experience anger (Items T11–T20). Factor-analytic studies of the 10 STAXI T-Anger items (Fuqua et al., 1991; Spielberger, 1988; Spielberger et al., 1983) have consistently demonstrated that this scale consists of two components: Angry-Temperament (T-Anger/T) and Angry-Reaction (T-Anger/R). Similar findings have also been reported for the Dutch (van der Ploeg, 1988), German (Schwenkmezger & Hodapp, 1989), Italian (Spielberger & Comunian, 1992), and Norwegian (Haseth, 1993) forms of the STAXI. The T-Anger/T subscale (Items T11, T12, T13, T16) measures a general disposition to experience angry feelings without specific provocation; the T-Anger/R subscale (Items T14, T15, T18, T20) assesses an individual's proneness to experience anger when criticized or treated unfairly by others.

Anger expression is measured with the STAXI by 3 eight-item scales. The STAXI AX/Out scale (Items AX22, AX27, AX29, AX32, AX34, AX39, AX42, AX43) assesses how often anger is expressed toward other persons or objects in the environment (e.g., When angry or furious, "I argue with others"; "I do things like slam doors"). Aggressive verbal behavior (e.g., insults, verbal threats, and the use of profanity) are considered expressions of anger-out, whether directed toward the source of provocation or frustration, or toward persons or objects associated with or symbolic of the provoking agent.

The eight items of the STAXI AX/In scale (Items AX23, AX25, AX26, AX30, AX33, AX36, AX37, AX41) assess individual differences in the frequency that a person holds in or otherwise suppresses angry feelings (e.g., When angry or furious, "I keep things in"; "I boil inside, but I don't show it"). Suppressed anger is experienced as an emotional state (S-Anger) that varies in intensity. The eight-item STAXI AX/Con scale (Items AX21, AX24, AX28, AX31, AX35, AX38, AX40, AX44) measures the extent to which a person consciously attempts to control anger by preventing its expression (e.g., When angry or furious, "I control my angry feelings"; "I keep my cool").

COMPONENTS OF ANGER IN SINGAPOREAN CHINESE

Means, standard deviations, and alpha reliability coefficients for the STAXI S-Anger, T-Anger, AX/In, AX/Out, and AX/Con scales, and for the two T-Anger subscales (i.e., T-Anger/T and T-Anger/R), are reported for males and females in Table 3.1. No significant gender differences were found in S-Anger, T-Anger, the two T-Anger subscales, or in AX/In or AX/Out. However, males scored significantly higher than females ($p < .01$) on the AX/Con

Table 3.1 STAXI scale and subscale means, standard deviations, and alpha
coefficients for female and male Singaporean Chinese adults

STAXI scales and subscales	No. of items	M	SD	Alpha
S-Anger	10			
Females		15.00	6.00	.92
Males		16.18	6.33	.89
T-Anger	10			
Females		19.91	4.88	.83
Males		20.01	5.24	.84
T-Anger/T	4			
Females		7.44	2.51	.87
Males		7.22	2.36	.80
T-Anger/R	4			
Females		9.15	2.42	.74
Males		9.03	2.41	.71
AX/In	8			
Females		16.62	3.41	.60
Males		16.86	3.72	.68
AX/Out	8			
Females		15.37	3.85	.79
Males		15.38	4.10	.79
AX/Con	8			
Females		19.54	4.39	.82
Males		21.36	4.32	.81

scale. Similarly, males also had higher AX/Con scores than females in the U.S.
normative sample (Spielberger, 1988) and in several European samples
(Schwenkmezger & Hodapp, 1986; Spielberger & Comunian, 1992).

Alpha reliabilities were .79 or higher for all of the STAXI scales, except for
AX/In and the T-Anger/R subscale. The alphas found for the four-item
T-Anger/R subscale, which were similar to those reported for the U.S. normative sample (Spielberger, 1988), are satisfactory for this brief measure. However, given the relatively low alpha for the AX/In scale, indicating marginal
internal consistency, scores on this measure should be interpreted with caution,
especially for the females.

State and Trait Anger

To examine the factor structure for the STAXI S-Anger and T-Anger scales,
the 20 S-Anger and T-Anger items were factored together in separate principal
components analyses for males and females. Scree plots indicated that the
resulting two-factor solutions provided the best fit for both sexes. For the
males, 47% of the total variance was explained (37% and 11%, respectively,

Table 3.2 STAXI S-Anger and T-Anger item loadings for males and females on the State and Trait Anger factors

STAXI items	Factor I, State Anger		Factor II, Trait Anger	
	M	F	M	F
S-Anger				
S1	.82	.69		
S2	.72	.74		
S3	.85	.79		
S4	.69	.78		
S5	.50	.82		
S6	.58	.60		
S7	.45	.85		
S8	.50	.83		
S9	.79	.66		
S10	.56	.79		
T-Anger				
T11			.82	.67
T12			.73	.75
T13			.74	.79
T14			.48	.48
T15			.57	.59
T16			.59	.70
T17			.63	.54
T18			.56	.57
T19		.37	.65	.36
T20			.50	.57

Note. Item loadings of less than .35 are omitted from the table.

for the first two unrotated factors); for females, 50% of the total variance was explained (36% and 14%, respectively, for the two unrotated factors).

Factor loadings for females and males in the two-factor Oblimin-rotated solutions are reported in Table 3.2. For both sexes, the 10 S-Anger items (S1–S10) all loaded exclusively on Factor I, and all 10 T-Anger items (T11–T20) loaded on Factor II. Only one item, T19 for females, had a dual salient loading (.35 or greater) on either the S-Anger or T-Anger factors, which were moderately correlated for both sexes ($r = .47$ for males, $r = .36$ for females). These results clearly indicate that the S-Anger and T-Anger factors for the Singaporean Chinese participants in this study were quite similar to those found for American and Western European subjects.

To determine whether Angry-Temperament and Angry-Reaction could be identified as distinguishable components of T-Anger, the 10 T-Anger items were factored in separate principal components analyses for males and females. The scree plots in both analyses indicated that the two-factor solutions were most meaningful for both sexes, explaining 54% of the total variance for males (42% and 12% for the first two unrotated factors) and 56% for females (40%

Table 3.3 STAXI T-Anger item loadings for males and females on the
Angry-Temperament and Angry-Reaction factors

STAXI T-Anger items	Factor I, Angry-Temperament		Factor II, Angry-Reaction	
	M	*F*	*M*	*F*
Temperament				
T11	.60	.78		
T12	.83	.92		
T13	.66	.81		
T16	.62	.82		
Reaction				
T14			.68	.50
T15			.88	.73
T18			.41	.77
T20			.76	.91
Nonsubscale				
T17	.75	.59		
T19	.82			

Note. Item loadings of less than .35 are omitted from the table.

and 16% for the first two factors). The Oblimin-rotated factor loadings for
each T-Anger item are reported in Table 3.3.

All eight T-Anger/T (T11, T12, T13, T16) and T-Anger/R (T14, T15, T18,
T20) items loaded exclusively on their respective target factors; none had any
secondary salient loadings. The correlations between the T-Anger/T and T-
Anger/R factors were .47 for males and .39 for females, confirming the presence of distinguishable, but substantially related, temperament and reaction
factors for the Singaporean Chinese subjects. These findings also provide concurrent evidence of the validity of the STAXI subscales for assessing these
factors.

In the U.S. normative sample (Spielberger, 1988), two items had dual or
ambiguous loadings on the T-Anger subscale (T17—"When I get mad, I say
nasty things"; T19—"When I get frustrated, I feel like hitting someone"). For
the Singaporean males, both of these items had strong loadings on the
T-Anger/T factor and no dual loadings (see Table 3.3). Item T17 also had a
moderately high loading on this factor for females. Consequently, it seems
plausible that the Singaporean subjects may interpret Item T17 as "Whenever
(each time) I get mad . . . ," which would explain the strong loadings on the
T-Anger/T factor. Although Item T19 appears to be interpreted in a similar
manner by the Singaporean males, the stated consequence of frustration for
Singaporean women (i.e., "feel like hitting someone") may be so unacceptable, as indicated by their very low scores, that this item failed to load on either
factor for them.

Table 3.4 STAXI AX/In and AX/Out item loadings for males and females on the Anger-In and Anger-Out factors

AX scale items	Factor I, Anger-In		Factor II, Anger-Out	
	M	F	M	F
AX/In				
AX23	.59		− .42	− .64
AX26	.63	.41		
AX30	.72	.38		− .68
AX33	.56	.58		
AX37	.63	.62		
AX41	.65	.65		
AX25		.43	.41	
AX36		.53	.37	
AX/Out				
AX22			.68	.67
AX27			.71	.66
AX32			.73	.61
AX34		.44	.65	.59
AX39			.65	.71
AX43			.35	
AX29			.64	.62
AX42			.71	.64

Note. Item loadings of less than .35 are omitted from the table.

Measuring Anger Expression

To evaluate the independence for the Singaporean subjects of the two components of anger expression—anger-in and anger-out—the 16 items comprising the STAXI AX/In and AX/Out scales were factored in separate principal components analyses for males and females. The scree plots for both sexes indicated that the total variance was best accounted for by the two-factor solutions, in which 42% of the total variance was explained for males (26% and 16%, respectively, for the unrotated factors) and 40% for females (27% and 14% for the unrotated solution). Because the two rotated factors in the Oblimin solution were essentially uncorrelated for both sexes ($r = .09$ for males, $r = .19$ for females), the orthogonal (Varimax) rotated loadings are reported for males and females in Table 3.4.

Although most of the AX/In and AX/Out items had primary loadings on their respective target factors, AX/In Item AX23 ("I keep things in") had a primary negative loading on the AX/Out factor for females and no salient loading on AX/In, and a secondary negative loading on AX/Out for males. AX/In Item AX30 ("I boil inside, but don't show it") also had a primary negative loading for females on the AX/Out factor, and a smaller but salient positive loading on AX/In. Thus, as assessed by these two items, keeping anger in for the Singaporean Chinese females was more strongly associated with the absence of anger-out than with the tendency to experience and suppress anger (anger-in).

AX/In Item AX25 ("I pout or sulk") and AX36 ("I am secretly quite critical of others") had appropriate primary loadings on the AX/In factor for females, whereas these items failed to load on the target factor for males, and had small primary loadings on the AX/Out factor. Item AX43 ("If someone annoys me, I'm apt to tell him or her how I feel") had a weak primary loading on the target AX/Out factor for males, but no salient loadings on either factor for females. Thus, harboring criticism may be equivalent to expressing anger-out for Chinese men, whereas telling someone off appears to be unacceptable as a means of expressing anger for Chinese women.

To examine the relation of anger-in and anger-out with anger control, the 24 items comprising the 3 eight-item AX scales were factored in separate principal components analyses for males and females. The scree plots in these analyses indicated that the three-factor solutions were most meaningful, explaining 45% of the total variance for males (23%, 15%, and 7%, respectively, for each factor in the unrotated solution) and 46% for females (27%, 12%, and 7%, respectively). Because the three factors in the Oblimin rotation were essentially uncorrelated for both sexes, the orthogonal-rotated factor solutions are reported in Table 3.5.

For both males and females, all eight anger control items had high loadings on the target factor and no salient nontarget loadings, as may be noted in Table 3.5. Moreover, all eight AX/Out items had primary loadings for males on the target factor, as did six of the eight AX/In items. With the exception of three AX/In items (AX23, AX25, AX36), the orthogonal three-factor structure for the Singaporean males was quite similar to that obtained for their U.S. counterparts. Thus, the findings for Singaporean males in the present study were quite similar to those for their U.S. counterparts.

In contrast to the similarities between Singaporean and U.S. males, important differences were found in the anger-in and anger-out factors for Singaporean Chinese women. Although six of the eight AX/Out items had substantial loadings on the target factor for the Singaporean females, five AX/Out items (AX22, AX27, AX29, AX39, AX42) also had strong negative loadings on the AX/Con factor. Moreover, four AX/In items (AX23, AX30, AX33, AX36) had nontarget primary loadings, and no salient loadings on the target factor. Of these, Items AX23 and AX30 had salient loadings on AX/Con rather than on AX/In, and Items AX33 and AX36 shifted from the AX/In factor in the two-factor solution (see Table 3.4) to the AX/Out factor in the three-factor solution reported in Table 3.5.

DISCUSSION AND CONCLUSIONS

The factor structure of the STAXI S-Anger and T-Anger scales for Singaporean Chinese, including the T-Anger/T and T-Anger/R subscales, closely resembled the findings for the U.S. normative sample. Because similar results have also been found in several European adaptations of the STAXI, these

Table 3.5 STAXI AX/In, AX/Out, and AX/Con item loadings for males and females on the Anger-In, Anger-Out, and Anger Control factors

AX scales	Factor I, Anger-In		Factor II, Anger-Out		Factor III, Anger Control	
	M	F	M	F	M	F
AX/In items						
AX23	.59		− .41			.58
AX26	.60	.53				
AX30	.65					.71
AX33	.56			.39		
AX37	.56	.70				
AX41	.68	.73				
AX25		.48	.37			
AX36			.39	.72		
AX/Out items						
AX22			.67	.42		− .45
AX27			.71	.59		− .36
AX32			.70	.57		
AX34			.66	.62		
AX39			.63	.56		− .48
AX43			.39	.56		
AX29		.44	.57			− .47
AX42		.40	.63		− .36	− .56
AX/Con items						
AX21					.61	.73
AX24					.48	.51
AX28					.70	.77
AX31					.70	.78
AX35					.62	.56
AX38					.57	.46
AX40					.73	.67
AX44					.67	.62

Note. Item loadings of less than .35 are omitted from the table.

findings provide further confirmation that the state–trait distinction in anger research can be generalized across gender, language, and culture.

The posited two- and three-factor structures for Anger-In, Anger-Out, and Anger-Control, as measured by the STAXI, for the Singaporean Chinese males were quite similar to those for both men and women in the United States and other Western cultures. For the Singaporean females, however, the primary loadings for several AX/In items shifted to the AX/Con factor; secondary negative loadings on AX/Con were also found for five of the eight AX/Out items.

The differences in the structure of the AX/In and AX/Out factors for the females in the two-factor solution, as compared with the three-factor solution, are especially interesting. For example, Item AX36 ("I am secretly quite critical of others") shifted from the AX/In factor in the two-factor analysis (Table 3.4) to AX/Out in the three-factor analysis (Table 3.5), and five of the eight AX/Out items had strong negative loadings on AX/Con. These findings suggest that the control of anger is a more dominant characteristic for Singaporean females than for Singaporean men. The expression of anger appears to be especially unacceptable to traditional Singaporean Chinese women.

Harmony in the family and in interpersonal relationships between friends and colleagues is very important in Chinese cultures. To achieve and maintain such harmony, a Chinese person must be able to "tolerate" unpleasant situations without the overt expression of negative emotions such as anger. This characteristic is referred to as *lun* in the Teochew and Hokkien dialects, and *yan* in Cantonese. In the traditional roles of men and women in Chinese society, the ability to tolerate unpleasantness is clearly more important for females.

Because similar shifts in some AX/In and AX/Out items have also been found in several independent German and Italian samples (Schwenkmezger & Hodapp, 1986; Spielberger & Comunian, 1992), the differences found in the expression of anger in this study cannot be attributed entirely to cultural factors. Nevertheless, in Chinese culture, "being critical of others" appears to be associated more with anger-out than with anger-in. Indeed, secretly harboring criticism regarding another person, even without directly confronting and embarrassing that person ("giving face"), is equivalent to expressing anger. Similarly, nonverbal facial expressions of displeasure, such as sulking or pouting, considered as anger-in in Western cultures, appear to be equivalent to the outward expression of anger in Chinese society. In the Teochew, Hokkien, and Cantonese dialects, such facial expressions are described by the denigrating metaphor *showing his black face*.

REFERENCES

Barefoot, J. C., Dodge, K. A., Peterson, B. L., Dahlstrom, W. G., & Williams, R. B., Jr. (1989). The Cook-Medley Hostility Scale: Item content and ability to predict survival. *Psychosomatic Medicine, 51,* 46–57.
Bond, M. (1991). *Beyond the Chinese face.* Hong Kong: Oxford University Press.
Carmody, T. P., Crossen, J. R., & Wiens, A. N. (1989). Hostility as a health risk factor: Relationships with neuroticism, Type A behavior, attentional focus, and interpersonal style. *Journal of Clinical Psychology, 45,* 754–762.
Colligan, R. C., & Offord, K. P. (1988). The risky use of the MMPI Hostility Scale in assessing risk for coronary heart disease. *Psychosomatics, 29,* 188–196.
Comunian, A. L. (1991, July). *Psychometric properties of the State-Trait Anger Expression Inventory in a college population.* Paper presented at the 12th International STAR Conference, Budapest, Hungary.
Dimsdale, J. E., Pierce, C., Schoenfeld, D., Brown, A., Zusman, R., & Graham, R. (1986). Suppressed anger and blood pressure: The effects of race, social class, obesity, and age. *Psychosomatic Medicine, 48,* 430–436.

Engebretson, T. O., Matthews, K. A., & Scheier, M. F. (1989). Relations between anger expression and cardiovascular reactivity: Reconciling inconsistent findings through a matching hypothesis. *Journal of Personality and Social Psychology, 57,* 513–521.

Forgays, D. G., Forgays, D. K., & Spielberger, C. D. (in press). Factor structure of the State-Trait Anger Expression Inventory. *Journal of Personality Assessment.*

Fuqua, D. R., Leonard, E., Masters, M. A., & Smith, R. J. (1991). A structural analysis of the State-Trait Anger Expression Inventory. *Educational and Psychological Measurement, 51,* 439–446.

Goldstein, H. S., Edelberg, R., Meier, C. F., & Davis, L. (1988). Relationship of resting blood pressure and heart rate to experienced anger and expressed anger. *Psychosomatic Medicine, 50,* 321–329.

Hambleton, R. K. (1991). Test translation for cross-cultural studies. *Bulletin of the International Test Commission, 18* (1 & 2).

Harburg, E., Gleiberman, L., Russell, M., & Cooper, M. L. (1991). Anger-coping styles and blood pressure in Black and White males: Buffalo, New York. *Psychosomatic Medicine, 53,* 153–164.

Haseth, K. (1993). *The factor structure of the Norwegian adaptation of Spielberger's State-Trait Anger Expression Scale.* Unpublished manuscript, University of Oslo.

Hearn, M. D., Murray, D. M., & Luepker, R. V. (1989). Hostility, coronary heart disease, and total mortality: A 33-year follow-up of university students. *Journal of Behavioral Medicine, 12,* 105–121.

Johnson, E. H. (1989). The role of the experience and expression of anger in elevated blood pressure among Black and White adolescents. *Journal of the National Medical Association, 81,* 573–584.

Karniol, R., & Heiman, I. (1987). Situational antecedents of children's anger experiences and subsequent responses to adult versus peer provokers. *Aggressive Behavior, 13,* 109–118.

Knight, R. G., Paulin, J. M., & Waal-Manning, H. J. (1987). Self-reported anger intensity and blood pressure. *British Journal of Clinical Psychology, 26,* 65–66.

Mesquita, B., & Frijda, N. H. (1992). Cultural variations in emotions: A review. *Psychological Bulletin, 112,* 179–204.

Mills, P. J., Schneider, R. H., & Dimsdale, J. E. (1989). Anger assessment and reactivity to stress. *Journal of Psychosomatic Research, 33,* 379–382.

Mook, J., van der Ploeg, H. M., & Kleijn, W. C. (1990). Anxiety, anger and depression: Relationships at the trait level. *Anxiety Research, 3,* 17–31.

Musante, L., MacDougall, J. M., Dembroski, T. M., & Costa, P. T., Jr. (1989). Potential for hostility and dimensions of anger. *Health Psychology, 8,* 343–354.

Schwenkmezger, P., & Hodapp, V. (1986). *Die deutsche Adaption der Anger Expression (AX) Scale nach C. D. Spielberger* [German adaption of C. D. Spielberger's Anger Expression Scale]. Trier, Germany: Fachbereich Psychologie, University of Trier.

Schwenkmezger, P., & Hodapp, V. (1989). *Das State-Trait Anger Expression Inventory (STAXI): Itemmetrische und faktorenanalytische Befunde und Un-*

tersuchungen zur Konstruktvalidität [The State-Trait Anger Expression Inventory: Psychometric and factoranalytic properties and some results on construct validity]. Trier, Germany: Fachbereich Psychologie, University of Trier.

Schwenkmezger, P., Hodapp, V., & Spielberger, C. D. (1992). *Das State-Trait Ärger-Ausdrucks-Inventar (STAXI). Handbuch* [Test Manual of the German Version of the State-Trait Anger Expression Inventory]. Bern: Huber.

Siegman, A. W., & Smith, T. W. (Eds.) (1994). *Anger, hostility and the heart.* Hillsdale, NJ: Lawrence Erlbaum Associates.

Smith, T. W., & Allred, K. D. (1989). Blood-pressure responses during social interaction in high- and low-cynically hostile males. *Journal of Behavioral Medicine, 12,* 135–143.

Spielberger, C. D. (1988). *State-Trait Anger Expression Inventory Research Edition. Professional Manual.* Odessa, FL: Psychological Assessment Resources.

Spielberger, C. D., & Comunian, A. L. (1992). *STAXI. State-Trait Anger Expression Inventory. Versione e adattamento italiano a curi di Anna Laura Comunian. Manuale* [Test Manual of the Italian Version of the State-Trait Anger Expression Inventory]. Firenze: Organizzazioni Speziali.

Spielberger, C. D., Crane, R. S., Kearns, W. D., Pellegrin, K. L., Rickman, R. L., & Johnson, E. H. (1991). Anger and anxiety in essential hypertension. In C. D. Spielberger & I. G. Sarason (Eds.), *Stress and emotion* (Vol. 14, pp. 266–283). New York: Hemisphere/Taylor & Francis.

Spielberger, C. D., Jacobs, G., Russell, S., & Crane, R. J. (1983). Assessment of anger: The State-Trait Anger Scale. In J. N. Butcher & C. D. Spielberger (Eds.), *Advances in personality assessment* (Vol. 2, pp. 159–187). Hillsdale, NJ: Lawrence Erlbaum Associates.

Spielberger, C. D., Johnson, E. H., Russell, S. F., Crane, R. J., & Worden, T. J. (1985). The experience and expression of anger: Construction and validation of an anger expression scale. In M. A. Chesney & R. H. Rosenman (Eds.), *Anger and hostility in cardiovascular and behavioral disorders* (pp. 5–30). New York: Hemisphere/McGraw-Hill.

Spielberger, C. D., Krasner, S. S., & Solomon, E. P. (1988). The experience, expression, and control of anger. In M. P. Janisse (Ed.), *Health psychology: Individual differences and stress* (pp. 89–108). New York: Springer.

Suarez, E. C., & Williams, R. B., Jr. (1989). Situational determinants of cardiovascular and emotional reactivity in high and low hostile men. *Psychosomatic Medicine, 51,* 404–418.

Tanzer, N. K., Sim, C. Q. E., & Marsh, H. W. (1992). Using personality and attitude inventories over cultures. Theoretical considerations and empirical findings. *Bulletin of the International Test Commission, 19,* 151–172.

Törestad, B. (1990). What is anger provoking?—Provokers and provoked in anger situations: Developmental trends and sex differences. *Aggressive Behavior, 16,* 353–359.

Treiber, F. A., Musante, L., Riley, W., Mabe, A. P., Carr, T., Levey, M., & Strong, W. B. (1989). The relationship between hostility and blood pressure in children. *Behavioral Medicine, 15,* 173–178.

van der Ploeg, H. M. (1988). The factor structure of the State-Trait Anger Scale. *Psychological Reports, 63,* 978.

Wu, D. Y. H. (1991). The construction of Chinese and non-Chinese identities. *Daedalus. Journal of the American Academy of Arts and Sciences, 120,* 159–179.

Yui Miao, E. S. C., & Lin, R.-F. (1990, July). *An exploratory study of the Anger Expression Scale: Comparing two groups of adolescents.* Paper presented at the 22nd International Congress of Applied Psychology, Kyoto, Japan.

4

Assessing Anger with the Minnesota Multiphasic Personality Inventory

Jaime L. Carr and John R. Graham
Kent State University, Kent, Ohio, USA

Abstract   *This chapter examines how anger has been assessed with the Minnesota Multiphasic Personality Inventory (MMPI) and the Minnesota Multiphasic Personality Inventory–2 (MMPI–2). The empirical correlates of the basic MMPI scales that are related to anger are reviewed, and several new content-based anger scales that were developed from the MMPI–2 item pool are described. The construction of the new MMPI–2 anger scales has involved: (a) the rational identification of content areas, (b) statistical verification of the inclusion of items in the new scales, (c) further statistical refinement of each new scale, and (d) writing interpretive descriptions. Correlations of the MMPI–2 anger scales with other MMPI–2 scales, and with external criteria such as the Anger Expression scale, the Anger Self-Report scale, the Cook–Medley Hostility scale, and the State–Trait Anger Expression Inventory (STAXI) are reported.*

Awareness of the importance of assessing anger accurately (Biaggio & Maiuro, 1985) has been greatly enhanced by increasing evidence that angry and hostile feelings may be related to high blood pressure (BP), coronary heart disease (CHD), cancer, and other health problems. In addition to health-related issues, a person's sense of well-being can be markedly and negatively affected by the inability to express angry feelings in adaptive ways. Conversely, the uncontrolled expression of anger can lead to problems and conflicts with other people and with society.

Many different approaches have been utilized to assess anger. During the past decade, psychometrically sound instruments, such as the State–Trait Anger Expression Inventory (STAXI; Spielberger, 1988), have been developed to assess the experience, expression, and control of anger. The potential benefits of being able to assess anger with instruments that are routinely administered in a variety of settings, such as the MMPI or MMPI–2, have also been long recognized.

The primary purpose of this chapter is to examine the ways in which anger has been assessed with the MMPI and MMPI–2. Several new content-based

The authors are grateful to Charles D. Spielberger for granting permission to modify the STAXI items for this study.

anger scales that have been developed from the MMPI–2 item pool are described. Directions for future research on the assessment of anger with the MMPI–2 are also suggested.

HISTORY OF ANGER ASSESSMENT WITH THE MMPI

Because the MMPI was originally developed to assess psychiatric symptom syndromes, the instrument did not include a scale designed specifically to assess anger. However, subsequent research efforts attempted to determine the extent to which inferences concerning anger could be made from the MMPI. Some of the research concerning empirical correlates of the basic MMPI scales indicated that anger was often associated with high scores on some scales (e.g., *Psychopathic Deviate*). Because the basic scales were so heterogeneous in content, it was difficult to know when high scores on a particular scale indicated anger and when they indicated other symptoms and characteristics. Other research attempted to develop new scales to assess anger, hostility, and related constructs.

Assessment of Anger with the Basic MMPI Scales

Numerous attempts have been made to identify characteristics of test subjects who obtain high scores on one or more of the basic scales of the MMPI (e.g., Boerger, Graham, & Lilly, 1974; Gilberstadt & Duker, 1965; Gynther, Altman, & Sletten, 1973; Lewandowski & Graham, 1972; Marks & Seeman, 1963). Although anger was not a specific focus of these studies, some of the empirical correlates of the scales and configurations of scales were related to anger. Table 4.1 summarizes some of the empirical correlates of the basic MMPI scales that are related to anger. High scorers on Scale 1 (Hypochondriasis) are said to express hostility indirectly. Indirect hostility is also a descriptor for high scorers on Scale 3 (Hysteria). However, high Scale 3 scorers may also have occasional periods of aggressive acting out. High scorers on Scale 4 (Psychopathic Deviate) are thought to be hostile and to act on aggressive impulses, with their aggressive outbursts sometimes accompanied by assaultive behavior. However, women who score high on Scale 4 are said to express aggression in indirect ways. High scorers on Scales 6 (Paranoia) and 8 (Schizophrenia) are described as resentful and hostile, and high scorers on Scale 9 (Hypomania) are described as having a low frustration tolerance and displaying episodes of irritability, hostility, and aggressive outbursts.

Various aspects of anger have also been associated with combinations of scores on the basic MMPI scales (i.e., code types; e.g., Dahlstrom, Welsh, & Dahlstrom, 1972; Graham, 1993). As reported in Table 4.1, persons with the 13/31 code type have been described as harboring resentment and hostility. Although they do not typically express anger directly, they occasionally lose their tempers and express themselves in angry, but nonviolent, ways. Persons with the 18/81 code type have been characterized as feeling hostile. They may

Table 4.1 Anger-related descriptors for MMPI scales and code types

MMPI	Descriptors
Clinical scales	
1 (Hypochondriasis)	indirect expression of hostility
3 (Hystria)	indirect expression of hostility; occasional aggressive acting out
4 (Psychopathic Deviate)	hostile, aggressive; limited frustration tolerance; aggressive acting out; women express aggression in passive, indirect ways
6 (Paranoia)	angry, resentful, hostile; argumentative
8 (Schizophrenia)	resentful, hostile, aggressive
9 (Hypomania)	low frustration tolerance; irritable, hostile; aggressive outbursts
Code types	
13/31	resentful, hostile; occasionally lose temper; express anger in nonviolent ways
18/81	feel hostility, aggression; inhibit expression of aggression or overly belligerent, abrasive
34/43	chronic, intense anger; hostile, aggressive impulses, but don't express them
36/63	repressed anger
45/54	low frustration tolerance; anger, resentment; aggressive acting out
46/64	repressed hostility and anger
48/84	angry, irritable, resentful; act out asocially/ antisocially; crimes, if committed, vicious/assaultive
49/94	angry, hostile; occasional emotional outbursts
89/98	resentful, hostile

either inhibit their expression of aggression or become overly belligerent and abrasive.

Persons with the 34/43 code type are thought to have hostile and aggressive impulses, especially toward their families. They also have brief episodes of aggressive, and sometimes violent, acting out. Persons with the 36/63 code type have been described as prone to repress anger. Low frustration tolerance, intense anger and resentment, and brief periods of aggressive acting out have been attributed to persons with the 45/54 code type. Persons with the 46/64 code type have been described as having repressed hostility and anger. Persons with a 48/84 code type have been characterized as angry, irritable, and resentful, and as acting out in asocial ways. Persons with the 49/94 code type have been described as irritable and harboring intense feelings of anger and hostility.

Finally, persons with the 89/98 code type have been found to be resentful and hostile when their demands are not met.

For these various scales and code types, anger-related characteristics have been listed along with many other possible problems and behaviors. It is difficult to know when the anger-related characteristics should be emphasized for any particular person who has high scores on these scales or who has one of these code types.

Specific MMPI Scales to Assess Anger and Hostility

Various attempts have been made to develop MMPI scales that specifically assess anger. Dahlstrom, Welsh, and Dahlstrom (1975) provided a comprehensive list of anger and hostility scales and indices for the MMPI. Special scales were developed to assess anger and anger-related constructs, including hostility, resentment, bitterness, belligerence, manifest hostility, overt hostility, and overcontrolled hostility. Although it is beyond the scope of this chapter to discuss all of these scales, we describe several of the more widely researched and utilized ones.

Megargee and his colleagues developed the Overcontrolled Hostility (O-H) scale to assess hostility, cynicism, and overt aggression (Megargee, Cook, & Mendelsohn, 1967). They believed that two different types of people commit acts of extreme physical aggression. Undercontrolled people have not developed appropriate means to control the expression of aggression and, when provoked, respond aggressively at the same intensity level as the provocation. Overcontrolled people exhibit rigid inhibition against aggressive expression. They typically do not express an appropriate amount of aggression, but occasionally respond to even minor provocation with exaggerated levels of aggression. Although there are data suggesting that the O-H scale is related to aggressive behavior in prison inmates, there is little evidence that high O-H scores in other settings are associated with violent acts (e.g., Biaggio & Maiuro, 1985; Buck & Graham, 1978).

The Cook–Medley Hostility (Ho) scale (Cook & Medley, 1954) was originally devised to identify teachers who had difficulty getting along with their students. Items in this scale were thought to reflect generalized hostility toward others. Since its development, the Ho scale has been used to assess hostility, aggression, and anger in various settings, and has also been used extensively as a predictor of health outcomes (Barefoot, Dodge, Peterson, Dahlstrom, & Williams, 1989). Several studies have reported that persons with lower Ho scale scores are less likely than persons with higher Ho scale scores to develop CHD (Graham, 1993). However, other studies have concluded that higher Ho scale scores are not associated with risk for CHD (Colligan & Offord, 1988). The Ho scale seems to be more effective in identifying hostile men than women, and it is not useful in predicting overt expression of anger (Cook & Medley, 1954).

The Manifest Hostility (HOS) scale is one of the Wiggins content scales (Wiggins, 1969); it was designed to assess anger. High scorers on the HOS scale are said to harbor hostile and aggressive impulses; express negative impulses in passive, indirect ways; and be cross, grouchy, and argumentative.

Assessment of Anger with the MMPI-2

Prior to the restandardization of the MMPI in 1989 (Butcher, Dahlstrom, Graham, Tellegen, & Kaemmer, 1989), the test had not been revised since its publication in 1943. There were concerns that the MMPI norms had become outdated, that some of its items were no longer appropriate for contemporary subjects, and that the item pool was not broad enough to assess characteristics that many test users felt were important (Graham, 1993). These concerns were addressed by collecting contemporary normative data, revising some outdated items, deleting some objectionable items, and adding news items to broaden the content dimensions of the item pool. To ensure continuity between the original MMPI and the revised version (MMPI-2), the standard validity and clinical scales were maintained with only minor deletions and modifications.

Because of the continuity between the MMPI and MMPI-2, one would expect that empirical correlates of the MMPI scales and code types would also apply to the MMPI-2. Some preliminary data suggest that this is in fact the case. Graham (1988) correlated MMPI-2 scores of normal subjects and hospitalized psychiatric patients with ratings of their behaviors and personality characteristics. Graham concluded that the MMPI-2 scales measure essentially the same characteristics as the corresponding MMPI scales. Similar conclusions were reached by Graham and Ben-Porath (1994), who utilized an outpatient mental health center sample. Moreland and Walsh (1991) reported correlates of some frequently occurring MMPI-2 code types that were similar to those previously reported for corresponding MMPI code types.

Of the supplementary MMPI scales developed to assess anger-related constructs, only the O-H scale is routinely scored on the MMPI-2. However, enough items from other MMPI anger scales remain in the MMPI-2 that the scales also can be scored. However, interpretation of these other scales would be difficult because norms are not readily available for them.

MMPI-2 CONTENT AND COMPONENT SCALES

As stated earlier, a psychometrically sound set of content scales, including one to assess manifest hostility, was available for the MMPI (Wiggins, 1969). However, due to deletion of old items and addition of new ones, these scales were no longer representative of the content domains represented in the MMPI-2 item pool.

Development of MMPI-2 Content Scales

The MMPI-2 content scales were developed using a multistage, multi-method procedure with a combination of rational and statistical methods (Butcher, Graham, Williams, & Ben-Porath, 1990). The first stage involved the rational identification of content areas. This stage included definition of content dimensions, independent rater selection of items to represent each dimension, and group consensus concerning items to be included in the preliminary scales. The second stage involved statistical verification of item-scale membership. This stage included identification and deletion of items not correlated with the preliminary scales, and identification and addition of items correlated with the scales but not previously selected for inclusion. The third stage involved a final rational review, including inspection and revision of changed content domains and deletion of statistically related, but content inappropriate, items. In the fourth stage, final statistical refinement of scales was accomplished, with elimination of items more highly correlated with scales other than the ones in which they had been provisionally included. The fifth and final stage consisted of writing interpretive descriptions for each of the content scales based on item content and correlations with other MMPI–2 scales and external criteria. These procedures resulted in the following 15 content scales: Anxiety, Fears, Obsessiveness, Depression, Health Concerns, Bizarre Mentation, Anger, Cynicism, Antisocial Attitudes, Type-A Behavior, Low Self-Esteem, Social Discomfort, Family Problems, Work Interference, and Negative Treatment Indicators. Interested readers should consult Butcher et al. (1990) for a complete listing of items in each content scale and their scoring directions.

Psychometric Characteristics of MMPI–2 Content Scales

The MMPI–2 content scales have respectable psychometric properties. Their test–retest reliabilities in the normative sample ranged from .78 (Bizarre Mentation) to .91 (Social Discomfort) for men, and from .79 (Type-A Behavior) to .91 (Work Interference) for women. Their internal consistency coefficients in the MMPI–2 normative sample ranged from .72 (Fears and Type-A Behavior) to .86 (Cynicism) for men, and from .68 (Type-A Behavior) to .86 (Depression) for women (Butcher et al., 1990).

Initial external validation involved correlating content scale scores with ratings of subjects in the normative sample that had been completed by spouses or other partners (Butcher et al., 1990). For most scales, the patterns of correlations suggested that the scales were measuring characteristics consistent with the original definitions of the constructs underlying the scales. Several subsequent studies indicated that the content scales significantly add to the clinical scales in predicting extratest characteristics such as psychiatric diagnosis (Ben-Porath, Butcher, & Graham, 1991); symptoms such as depression, anxiety, and disturbed thinking (Dwyer, Graham, & Ott, 1992); and personality characteristics such as anger (Schill & Wang, 1990).

MMPI–2 Component Scales

Using factor-analytic procedures, Ben-Porath and Sherwood (1993) developed component scales for some of the content scales. Empirical and rational analyses were used to detect clusters of items within each MMPI–2 content scale. Specifically, principal component analyses were conducted within each of the content scales using the data sets collected as part of the MMPI–2 restandardization project. Rational analyses of the candidate clusters were then performed. Twenty-seven subscales for 12 of the 15 content scales were identified. Analyses indicated that component scales could not be developed for the Anxiety, Obsessiveness, and Work Interference content scales. Ben-Porath and Sherwood presented correlations between component scales and extratest measures, suggesting that the use of the component scales added significantly to the parent content scales.

THE MMPI–2 ANGER CONTENT SCALE AND COMPONENT SCALES

One of the MMPI–2 content scales was developed specifically to assess anger. It is a 16-item scale whose items, for the most part, have content that is obviously related to the experience and expression of anger. Some items seem to be measuring outward expressions of anger (e.g., "At times I feel like swearing" [T]; "I almost never lose self-control" [F]; and "I am often said to be hotheaded" [T]). Other items seem to be measuring angry feelings (e.g., "It makes me angry to have people hurry me" [T]; and "I have become so angry with someone, that I have felt as if I would explode" [T]).

Ben-Porath and Sherwood (1993) developed two component scales for the Anger content scale: Explosive Behavior and Irritability. Persons scoring high on the Explosive Behavior scale are thought to have violent and explosive tendencies; those scoring high on the Irritability scale are thought to have a general tendency toward irritability and grouchiness, and are easily annoyed. Correlations between the Anger component scales were .51 for men and .54 for women, indicating the discriminative capacity of these scales.

Reliability of the Anger Content Scale and Component Scales

Butcher et al. (1990) reported reliability data for the Anger content scale for the subjects in the MMPI–2 normative sample. Test–retest reliability coefficients for men and women were .85 and .82, respectively. Internal consistency coefficients for men and women were .76 and .73, respectively. Ben-Porath and Sherwood reported reliability data for the Anger component scales for subjects in the MMPI–2 normative sample. Test–retest reliability coefficients for the Explosive Behavior component scale for men and women were .84, and .79, respectively. Test–retest reliability coefficients for the Irritability component scale for men and women were .80 and .78, respectively. Internal consistency coefficients for the Explosive Behavior component scale for men and women were .63 and .56, respectively. For both men and women, an internal consistency coefficient of .65 was reported for the Irritability component scale.

Table 4.2 Correlations between Anger content and component scales and MMPI–2 clinical and validity scales for men (*n* = 46) and women (*n* = 96)

Scale	Anger		Explosive behavior		Irritability	
	M	W	M	W	M	W
L	−.39**	−.23*	−.32*	−.09	−.35*	−.29**
F	.45**	.59**	.46**	.53**	.34*	.49**
K	−.64**	−.59**	−.47**	−.51**	−.68**	−.57**
Hs	.23	.22*	.20	.19	.18	.20*
D	.12	.24*	.04	.18	.26	.29**
Hy	.05	.17	−.01	.11	.10	.18
Pd	.09	.32**	.07	.35**	.11	.22*
Mf	−.13	.16	−.27	.20	.03	.03
Pa	.29*	.38**	.27	.34**	.28	.35**
Pt	.48**	.43**	.34*	.31**	.49**	.45**
Sc	.43**	.49**	.39**	.42**	.36*	.46**
Ma	.38**	.42**	.29*	.37**	.35*	.36**
Si	.26	.28**	.19	.16	.33*	.36**

Note. M = men, W = women.
*$p < .05$. **$p < .01$.

Relationships Between Anger Content and Component Scales and Other MMPI–2 Scales

Correlations of the MMPI–2 Anger content scales with other MMPI–2 scales can provide some information concerning the construct validity of the scales. According to Butcher et al. (1990), in the MMPI–2 normative sample, the Anger content scale was consistently correlated with other MMPI–2 scales that relate to the expression of anger or hostility. For example, the Anger content scale was correlated .79 for men and .80 for women with the HOS scale. Butcher et al. (1990) also reported correlations between the Anger content scale and the MMPI–2 clinical scales. Anger content scale scores were positively correlated with Scale 7 (Psychasthenia) scores (.55 for men, .62 for women) and Scale 8 (Schizophrenia) scores (.53 for men, .60 for women).

Table 4.2 reports correlations between the Anger content and component scales and the validity and clinical scales of the MMPI–2 for college student subjects in a study by Carr and Graham (1993). Several observations can be made about these data. The pattern of correlations is similar to that reported by Butcher et al. (1990) for subjects in the MMPI–2 normative sample. The Anger content scale and component scales were negatively correlated with the L and K scales, suggesting that persons who endorsed items indicating more anger and more problems in controlling anger were less defensive. This relationship with scales assessing defensiveness has also been found for many other MMPI–2 scales. It makes sense that persons who are being less defensive are likely to endorse more items indicative of anger, and probably many other problems and symptoms as well.

The highest correlations between the Anger scales and the clinical scales were for Scales 7 and 8. Because both of these scales are suggestive of general maladjustment, it can be inferred that persons who report experiencing more anger and more problems with anger control are generally more maladjusted than persons who report experiencing less anger and fewer problems with anger control. Put another way, problems with anger and anger control may often be part of a larger picture of psychological maladjustment.

The patterns of correlations for the component scales were similar to those of the parent Anger content scale. This would suggest that the component scales may be assessing many of the same characteristics as the parent Anger content scale.

Although most correlations were similar for men and women, there were some notable differences. For both the Anger content scale and the Explosive Behavior component scale, higher scores for women were related to higher scores on Scale 4. This would suggest that these two anger scales may be assessing some aspects of asocial or antisocial behavior for women. For both the Anger content scale and the Irritability component scale, higher scoring women tended to have higher scores on Scales 1 and 2. This would suggest that these two anger scales may be measuring some neurotic tendencies, including depression and somatization.

External Validity of the Anger Content Scales and Component Scales

Butcher et al. (1990) reported behavioral correlates for the Anger content scale for subjects in the MMPI–2 normative sample. For both men and women, higher scores were associated with moodiness and problems with anger control. Men who scored higher on the Anger content scale were described by their partners as hostile and overbearing, and as having significant interpersonal adjustment problems. Behavioral characteristics for men scoring higher on the Anger scale also included having temper tantrums, getting very angry, getting annoyed easily, swearing and cursing, smashing things in anger, getting upset by small events, and being generally hostile. Both internal and external expressions of anger were noted (e.g., having angry thoughts, displaying aggressive physical acts). Most of these behavioral correlates were also found for women scoring higher on the Anger content scale. However, higher scoring women were also described as antisocial and feeling sad or blue.

Schill and Wang (1990) examined correlations between the Anger content scale and the Anger Expression scale (Spielberger, 1988), the Anger Self-Report scale (Zelin, Adler, & Myerson, 1972) and the Cook–Medley Ho scale (Cook & Medley, 1954). Their subjects were 32 men and 33 women. The Anger content scale correlated positively with anger expression and negatively with anger control. The form that anger expression took was different for men and women. Higher Anger scale scores for men were associated with verbal expression, whereas higher scores for women were associated with physical expression.

Validity of the Anger component scales was assessed using partner ratings from the MMPI–2 normative sample (Ben-Porath & Sherwood, 1993). Results indicate that explosive acting-out behaviors (e.g., having temper tantrums and breaking things) were most strongly associated with the Explosive Behavior scale. Less extreme behaviors (e.g., arguing about minor things, moodiness, and stubbornness) were associated with higher scores on the Irritability scale.

Carr and Graham (1993) examined the construct validity of the Anger content and component scales. Scores on the Anger scales were correlated with scores on the STAXI (Spielberger, 1988). By utilizing the STAXI, which assesses both angry feelings and anger expression, it was hoped that the facets of anger being assessed by the Anger content scale and its component scales would be clarified.

Subjects were 46 male and 96 female college students. Each subject participated with a partner, and was asked to indicate the type of relationship that he or she had with the partner, the length of time he or she had known the partner, and the closeness of the relationship with the partner. Most of the subjects (78.8% of men, 69.8% of women) indicated that their partner was a friend, and that they had known their partner for more than 6 months. However, a significant number of subjects indicated that they had known their partner for less than 6 months. The closeness of the relationship was rated on a 7-point scale, ranging from *not close at all close* to *extremely close*. Subjects were eliminated from final analyses if they rated their relationship as less than *somewhat close*.

Although subjects completed the entire MMPI–2, the Anger content scale and its component scales (Explosive Behavior and Irritability) were of primary interest. The STAXI is a multidimensional assessment instrument for identifying various components of anger. In addition to the five subscales used here, there are three other subscales that were not used due to their perceived inappropriateness, given what the Anger content and component scales were assumed to be measuring. We used the Angry-Temperament, Angry-Reaction, Anger-In, Anger-Out, and Anger Control subscales. Angry-Temperament and Angry-Reaction are subscales of the Trait Anger (T-Anger) scale, and have to do with the experience of angry feelings. Angry-Temperament (T-Anger/T) measures the frequency of the experience of angry feelings in a wide variety of situations, regardless of provocation. Angry-Reaction (T-Anger/R) measures the frequency of the experience of angry feelings in more specific anger-provoking situations, such as when criticized or treated unfairly by other people. Anger-In, Anger-Out, and Anger Control measure the way in which anger is expressed when it is already recognized that angry feelings are present. Anger-In measures the frequency of the expression of anger toward the self, and Anger-Out measures the frequency of the expression of anger toward other people or objects in the environment. Finally, Anger Control measures the frequency with which an individual attempts to control the expression of anger, with higher scores indicating greater control and lower scores indicating less control. Spielberger (1988) reported test–retest and internal consistency coefficients for the STAXI subscales. Test–retest coefficients ranged from .62 for T-Anger/T for men to .81 for T-Anger/T and Anger-Out for women. Internal consistency coefficients ranged from .70 for T-Anger/R for women to .89 for T-Anger/T for women.

Table 4.3 Means and standard deviations for the MMPI–2 Anger content and component scales and the STAXI subscales

Scales	Men (n = 46)			Women (n = 96)		
	M	SD	Range	M	SD	Range
MMPI–2						
Anger	56.70	11.44	36–86	55.60	11.76	36–84
Explosive Behavior	59.11	11.11	39–84	54.17	12.36	40–84
Irritability	54.32	10.75	36–72	56.07	9.87	34–70
STAXI						
State Anger	13.45	5.00	10–31	13.58	5.19	10–33
T-Anger/T	7.32	3.43	2–16	6.72	3.07	4–16
T-Anger/R	9.13	3.22	3–15	9.61	2.89	4–16
Anger-In	17.00	4.06	10–27	17.18	4.25	8–26
Anger-Out	17.45	3.68	12–29	16.77	4.44	8–30
Anger Control	20.68	4.88	11–31	21.79	5.19	9–32

Subjects completed the entire STAXI under standard directions. In an attempt to further assess the validity of subjects' self-reports of anger, the STAXI was also modified so that it could be completed by each member of the pair of subjects to describe the other member of the pair. For example, the self-rated item "I have a fiery temper" was rewritten for the partner rating scale as "My partner has a fiery temper." Because the S-Anger scale assesses the subjective intensity of angry feelings at any particular time, we felt that it would not be possible for partners to assess the state anger of the other member of the pair. Thus, a modified version of this scale was not developed.

Table 4.3 reports the means and standard deviations for the MMPI–2 Anger content and component scales and for the STAXI subscales for men and women. The men and women obtained somewhat above average T scores on the Anger content scale and the Explosive Behavior and Irritability component scales. This is not surprising because college students, in general, score higher on other MMPI–2 scales (Butcher et al., 1990).

Table 4.4 reports correlations between scores on self-rated STAXI subscales and MMPI–2 Anger content and component scales for men. All correlations were in the expected direction. For men, the Anger content scale was significantly correlated with T-Anger/T, Anger-In, and Anger-Out. Based on Spielberger's (1988) definition of *angry-temperament,* in the present study, men who scored higher on the Anger content scale reported that they experienced angry feelings more frequently than lower scoring men, regardless of whether the feelings were provoked. Men who scored higher on the Anger content scale were equally likely to direct the expression of their anger toward themselves and toward people and objects in their environment.

To summarize results for men, higher scoring men reported experiencing more anger in general. However, it was not possible to predict from Anger content scale scores how men will express their angry feelings. High scorers are equally likely to express their angry feelings inwardly and outwardly.

Table 4.4 Correlations between MMPI–2 Anger content and component scales and self-rated STAXI subscales for men ($N = 46$)

STAXI subscales	MMPI–2 scales		
	Anger	Explosive behavior	Irritability
T-Anger/T	.60*	.52*	.52*
T-Anger/R	.35	.20	.36
Anger-In	.52*	.38*	.48*
Anger-Out	.60*	.60*	.44*
Anger Control	− .24	− .36	− .24

*$p < .01$.

Table 4.5 reports correlations between the Anger content scale and component scale scores and the STAXI subscale scores for women. The Anger content scale correlated significantly and positively with T-Anger/T, T-Anger/R, and Anger-Out, and negatively and significantly with Anger Control. Women who scored higher on the Anger content scale reported experiencing angry feelings more frequently both with and without specific provocation.

The pattern of the correlations for women was different from that for men. Both men and women who scored higher on the Anger content scale reported experiencing anger more frequently than lower scoring men and women, regardless of whether they were provoked (T-Anger/T). However, higher scoring women were also more likely than lower scoring women to report experiencing anger in more specific anger-provoking situations. This was not the case for men.

The significant positive correlation between the Anger content scale and the Anger-Out subscale suggests that women who scored higher on the Anger content scale were more likely than lower scoring women to report expressing their angry feelings outwardly toward people and objects in the environment. This finding is consistent with the significant negative correlation for women between the Anger content scale and the Anger Control scale.

Table 4.5 Correlations between MMPI–2 Anger content and component scales and self-rated STAXI subscales for women ($N = 96$)

STAXI subscales	MMPI–2 scales		
	Anger	Explosive behavior	Irritability
T-Anger/T	.62*	.51*	.55*
T-Anger/R	.41*	.23*	.32*
Anger-In	.23	.26	.14
Anger-Out	.48*	.33*	.47*
Anger Control	− .47*	− .46*	− .38*

*$p < .01$.

In summary, women who scored higher on the Anger content scale reported experiencing angry feelings with and without specific provocation. These women reported that they lacked control of their angry feelings and expressed their anger outwardly. Comparing these last two findings to the findings for high scoring men, the direction of the expression of anger (in or out) cannot be predicted for high scoring men, whereas high-scoring women, when angry, are likely to lack control of their expression of anger and to express it outwardly.

The pattern of correlations between the Explosive Behavior and Irritability component scales and the STAXI subscales for men was markedly similar to that of the Anger content scale. It would appear from these data that the component scales did not add much to the understanding of how these subjects reported experiencing and expressing anger.

Unfortunately, the results of the partner ratings yielded little useful information. There was not a single significant correlation between the Anger content scale or component scales and the modified STAXI subscale scores. One possibility is that partners did not know each other well enough to assess reactions to anger accurately. The fact that approximately 20% of men and 30% of women in the study indicated that they had known their partners less than 6 months lends support to this possibility. Another possible reason for lack of significant results is that the STAXI may not lend itself to modification for partner ratings. The experience of anger may be a relatively private matter that cannot be assessed accurately by other people.

CONCLUSIONS AND RECOMMENDATIONS FOR FUTURE RESEARCH

Several kinds of validity data suggest that scores on the Anger content scale appear to be related to the ways people report experiencing and expressing anger. However, there are some differences between men and women. Men scoring higher on the Anger content scale report experiencing anger more frequently than lower scoring men, regardless of provocation, and it is not possible to predict whether higher scoring men will express their angry feelings inwardly or outwardly. Higher scoring women on the Anger content scale also reported experiencing anger more frequently, both with and without specific provocation. However, they also reported lacking anger control, and, not surprisingly, they expressed their anger outwardly. For the college student sample in the Carr and Graham (1993) study, the component scales did not add significantly to an understanding of how people report experiencing and expressing anger. Perhaps with larger, more heterogeneous samples, or in clinical settings, the component scales will prove to have incremental validity.

The Anger content scale appears to have the potential to assess the expression of anger in both men and women. The scale has adequate temporal stability and internal consistency. The scale seems to be related to how anger is experienced and expressed. However, more data are needed to know the extent to which the scale will be useful in clinical settings. Studies with clinical subjects for whom reliable extratest measures of anger-related behaviors are available are indicated. Of special interest would be studies utilizing behavioral observations (e.g., administering electric shock in response to varying degrees of provocation) or physiological reactions to provocation. A significant research issue, which plagues most anger research, is that the experience of anger is a relatively private experience. As such, it is difficult to choose criterion measures other than self-report. However, when self-report criterion measures are used, one cannot determine to what extent relationships between MMPI–2 scales and other self-reports are due to method variance. For the Anger content and component scales to be useful for clinical purposes, it is necessary to demonstrate that the scales add significantly to the prediction of relevant behaviors above and beyond what can be accomplished with the more familiar MMPI–2 clinical scales.

Although the Ho scale is not routinely scored on the MMPI–2, there is enough evidence to warrant additional research concerning its relationship to health problems. Prospective studies with sound outcome measures (e.g., angiography or autopsy) are needed to clarify the extent to which the Ho scale will be useful in identifying persons who are at risk for significant medical problems.

REFERENCES

Barefoot, J. C., Dodge, K. A., Peterson, B. L., Dahlstrom, W. G., & Williams, R. B., Jr. (1989). The Cook–Medley Hostility scale: Item content and ability to predict survival. *Psychosomatic Medicine, 51,* 46–57.

Ben-Porath, Y. S., Butcher, J. N., & Graham, J. R. (1991). Contribution of the MMPI–2 content scales to the differential diagnosis of schizophrenia and major depression. *Psychological Assessment: A Journal of Consulting and Clinical Psychology, 3,* 634–640.

Ben-Porath, Y. S., & Sherwood, N. E. (1993). *The MMPI–2 content component scales: Development, psychometric characteristics, and clinical application.* Minneapolis: University of Minnesota Press.

Biaggio, M. K., & Maiuro, R. D. (1985). Recent advances in anger assessment. In C. D. Spielberger & J. N. Butcher (Eds.), *Advances in personality assessment* (Vol. 5, pp. 71–111). Hillsdale, NJ: Lawrence Erlbaum Associates.

Boerger, A. R., Graham, J. R., & Lilly, R. S. (1974). Behavioral correlates of single-scale MMPI code types. *Journal of Consulting and Clinical Psychology, 42,* 398–402.

Buck, J. A., & Graham, J. R. (1978). The 4-3 MMPI profile type: A failure to replicate. *Journal of Consulting and Clinical Psychology, 46,* 344.

Butcher, J. N., Dahlstrom, W. G., Graham, J. R., Tellegen, A., & Kaemmer, B. (1989). *Minnesota Multiphasic Personality Inventory–2 (MMPI–2); Manual for administration and scoring.* Minnesota: University of Minnesota Press.

Butcher, J. N., Graham, J. R., Williams, C. L., & Ben-Porath, Y. S. (1990). *Development and use of the MMPI–2 content scales.* Minneapolis: University of Minnesota Press.

Carr, J. L., & Graham, J. R. (1993, March). *The MMPI–2 Anger content scale: A construct validity study.* Paper presented at the 28th annual symposium on Recent Developments in the Use of the MMPI (MMPI–2 and MMPI–A), St. Petersburg Beach, FL.

Colligan, R. C., & Offord, K. P. (1988). The risky use of the MMPI Hostility scale in assessing risk for coronary heart disease. *Psychosomatics, 29,* 188–196.

Cook, W. N., & Medley, D. M. (1954). Proposed hostility and pharisaic-virtue scales for the MMPI. *Journal of Applied Psychology, 38,* 414–418.

Dahlstrom, W. G., Welsh, G. S., & Dahlstrom, L. E. (1972). *An MMPI–2 handbook: Vol. I. Clinical interpretation.* Minneapolis: University of Minnesota Press.

Dahlstrom, W. G., Welsh, G. S., & Dahlstrom, L. E. (1975). *An MMPI handbook: Vol. II. Research applications.* Minneapolis: University of Minnesota Press.

Dwyer, S. A., Graham, J. R., & Ott, E. K. (1992). *Psychiatric symptoms associated with the MMPI–2 content scales.* Unpublished manuscript, Kent State University, Kent, OH.

Gilberstadt, H., & Duker, J. (1965). *A handbook for clinical and actuarial MMPI interpretation.* Philadelphia: Saunders.

Graham, J. R. (1988, August). *Establishing validity of the revised form of the MMPI.* Symposium presentation at the 96th annual convention of the American Psychological Association, Atlanta, GA.

Graham, J. R. (1993). *MMPI–2: Assessing personality and psychopathology (2nd ed).* New York: Oxford.

Graham, J. R., & Ben-Porath, Y. S. (1994, May). *Empirical correlates of MMPI–2 scales in an outpatient mental health center setting.* Paper presented at the 29th annual symposium on Recent Developments in the Use of the MMPI (MMPI–2 and MMPI–A), Minneapolis, MN.

Gynther, M. D., Altman, H., & Sletten, I. W. (1973). Replicated correlates of MMPI two-point types: The Missouri Actuarial System. *Journal of Clinical Psychology* (Suppl. 39).

Lewandowski, D., & Graham, J. R. (1972). Empirical correlates of frequently occurring two-point code types: A replicated study. *Journal of Consulting and Clinical Psychology, 39,* 467–472.

Marks, P. A., & Seeman, W. (1963). *Actuarial description of abnormal personality.* Baltimore, MD: Williams & Wilkins.

Megargee, E. I., Cook, P. E., & Mendelsohn, G. A. (1967). The development and validation of an MMPI scale of assaultiveness in overcontrolled individuals. *Journal of Abnormal Psychology, 72,* 519–528.

Moreland, K. L., & Walsh, S. (1991, August). *Comparative concurrent validity of the MMPI–2 using MMPI and MMPI–2 based descriptors.* Symposium presentation at the 99th annual convention of the American Psychological Association, San Francisco, CA.

Schill, T., & Wang, S. (1990). Correlates of the MMPI–2 Anger content scale. *Psychological Reports, 67,* 800–802.

Spielberger, C. D. (1988). *State–Trait Anger Expression Inventory.* Odessa, FL: Psychological Assessment Resources.

Wiggins, J. S. (1969). Content dimensions in the MMPI. In J. N. Butcher (Ed.), *MMPI: Research developments and clinical applications* (pp. 127–180). New York: McGraw-Hill.

Zelin, M., Adler, G., & Myerson, P. (1972). Anger self-report: An objective questionnaire for the measurement of aggression. *Journal of Consulting and Clinical Psychology, 39,* 340.

5

The Norwegian Adaptation of the State–Trait Anger Expression Inventory

Kjell J. Håseth
University of Oslo, Oslo, Norway

Abstract *In studies that have investigated the relationship of psychological variables to cancer and coronary heart disease, anger has been identified as a significant factor among possible causal links. Consequently, the measurement of anger has become increasingly important during the last two decades. This chapter presents the psychometric properties of the Norwegian adaptation of Spielberger's State–Trait Anger Expression Inventory (STAXI-N) based on large samples of young adults (N = 1,235). The results show that the psychometric properties and the factor structure of the Norwegian STAXI are quite similar to the American original and STAXI adaptations in other European countries. In addition to the three traditional anger expression factors, the factor structure of the Norwegian STAXI includes an additional anger control factor related to inwardly directed anger (AX/Con-In). Examination of gender differences shows that Norwegian female college students, in contrast to American female students, have higher trait anger scores than their male counterparts.*

During the past two decades many psychologists have focused their attention on the study of negative emotions, particularly on anxiety and anger (Smedslund, 1993). Increasingly, research efforts have concentrated on the experience, expression, and control of anger, and on relationships between these factors and a variety of disorders such as alcoholism, hypertension, coronary heart disease, and cancer (Spielberger, 1988). Anger, especially inhibited anger, appears to contribute to the etiology of hypertension and other psychosomatic disorders (Alexander, 1948), and to psychiatric disorders such as depression (Novaco, 1977).

The increased importance of anger as an explanatory factor in cardiovascular disorders has created a renewed interest in developing valid and reliable anger measures. Tests with well-established reputations, such as the Buss–Durkee (1957) Hostility Inventory (BDHI) and the Novaco (1975) Anger Inventory, have been recently revised and improved (Buss & Perry, 1992; Novaco, 1994). Other anger measures were also developed in the 1970s, for example, the Reaction Inventory (RI; Evans & Stangeland, 1971) and the Anger Self Report (ASR; Zelin, Adler, & Myerson, 1972), but have not been revised. Based on extensive analyses of the psychometric properties of the anger measures developed in the 1970s, Biaggio, Supplee, and Curtis (1981) concluded that all of these instruments had severe limitations in both reliability and validity, resulting from lack of clarity in the conceptual definitions of anger, hostility, and aggression.

Spielberger, Jacobs, Russell, and Crane (1983) pointed out the need for a better theoretical understanding and clearer working definitions of the concepts of anger, hostility, and aggression. Anger, considered the most fundamental of these concepts, was described as the feeling/experience core of an emotional state. Hostility was conceptualized as a complex set of attitudes connected to anger; aggression was defined as destructive and punitive behavior directed at other persons. More recently, Spielberger has referred to the three interrelated concepts as the "AHA! Syndrome" (Spielberger & Sydeman, 1994), suggesting that they constitute a complex entity with synergistic effects on behavior.

Spielberger's (1988) theoretical analysis and definition of anger led to the construction of the State–Trait Anger Expression Inventory (STAXI). The State–Trait Anger Scale (STAS; Spielberger et al., 1983), a forerunner of the STAXI, was analogous in concept and format to the State–Trait Anxiety Inventory (STAI); Spielberger, Gorsuch, & Lushene, 1970). The second part of the STAXI, the Anger Expression (AX) scale (Spielberger, Johnson, Russell, Crane, Jacobs, & Worden, 1985), assesses how anger is expressed and controlled. Interest around the world in using the STAS, the AX scale, and the STAXI seems to be growing, as reflected in the fact that these tests have been standardized for use in Brazil and Portugal (Spielberger & Biaggio, 1992), Germany (Schwenkmezger, Hodapp, & Spielberger, 1992), The Netherlands (van der Ploeg, van Buuren, & van Brummelen, 1988), and Italy (Spielberger & Comunian, 1992).

THE NORWEGIAN ADAPTATION OF THE STAXI

Before 1990 very few instruments were available in Norway for measuring any of the components of the AHA! Syndrome. Projective techniques such as the Rorschach (1932) Inkblots and the Rosenzweig Picture Frustration Test (Rosenzweig, 1950) were available for assessing aggression in the context of the psychoanalytic meaning of this term. The Buss–Durkee Hostility Inventory was also translated at the University of Oslo (K. Berg Kveim, personal communication, March 1993) for use in psychophysiological research.

During a project that focused on constructing a Norwegian adaptation of the STAI (Håseth, Hagtvet, & Spielberger, 1990), it was considered feasible and time-efficient also to collect data for developing a Norwegian adaptation of the STAXI. The correlations of anxiety and anger measures would give valuable validation information for both Norwegian adaptations, because relations between the STAI and STAXI scales and subscales had already been established in a number of studies in which both instruments were administered to the same subjects (Spielberger, 1988).

Developing the Norwegian Adaptation of the STAXI

The development of a Norwegian form of the STAI with good psychometric properties turned out to be much easier than adapting the STAXI to the same standards. Partly because social desirability seemed to have a greater influence on self-reports of anger than of anxiety, more time and effort were required to formulate good anger items. Difficulties were also encountered in translating anger terms from English to Norwegian; several key words in the American STAXI had no direct equivalent in Norwegian.

Our overall impression was that the Norwegian language, compared with English, has fewer commonly used words for describing the experience and expression of anger. For example, two English expressions, "to be mad" and "to be furious," had only one equivalent expression in Norwegian: "å være rasende," which is almost identical with "to be furious." Moreover, the English expression, "I am burned up," could not be directly translated. As was often the case in our translation of anger items, we had to combine the most frequently used Norwegian anger adjective "sint" ("anger") with an additional more idiomatic adjective. To compensate for the scarcity of Norwegian terms for anger, we used combinations of words to ensure richness in the Norwegian vocabulary of emotions. For example, in the case of "burned up," we replaced "burned" with "flammende" ("flaming"). Combining "flaming" with "angry" makes "Jeg er flammende sint" ("I am flaming with anger").

There are, however, metaphors commonly used in Norwegian that are rarely if ever used in English. For example, "Jeg er forbannet" ("I am cursed") communicates that the speaker is angry to some degree but not furious. In German, the same expression is "Ich bin entauscht." Another example is "Jeg er hissig," for which the English counterpart would be "I can hiss"; the German equivalent would use the verb "zichen." Whereas in Norwegian this adjective seems to be at the core of trait-anger (T-Anger), in English and German these words are rarely used to express anger and are not used as test items in the STAXI.

For idiomatic expressions, we tried to replace English idioms with Norwegian idioms when possible. The English idiom "I am a hothead," was translated into "Jeg er en sinnatagg" ("I am a Sinnatagg"), where "sinnatagg" means an angry small person, that is, a toddler. "Sinnatagg," the name given to a famous statue by the great Norwegian sculptor, Gustav Vigeland, is one of the best-known pieces in a sculptor park in the center of Oslo. It pictures the embodiment of anger in a male toddler and is well known to all Norwegians through pictures in history books and sightseeing. However, the test item containing "sinnatagg" had mediocre-to-bad psychometric properties in spite of, or perhaps because of, its well-known anchoring to anger expression. Initially left out of the preliminary Norwegian STAXI (STAXI-N), this item was later rewritten, using a similar but not identical idiomatic expression, "Jeg er en hissigpropp."

"Hissigpropp" combines "hissig," that is, "tend to hiss," the sound a snake makes before it bites (it hisses), with "propp," which signifies a small device for locking a container. Thus, "hissigpropp" connotes someone who easily becomes angry, keeps it in for a short moment, and then blows the anger out. The combination of words makes the self-description non-serious and a bit humorous, without the connotation of the famous sculpture depicting a child's anger. "Hissigpropp" also points to a snake's signal, its hiss, that it is going to bite. The association of "hissigpropp" with human reactions is obvious, constituting an allegory with a euphemistic effect, and making it less derogatory as a self-description. On the other hand, "Sinnatagg" bluntly signifies that one has lost control of one's anger and behaves in an infantile way. The new test item based on the revised idiomatic expression, which turned out to have excellent psychometric properties as a measure of T-Anger, was included in the final version of the STAXI-N.

In developing the Norwegian adaptation of the STAXI, all of the original American STAXI test items were translated, often with several alternative formulations of some items. In addition, as previously noted, a number of entirely new test items were formulated in accordance with the constructs defined by the STAXI scales and subscales. Thus, the pool of test items for the STAXI-N consisted of a much larger number of items than would be required for the final version of this measure.

The format for the Norwegian STAXI was made to match the original American form of the scale (Spielberger, 1988). The instructions were translated, as closely as possible, to approximate the English instructions in both content and layout. The intensity rating scale used in the STAXI-N to assess state-anger (S-Anger) was essentially the same as the one used in the Norwegian adaptation of the STAI (Håseth, Hagtvet, & Spielberger, 1990), with the following four response alternatives: (1) *Aldeles ikke* (Not at all); (2) *Litt* (Somewhat); (3) *Nokså mye* (Moderately); and (4) *Svaert mye* (Very much so). The 4-point frequency rating scales used to assess T-anger and anger expression was also essentially the same as the trait scale used in the Norwegian STAI: (1) *Nesten aldri* (Almost never), (2) *Noen ganger* (Sometimes), (3) *Ofte* (Often), (4) *Nesten alltid* (Almost always).

The preliminary Norwegian STAXI, along with the Norwegian STAI, was administered to a large group of medical and psychology students at the University of Oslo during regular classes, and to a smaller group of recruits at the Oslo Police Academy. Following the procedure recommended by Spielberger (1983), the STAXI-N S-Anger scale was administered before the T-Anger and AX scales.

The students were first asked to respond to the S-Anger items by reporting their feelings at the moment (standard instruction), and were then asked to respond to the S-Anger scale while they imagined themselves to be in an anger-provoking situation (waiting in a line when somebody passes you without giving any explanation or excuse). After completing the STAXI-N S-Anger scale with standard and anger-provoking instructions, the students were given the T-Anger and AX scales. Because these procedures were similar to those used by Spielberger in developing the STAI and the STAS, the internal consistency reliability when the test was given under relaxed and imagined test-taking conditions could be compared for Norwegian and American students.

On the basis of the results from the initial study of the preliminary STAXI-N, the inventory was revised and a second preliminary form was created. This revised preliminary STAXI-N was administered with standard instructions to 10th-grade students and to recruits at the Norwegian Military Air Pilot Academy. Test–retest data were also obtained for these two samples. On the basis of the findings with these samples, several items were deleted and new items were written to form the third preliminary version of the STAXI-N. This third preliminary form of the STAXI-N, along with the Eysenck Personality Inventory (EPI; Håseth, 1992), was administered to 444 students entering the University of Oslo, who were enrolled in a mandatory history of philosophy class required of all undergraduate students.

Psychometric Properties of the STAXI-N

For the first preliminary version of the STAXI-N that was administered to medical and psychology students during an ordinary lecture, the age range was 19–35 (63 males, $\overline{X} = 28.7$; 141 females, $\overline{X} = 25.9$). The age range for the small group of recruits tested at the Police Academy was also 19-25 (35 males, $\overline{X} = 22.8$; 14 females, $\overline{X} = 22.7$). For the second preliminary form of the STAXI-N, administered at the Military Air Pilot Academy, the age range was 19–23 (212 males, $\overline{X} = 20.1$; 19 females, $\overline{X} = 20.8$); 100 participants in this study were retested 1 month later. The age range for the 10th-grade students was 16–18 (115 males, $\overline{X} = 17.1$; 139 females, $\overline{X} = 17.2$); 50 of these students were retested after 1 month.

The means, standard deviations, and alpha coefficients for the S-Anger and T-Anger scales for the four groups of subjects who participated in the three STAXI adaptation studies are reported in Table 5.1. Substantial differences were found in the anger scores of the four normative groups. Recruits at the Police and Air Pilot Academies generally had lower scores on all subscales except Anger-Control. These findings could have been influenced by social desirability because young people who are in the process of being selected to become police officers and air pilots have a natural capacity and interest in controlling their temper.

As can be seen in Table 5.1, the 10th-grade students had significantly higher scores on the T-Anger and Angry Temperament (T-Ang/T) scales, and tended to score somewhat higher than the university students on S-Anger, although this difference was not statistically significant. Females also had substantially higher scores than males on the T-Anger scales; these gender differences were strongest for both groups of students and almost negligible for the recruits. A similar tendency for younger subjects to have higher S-Anger and T-Anger scores was reported by Spielberger (1988) for American subjects, and by Spielberger and Comunian (1992) for Italians.

Gender differences in scores on the Anger Expression (AX) scales were mixed and more complicated, as can be seen in Table 5.2. In analyses of variance (ANOVAs) that included the four norm groups, significant gender differences ($p < .001$) were found for all three AX scales. Females had higher

Table 5.1 Means, standard deviations, and alphas of the Norwegian S-Anger and T-Anger scales for the norm groups

Scales	University students		High school students		Air Pilot Academy recruits		Police Academy recruits	
	M (N = 63)	F (N = 131)	M (N = 114)	F (N = 137)	M (N = 212)	F (N = 19)	M (N = 35)	F (N = 14)
S-Anger								
M	11.91	11.79	12.21	12.63	10.41	10.36	10.57	10.42
SD	3.15	3.4	3.8	5.3	1.18	.83	1.03	.85
Alpha	.90	.93	.88	.94	.81	—	—	—
T-Anger								
M	17.85	19.82	20.33	22.32	15.86	16.31	16.14	16.71
SD	4.2	4.4	5.1	5.7	2.91	3.36	2.51	3.75
Alpha	.84	.87	.84	.86	.70	—	—	—
T-Anger/T								
M	6.23	7.28	6.77	7.90	5.55	6.00	5.34	6.85
SD	4.2	4.4	5.1	2.8	1.60	1.53	1.37	2.47
Alpha	.84	.87	.84	.84	.71	—	—	—
T-Anger/R								
M	8.25	9.09	7.54	8.45	6.91	7.00	7.77	7.14
SD	2.3	2.2	2.1	2.3	1.79	1.91	1.33	1.46
Alpha	.72	.75	.69	.71	.69	—	—	—

Note. Alphas not reported when *N* is less than .35.

Table 5.2 Means, standard deviations, and alphas of the AX scales for the Norwegian norm groups

Scales	University students		High school students		Air Pilot Academy recruits		Police Academy recruits	
	M (N = 97)	F (N = 141)	M (N = 114)	F (N = 137)	M (N = 212)	F (N = 19)	M (N = 35)	F (N = 14)
AX/In								
M	17.30	18.25	15.21	16.09	16.86	16.89	16.65	16.54
SD	4.1	4.2	4.2	4.0	3.30	3.28	3.81	3.77
Alpha	.74	.66	.76	.66	.73	—	—	—
AX/Out								
M	17.03	16.59	16.66	18.25	13.75	14.57	13.93	14.82
SD	3.3	4.0	4.0	5.3	2.91	2.79	2.94	3.43
Alpha	.77	.79	.70	.79	.70	—	—	—
AX/Con								
M	24.00	21.79	24.74	22.19	28.50	27.52	28.11	25.01
SD	4.5	5.5	4.4	4.2	3.45	3.50	3.32	4.34
Alpha	.89	.81	.69	.76	.77	—	—	—

Note. Alphas not reported when *N* is less than .35.

Table 5.3 Test–retest correlations after 2 weeks (50 high school students) and 4 weeks (100 Air Pilot Academy recruits)

No. of weeks	S-Anger	T-Anger	T-Ang/T	T-Ang/R	AX/In	AX/Out	AX/Con
2	.01	.77	.69	.64	.82	.84	.67
4	.17	.75	.71	.72	.67	.70	.52

scores on Anger-In (AX/In) and Anger-Out (AX/Out), whereas males scored higher on Anger-Control (AX/Con). However, these differences were not always significant in one-way ANOVAs for each norm group.

Reliability and Validity of the STAXI-N

The reliability of the STAXI-N was evaluated by calculating test–retest correlations, and by examining the internal consistency of each scale and subscale. In applying state–trait theory to measures of anger (Spielberger, 1988), S-Anger is expected to fluctuate over time as a function of frustration, perceived injustice, or other anger provocations in a given situation. Rather than indicating a lack of reliability, small correlations between S-Anger scores on two different occasions reflect differences in the perceived provocations that activate angry feelings.

In contrast to expected fluctuations in S-Anger, measures of T-Anger assess relatively stable individual differences in anger proneness. Therefore, relatively high test–retest correlations would be expected for the T-Anger scales and the three AX scales. Table 5.3 shows that the test–retest stability correlations for the two subsamples on which these data were collected over the 2- and 4-week time periods varied from .01 for S-Anger to .84 for AX/Out. The test–retest correlations for the S-Anger scale were very weak as expected; those for all six trait scales were much larger. Although the samples were small and the subjects were tested under rather different circumstances, the test–retest reliability coefficients for the STAXI-N T-Anger and AX scales were quite consistent with what would be expected for trait measures (Spielberger, 1988).

The Cronbach alpha coefficients presented in Tables 5.1 and 5.2 are quite similar to those reported by Spielberger (1988) for the American normative samples, and provide strong evidence of the internal consistency of the STAXI scales and subscales. Table 5.1 shows that the reliability of the S-Anger scale varies between .81 and .94; three of the five norm groups had reliabilities of .90 or higher. For the T-Anger and T-Ang/T scales, the reliabilities for the four norm groups were in the .80s; for the 4-item T-Ang/R scale, all but one of the alphas were in the .70s. The median alpha for the AX scales, each consisting of only 8 items, was .76; an alpha higher than .80 with such a small number of items would be quite unusual.

The alphas for the male Air Pilot Academy recruits were lower on all four scales than for the other groups, as can be noted in Table 5.1. One possible reason for the lower consistency of these students is that they were tested in a more stressful situation. Given the fact that they were being evaluated for admission to a military academy, some of them might have tried to appear to have flawless personalities, thus causing inconsistencies in their responses.

The item-total correlations for the preliminary STAXI-N S-Anger and T-Anger items were generally .40 or higher for university, high school, and Police Academy students; with only a few exceptions, each item correlated .30 or higher with the scale as a whole in all four norm groups. The median item-scale correlations for the three AX scales varied between .40 and .70. An item-scale correlation of .30 or higher was used as an important criterion for including an item in one of the STAXI-N scales.

Evidence of the construct validity of the Norwegian STAXI was provided by having the university students and police recruits complete the S-Anger scale with standard instructions, and then respond to this scale while imagining themselves as being provoked and angered. As predicted by state–trait theory, the means for the S-Anger scale were significantly higher ($p < .001$) in the imagined anger-provoking condition, providing evidence of the construct validity of the STAXI S-Anger scale.

In the relatively nonstressful classroom situation, elevations in the scores for most S-Anger items were very small. Although these items [#4 ("I am irritated"), #5 ("I am frustrated"), and #14 ("I am resentful")] showed some elevation, the distributions of the scores for the S-Anger items were all clearly skewed toward the report of "no anger," suggesting that the STAXI-N S-Anger scale appears to have a "floor" effect. However, this might not be the case because students volunteered to participate in the study, rather than attending a lecture. Because the test situation could hardly be said to be anger provoking unless interpreted in some paranoid way, the low S-Anger item means may simply reflect the fact that little or no anger was provoked. The psychoanalytic view that everyone harbors anger and aggression most of the time might be wrong. Perhaps a necessary condition for experiencing anger is the perception, recall, or imagination of situational anger provocation (Averill, 1982; Lazarus, 1993).

Our validation study showed that, even when there was only imagined provocation, the STAXI-N S-Anger items are differentially sensitive to measuring different degrees of experienced anger. Items #4 ("I feel irritated") and #14 ("I am resentful") appear to be the most sensitive to mild provocation, as reflected in the highest means for these items. Items #12 ("I feel like hitting someone") and #13 ("I feel like breaking things") showed little or no elevation under this kind of provocation.

In evaluating S-Anxiety as measured by the STAI, Spielberger et al. (1970) noted variations in the sensitivity of individual items to different degrees of stress, which they referred to technically as *item intensity specificity*. This item intensity specificity hypothesis also seems to apply to the measurement of S-Anger as related to perceived differences in the extent of anger provocation. Our findings provide evidence that the STAXI-N S-Anger items were differentially sensitive at low levels of anger provocation. However, when anger was activated when subjects imagined themselves to be in an anger-provoking situation, the responses to most S-Anger items were in the middle of the 4-point intensity scale.

Correlations between the STAXI-N scales and subscales based on the pooled data from the Norwegian norm groups are reported in Table 5.4. T-Anger correlated positively with AX/Out and negatively with AX/Con: The correlation between T-Anger and AX/Out was also higher for the STAXI-N than the American STAXI. A small but significant negative correlation between AX/In and AX/Out was found for the Norwegian STAXI, as compared with no correlation between these scales in the original STAXI. Nevertheless, the pattern of correlations for the STAXI-N was generally similar to that reported by Spielberger (1988).

Concurrent evidence of the validity of the STAXI-N was investigated in the normative sample of 10th-grade Norwegian students. The intercorrelations of the STAXI-N AX scales with the state and trait anxiety and curiosity scales of an experimental Norwegian version of the State–Trait Personality Inventory (STPI; Håseth, 1990a) are reported in Table 5.5. The correlations for AX/In and AX/Out with T-Anxiety were positive, but there were substantial gender differences in these correlations. Although the correlations for Norwegian females were generally similar to those reported by Spielberger (1988) and Spielberger and Biaggio (1992), T-Anxiety was more strongly associated with AX/Out than AX/In for the Norwegian males, whereas the reverse was true for the Norwegian females. In general, these correlations seem to indicate that persons who either suppress or openly express anger tend to experience anxiety more often than those with low AX scores, as was previously noted by Spielberger and others working with the STAXI (Spielberger & Sydeman, 1994).

The STAXI-N AX/Con scale had moderately high, negative correlations with T-Anxiety, as was expected from earlier findings. The correlations of the AX scales with T-Curiosity were essentially zero, providing evidence of discriminant validity. The small positive but highly significant correlations between AX/Con and T-Curiosity were surprising; Spielberger and Sydeman (1994) reported essentially zero correlations between these measures. Our findings can be interpreted as indicating that curiosity is accompanied by tendencies to control anger expression, which in turn inhibit the experience of anxiety, thus enhancing more adequate environmental exploration.

Correlations are also reported in Table 5.5 between the STAXI-N AX scales and the Norwegian version of Carver and Scheier's Life Orientation Scale (LOT; Håseth, 1990b), which measures optimism. The LOT scale correlates negatively with the EPI Neuroticism (N) scale, indicating that low LOT scores, that is, lack of optimism (pessimistic outlook), are associated with a neurotic personality style. In Table 5.5, it can be noted that the correlations between LOT and AX/Out scores were essentially zero, whereas statistically significant ($p < .001$) negative correlations were found between the LOT and AX/In scores for females, similar to those found between AX/In and EPI N scores (see Table 5.6). Together with the positive correlation between LOT and AX/Con scores, these results provide further evidence of differences in the gender correlates of anger expression.

Table 5.4 Intercorrelations of the STAXI subscales based on the total number of subjects in the STAXI-N

Subscales	S-Anger	T-Anger	T-Ang/T	T-Ang/R	AX-Out	AX-In	AX-Con
S-Anger	—	.26**	.22**	.21**	.21**	.12	−.18**
T-Anger	.36**	—	.81**	.71**	.68**	.04	−.54**
T-Ang/T	.26**	.74**	—	.37**	.63**	−.11	−.54**
T-Ang/R	.29**	.77**	.38**	—	.32**	.15*	−.32**
Anger-Out	.28**	.66**	.51**	.48**	—	−.23**	−.61**
Anger-In	.07	.01	−.02	.11*	−.11*	—	.15*
Anger-Control	−.31**	−.56**	−.49**	−.37**	−.55**	.13**	—

Note. $N = 1,235$; 60% males. Female correlations in top section of table.
*$p < .01$. **$p < .001$.

Table 5.5 Intercorrelations between the AX scales with the LOT and the Anxiety and Curiosity scales of STPI–N for 254 high school students

STAXI scales	AX/In			AX/Out			AX/Con		
	M	F	Total	M	F	Total	M	F	Total
S-Anxiety	.23**	.26**	.22**	.13**	.06	.15**	−.19**	−.24**	−.24**
T-Anxiety	.24**	.35**	.31**	.31**	.18**	.20**	−.43**	−.34**	−.35**
S-Curiosity	.01	−.02	−.03	−.13*	−.16*	.04	.28**	.26**	.18
T-Curiosity	−.09	−.10	−.07	.05	.04	.02	.26**	.27**	.26
LOT (Optimism)	−.14	−.36**	−.25**	−.04	.09	−.10	.10	.33**	.30

*p < .01. **p < .001.

94

Table 5.6 Intercorrelations between the EPI scales and the STAXI–N scales based on 444 college students

EPI scales	S-Anger	T-Anger	AX/In	AX/Out	AX/Con
Neuroticism	.08	.11	.28*	−.17*	−.07
Extraversion	.19	.13*	−.22*	.29*	−.23*
Lie	.00	−.21**	−.14*	−.08	.27**

*$p < .01$. **$p < .001$.

In a recent validation study, the STAXI-N was administered together with the Norwegian EPI (Håseth, 1992) to 444 students just admitted to the University of Oslo. Correlations between the STAXI-N and EPI Neuroticism (N), Extraversion (E), and Lie (L) scales are reported in Table 5.6. The correlations between S-Anger and the EPI N and L scales were close to zero; a small positive correlation was found with the EPI E scale. The correlation between T-Anger and N was surprisingly low, but positive as expected: Spielberger (1988) found moderately high positive correlations between N and T-Anger. The small positive correlation between T-Anger and E corresponds to similar findings in other studies (Spielberger & Biaggio, 1992).

A moderate positive correlation between AX/In and N, and a small but significant negative correlation between AX/In and E, can be noted in Table 5.6. Correlations of similar magnitude but opposite in direction were found for AX-Out with E and N, as expected. The significant negative correlation between the T-Anger and the EPI L scale further suggests that T-Anger scores might be influenced by socially desirable test-taking attitudes, which might also be reflected in the positive correlation between L and AX/Con.

The intercorrelations between the STAXI-N and EPI scales were not always consistent with results reported by other investigators. It should be noted, however, that the correlations in the present study were between the STAXI-N and the EPI, rather than the Eysenck Personality Questionnaire (EPQ; Eysenck & Eysenck, 1975), which was used in most other studies. If one disregards the actual size of the correlations and looks primarily at their direction, the observed relations were generally in accord with theoretical expectations and similar to those found in other studies, thus providing concurrent evidence of the validity of the STAXI-N.

THE FACTOR STRUCTURE OF STAXI-N

The participants in our initial study of the factor structure of the STAXI-N were 444 freshmen at the University of Oslo (160 males, $\overline{X}$ age = 20.29; 284 females, $\overline{X}$ age = 20.26). A preliminary version of the STAXI-N, together with the EPI, was administered to these students during ordinary lectures. The factor structure of the STAXI-N State and Trait Anger scales was investigated by factoring the S-Anger and T-Anger items together, in separate analyses for males and females. The three factors extracted for both sexes, one S-Anger and two T-Anger factors, Angry Temperament (T-Ang/T) and Angry Reaction (T-Ang/R), were essentially the same as those reported by Spielberger (1988), and similar to the findings reported by Schwenkmezger et al. (1992) for the German adaptation of the STAXI. Moreover, the Norwegian and American test items that defined these factors were almost identical.

Fuqua et al. (1991) were the first to report the results of a factor study of all 44 items of the original American STAXI, but they combined the data for both sexes in the same analysis. Because significant gender differences have been reported by Spielberger (1988) and were also found with Norwegian subjects for several STAXI-N subscales, the STAXI-N items were factored in separate analyses for males and females. For both sexes, the six-factor solutions, which are reported in Table 5.7, resulted in the best fit for the data, reproducing the six factors that were incorporated in the STAXI when constructing the inventory (Spielberger, 1988). As may be noted in Table 5.7, two S-Anger items, #5 ("feel like breaking things") and #8 ("feel like hitting someone"), had the smallest loadings for females on the S-Anger factor, but much higher loadings for males. Fuqua et al. (1991) found that these items had salient loadings on a seventh factor, which was subsequently expanded by Spielberger (personal communication, November 1994) to assess "feeling like expressing anger."

As previously noted, the STAXI-N S-Anger scale may have a "floor effect," which makes it difficult to identify two S-Anger factors in situations that do not provoke much anger. Moreover, "feeling angry" items appear to be more sensitive to lower levels of anger intensity, whereas the "feeling like expressing anger" items may require greater anger provocation to be activated in order to have sufficient influence to produce a seventh factor. The development of a Norwegian S-Anger scale with "feeling angry" and "feeling like expressing anger" components will require constructing additional items with "feeling like expressing anger" content, but this may not be necessary because the original S-Anger scale consists of items that assess a wide range of angry feelings, providing a well-defined measure of S-Anger with a high degree of internal consistency. Moreover, taken together with an individual's score on the AX/Out scale, the STAXI-N S-Anger scale provides information regarding the probability that angry feelings will be expressed in aggressive behavior.

The findings of the factor analyses of the STAXI-N items reported in Table 5.7 are quite similar to the factor structure reported by Fuqua et al. (1991), apart from the seventh factor identified by Fuqua, which was not found for Norwegian subjects. These results also provide strong support for the multidimensional anger concepts defined and assessed by Spielberger (1988) that underlie the construction of the STAXI. However, they also raise some interesting questions concerning gender that must be considered, along with possible cultural differences in relation to the experience, expression, and control of anger.

The six STAXI-N factors for Norwegian males, in descending order of magnitude, were S-Anger, Anger-Control, Anger-In, Anger-Out, T-Ang/T, and T-Ang/R. For Norwegian females the same six factors were identified, but

Table 5.7 Factor loadings of the STAXI-N items in the six-factor solutions with oblimin rotation for male (*N* = 160) and female (*N* = 284) university students

Item	S-Anger		AX/Con		AX/In		AX/Out		T-Ang/T		T-Ang/R	
	M-1	F-2	M-2	F-3	M-3	F-1	M-4	F-5	M-5	F-4	M-6	F-6
1. Furious	.85	.71										
2. Irritated	.44	.49										
3. Angry	.90	.75										
4. Feel like yelling	.79	.74										
5. Feel like breaking things	.58	.23										
6. Mad	.82	.67										
7. Feel like banging	.62	.78										
8. Feel like hitting someone	.75	.41										
9. Burned up	.86	.60										
10. Feel like swearing	.36	.60										
24. Patient with others			.57	.37								
28. Keep my cool			.57	.50								
31. Control my behavior			.67	.67								
31. Control my temper			.66	.46								
35. Stop self from temper			.48	.67								
40. Tolerant			.64	.46								
44. Control anger			.50	.66								
23. Keep things in					.61	.68						
25. Clench my teeth					.54	.69						
26. Withdraw from people					.56	.71						
30. Boil inside					.53	.65						
33. Harbor grudges					.68	.63						
36. Secretly critical					.22	.30						
37. Angrier than admit					.57	.46						
41. Irritated, not show					.56	.48						

(*continued*)

Table 5.7 Factor loadings of the STAXI-N items in the six-factor solutions with oblimin rotation for male (N = 160) and female (N = 284) university students (continued)

Item	S-Anger		AX/Con		AX/In		AX/Out		T-Ang/T		T-Ang/R	
	M-1	F-2	M-2	F-3	M-3	F-1	M-4	F-5	M-5	F-4	M-6	F-6
17. Mad, say nasty things							.72	.74				
22. Express my anger						-.56	.33			.31		
27. Sarcastic remarks							.46	.35				
29. Slam doors							.36	.20				
32. Argue with others							.31	.22				
34. Strike out						-.29	.40	.27				
39. Say nasty things							.81	.80				
42. Lose my temper							.32	.27				
43. If someone annoys me				-.37	-.51	-.57	.47					
11. Quick tempered									.66	.62		
12. Fiery tempered									.65	.75		
13. Hotheaded person									.67	.65		
16. Fly off the handle									.34	.54		
19. Hit when frustrated									.50	.25		
14. Slowed down											.46	.55
15. Annoyed work											.48	.61
18. Criticized											.56	.39
20. Poor evaluation											.56	.61
Eigenvalue												
Males	7.18		5.26		2.31		1.97		1.47		1.14	
Females		4.31		2.38		6.93		1.18		1.98		1.00

Note. The order of extraction for each factor for males (M) and females (F) is indicated by the number following the letter signifying gender. Only dominant loadings for each item and nondominant salient loadings of .30 or higher are reported.

with the following somewhat different order of factor strength: Anger-In, S-Anger, Anger-Control, T-Ang/T, Anger-Out, and T-Ang/R. The differences between Norwegian men and women in the magnitude and order of extraction of the STAXI factors may be due to ambiguity in several AX/Out items, especially for the females. The items with the clearest loadings on the Anger-Out factor for Norwegian females describe the verbal expression of anger, whereas items describing anger directed outwardly had strong negative loadings on the Anger-In factor.

Although there were gender differences in the factor structure of the STAXI-N (Håseth & Spielberger, 1993), the meanings of such differences have not been fully explored. One possible interpretation of the observed gender differences for Norwegian subjects is that Anger-In and Anger-Out are not entirely independent dimensions, but represent divergent modes of a single dimension of anger expression. The hypothesis that there is only one dimension of anger expression is, of course, not new (Funkenstein, King, & Drolette, 1954). When Spielberger initiated construction of the AX scale, his working definition assumed a unidimensional conception of anger expression (Spielberger, Reheiser, & Sydeman, 1995). During the test construction process, he identified two relatively independent anger-expression factors and developed separate scales to measure the underlying constructs. Thus, although anger expression was initially conceptualized by Spielberger as a unidimensional, bipolar construct, items with unclear loadings and/or gender differences were eliminated in his empirical analyses, resulting in a multidimensional scale.

In several European adaptations of the STAXI, problems were also encountered in the relations between the AX/Out scale and other dimensions of anger expression. In the German adaptation (Schwenkmezger et al., 1992), for example, several AX/Out items had dual loadings on the Anger-Control factor, and significant *positive* correlations were found between AX/Out and AX/In. For Norwegian males this correlation was negligible, but it was *negative* and highly significant for Norwegian females ($R = -.23$, $p < .001$). A similar pattern was also found in the Italian adaptation of the STAXI (Spielberger & Comunian, 1992).

Factor Structure of the Revised STAXI-N Anger Expression Scale

Inconsistencies in the factor structure of the STAXI-N AX/Out scale were most pronounced for the female university students, for whom 3 of the 8 AX/Out items had primary loadings on the AX/In scale. Similar results were also found in the male sample but to a lesser degree, suggesting that Anger-Out and Anger-In might not be separate dimensions. Because we relied heavily on verbatim translations from English to Norwegian, it was possible that our item pool was not large enough to eliminate ambiguity in the selection of items. However, the main argument against attributing the observed gender difference to this psychometric technicality is that only one scale, AX/Out, was affected. Why this should be the case if language and item wording alone accounted for the observed gender differences in anger expression was not evident. Nevertheless, it seemed reasonable to construct additional AX/Out items to determine if an AX/Out scale could be developed with no dual loadings on the other AX factors. Therefore, seven new AX/Out items were written, using colloquial Norwegian words and expressions.

The Norwegian AX/Con scale was designed to measure the control of outwardly directed anger, as in the original STAXI. The only STAXI-N AX/Con item measuring the control of suppressed anger, "I calm down faster than most people," was omitted from the Norwegian STAXI because the correlations of this item with the AX/Con scale was quite small in the samples studied. However, recent research (Spielberger, Reheiser, & Sydeman, 1995) has indicated that it is possible to measure the control of suppressed anger. In the Dutch adaptation of the AX scale, a new scale was developed to assess the reduction of suppressed anger, with the item, "calm down faster" as its core or anchor. Based on the Dutch scale and its American translation (Spielberger et al., 1995), 16 new anger-control items were written, using Norwegian expressions relating to the basic concept of controlling Anger-In by reducing the intensity of suppressed anger. Each new anger-control item was placed at every fourth position in the STAXI-N AX scale, following an AX/In item and immediately before an AX/Con item. The remainder of the items were placed at the end of the 24-item AX scale, alternating with the new AX/Out items.

The revised STAXI-N, which included the 47 experimental AX items, was administered to 404 introductory psychology students and freshmen entering the University of Oslo (122 men, $\overline{X}$ age 20.93; 282 females, $\overline{X}$ age 22.17). Based on the results of the exploratory factor analyses and item-scale correlations, 8 items were selected to form the new Norwegian STAXI-N AX/Con-In scale. Of the 7 AX/Out items added to the item pool, 5 items with better psychometric properties than the original AX/Out items were used as replacements to improve this scale. Separate factor analyses for males and females of the 32 items constituting the four 8-item AX scales were performed. Because there were no gender differences in the factor structures, the data for men and women were combined.

The 4-factor solutions with oblimin rotation, which fitted the data equally well for both sexes and had the best simple structure, are reported in Table 5.8. In addition to the three established anger expression factors (Anger-In, Anger-Out, Anger-Control), a strong AX/Con-In factor similar to the one identified by Spielberger et al. (1995) was also found; all 8 AX/Con-In items had clear and salient loadings on this factor. The correlation between the AX/Con-In and AX/Con-Out scales was .48.

Alphas for the three STAXI-N scales were at the same levels or slightly higher than those reported in Table 5.2. For the new AX/Con-In scale, the alphas were .81 for both sexes. The median item-total correlations for the 32 items in the revised AX scale were .54 and .53, respectively, for males and females. For the revised AX/Out scale, the alphas were .81 for males and .79 for females; the median item-total correlations were .55 and .49, respectively, for males and females.

Table 5.8 Four-factor solution (PC, Promax rotation) for revised AX scale in STAXI–N based on 404 Norwegian college students

Test items		AX/Con-Out Factor 1	AX/In Factor 2	AX/Out Factor 3	AX/Con-In Factor 4
AX1	Control my temper	.55	.38		
AX5	Patient with others	.51			
AX10	Keep my cool	.61			
AX14	Control my behavior	.61			
AX19	Stop myself from losing temper	.71			
AX23	Calm down quickly	.64			
AX31	Control angry feelings	.50			
AX36	Anger quickly under control	.76			
AX3	Keep things in		.72		
AX6	Clench my teech		.61		
AX7	Withdraw from other people		.71		
AX13	Boil inside, but hide it		.62		
AX17	Harbor grudges without telling		.76		
AX21	Secretly critical of others		.54		
AX22	Angrier than admit		.66		
AX27	More irritated than people know		.66		

(*continued*)

Table 5.8 Four-factor solution (PC, Promax rotation) for revised AX scale in STAXI–N based on 404 Norwegian college students (continued)

Test items		AX/Con-Out Factor 1	AX/In Factor 2	AX/Out Factor 3	AX/Con-In Factor 4
AX9	Make sarcastic remarks			.77	
AX15	Argue with others			.33	
AX18	Fight back when angry			.46	
AX25	Can say nasty things			.52	
AX33	Can bang on the table			.56	
AX35	Use sharp utterances			.80	
AX43	Yell at somebody provoking			.67	
AX45	Easily starts bickering			.64	
AX8	I try to calm down				.74
AX12	Calm down as soon as possible				.68
AX16	Let temper ease off				.85
AX20	I try to simmer down				.69
AX32	I try to relax				.58
AX34	Do something attractive				.53
AX40	Soothe angry feelings				.47
AX47	Think of something else				.48
Eigenvalue		8.11	3.62	2.81	2.06
% of variance		21.9	9.8	7.6	5.6
Alpha		85	81	80	81

Note. Loadings < .35 not reported. Males = 122, Females = 286.

DISCUSSION AND CONCLUSIONS

The factorial independence of the six Norwegian STAXI scales reproduces the well-known factor structure of the original American and several recent European adaptations of the STAXI. The revised STAXI-N AX/Out scale was also factorially independent of the AX/In scale, and had better psychometric properties than the original scale; none of the items in the revised STAXI-N AX/Out had dual loadings on the Anger-In factor. Nevertheless, small but highly significant ($p < .001$) negative correlations of .26 for males and .30 for females were found between the STAXI-N AX/In and AX/Out scales, suggesting a single Anger-In/Anger-Out dimension. It is possible that cultural factors contributed to the negative correlations between the two scales.

Given the negative correlation between STAXI-N AX/In and AX/Out scales, it is still possible that anger expression consists of two dimensions. This interpretation is supported by the substantial correlation that was found between the AX/In and T-Anxiety scales (Table 5.5). Because expressing Anger-Out can be threatening because of possible retaliation by others, anxiety may be provoked that activates the suppression of anger as a defensive strategy. Thus, anxiety may be the mediating variable that contributes to the correlation between AX/In and AX/Out. Assuming that the tendency to experience anxiety is stronger in females than males, women may be more prone to use Anger-In as a defense strategy.

Gender differences were most pronounced for the youngest Norwegian subjects, that is, the 10th-grade high school students. On T-Anger and the AX/Out scales, the 10th-grade girls scored much higher than the boys ($p < .001$). Thus, contrary to what might be expected according to popular conjectures, the young Norwegian females scored higher than the males in the experience and expression of anger.

In all of the studies with the STAXI-N, males consistently scored higher than females on the AX/Con scale, indicating a stronger need to keep anger expression within socially acceptable limits. Apart from the finding on S-Anger, similar tendencies have been observed for students in the standardization of the German STAXI (Schwenkmezger et al., 1992). Female German students scored significantly higher than males on T-Anger and Anger-Out, whereas males scored higher on Anger-Control. As previously noted, this pattern was different from that reported by Spielberger (1988) based on extensive studies with the original STAXI, in which American males and females were equally likely to experience anger, and males showed a stronger tendency to express their anger.

Differences in the findings for Norwegian/German and American students with regard to gender could be due to cultural factors. However, these differences might also be by-products of transforming and adapting a measuring instrument to another language. Further studies utilizing the STAXI and additional, independent ways of measuring anger will be needed to clarify these issues.

REFERENCES

Alexander, F. (1948). *Psychosomatic medicine.* New York: Norton.

Averill, J. R. (1982). *Anger and aggression: An essay on emotion.* New York: Springer-Verlag.

Biaggio, M. K., Supplee, K., & Curtis, N. (1981). Reliability and validity of four anger scales. *Journal of Personality Assessment, 45,* 639–648.

Buss, A. B., & Perry, M. (1992). The aggression questionnaire. *Journal of Personality and Social Psychology, 63,* 452–459.

Buss, A. H., & Durkee, A. (1957). An inventory for assessing different kinds of hostility. *Journal of Counseling Psychology, 21,* 343–349.

Evans, D. R., & Stangeland, M. (1971). Development of the reaction inventory to measure anger. *Psychological Reports, 29,* 412–414.

Eysenck, H. J., & Eysenck, S. B. G. (1975). *Manual of the Eysenck Personality Questionnaire.* London: Hodder & Stroughton.

Funkenstein, D. H., King, S. H., & Drolette, M. E. (1954). The direction of anger during a laboratory stress-inducing situation. *Psychosomatic Medicine, 16,* 404–413.

Fuqua, D. R., Leonard, E., Masters, M. A., Smith, R. J., Campbell, J. L., & Fischer, P. C. (1991). A structural analysis of the State–Trait Anger Expression Inventory (STAXI). *Educational and Psychological Measurement, 51,* 439–446.

Håseth, K. (1990a). *Preliminary manual for the Norwegian adaptation of Spielberger's State–Trait Personality Inventory (STPI).* Unpublished manuscript, Department of Psychology, University of Oslo, Norway.

Håseth, K. (1990b). *Preliminary manual for the Norwegian adaptation of Carver and Scheier's Life Orientation Test (LOT).* Unpublished manuscript, Department of Psychology, University of Oslo, Norway.

Håseth, K. (1992). *Preliminary manual for the Eysenck Personality Inventory (EPI).* Unpublished manuscript, Department of Psychology, University of Oslo, Norway.

Håseth, K., Hagtvet, K. A., & Spielberger, C. D. (1990). Psychometric properties and research with the Norwegian State–Trait Anxiety Inventory. In C. D. Spielberger, R. Diaz-Guerrero, & J. Strelau (Eds.), *Cross-cultural anxiety* (Vol. 4, pp. 169–181). Washington, DC: Hemisphere.

Håseth, K., & Spielberger, C. D. (1993). *Manual for Norsk Tilstands-Trekk Sinneuttrykks Inventorium (STAXI–N).* Unpublished manuscript, Department of Psychology, University of Oslo, Norway.

Lazarus, R. (1993). Why we should think of stress as a subset of emotion. In L. Goldberger & S. Breznitz (Eds.), *Handbook of stress: Theoretical and clinical aspects* (2nd ed., pp. 21–39). New York: The Free Press.

Novaco, R. W. (1975). *Anger control: The development and evaluation of an experimental treatment.* Lexington, MA: Lexington Books/D.C. Heath.

Novaco, R. W. (1977). Stress inoculation: A cognitive therapy for anger and its application to a case of depression. *Journal of Consulting and Clinical Psychology, 45,* 600–608.

Novaco, R. W. (1994). Assessing anger among mentally disordered persons as a violence risk factor. In J. Monahan & H. J. Steadman (Eds.), *Violence and mental disorder: Developments in risk assessment* (pp. 21–59). Chicago: University of Chicago Press.

Rorschach, H. (1932). *Psychodiagnostik: Methodik und Ergebnisse eines wahrnehmungs-diagnostischen experiments* [Psychodiagnostics: Method and findings in a perceptual-diagnostic experiment] (2nd ed.). Bern: Huber.

Rosenzweig, S. (1950). Revised norms for the adult form of the Rosenzweig Picture-Frustration Study. *Journal of Personality, 3,* 344–346.

Schwenkmezger, P., Hodapp, V., & Spielberger, C. D. (1992). *Das State–Trait–Argerausdrucks-Inventar (STAXI)* [The State–Trait Anger Expression Inventory]. Bern: Huber.

Smedslund, J. (1993). How shall the concept of anger be defined? *Theory and Psychology, 3,* 5–33.

Spielberger, C. D. (1983). *Manual for the State–Trait Anxiety Inventory: STAI: (Form Y).* Palo Alto, CA: Consulting Psychologists Press.

Spielberger, C. D. (1988). *Manual for the State–Trait Anger Expression Inventory (STAXI).* Odessa, FL: Psychological Assessment Resources.

Spielberger, C. D., & Biaggio, M. B. (1992). *Manual do Inventário de Expressao de Raiva Como Estado e Traço (STAXI)* [Manual of the State–Trait Anger Expression Inventory]. Alameda Jau, Brazil: Vetor Editora Psico-Pedagogica Ltda.

Spielberger, C. D., & Comunian, A. L. (1992). *STAXI, State–Trait Anger Expression Inventory (STAXI) Manuale.* Firenzi: Organizzazioni Speciali.

Spielberger, C. D., Gorsuch, R. L., & Lushene, R. (1970). *Manual for the State–Trait Anxiety Inventory: STAI ("Self-Evaluation Questionnaire").* Palo Alto, CA: Consulting Psychologists Press.

Spielberger, C. D., Jacobs, G. A., Russell, S. F., & Crane, R. S. (1983). Assessment of anger: The State–Trait Anger Scale. In J. N. Butcher & C. D. Spielberger (Eds.), *Advances in personality assessment* (Vol. 2, pp. 159–187). Hillsdale, NJ: Lawrence Erlbaum Associates.

Spielberger, C. D., Johnson, E. H., Russell, S. F., Crane, R. S., Jacobs, G. A., & Worden, T. J. (1985). The experience and expression of anger: Construction and validation of an anger expression scale. In M. A. Chesney & R. H. Rosenman (Eds.), *Anger and hostility in cardiovascular and behavioral disorders* (pp. 5–30). New York: Hemisphere/McGraw-Hill.

Spielberger, C. D., Reheiser, E. C., & Sydeman, S. J. (1995). Measuring the experience, expression and control of anger. In H. Kassinove (Ed.), *Anger disorders: Definition, diagnosis, and treatment* (pp. 49–72). Washington, DC: Taylor & Francis.

Spielberger, C. D., & Sydeman, S. J. (1994). State–Trait Anxiety Inventory (STAI) and State–Trait Anger Expression Inventory (STAXI). In M. Maruish (Ed.), *The use of psychological testing for treatment planning and outcome assessment* (pp. 292–321). Hillsdale, NJ: Lawrence Erlbaum Associates.

van der Ploeg, H. M., van Buuren, E. T., & van Brummelen, P. (1988). The factor structure of the State–Trait Anger Scale. *Psychological Reports, 63,* 978.

Zelin, M. L., Adler, G., & Myerson, P. G. (1972). Anger self-report: An objective questionnaire for the measurement of aggression. *Journal of Consulting and Clinical Psychology, 39,* 340.

II

STRESS AND EMOTION IN THE WORKPLACE

6

Occupational Stress, Personnel Adaptation, and Health

Anna B. Leonova
Moscow State Lomonosov-University, Russia

Abstract *The multidimensional effects of occupational stress on job performance and the development of stress-related symptoms during prolonged work in a demanding work environment were investigated in a longitudinal study of operator managers of a complex automated system. Thirty-one highly educated and experienced specialists were followed for 6 years, using a widespread-netting research paradigm. Measures of job performance, job satisfaction and well-being, emotional strain, chronic negative states, and psychosomatic symptoms and disorders were obtained at three different stages of adaptation to technological innovations in the workplace. Following automatization, the parameters of job performance improved significantly as compared with the initial semiautomated working conditions. Technical modernization also reduced manifestations of a fatigue-boredom syndrome, but resulted in cognitive and emotional overstrain. Progressive development of occupational stress was reflected in acute and chronic stress-related manifestations of negative states, and in psychosomatic symptoms and disorders. Mobilization of the resources required for efficient job performance to meet the increased cognitive demands of the more complex, automated work environment resulted in emotional overstrain, fatigue, and other cumulative negative effects of occupational stress.*

Occupational stress refers to the complex, multidimensional effects of professional life on a working person (Cooper & Payne, 1978; Frankenhaueser, 1986; Karasek & Theorell, 1990). In addition to traditional analyses of changes in job efficiency and physical health under demanding work conditions (Frese, 1986; Kasl, 1978; Rohmert & Luczak, 1979), recent investigations have directed attention to many other stress-related occupational problems (Appley & Trumbull, 1986). Characteristics such as subjective comfort and well-being, emotional reactions, job satisfaction, self-esteem, and personal resources for coping and adaptation have moved from the periphery to the center of interest in empirical studies of stress in the workplace.

Research on occupational health has been guided by transactional process models, in which stress is conceptualized as the "meeting point" for environmental demands and personal reactions to them (Appley & Trumbull, 1986; Cox & Mackay, 1981; Lazarus, 1966). According to Lazarus (1977), the stress process involves subjective appraisal of stressor situations, activation of an individual's coping resources, and the use of available external tools and internal resources to cope with stress-related emotional reactions.

Stressor → Appraisal → Emotional and Coping Responses

Although transactional process approaches are better suited than classical theories to the analysis of everyday work-related stressors, the simple research paradigm of these models is not sufficiently comprehensive for the analysis of complex constellations of sociopsychological and personal events. For longitudinal field studies, especially, the methodology of "widespread netting" would seem to be more productive in providing a comprehensive understanding of the complex impact of a variety of personal and sociopsychological factors on occupational stress.

When using the widespread-netting methodology, four aspects of occupational stress must be considered. First, a detailed job analysis is required to provide a clear description of the demands of the work environment that may provoke stress reactions (Algera, 1988; Rohmert & Luczak, 1979). Second, multidimensional assessment is needed to evaluate various manifestations of stress and their effects on performance and health (Cox, 1985; Frankenhaueser, 1986; Leonova, 1994). Third, strategies for data integration must be developed to allow a comprehensive interpretation of heterogeneous facts and events (Hockey & Hamilton, 1983; Leonova, 1993). Finally, observations of dynamic patterns of change over long periods of time must be considered to differentiate situational reactions from more stable adaptation mechanisms and personal strategies for coping with stress.

In addition to comparative analyses of demographic and epidemiological factors for different occupations (Johanssen & Gardell, 1988; Karasek & Theorell, 1990; Kasl, 1978), longitudinal studies based on observations of the same group over an extended period of time are needed to follow the sequence of transformations that link delayed stressor effects to personal health and well-being. Longitudinal research also facilitates defining risk zones, and permits the application of effective interventions that can correct any emerging negative tendencies.

Changes in job requirements that result from the implementation of new technologies are frequently encountered in occupational settings in modern society (Blackler, 1988; Salvendy, Sauter, & Hurrel, 1987). These potential sources of occupational stress encompass the whole spectrum of personal reactions and attitudes toward modernization, including emotional and motivational factors and spontaneous adaptation. Investigations of the effects of technical innovation also permit evaluation of the "internal costs" of such changes from both engineering and psychological perspectives (Appley & Trumbull, 1986).

This chapter reports findings based on a longitudinal study of the operator managers of a complex automated system. A widespread-netting research paradigm was used to investigate the effects of workplace technological innovations on performance and job satisfaction for these workers over 6 years. The development of stress-related symptoms and disorders during this period was also evaluated.

LONGITUDINAL STUDY OF OPERATOR MANAGERS

Operator managers with assigned control functions for monitoring a complex telecommunications network were evaluated at three time periods during a 6-year investigation of occupational stress. The operators' job consisted of assessing both technical reliability and deviations from normal functioning of complex equipment. Because the technical objects were distanced from the observers, monitoring operations (controlling, manipulation, correction, etc.) were managed using telemetric data supplied by a control computerized system (CCS). Consequently, the operators had to work with informational models of the actual technological processes, and without prompt feedback links. The requirements of this type of job were typical of the activities of managers of automated systems, which are now widespread in both production industries and the service sector (Blackler, 1988; Roe, 1988).

One important aspect of the operators' job was in the specificity of the work's temporal organization. The opportunity for management and control of the technological processes was provided only intermittently, often during night hours, and for strictly limited time periods. Thus, the operators worked a shift regime, with a rigorously defined sequence of working sessions and a machine-paced flow of information. Time limits, forced work rate, repetitive informational overload, and inverted day-and-night work schedules were among the critical aspects of this highly stressful job.

The operator managers occupied a key leadership position in the functioning of the entire CCS. Supported by lower levels of the CCS, their daily work provided the initial data for the realization of numerous vital control operations performed by supplementary personnel (engineers, programmers, technical assistants, etc.). However, each operator manager was personally responsible for a final decision in regard to the reliability and safety of the technical operations. These job conditions were highly demanding, often evoking intense levels of emotional tension in the operator managers. Moreover, the cost of an operator error was very expensive, both from a material and a personal perspective.

The group of operator managers participating in the study consisted of highly educated and experienced specialists who were relatively well remunerated. Given their prestigious position in the organizational hierarchy, ensuring the safety of and providing good working conditions for this professional group were highly valued by the administration. Consequently, medical observations of an increasing sick rate among operator manager personnel, mostly from stress-related complaints and psychosomatic disorders, stimulated management interest in the psychological determinants of these problems, and prompted efforts to provide psychological support to enhance the operators' health and well-being.

Technical Innovations in Operator Managers' Job

During the course of the study, conducted from 1985 to 1991, a general modernization of the CCS took place. More effective program tools and technical devices were installed to modify the human–computer interface, which produced substantial changes in the operator managers' job. Before modernization, the operator managers received displays of a long list of raw telemetric parameters that reported on technical characteristics of the equipment. The operators screened these displays sequentially for defects or potential hazards, and then transferred summarized information to superiors and subordinates at lower levels of the CCS (see Fig. 6.1A). Computerized tools supported only a part of the human actions involved in screening and detection; other operations were performed by verbal or written activities. Thus, the operator managers were an integral part of the online data processing designed to monitor, detect, and compensate for deficiencies in the CCS. Such working conditions can be classified as *semiautomated*.

After modernization, a more comprehensive informational control model was available to the operators, in which all routine operations and telemetric parameters were automated. The operators worked with modernized equipment, which provided representations of the technological systems to test their reliability. Thus, more detailed and comprehensive technological information was available for implementing adequate correction procedures (see Fig. 6.1B), placing the operators in a better position to supervise and perform the functions of decision making, strategic planning, and so on. The modernized job design corresponded more closely to automatization.

Technical modernization did not change either the operator managers' organizational structure or the external work conditions. Most operator managers remained in their positions and attended retraining courses during the installation of the new equipment. Adapting to changes in the job required acquisition of new skills, which were needed to master the automated tasks, and the duties and demands of the job. This adaptation took a relatively long period of time (usually at least 1 year), and was considered a transitional stage. Thus, in the course of the longitudinal study, there were three main stages: (a) before automatization, (b) the transition stage, and (c) after automatization.

A number of factors that generally provoke stress responses were common to all three stages: cognitive overload, repetitive work, time pressures associated with machine-paced performance, delayed feedback, shift work, prolonged working hours, and a high level of personal responsibility. Automatization of the operators' job also added an important new factor to this complex picture—namely, the predominance of creative cognitive functions (e.g., decision making and problem solving, as contrasted with simpler perceptual search and monitoring, which were required in the semiautomated stage).

While these important job structure changes were taking place, operators' performance, well-being, emotional strain, and health in this stressful work environment were evaluated. For the multidimensional assessment of stress reactions, the following groups of indicators were utilized:

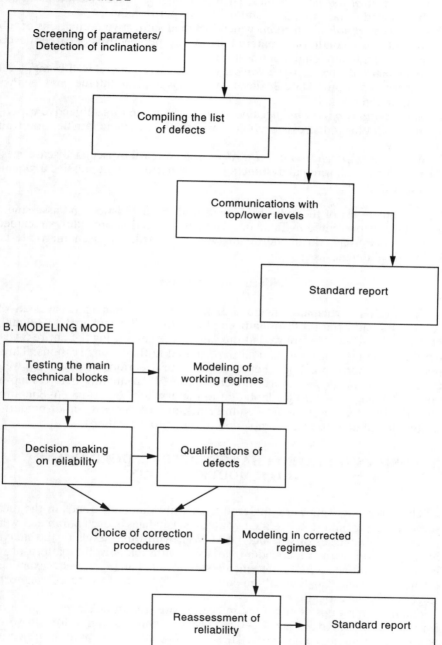

Figure 6.1 Operator's work on functional control of dynamic technological object (functional structure of one working cycle).

1. *Parameters of job performance,* such as numerous executed job tasks per shift, speed of performance, and quality of performance.
2. *Parameters of job satisfaction,* which included subjective evaluations of job content, work conditions, material prosperity, perspectives of career development, and emotional identification.
3. *Assessment of current psychological states,* such as general well-being, level of emotional strain (state anxiety), symptoms of acute fatigue, and feelings of monotony.
4. *Manifestations of chronic negative states,* as indicated by subjective experience of prolonged stress reactions, symptoms of chronic fatigue, and trait anxiety.
5. *Symptoms of psychosomatic disorders,* such as cardiovascular disease, gastric disorders, hormonal dysfunction, and symptoms of depressive and neurotic reactions.

A complete list of the indicators, measured characteristics, and assessment procedures is presented in Table 6.1. The data-collection procedures included direct observations, chronometric analyses, standardized psychometric tests, and medical diagnoses.

Subjects and Procedures

The study's participants included 31 male operator managers, ages 28–49 years, who had been professionally employed for 6–19 years at the beginning of the study. All were employed at the same work site during the entire 6-year period of the investigation, and all participated in the testing sessions. Three sets of data, corresponding to each of the critical periods of the study, were collected: (a) *Stage 1*—before modernization (9–12 months before innovations), (b) *Stage 2*—during adaptation to the new job conditions (6–8 months after the installation of the new equipment), and (c) *Stage 3*—after modernization (18–20 months after completion of the automatization).

STRESS-RELATED CHANGES BEFORE, DURING, AND AFTER MODERNIZATION

The three data sets were analyzed to identify the main trends in the measured indicators and stress-related symptoms. Changes in each parameter were evaluated in analyses of variance (ANOVA), with three levels of the *state of modernization* as the independent variable. Differences in the pattern of relationships among stress-related manifestations of change were also examined by means of factor analyses of the data matrix for each of the three diagnostic stages of the investigation.

Changes in groups of measured indicators over the three stages of modernization are presented in Figs. 6.2–6.6, in which significant trends for a majority of the indicators can be observed. These included changes in both the objective parameters of job performance and the subjective measures of psychological

Table 6.1 List of measures and indicators

Type of Measures	Indicators	Procedures
Job performance	Productivity	Number of performed working cycles per shift
	Speed of performance	Average time of performing one working cycle (min)
	Quality of performance (errors)	Average number of errors and false decisions per month
Job satisfaction	General index of subjective attitudes to job	Multidimensional checklist for job satisfaction (Fomicheva, 1982)
Current psychological states	Actual well-being	Subjective scale for general well-being (Leonova et al., 1987)
	Emotional strain	Spielberger state anxiety scale (Spielberger et al., 1970)
	Acute fatigue	Checklist for acute fatigue (Leonova et al., 1987)
	Monotony	Subjective scale for boredom and monotony (Fetiskin, 1992)
Chronic psychological states	Prolonged stress reactions	Checklist for neuro-mental tension (Nemchin, 1981)
	Chronic fatigue	Chronic fatigue (Leonova et al., 1987)
	Trait anxiety	Spielberger trait anxiety scale (Spielberger et al., 1970)
Psychosomatic diseases	Heart-vascular diseases	Data of medical control
	Gastric disorders	Data of medical control
	Hormonal dysfunction	Data of medical control
	Neurotic reactions	Data of medical control

states. As can be noted, some of these changes appear to be contradictory, reflecting contrasts of improved performance and enhanced feelings of well-being associated with the accumulation of chronic negative effects.

Productivity in Job Performance

All parameters of job performance improved significantly following automatization as compared with the initial semiautomatized working conditions (see Fig. 6.2). The operator managers were more productive, performing more tasks per shift. Speed of task execution increased and quality of performance improved, as reflected in a gradual reduction in the number of errors.

From the program administrators' perspective, the observed changes indicated that the operators had sufficient resources to master the new techniques.

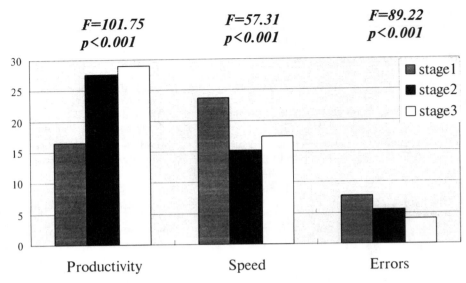

Figure 6.2   Dynamics in parameters of job performance during stages of modernizations.

However, work load also increased as a function of the greater cognitive demands of the automated work setting. Evidence for this was seen in changes
in the type of operator errors as the study progressed. During the initial stage,
"perceptual" errors dominated (e.g., omissions and false alarms, 69%); after
modernization, mistakes in strategic choices and observed technical deficiencies became more frequent (62%).

Job Satisfaction

Although relatively high at the beginning of the study, level of job satisfaction increased after modernization, as may be noted in Fig. 6.3. An "enthu-
siastic" spike in the transitional stage settled into a more stable improved level
in Stage 3 (see Fig. 6.3A). This positive change resulted from increased satisfaction with a number of job components, such as more challenging content
and better working conditions. It was also reflected in reports of significant
subjective benefits, such as the perception of enhanced possibilities for realizing greater personal growth and professional potential.

In contrast, subjective measures of several external components of job satisfaction (e.g., appraisals of material prosperity and career development prospects) reflected a decline in satisfaction. However, decrements in these qualities
might have been related to turbulence in the broader social environment at
the time of the investigation, rather than growing dissatisfaction with the job.
Whatever their cause, such problems did not detract from the operator managers' enhanced positive motivation toward work.

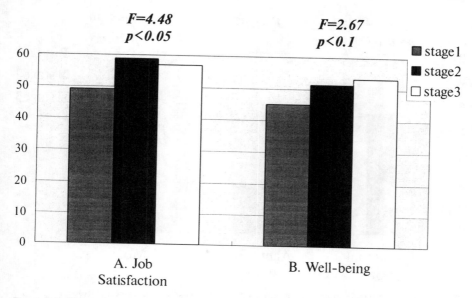

Figure 6.3 Dynamics in job satisfaction and well-being during stages of modernization.

Well-Being and Current Psychological States

Although job satisfaction and the subjective experience of well-being both improved, symptoms of negative reactions (e.g., acute fatigue, state anxiety) indicated that there were negative as well as positive changes (see Fig. 6.4). During Stage 1, slightly higher manifestations of acute fatigue were observed (e.g., symptoms of mental exhaustion, physical discomfort, difficulty in visual information processing), and feelings of monotony were much higher. Level of emotional strain was moderate during Stage 1, as indicated by a mean score of 42 on the Russian adaptation of the State Anxiety (S-Anxiety) scale of the State–Trait Anxiety Inventory (STAI; Spielberger, Gorsuch, & Lushene, 1970).

During Stages 2 and 3, the indicators of well-being tended to improve (see Fig. 6.3B) but these changes were only marginally significant ($p < .10$). Although symptoms of acute fatigue remained at about the same level, subjective feelings of monotony were substantially reduced (see Fig. 6.4), apparently because of job content, which was more challenging after modernization. In contrast to these positive trends, emotional strain was greater (see Fig. 6.4), as reflected in S-Anxiety scores that increased in Stages 2 and 3 to an average of more than 45 points on the STAI S-Anxiety scale.

The conflict between disparate appraisals of greater subjective comfort, in parallel with increased emotional tension, indicated the operator managers' spontaneous adaptation to better organized and more appealing work, which was also more mentally demanding. Thus, emotional overstrain resulted from the need to cope with more complex tasks and increased work load.

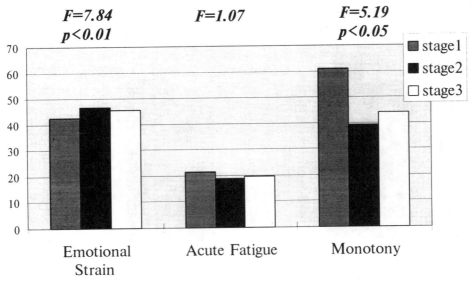

Figure 6.4   Dynamics in indicators of current states during stages of modernization.

Indicators of Chronic Negative States

Unlike the conflicting trends in current subjective states during modernization (see Fig. 6.4), the various symptoms of chronic negative states progressively accumulated over the three stages of the study, as noted in Fig. 6.5. Prolonged stress reactions, such as physiological complaints, behavioral disturbances, loss of motivation, and confusion in social contacts, increased from

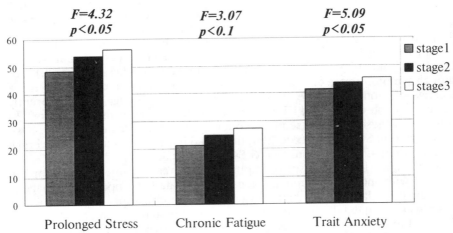

Figure 6.5   Dynamics in indicators of chronic states during stages of modernization.

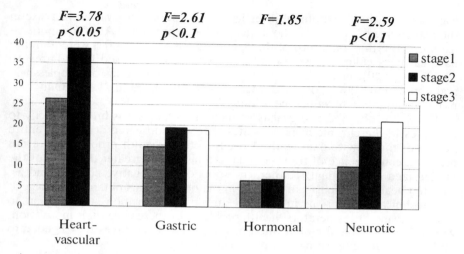

Figure 6.6 Dynamics in psychosomatic symptoms during stages of modernization.

Stage 1 to Stage 3 ($p < .05$). These indicators also correlated positively and significantly ($p < .01$) with increased emotional tension.

The effects of prolonged stress were also reflected in the accumulation of chronic fatigue symptoms (see Fig. 6.5). Although this tendency only approached significance ($p < .10$), signs of exhaustion and asthenic changes were observed in both the somatic and mental spheres. Level of trait anxiety also increased from Stage 1 to Stage 3, reaching a critically high value in Stage 3, as indicated by a mean score of 45 on the Spielberger STAI Trait Anxiety (T-Anxiety) scale.

Psychosomatic Symptoms and Disorders

The health of the operator managers was not good at the beginning of the study, as noted in Fig. 6.6. More than half had one or more of the following medical problems: (a) cardiovascular diseases, mostly hypo- or hypertension (26.2%); (b) gastric disorders, including gastritis, colitis, and gastric ulcers (14.6%); (c) hormonal dysfunction, mainly some form of glycogen-storage disorder (6.7%); and (d) neurotic or depressive reactions (10.3%). These psychosomatic disorders emerged while the study participants were employed as operator managers because the personnel procedures by which they were selected required that only healthy people could be hired. Thus, individuals with preexisting medical and psychological conditions were excluded. Because the frequency of psychosomatic complaints and disorders correlated with length of time on the job ($r = .40, p < .05$), the onset and progression of the operator managers' medical problems may be regarded as the internal price that was paid for their prolonged employment in a stressful work environment.

In addition to the observed increase in the incidence of psychosomatic disorders, the general health status of the operator managers declined during each stage of this longitudinal investigation. Most notable was an increase in the percentage of operators who developed heart problems. After job modernization, more than one third of the operators (38.5%, $p < .05$) were found to have cardiovascular disease. Gastric disorders also increased from 14.6% to 18.7% ($p < .10$). Neurotic reactions, indicated by symptoms of sleeplessness and depression, almost doubled, increasing from 10.3% to 21.4%. Only hormonal dysfunction remained near initial levels.

The rise in the operator managers' health problems was linked directly to increases in the chronic negative states that were observed across the entire period of this longitudinal study. Moreover, these health problems were not merely a consequence of transient adaptations to the greater demands of the modernized environment. Rather, the roots of the negative changes and associated health problems can be seen in the observations obtained in Stage 1. The technical innovations introduced during the transition stage appear to have intensified the operators' health problems by increasing their motivation, which then stimulated mobilization of the personal resources they needed to perform a more interesting, but more demanding, job.

TRANSFORMATIONS IN THE STRUCTURE OF STRESS-RELATED MANIFESTATIONS

Transformations in the complex patterns of relationships across the entire set of measures and indicators were examined by factor analysis. The raw data matrices for the measures obtained in each stage of the study were transformed to standard scores, and then factored separately for the diagnostic cuts at each stage. The factor structures for the initial and final stages were then compared. The data for the intermediate transitional stage were not considered because of their diffuse picture, which was due as much to the establishment of new regulations as to job parameters. The findings obtained for the initial and final factor structures are presented in Fig. 6.7, in which the dynamics of the relations among the individual variables may be noted.

The factor analysis of the data collected during the initial stage of the study identified five distinct factors. Factor 1 was defined by a variety of somatic complaints and disorders, and by feelings of subjective discomfort, fatigue, monotony, and emotional tension. In essence, this factor reflected a psychosomatic syndrome resulting from exhaustive work under monotonous conditions. Factor 2 included positive appraisals of job satisfaction associated with acute fatigue. A number of job performance characteristics (productivity, speed, number of errors) were linked in Factor 3 to level of emotional tension, which had a negative loading. The two remaining factors consisted of gastric symptoms and neurotic reactions (Factor 4), and hormonal dysfunction accompanied by manifestations of prolonged stress (Factor 5).

Following the technical innovations associated with modernization and the time required to adapt to them, a somewhat different factor structure emerged in the final stage of the study. The Stage 3 factor structure consisted of six factors; only three of these factors were similar to those obtained in the initial

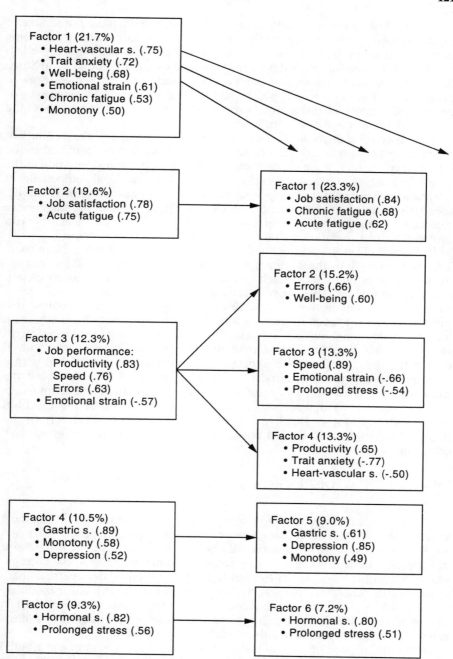

Figure 6.7 Transformation in factor structures of indicators from the beginning until the end of observations.

stage. The first factor in the initial stage, which reflected fatigue-boredom and psychosomatic symptoms, completely disappeared as its various components migrated to other factors. Factor 2 in the initial stage was basically a job satisfaction factor. Although this factor remained essentially the same in Stage 3, the connection to feelings of fatigue—both acute and chronic—was more pronounced. Factors 4 and 5, which were defined in Stage 1 by symptoms of gastric and neurotic disorders and hormonal dysfunction, also stayed about the same in the final stage of the study.

The observed changes in the factor patterns from Stage 1 to Stage 3 did not result from any simple addition or subtraction of the factors identified in the initial stage. Rather, these changes represented a deeper transformation in the core relationships between job performance and the emotional components of adaptation to a stressful work environment. Direct links among productivity, speed, and quality of performance, which was typical in the initial stage, were replaced by more complex interrelations of the performance measures with prolonged stress, emotional strain, and psychosomatic symptoms.

In Stage 1, Factor 3 was defined by three parameters of job performance. This factor split into three separate factors in Stage 3: (a) quality of performance (number of errors), which was correlated with level of subjective comfort and well-being; (b) job productivity, which was associated with more frequent elevations in worry, increased trait anxiety, and cardiovascular disturbances; and (c) speed of performance, which was inversely correlated with increasing emotional tension as assessed by state anxiety and prolonged stress reactions. Thus, the three new factors that emerged in Stage 3 each involved one of the three performance indicators, which were now associated with a different facet of the operators' emotional feelings and attitudes about the work situation. This intertwining of the behavioral and emotional components of job-related activities seemed to reflect a mobilization of the essential emotional and motivational resources needed to work effectively in the highly demanding, overloaded conditions of the operators' stressful work environment.

DISCUSSION AND CONCLUSIONS

The operator managers' professional life changed substantially during the 6 years of this study. These changes were reflected in greater productivity and work satisfaction, which, paradoxically, were associated with the progressive development of acute occupational stress-related manifestations, the accumulation of chronic negative states, and the deterioration of the operator managers' health. These dynamic changes were provoked by: (a) major modifications in job content as a consequence of automatization, which resulted in increased cognitive demands; and (b) prolonged work in a stressful job environment, with excessive demands and continuous overload.

In the initial stage of the study, the stressful work environment contributed to the development of a fatigue-boredom syndrome, as is often found in jobs that require continuous monitoring of semiautomated systems (Salvendy et al.,

1987). This syndrome was composed of strong feelings of monotony, acute and chronic fatigue, and a lowered state of well-being. High levels of anxiety and cardiovascular symptoms associated with the fatigue-boredom syndrome placed it in the psychosomatic range. Nevertheless, the operator managers' enhanced work-related motivation produced an acceptable level of performance and relatively high levels of intrinsic job satisfaction. The factor structure of the study measures in the initial stage, which was based on multiple sources of data, provides impressive evidence to support these conclusions.

After modernization, the revised specification of the operator managers' duties and responsibilities reduced the monotonous and exhaustive work load, but many new work tasks were added. The net effect of these changes was to increase the cognitive demands of the job while other important sources of job stress remained at high levels (e.g., limited time, machine-paced activities, shift work, personal responsibility for critical decisions). The inherent conflict between the enrichment of job content and the increased cognitive complexity of the work produced contradictory changes in the pattern of the operators' responsibilities.

The effects of automatization on the operators' job performance and psychological adjustment were primarily positive, as was reflected in enhanced motivation and performance and improved job satisfaction. The major negative effect was an increased level of emotional strain, suggesting that the delayed distressing effects of working under such stressful conditions were cumulative. Greater emotional strain was also indicated by an increase in chronic negative states and deterioration of personal health, as reflected in cardiovascular symptoms and psychosomatic disorders.

Contradictory tendencies were observed during the transitional stage of adaptation to the modernization of the work environment. On the one hand, improvement in the situational characteristics of the job contributed to the operator managers' positive feelings of well-being. On the other hand, a gradual accumulation of health problems was also observed. Transformations after modernization were consolidated in the final stage of the investigation, as reflected in the factor structure of the indicators in the automated stage. This helps explain how the operators endeavored to adapt to their new working conditions.

Emotional overstrain, as indicated by somatic reactions and high levels of state anxiety, was a critical factor in the changes that were observed in the health indicators. Increased emotional arousal provided the impetus to mobilize the internal resources needed to perform a more complex job, while also contributing to enhanced work motivation and personal interest in the job. But emotional overload without adequate release also resulted in a chronic imbalance in basic regulatory mechanisms, both emotional and somatic. Consequently, increased trait anxiety and psychosomatic symptoms were not surprising reactions to the nonstop emotional hypermobilization required to carry out the demanding and complex requirements of the operator managers' job.

Perhaps emotional overstrain was a consequence of the greater cognitive, temporal, and personal demands of the job after modernization, as well as the operator managers' efforts to adapt to them. From the perspective of the operators' long-term health and well-being, these spontaneously developed mechanisms for coping with the complex occupational stressors of a demanding job are unacceptable. One approach to improving the situation would be to reduce occupational stress by increasing the number of operators and/or by giving them more breaks and rest periods. Another alternative would be to increase the operators' stamina and resistance by helping them develop more effective regulatory habits for coping with occupational stress.

In conclusion, long-term adaptation to a complex, demanding, and changing professional work environment will depend on how individuals personally deal with job requirements and technical innovations. Irrespective of increasing job demands, employees' professionalism, commitment, and strong job-oriented motivation can help them maintain efficient performance over long periods of time while contributing to feelings of well-being and positive attitudes toward work. However, complex cognitive demands and overload can also result in persistent emotional strain, as well as accumulation of chronic negative states and psychosomatic symptoms. This study's findings suggest that more effective coping strategies and/or increased operator resistance are needed to deal with the occupational stress associated with the persistent demands of a highly complex work environment.

REFERENCES

Algera, J. A. (1988). Task analysis and new technologies. In V. E. de Keyser, T. Qvale, B. Wilpert, & S. A. R. Quintanilla (Eds.), *The meaning of work and technological options* (pp. 131–145). Chichester: Wiley.

Appley, M. H., & Trumbull, R. (1986). Development of the stress concept. In M. H. Appley & R. Trumbull (Eds.), *Dynamics of stress* (pp. 3–18). New York: Plenum.

Blackler, F. (1988). Information technologies and organizations: Lessons from 1980s and issues for the 1990s. *Journal of Occupational Psychology, 61,* 113–127.

Cooper, C. L., & Payne, R. (Eds.). (1978). *Stress at work.* Chichester: Wiley.

Cox, T. (1985). The nature and measurement of stress. *Ergonomics, 28,* 1155–1163.

Cox, T., & Mackay, C. (1981). A transactional approach to occupational stress. In E. N. Corlett & J. Richardson (Eds.), *Stress, work design, and productivity* (pp. 91–113). Chichester: Wiley.

Frankenhaueser, M. (1986). A psychobiological framework for research on human stress and coping. In M. H. Appley & R. Trumbull (Eds.), *Dynamics of stress* (pp. 101–116). New York: Plenum.

Frese, M. (1986). Coping as a moderator and mediator between stress at work and psychosomatic complaints. In M. H. Appley & R. Trumbull (Eds.), *Dynamics of stress* (pp. 183–206). New York: Plenum.

Fomicheva, N. I. (1982). A complex scale for evaluations of job satisfaction. *A use of ergonomic methods and norms in technical design: Methodical recommendations.* Moscow: Ekonomika. [In Russian]

Hockey, G. R. L., & Hamilton, P. (1983). The cognitive patterning of stress states. In G. R. L. Hockey (Ed.), *Stress and fatigue in human performance* (pp. 331–362). New York: Academic Press.

Johanssen, G., & Gardell, B. (1988). Work-health relations as mediated through stress reactions and job socialisation. In S. Maers (Ed.), *Topics in health psychology* (pp. 271–285). London: Wiley.

Karasek, R., & Theorell, T. (1990). *Healthy work, stress, productivity, and the reconstruction of working life.* New York: Basic Books.

Kasl, S. V. (1978). Epidemiological contributions to the study of work stress. In C. L. Cooper & R. Payne (Eds.), *Stress at work* (pp. 3–48). Chichester: Wiley.

Lazarus, R. S. (1966). *Psychological stress and the coping process.* New York: McGraw-Hill.

Lazarus, R. S. (1977). Cognitive and coping processes in emotion. In A. Monat & R. S. Lazarus (Eds.), *Stress and coping: An anthology* (pp. 145–159). New York: Columbia University Press.

Leonova, A. B. (1993). Psychological means for the control and prevention of industrial stress in computerized working places. *European Work and Organizational Psychologist, 3,* 11–27.

Leonova, A. B. (1994). Industrial and organizational psychology in Russia: The concept of human functional states and applied stress research. In C. L. Cooper & I. T. Robertson (Eds.), *International review of industrial and organizational psychology: 1944* (Vol. 9). Chichester: Wiley.

Roe, R. A. (1988). Acting systems design: An action theoretical approach to the design of man-computer systems. In V. E. de Keyser, T. Qvale, B. Wilpert, & S. A. R. Quintanilla (Eds.), *The meaning of work and technological options* (pp. 179–195). Chichester: Wiley.

Rohmert, W., & Luczak, H. (1979). Stress, work, and productivity. In V. Hamilton & D. M. Warburton (Eds.), *Human stress and cognition* (pp. 339–379). Chichester: Wiley.

Salvendy, G., Sauter, S. L., & Hurrel, J. J. (Eds.). (1987). *Social, ergonomic and stress aspects of work with computers.* Amsterdam: Elsevier.

Spielberger, C. D., Gorsuch, R. L., & Lushene, R. E. (1970). *Manual for the State–Trait Anxiety Inventory (STAI).* Palo Alto, CA: Consulting Psychologists Press.

7

Time Urgency and Its Relation to Occupational Stressors and Health Outcomes for Health Care Professionals

Shanker Menon, Lakshmi Narayanan, and Paul E. Spector
University of South Florida, Tampa, USA

Abstract   *The present study examined the nature of the construct of time urgency in a sample of 108 full-time nurses and 116 physicians. Time urgency was found to decompose into two separate and interpretable factors. The first factor was interpreted as the Strategic Time factor of time usage, and the second factor was interpreted as the Obsession Time factor of time usage. For both samples of nurses and physicians, the Strategic Time factor was positively related to job satisfaction and negatively related to the job stressors of interpersonal conflict and situational constraints. The Obsession Time factor was positively related to interpersonal conflict and negatively related to job satisfaction. There were significant differences in stressors reported between the two professions. For both samples, age was positively related to the Obsession Time factor of time usage. Results are discussed in the light of past research and future implications for stress research in organizational settings.*

In the past decade, a high level of interest has been displayed in understanding the dynamics of employee job stress. A research stream in occupational stress that has come from the health sciences has focused on understanding the stress-prone behavior syndrome called the Type-A Behavior Pattern (TABP). Since Friedman and Rosenman's (1959) pioneering work on Type-A behavior and its consequences over 30 years ago, a vast amount of literature has accumulated on the topic. They described TABP as an action-emotion complex that can be observed in any person who is aggressively involved in a chronic, instant struggle to achieve more and more in less and less time. The components of Type-A behavior involve hostility, aggressiveness, competitiveness, and a sense of time urgency.

Although Type-A behavior has been widely researched, results show non-significant or weak relationships between Type-A behavior and outcome variables such as performance and several affective reactions (Lee, Earley, & Hanson, 1988; Matteson, Ivancevich, & Smith, 1984; Matthews, 1988). It has now been suggested that certain Type-A behavior components may yield positive consequences, whereas others may be responsible for health risks typically

associated with Type-A behavior (Matthews, 1982; Wright, 1988). Some researchers have suggested that, to enhance its predictive qualities, the various
components of Type-A behavior should be studied separately (Helmreich,
Spence, & Pred, 1988; Spence, Helmreich & Pred, 1987; Spence, Pred, &
Helmreich, 1989). In this chapter, one such component, called *time urgency,* is
examined.

THE CONCEPTS OF TIME AND TIME URGENCY

For some time, researchers have recognized the importance of the time
dimension of work, as well as the temporal dimensions of norms and work
processes. For example, in an organizational context, it has been suggested
that norms about time can be viewed as characteristics of culture (Schriber,
1985). Researchers have shown how differences in organizational cultures can
lead to different views and assumptions about time (Schein, 1983). Similarly,
Schriber and Gutek (1987) pointed out that "time is a basic dimension of
organizations," and that organizations and the people who work in them are
influenced by how time is partitioned and scheduled.

The concept of *time urgency* has been around for a long time. However, in
recent years, researchers have focused more on this construct for several reasons, including the relationship between time as a scarce resource and strains
experienced in the workplace. There is the idea that some people are more
time urgent than others, and, as a result, may be more prone to suffer the
physical and psychological consequences associated with strain when time demands are high.

Time urgency as a component of Type-A behavior is reflected in the definition of TABP provided by Friedman and Rosenman (1974, p. xx): ". . . a
characteristic action-emotion complex which is exhibited by those individuals
who are engaged in a relatively chronic struggle to obtain an unlimited number of poorly defined things from their environment in the shortest possible
time. . . ." The emphasis on the time-urgent dimension of TABP is apparent
from this definition. Burnam, Pennebaker, and Glass (1975) defined *time urgency* as a tendency on the part of an individual to consider time as a scarce
resource and to plan its use carefully. In contrast, the Type-B behavior pattern
is characterized as a more relaxed and noncompetitive approach to life. Thus,
by the way it is defined, *time urgency* is an integral part of Type-A behavior
patterns.

The typical instruments used to measure time urgency have been self-report
measures of TABP, such as the Jenkins Activity Survey (JAS; Jenkins, Zyzanski, & Rosenman, 1971) and the Framingham scale (Haynes, Levine, Scotch,
Feinleib, & Kannel, 1978). However, a recent study by Edwards, Baglioni, and
Cooper (1990) revealed numerous problems with these scales. Edwards et al.
(1990) examined three current measures of TABP (and time urgency): the
JAS, the Framingham scale, and the Bortner questionnaire. Their analysis
revealed that none of these constructs was psychometrically sound because
they tapped different underlying constructs, contained substantial measure-

ment error, and did not truly reveal the multidimensional nature of the Type-A construct. These findings are supported by other researchers who have not been able to achieve high levels of prediction of coronary heart disease (CHD) with self-reports of Type-A behavior (Booth-Kewley & Friedman, 1987; Matthews, 1988).

The weak relationships that have been found between Type-A behavior and CHD and other variables may have resulted from using a global undifferentiated concept of Type-A behavior (Barling & Charbonneau, 1988; Helmreich et al., 1988; Spence et al., 1987). For example, the relationship between Type-A behavior and job satisfaction has not been clear (Matteson et al., 1984). Although some studies have reported a negative correlation between Type-A behavior and job satisfaction (Dearborn & Hastings, 1987), others have reported no relationship between these variables (Burke & Weir, 1980; Greenglass, 1987; Howard, Cunningham, & Rechnitzer, 1977; Matteson et al., 1984). One reason for this inconsistency may be that Type-A behavior has been assessed as a global, rather than a multifaceted, construct. It is also possible that the different components of Type-A behavior are differentially related to work-related attitudes (see Wright, 1988).

Although there is sufficient literature on time estimation and perception in experimental settings (Fraisse, 1963; Frankenhauser, 1959), the treatment of time orientation in organizational settings has not been as detailed, and there have been virtually no empirical studies related to actual time usage. There is the notion that some people are more time urgent than others, and, as a result, may be more prone to suffer the physical and psychological consequences associated with strain when time demands are high. Research on these aspects has been limited.

However, several studies have demonstrated that time urgency has been implicated in dissatisfaction and burnout in the nursing profession (Dewe, 1988; Maslach & Jackson, 1984; Moses & Rothe, 1979). Recent studies related to time-urgent professions indicate that female physicians tend to score higher than male physicians, especially on time urgency and other coronary-prone behaviors, due to various psychosocial factors (Smith & Sterndorff, 1992). Other studies (Streufert, Streufert, & Gorson, 1981) have indicated that managerial activities requiring complex decision making and long-term future planning are hindered, rather than aided, by time urgency. A study conducted by Friend (1982) found that, in problem-solving or other tasks requiring novel responses, increases in psychological stresses (such as subjectively high work load) and time urgency uniformly impair performance across a whole range of variables. Other studies have examined the construct of time urgency in relation to health outcomes. Coronary-prone individuals have been found to be more time urgent than others (Yarnold & Mueser, 1984).

Research also indicates that Type-A individuals are attracted to environments that are fast paced and competitive, and that have excessive work loads (Baker, Dearborn, Hastings, & Hamburger, 1984). This implies that these individuals are likely to resign if the work environment does not possess these characteristics. However, the reported correlations have been low again, indicating that it would be useful to examine some of the underlying dimensions of Type-A behavior (e.g., time urgency), which may provide a better explanation of such behavior.

Recognizing this problem, Landy, Rastegary, Thayer, and Colvin (1991) recently developed a behaviorally anchored rating scale (BARS) to measure time urgency, in which behavioral statements were used to measure the construct of time urgency. Their BARS technique produced multidimensional measures of time urgency, with adequate reliability and construct validity.

THE CURRENT STUDY

This study explored the multidimensional nature of time urgency using the BARS (Landy et al., 1991). The study sought to determine whether these multiple dimensions were, indeed, independent, or if they formed factors that would improve the predictability of these scales. Landy et al. examined the relationship between time urgency (using the new BARS technique) and job satisfaction as part of their construct validation process. This study went further. This new multidimensional scale was used to examine its relationship with some organizational variables related to job stressors. Furthermore, the study was interested in finding out whether these different factors differentially predicted outcome measures such as job satisfaction, intent to turnover, and physiological symptoms for health care professionals for whom time would be very relevant: nurses and physicians.

METHOD

Subjects

Nurse sample. The subjects consisted of 108 nurses from two major hospitals. The nurses had similar demographic characteristics, thus the data were combined. There were 28 male and 80 female nurses in the sample. The mean age of the subjects was 36.8 years. Surveys were distributed to 205 nurses, and 123 responses were returned—achieving a response rate of about 60%. Only 108 were usable because 15 of the surveys had incomplete information.

Physician sample. The subjects consisted of 116 physicians from three major hospitals. The three samples had similar demographic characteristics, therefore the data were combined. There were 80 male and 46 female physicians in the sample. The mean age was 44.9 years. Surveys were distributed to 250 physicians, and 116 were returned—achieving a response rate of about 46%.

Measures

Time urgency. Time urgency was measured by the BARS developed by Landy et al. (1991). Dimensions of time-urgent behavior measured by this scale are: Awareness of Time, Speech Patterns, Scheduling, Nervous Energy,

List Making, Eating Behavior, and Deadline Control. For each dimension, behavioral statements were used as qualitative anchors. Examples of behavioral statements for each dimension include: "I glance at my watch frequently during the day" for Awareness of Time; "I never interrupt or rush others when they are speaking" for Speech Patterns; "I allow a specific amount of time for each activity that I engage in" for Scheduling; "I tend to pace when I talk or think" for Nervous Energy; "If I get bogged down, I make a 'things to do' list" for List Making; "I am often the first person finished eating at the table" for Eating Behavior; and "I am always preparing for some event" for Deadline Control. Landy et al. (1991) reported test–retest reliabilities ranging from .79 to .84.

Stressors

Interpersonal conflict. A four-item scale developed by Spector (1987) assessed the degree of interpersonal conflict in the workplace. Examples of scale items include: "How often do you get into arguments with others at work?" and "How often do other people yell at you at work?" Responses were made on a 5-point scale, with response choices *never, rarely, sometimes, quite often,* and *extremely often.*

Work load. Work load was measured by a six-item scale developed by Spector, Dwyer, and Jex (1988). Examples of scale items include: "How often does your job require you to work very hard?" and "How often does your job leave you with little time to get things done?" Response choices were *never, rarely, sometimes, quite often,* and *extremely often.* The authors reported an alpha coefficient of .85.

Situational constraints. This organizational stressor was measured by an 11-item scale (Spector et al., 1988). Items dealt with the way in which aspects of the work situation impeded work progress (e.g., "How often do you find it difficult or impossible to do your job because of lack of equipment or supplies?"). Each item had five response choices: *less than once per month or never, once or twice per month, once or twice per week, once or twice per day,* and *several times per day.*

Outcome Measures

Job satisfaction. General satisfaction was measured using the three-item Overall Job Satisfaction scale from the Michigan Organizational Assessment Questionnaire (Camman, Fichman, Jenkins, & Klesh, 1979). An example item is: "In general, I like working here." This scale had six response choices: *strongly agree, disagree, slightly disagree, slightly agree, agree,* and *strongly disagree.* Spector (1987) reported an alpha coefficient of .83.

Turnover motivation. This variable was assessed by a one-item question asking how often respondents had seriously considered quitting their present jobs (Spector et al., 1988).

Health symptoms. Health symptoms were measured with a checklist of 16 symptoms (Spector et al., 1988). This checklist included symptoms most sen-

Table 7.1 Rotated factor loadings

Variable	Factor 1	Factor 2
Nurses		
List	.786	− .048
Deadline	.750	− .129
Schedule	.631	.111
Aware	.409	.304
Speech	.076	.589
Eat	.056	.453
Nervous	− .146	.707
% Variance	31.4	21.6
Physicians		
List	.645	− .158
Deadline	.610	− .111
Schedule	.531	.120
Aware	.428	.294
Speech	.152	.510
Eat	.141	.491
Nervous	− .102	.399
% Variance	26.1	19.1

Note. Underline indicates all factor loadings above .30.

sitive to stress (e.g., "During the past 30 days, did you have an upset stomach or nausea?"). Respondents were asked if they had experienced any of these symptoms in the last 30 days. Response alternatives were: *No, I didn't, Yes, I did, but did not see a doctor,* and *Yes, I did, and I saw a doctor.*

RESEARCH RESULTS

The time-urgency dimensions of Awareness of Time, List Making, Scheduling, and Deadline Control were all positively and significantly correlated with each other. These results held across both samples. The Speech Patterns, Nervous Energy, and Eating Behavior dimensions were positively correlated with each other and negatively correlated with Awareness of Time, List Making, Scheduling, and Deadline Control. These results suggest that there could be two distinct underlying factors to explain the relationship among the different dimensions of the time-urgency scale. An attempt was made to reduce the items to their underlying dimensions by using principal axis factoring and Varimax rotation. Based on the scree test, a two-factor solution was rotated.

Table 7.1 presents the rotated factor loadings from the analysis for the different time-urgency scales for both samples. These results show a distinct two-factor structure. The dimensions of Awareness of Time (Aware), List Making (List), Scheduling (Schedule), and Deadline Control (Deadline) loaded on Factor 1, whereas the dimensions of Speech Patterns (Speech), Nervous Energy (Nervous), and Eating Behavior (Eat) loaded on Factor 2. Factor 1 was labeled

Table 7.2 Means, standard deviations, and alpha coefficients

Variable	Nurses			Physicians			T
	M	SD	Alpha	M	SD	Alpha	
Strategic Time factor	19.24	3.69	0.76	16.82	3.10	0.79	5.29*
Obsession Time factor	12.88	2.53	0.69	10.40	2.74	0.65	7.04*
Job satisfaction	13.91	2.34	0.74	14.32	3.12	0.82	ns
Turnover	2.24	0.93	—	2.01	0.87	na	ns
Physiological symptoms	3.81	2.41	—	2.91	0.92	na	3.63*
Work load	19.34	2.81	0.73	16.36	3.74	0.79	6.77*
Interpersonal conflict	6.83	1.64	0.71	7.98	2.32	0.81	4.31*
Situational constraints	23.27	7.91	0.88	19.21	6.45	0.84	4.19*
Age	36.76	11.08	—	38.80	10.41	—	ns
Sample size	108			116			

*$p < .01$.
ns = nonsignificant.

as a Strategic Time factor because it consisted of items related to the effective planning and utilization of time. Factor 2 was labeled as an Obsession Time factor because it displayed characteristics that signify an obsession with, or a continuous preoccupation with, time.

Individuals who display a strategic time orientation (Factor 1) are more likely to display a tendency to plan their activities well in advance, including: scheduling activities, having an awareness of time, making lists, and exerting deadline control into their daily activities. Individuals who display characteristics related to an obsession time orientation (Factor 2) expend nervous energy, exhibit fast speech patterns, and display rushed eating behavior. Following the results of the factor analysis, the scales representing the Strategic Time factor were combined into one subscale, and the scales representing the Obsession Time factor were combined into a second subscale. To obtain a Strategic Time score, the four dimensions of Aware, List, Schedule, and Deadline were summed. Similarly, scores obtained on Speech, Nervous, and Eat were combined to get an Obsession Time score. The following analyses involved these two factors.

Descriptive statistics for all variables used in this study are presented in Table 7.2. These include sample size, mean, standard deviations, and t tests comparing the two samples. Internal consistency reliability coefficients (alpha coefficient) are also reported where appropriate. As can be seen, the means obtained by the nurses on time-urgency measures were somewhat higher than those of the physician sample. Nurses had significantly higher scores on the Strategic Time factor ($t = 5.29$, $p < .01$) and the Obsession Time factor ($t = 7.04$, $p < .01$). For stressors, nurses appeared to perceive a significantly higher degree of work load ($t = 6.77$, $p < .01$), and reported having more situational constraints ($t = 4.19$, $p < .01$) than physicians. However, physicians appeared to perceive a higher degree of interpersonal conflict ($t = 4.31$, $p < .01$) when compared with the nurses.

Table 7.3 presents correlations among all scales, as well as some demographic variables used in this study for nurses. As can be seen, the two derived scales of time urgency were significantly and negatively correlated with each other. When the relationship with outcome variables was examined, the Strategic Time factor was correlated positively with job satisfaction and negatively with turnover. The Obsession Time factor was positively correlated with turnover and physical symptoms and negatively with job satisfaction. Although the Strategic Time factor was negatively correlated with the stressors of interpersonal conflict and situational constraints, the Obsession Time factor was positively correlated with interpersonal conflict. The correlation with situational constraints was also positive in direction, but nonsignificant.

Table 7.4 presents the correlation results for the physician sample. The Strategic Time factor was positively related to job satisfaction and negatively to the stressors of interpersonal conflict and situational constraints. Conversely, the Obsession Time factor was significantly and positively related to interpersonal conflict and negatively to job satisfaction. Unlike the nurse sample, there was no significant relationship with turnover for either time-urgency dimension. It is interesting to note that age was positively related to the Obsession Time factor for both samples.

A series of z tests were done to determine whether the strength of correlations was significantly different for the two samples. In general, the strength of associations was significantly higher for nurses in comparison with the physicians. The correlation between the two time-urgency dimensions was significantly higher for the nurses than the physicians. Similarly, the correlation between job satisfaction and the Strategic Time factor was significantly higher. The outcome of turnover intent had a significantly higher relationship with both time urgency dimensions and all stressors when compared with the correlation coefficients obtained in the physician sample. Finally, the association between physical symptoms and the Obsession Time factor was also significantly higher for nurses. Correlations of the seven time-urgency subscales with stressors and outcome measures are listed in Table 7.5.

Regression Analyses

A series of regression analyses were performed to investigate the predictive effect of the Strategic Time factor and the Obsession Time factor on the outcome variables of the study—namely, job satisfaction, turnover motivation, and physiological symptoms. Each outcome variable and stressor was regressed on both time dimensions. Table 7.6 summarizes the results of regression analyses.

Table 7.6 reveals that there were some significant effects for all three outcome variables (job satisfaction, turnover, and physiological symptoms). For nurses, both of the time dimensions significantly predicted job satisfaction, with the Strategic Time factor being a better predictor of job satisfaction. When these two dimensions were combined, it accounted for a larger proportion of variance in job satisfaction scores than each one alone. Similarly, for turnover motivation, both time dimensions contributed significantly to the

Table 7.3 Correlations between scales and demographic variables for nurses

Variable					Scales					
	1	2	3	4	5	6	7	8	9	10
Strategic Time factor	1.00									
Obsession Time factor	-.317**a	1.00								
Interpersonal conflict	-.353**	.454**	1.00							
Situational constraints	-.245*	.144	.090	1.00						
Work load	.030	.057	.053	.523**	1.00					
Job satisfaction	.522**a	-.341**	-.273**	-.237*	-.170	1.00				
Turnover motivation	-.324**a	.317**a	.335**a	.285**a	.404**a	-.515**	1.00			
Physical symptoms	-.165	.417**a	.513**	.270**	.197	-.383**	.415**	1.00		
Age	-.010	.225*	.148	-.114	-.083	-.100	.034	.129	1.00	
Sex	.003	.058	.139	-.207*	-.053	.043	.017	.099	.074	1.00

Note. N = 108.
[a]Significant differences in correlation between samples.
$*p < .05.$ $**p < .01.$

135

Table 7.4 Correlations between scales and demographic variables for physicians

Variable	Scales									
	1	2	3	4	5	6	7	8	9	10
Strategic Time factor	1.00									
Obsession Time factor	−.132ᵃ	1.00								
Interpersonal conflict	−.251*	.284**	1.00							
Situational constraints	−.219*	.035	.097	1.00						
Work load	.092	−.112	.064	.420**	1.00					
Job satisfaction	.341**ᵃ	−.212*	−.223**	−.185*	−.179	1.00				
Turnover motivation	−.019ᵃ	.081ᵃ	.037ᵃ	.085ᵃ	.136ᵃ	−.381**	1.00			
Physical symptoms	−.113	.111ᵃ	.421**	.170**	.297	−.213*	.316**	1.00		
Age	−.019	.215*	.133	−.014	−.092	−.112	.102	.029	1.00	
Sex	.012	.009	.118	−.153*	−.009	.021	.025	.018	.063	1.00

Note. N = 108.
ᵃSignificant differences in correlation between samples.
*p < .05. **p < .01.

Table 7.5 Correlations of the TABP's time-urgency scales with outcome variables

Scale	Outcome variables					
	Job satisfaction	Turnover motivation	Physical symptoms	Interpersonal conflict	Situational constraints	Work load
Nurses						
Aware	.19*	−.02	.07	.06	.06	.10
Speech	−.20*	.36**	.27**	.26**	.05	.08
Schedule	.28**	−.21*	−.17	−.31**	−.30**	.02
Nervous	−.20*	.13	.21*	21*	.19*	.06
List	.36**	−.19*	−.08	−.17	−.21*	.06
Eat	−.15	.09	.21*	.33**	−.09	−.14
Deadline	.33**	−.28**	−.15	−.21*	−.19*	−.17
Physicians						
Aware	.21*	−.12	−.19*	−.03	−.10	.10
Speech	−.21*	.13	.13	.19*	.08	.19*
Schedule	.25*	−.16	−.18	−.22*	−.23*	−.22*
Nervous	−.19*	.22*	.17	.18	.15	.25*
List	.30**	−.12	.18	.10	.19*	.16
Eat	−.11	.10	.15	.23*	−.07	−.13
Deadline	.29	.13	−.19*	−.19	−.16	−.16

$*p < .05. **p < .01.$

prediction of this outcome variable. Finally, only the Obsession Time factor made a significant contribution to the prediction of physiological symptoms. Both time dimensions significantly contributed to the prediction of interpersonal conflict, and together these two predictors account for a substantial proportion of variance. Only the Strategic Time factor was able to significantly predict situational constraints, and neither predictor reached significance for the stressor work load.

For the physician sample, there were similar results. The Strategic Time factor again significantly predicted the outcome of job satisfaction. Both dimensions together contributed significantly to the prediction of the interpersonal conflict stressor.

DISCUSSION AND CONCLUSIONS

This study resulted in some interesting findings. First, there were significant differences in perceived stressors for the two different professions. The stressors of situational constraints and work load were perceived to a significantly higher degree by the nurses, whereas interpersonal conflict was reported to a higher degree by the physicians. Stressors appeared to differ as a function of job and job level. There could be a number of reasons for this finding. A higher level job, such as that of a physician, may be characterized by more decision latitude and autonomy when compared with a lower level job, such as that of a nurse. It is conceivable that in lower level jobs, where there is limited au-

Table 7.6 Regression analysis

	Outcome variables					
	Job satisfaction		Turnover motivation		Physical symptoms	
Predictors	Beta	*t*	Beta	*t*	Beta	*t*
Nurses						
Strategic Time factor	.459	2.199**	−.245	−2.54*	−.037	−0.365**
Obsession Time factor	−.195	5.185**	.235	2.35*	.405	4.189**
Multiple *R*	(.554)		(.392)		(.418)	
Physicians						
Strategic Time factor	.332	3.458**	ns		ns	
Obsession Time factor	−.193	2.047*				
Multiple *R*	(.393)					

	Interpersonal conflict		Situational constraints		Work load	
Stressors	Beta	*t*	Beta	*t*	Beta	*t*
Nurses						
Strategic Time factor	−.232	−2.514*	−.222	−2.098*		ns
Obsession Time factor	.380	4.112**				
Multiple *R*	(.505)		(.255)			
Physicians						
Strategic Time factor	−.296	−3.082**	ns			ns
Obsession Time factor	.265	2.754*				
Multiple *R*	(.388)					

Note. ns = nonsignificant.
*p < .05. **p < .01.

thority and less room for individual discretion and initiative, employees may have feelings of powerlessness and lack of control. These job conditions could enhance perceived stress, and thus individuals may feel they have too much work to do and too many constraints. This could explain the higher scores obtained by the nurses on work load and situational constraints.

Conversely, in a higher level job, one may be more likely to perceive that one has control and autonomy over one's job conditions, and thus job stress may be perceived to a lesser degree. These findings lend additional support to an earlier study done by the present authors (Narayanan, Menon, & Spector, 1994), where stressors were found to differ as a function of job level across three occupations: clerical, academic, and sales. In that study, lower level clerical employees reported lack of autonomy and work load as greater sources of stress, whereas higher level academics reported interpersonal conflict as a major source of stress. The present study also found a higher degree of interpersonal conflict reported by physicians in comparison with nurses. There could be any number of reasons for interpersonal conflict being more prevalent in higher level jobs. It is conceivable that, as control and status in one's occupation increase, there is also more potential for conflict. Future research is needed to understand this in more depth.

Another important finding was the result of the factor analyses, which identified two distinct factors associated with time urgency as assessed with the BARS measure (Landy et al., 1991). The first factor (Strategic Time) indicated a tendency on the part of the subject to plan and organize work in advance. The second factor (Obsession Time) reflected a continuous and nervous preoccupation with time. Further support for the meaningfulness of these two dimensions came from their different patterns of associations with job stressors and strains. The results of the study indicate that both time dimensions were significantly related to the various stressors and strains in the samples of nurses and physicians. However, there were some differences in the results for the two professions. Overall, the strength of associations between time-urgency dimensions and strains was significantly higher for nurses in comparison with physicians.

Some researchers have suggested that the degree of autonomy an employee exercises can counterbalance the negative components of work (Gerber, 1983). It is possible that, for lower jobs high in stress, combined with high psychological demands and low decision latitude, such as a nurse's job, individuals will make efforts to decrease their stress by seeking control with other coping strategies (e.g., planning and scheduling time, trying to meet deadlines). However, with individuals who are obsessed with time, the relationship between the Obsession Time factor and outcome variables becomes detrimental. In a lower level job, high stress and low autonomy, combined with an obsession with time, may result in a perception of loss of control, where the individual seems to be engaged in a continuous struggle to meet deadlines, resulting in stress and anxiety. The employee may cope with this situation by withdrawing from it, expressed in terms of turnover intentions, and/or suffer from physiological symptoms of stress. The physician's job, despite being high on psychological demands, typically permits higher decision latitude and autonomy (Gerber, 1983; Mawardi, 1979). This could explain the lack of any significant relationship found between the Obsession Time factor and the outcome measures of turnover intention. Because of their higher decision latitude, physicians are less likely to withdraw from the situation. The higher decision latitude may also explain the nonsignificant relationship between the Obsession Time factor and physiological symptoms for the physicians in this study, although this may also be the result of physicians' underreporting symptoms.

One demographic variable that appeared to be important was age, which was positively related to the Obsession Time factor in both samples. This finding warrants more examination in future studies, where some of the reasons why age appears so relevant for individuals obsessed with time could be explored.

A note of caution is warranted about these results because of the perceptual nature of measures assessed in the present study. The finding that physiological symptoms are related to job stressors and personality (Obsession Time factor) goes well in accordance with previous research (Dearborn & Hastings, 1987; Lawler & Schmeid, 1987). Although self-report measures of health were employed in this study, it is encouraging that the magnitude of relationships appears to be comparable or stronger than previous studies that used objective measures of health (Caplan, Cobb, French, Harrison, & Pinneau, 1975; Hennigan & Wortham, 1975; Howard et al., 1977). Further research is essential to determine why the two time dimensions correlated with perceptual job stressors and job strains, and if they might relate to objective features of the job.

In line with past research (Edwards et al., 1990; Landy et al., 1991), these findings support the use of separate component scores rather than global Type A. The correlations of time-urgency dimensions with job stressors and strains had opposite signs and somewhat different patterns. Moreover, the dimension of time urgency may need to be further subdivided into at least two subdimensions. These different patterns of correlations of time-urgency dimensions with job stressors and strains underscore the need to treat them as different aspects of time urgency.

REFERENCES

Baker, L. J., Dearborn, M., Hastings, J. F., & Hamburger, K. (1984). Type-A in women: A review. *Health Psychology, 3,* 477–497.

Barling, J., & Charbonneau, D. (1988). *Disentangling the relationship between Type-A behavior, performance and health.* Manuscript submitted for publication.

Booth-Kewley, S., & Friedman, H. S. (1987). Psychological predictors of heart disease: A quantitative review. *Psychological Bulletin, 101,* 343–362.

Burke, R. J., & Weir, T. (1980). The Type-A experience: Occupational and life demands, satisfaction and well-being. *Journal of Human Stress, 6,* 28–38.

Burnam, M. A., Pennebaker, J. W., & Glass, D. C. (1975). Time consciousness, achievement striving, and the Type-A coronary prone behavior pattern. *Journal of Abnormal Psychology, 84,* 76–79.

Camman, C., Fichman, M., Jenkins, D., & Klesh, J. (1979). *The Michigan Organizational Assessment Questionnaire.* Unpublished manuscript, University of Michigan, Ann Arbor.

Caplan, R. D., Cobb, S., French, J. R. P., Harrison, R., & Pinneau, S. R. (1975). *Job demands and worker health.* Washington, DC: U.S. Government Printing Office.

Dearborn, M. J., & Hastings, J. E. (1987). Type-A personality as a mediator of stress and strain in employed women. *Journal of Human Stress, 13,* 53–60.

Dewe, P. J. (1988). Investigating the frequency of nursing stressors: A comparison across wards. *Social Science and Medicine, 26,* 375–380.

Edwards, J. R., Baglioni, A. J., & Cooper, C. L. (1990). Examining relationships among self-report measures of Type-A behavior pattern: The effects of dimensionality, measurement error, and differences in underlying constructs. *Journal of Applied Psychology, 75*, 440–454.

Fraisse, P. (1963). *The psychology of time.* New York: Harper & Row.

Frankenhauser, M. (1959). *The estimation of time: An experimental study.* Stockholm: Almquist & Wiksell.

Friedman, H. S., & Rosenman, R. H. (1959). Association of specific overt behavior patterns with blood and cardiovascular findings. *Journal of American Medical Association, 169*, 1286–1296.

Friedman, H. S., & Rosenman, R. H. (1974). *Type-A behavior and your heart.* New York: Knopf.

Friend, K. E. (1982). Stress and performance: Effects of subjective work load and time urgency. *Personnel Psychology, 35*, 623–633.

Gerber, L. A. (1983). *Married to their careers and family dilemmas in doctors' lives.* Tavistock: New York.

Greenglass, E. R. (1987). Anger in Type-A women: Implications for coronary heart disease. *Personality and Individual Differences, 8*, 639–650.

Haynes, S. G., Levine, S., Scotch, N., Feinleib, M., & Kannel, W. B. (1978). The relationship of psychosocial factors to coronary heart disease in the Framingham study: I. Methods and risk factors. *American Journal of Epidemiology, 107*, 362–383.

Helmreich, R. L., Spence, J. T., & Pred, R. S. (1988). Making it without losing it: Type-A, achievement motivation, and scientific attainment revisited. *Personality and Social Psychology Bulletin, 14*, 495–504.

Hennigan, J. K., & Wortham, A. W. (1975). Analysis of workday stresses on industrial managers using heart rate as a criterion. *Ergonomics, 18*, 675–681.

Howard, J. H., Cunningham, D. A., & Rechnitzer, P. (1977). Work patterns associated with Type-A behavior. *Human Relations, 30*, 825–836.

Jenkins, C. D., Zyzanski, S. J., & Rosenman, R. H. (1971). Progress toward validation of a computer-scored test for the Type-A coronary-prone behavior pattern. *New England Journal of Medicine, 33*, 1271–1275.

Landy, F. L., Rastegary, H., Thayer, J., & Colvin, C. (1991). Time urgency: The construct and its measurement. *Journal of Applied Psychology, 76*, 644–657.

Lawler, K. A., & Schmeid, L. A. (1987). The relationship of stress, Type-A behavior and powerlessness to physiological responses in female clerical workers. *Journal of Psychosomatic Research, 31*, 555–566.

Lee, C., Earley, P. C., & Hanson, L. A. (1988). Are Type-As better performers? *Journal of Organizational Behavior, 9*, 263–269.

Maslach, C., & Jackson, S. E. (1984). Burnout in organizational settings. *Applied Social Psychology Annual, 5*, 133–153.

Matteson, M. T., Ivancevich, J. M., & Smith, S. V. (1984). Relations of Type-A behavior to performance and satisfaction among sales personnel. *Journal of Vocational Behavior, 25*, 203–214.

Matthews, K. A. (1982). Psychological perspectives on the Type-A behavior pattern. *Psychological Bulletin, 91*, 293–323.

Matthews, K. A. (1988). Coronary heart disease and Type-A behaviors: Update on an alternative to the Booth-Kewley and Friedman (1987) quantitative review. *Psychological Bulletin, 104,* 373–380.

Mawardi, B. L. (1979). Satisfaction, dissatisfaction, and causes of stress in medical practice. *Journal of American Medical Association, 241,* 1483–1486.

Moses, B., & Rothe, A. (1979). Nursepower. *American Journal of Nursing, 81,* 1745–1756.

Narayanan, L., Menon, S., & Spector, P. E. (1994). *Stress at work: A comparison of gender and occupations.* Manuscript submitted for publication.

Schein, E. H. (1983). The role of the founder in creating organizational culture. *Organizational Dynamics, 12,* 13–28.

Schriber, J. B. (1985). *An exploratory study of the temporal dimensions of work organizations.* Unpublished doctoral dissertation, The Claremont Graduate School, Claremont, CA.

Schriber, J. B., & Gutek, B. A. (1987). Some time dimensions of work: Measurement of an underlying aspect of organization culture. *Journal of Applied Psychology, 72,* 642–650.

Smith, D. F., & Sterndorff, B. (1992). Female physicians outscore male physicians and the general public on Type A scales in Denmark. *Behavioral Medicine, 17,* 184–189.

Spector, P. E. (1987). Interactive effects of perceived control and job stressors on affective reactions and health outcomes for clerical workers. *Work and Stress, 1,* 155–162.

Spector, P. E., Dwyer, D. J., & Jex, S. M. (1988). Relation of job stressors to affective, health, and performance outcomes: A comparison of multiple data sources. *Journal of Applied Psychology, 73,* 11–19.

Spence, J. T., Helmreich, R. L., & Pred, R. S. (1987). Impatience versus achievement strivings in the Type-A pattern. *Journal of Applied Psychology, 74,* 176–178.

Spence, J. T., Pred, R. S., & Helmreich, R. L. (1989). Achievement strivings, scholastic aptitude, and academic performance: A follow-up to "Impatience versus achievement strivings in the Type-A pattern." *Journal of Applied Psychology, 74,* 176–178.

Streufert, S., Streufert, S. C., & Gorson, D. M. (1981). Time urgency and coronary-prone behavior: The effectiveness of a behavior pattern. *Basic and Applied Psychology, 2,* 161–174.

Wright, L. (1988). The Type-A behavior pattern and coronary artery disease. *American Psychologist, 43,* 2–14.

Yarnold, P. R., & Mueser, K. (1984). Time urgency of Type A individuals: Two replications. *Perceptual and Motor Skills, 59,* 334.

8

Causes and Consequences of Familial Role Stress Among Working Women: A Case Study in India

Y. K. Bhushan and Sandhya Karpe
Narsee Monjee Institute of Management Studies, Bombay, India

Abstract *In the peak stages of the family life cycle, working women must grapple with the Herculean task of balancing organizational and familial roles. Factors such as socioeconomic status (SES), family structure, behavioral dynamics in the family, attitude of the spouse, and self-perceptions influence the type and amount of stress experienced by working women. To enhance organizational role performance and achieve an emotionally satisfying family life, it is essential for working women to address those stressors that significantly affect performance in their familial role. This chapter investigates psychosocial and cultural factors contributing to familial role stress in an exploratory study of working women in Bombay, India. The target group consisted of 45 married women, ages 25–40 years, who worked full time or were self-employed. The type and magnitude of stress experienced at the workplace and in the home, and its effects on the marital relationship and on relations with children and other family members, were examined. Causes of familial role stress, its direct and indirect consequences, and the various strategies that working women use to cope with stress were identified. Recommendations for reducing familial role stress were also offered.*

Across the globe, women are stepping out of their homes into the world of organizational challenges. They are shedding their aprons and heading for the board rooms. As they shift their paradigms beyond the realms of homemaking, they may not necessarily achieve the requisite changes in their self-perception. Similarly, social conditioning is slow to change. As a consequence, working women's role expectations are often conflicting and difficult to fulfill. The cumulative effect of various factors contributes to the stress, anxiety, and emotional trauma experienced by working women.

Working women the world over, particularly those in the peak stages of their family life cycle, are grappling with the Herculean task of balancing their organizational and familial roles. Stress experienced during the performance of the familial role, or "family role stress," can take a severe psychological and physical toll in terms of organizational role performance. To enhance organizational role performance consistent with an emotionally satisfying family life, it is useful to address the stressors that directly and significantly affect the effective performance of woman's familial role. Equally, it could seriously jeopardize the quality of the working woman's family life, which is not only the cornerstone of any society, but also the primary source of her mental peace and socioemotional support.

WORKING WOMEN'S STRESS IN INDIA—
SOME RESEARCH STUDIES

Certain studies, such as those by Kapur (1969), Surti (1982), and Surti and Sarupria (1981), have focused on the causes of stress among working women in India, and Pestonjee (1992) has also reported research in this area. Srivastava and Srivastava (1985) compared self-perception and belief differences between dual-career and traditional couples. They also showed that more women are participating in the work force as a result of higher education. Surti (1982) studied the psychological correlates of stress in working women belonging to different occupational groups.

Srivastava and Srivastava (1985) also observed that Indian men have shown a preference for working women. The present study confirms husbands' largely "supportive" attitudes, with minimal participation in household chores, except in the case of those that have social legitimacy.

Differences studied between stress levels of dual-income versus traditional couples revealed a greater amount of role conflict and ambiguity experienced by dual-career husbands. Dual-career couples also experienced lower levels of marital adjustment, and social relations involving more neurotic and hysteric symptoms. The recommendations offered by the authors address these issues.

Kapur (1969), who studied role conflict among employed housewives, found that working women felt their professional and personal roles were conflicting. The author's sample expressed only a moderate effect of their careers on their family lives. Gupta (1982) and Gupta and Murthy (1984), who studied the effects of women's careers on marital adjustment, found that role conflict was a reality, and that the highest incidence of role conflict was found among women who had preschool-age children and who were at the "peak" stages of their family lives.

SCOPE OF THE CHAPTER

The stress emanating from familial role performance is the focus of this chapter, which explores the sociological, psychological, and cultural factors that contribute to familial role stress in the case of Indian working women. The chapter is exploratory in nature, and highlights several areas that can be researched further in the future.

Sociological factors in the Indian context are extremely relevant to understanding the sources of stress. The type of family structure, of which working women are a part, influences the level and type of stress experienced. For example, the "joint" or "extended" family holds a completely different set of behavioral dynamics than the nuclear family. Social conditioning regarding the status of women, reflected in the attitudes of males and "significant others" toward women, contributes both directly and indirectly to working women's role stress. Women's self-perception, which is a consequence of the subservient role they have played for generations, is another major factor. The psyche of Indian women and their beliefs about their familial role are the other critical factors that have a direct bearing on the "stress experience."

This chapter identifies sources and consequences of family role stress, explores coping strategies used by women, and offers suggestions for effective stress management. The goal is for dual-career couples, especially those in nuclear family units, to become socially and emotionally viable, and to provide an environment conducive to career women's professional development.

THE BACKDROP:
HISTORICAL AND SOCIOLOGICAL EVOLUTION

To understand the causes of familial role stress experienced by Indian married working women, it is useful to delve into the sociological, psychological, and historical contexts in which their identity and effectiveness are established.

Traditionally, Indian women have derived their identity from their family or group of origin. They have always been viewed as wives, daughters, or mothers, but rarely, if at all, as individuals in their own right. The perception of girl children as lesser beings (i.e., more of a liability than an asset) has been prevalent in all strata of Indian society. In fact, the tremendous rejoicing at the birth of male children and the lamenting in the case of females were the beginning of the attitudinal discrimination of society. The deplorable practice of female infanticide was another "dark" chapter in the sociological evolution of Indian women, reflecting the deep-seated prejudices that have existed in the society.

The process of social reform, which began in the 19th century, emphasized the improvement of women's status in society. It stressed that large-scale societal uplifting was not possible unless women's secondary status in Indian society was addressed. The Indian Constitution, which was adopted in 1949 and came into effect in 1950, conferred a preferred status on women, identifying them as one of the "weaker sections" of society.

It was felt that laws that protected women's interests were necessary to catalyze the change process. Social legislation, such as the Prevention of Female Infanticide Act (1912), The Child Marriages Restraint Act (1929), the Dowry Prohibition Act (1986), and the Hindu Women's Right to Property Act (1937), were introduced as serious attempts to accelerate the upliftment process. Unfortunately, these laws, either because of women's ignorance of them or because of rigid mind sets, were unable to bring about the desired quantum of social change, indicating, in some ways, that they were perhaps ahead of their time.

Women in India, like elsewhere, have relegated themselves to the background, content to perform domestic roles. However, with the passage of time, they ventured to join the work force, restricting themselves to traditional professions, such as nursing and teaching, as well as jobs at lower levels in the organizational hierarchy. With industrialization, modernization, urbanization, and the rapid spread of literacy across the country, Indian women have come a long way. The 1991 All Indian Census Report figures indicated 39% literacy among women in India and 46% in urban centers. Exposure to Western ideas through easily accessible literature, higher education, and media has resulted in significant changes. Women's aspiration and ambition levels, attitudes, and values have changed, as have others' attitudes toward women.

Modern Indian women, located largely in cosmopolitan cities and earlier confined to the conventional roles of homemaking and childrearing, have gradually emerged from the shadows and are coming to their own. Women's perception of their familial role was an important factor that prevented them from realizing their true self. As a result of the strong social conditioning, women were reconciled to secondary status; this prevented them from breaking out of their traditional mold. Almost like a "self-fulfilling prophecy," women's mental and emotional reconciliation to their subservience perpetrated this attitude of others toward women.

As a consequence of Indian women shifting their own paradigms about their familial role concept, they are now seeking ambitious, and even unconventional, careers. Social norms have evolved to accept women as an integral and legitimate part of the total work force. Today, many women have moved on to newer frontiers—into nontraditional fields such as engineering, medicine, and small enterprise. They are also aspiring to move up the rungs of the corporate ladder.

THE NEW FAMILY SYSTEM

Historically, the extended family has been the typical family unit in rural and urban India. In the extended or "joint" family, several nuclear units coexist. Household chores are typically shared by all members, and all resources, including financial ones, are pooled. There are often three generations of family members living under the same roof, each with its own set of values, attitudes, and belief systems. The extended family is based on the concepts of group living, mutual interdependence, a high sense of duty (*dharma*), respect for elders, and subordination of individual goals to the priorities of the family, which are generally stipulated by the family's patriarchs.

With the rapid pace of urbanization in India, the family system has undergone a radical transformation. The conventional extended family is quickly breaking up in the urban centers. The prime metropolitan cities in India, such as Bombay, Delhi, Madras, Calcutta, and Bangalore, have seen a large-scale migration of rural population driven by the quest for quality higher education, better job prospects, larger pay packets, and more satisfying work environments. As a result of urbanization, the rise in the cost of living, and changes in role perception, India's urban centers are seeing a trend toward an increased number of "nuclear," as opposed to "extended," family units. As a consequence, the familial role of working women has also undergone a change, which is manifested in the following ways:

1. They are the prime caregivers—of the home and family members' needs.
2. They must now perform their role independently, without socioemotional support of the other members, especially elders.
3. They are required, in addition, to provide socioemotional support to their spouse and children.
4. They are the "second engine" of the "family train," pushing it with their earnings to augment the income of the male breadwinner.

The "nuclear family" system, for reasons mentioned earlier, is inherently a great source of pressure that is spilling over into stress for working women. Research findings indicate a much higher level of role stress experienced by women who live in nuclear families. For women in nuclear families, the act of balancing personal and professional roles is a much more challenging and even daunting experience, and takes a heavier psychological and physical toll than for women in extended families.

In India, women may marry into a joint family or start their own nuclear unit. In either case, more so in the joint family, the husband's family is included in the "significant others" who affect women's perception of their familial role. For instance, the spouse may be supportive of his wife's organizational career and be willing to contribute to reduction of role stress by assisting her in its performance. But the other members of her family may exert pressures on her to conform to the traditional familial role—by making her feel guilty about leaving her home, spouse, and/or children in the care of others.

These "role senders" (i.e., the significant others around her) may include women who are domestically oriented and denounce career women for being mindless of their familial roles. In reality, these women are often envious of working women's achievements and opportunities to socialize with persons outside the family, and, sometimes, they are in awe of their multifaceted lifestyles.

Marriages are often arranged by elders, friends, or relatives, rather than mutually by the couple. Therefore, the wedded partners are often relative strangers to each other. The woman is likely to suppress opinions and feelings, rather than express them openly.

FAMILY HIERARCHY AND LOCATION

In the majority of Indian families, whether extended or nuclear, the patriarchal structure has been the norm. The eldest male member has been the decision maker. Decisions regarding every aspect of the family are made by him. The patriarchal family structure has successfully reinforced the subservient role of women in the home over several generations, conditioning them to accept the supremacy of their spouse unquestioningly. The modern Indian family is still patriarchal in nature, although the patriarch's decision-making style has tended to become more consultative and participative.

Family residence is largely "patrilocal," in which brides move into their husband's family home and inevitably learn to live, in the case of the extended family, with their in-laws. Due to the high emphasis placed on group living and subjugation of individual goals to familial goals, women are forced to completely adapt to the new set of role expectations. The renaming of the bride during the Hindu marriage ceremony is symbolic of the identity change that women are expected to undergo.

Marriage is viewed as a holy institution, and the view that "marriage is for keeps" is largely prevalent. As a result, partners are more inclined to tolerate conflict and differences in the larger interest of keeping the marriage intact. Divorces are frowned on, and divorcees experience a subtle form of social ostracization.

Although several religious communities (e.g., Hindus, Muslims, Sikhs, Parsis, and Christians) coexist peacefully in India, 80% of the population follows the Hindu religion. For Hindus, Hinduism is a way of life; hence its influence on Indian people's values and lifestyles has been profound.

The Hindu religion encourages women to be subservient, self-sacrificing, and self-denying. The Hindu concepts of *sati savitri* (silent suffering wife) and *pativrata* (husband worshipper) are an integral part of the Indian sociocultural ethos. A woman's family views their girl child as *paraya dhan* (another's property held in trust). This manifests itself repeatedly in the form of a much lower level of investment in female offspring in terms of finances, time, and attention, compared with male siblings.

Parental attitudes toward girl children who will soon become another's property (marriage is patrilocal), contributes significantly to girls' own conditioning and self-perception. They internalize their status as being inferior to male counterparts, and often willingly subvert their interests to those of their spouse and family as they grow into adulthood.

This chapter's frame of reference is married working women living in metropolitan cities, experiencing the early stages of married life, and upholding middle-class values that are somewhat influenced by Western ideas. Most of these women have had their education in the English language, have grown up in relatively liberal homes, and have been exposed to Western values of independence, ambition, and self-reliance.

ROLE AMBIGUITY AMONG URBAN WORKING WOMEN

It is evident that the role stress that women experience is dependent, to a large extent, on individuals' perceptions and beliefs about the role in question. Middle-class urban Indian women are brought up in a rather conventional family structure. At the same time, their parents are generous with freedom, autonomy, and encouragement—these women are allowed to pursue nontraditional career interests, which their mothers never had the freedom to explore.

Interestingly enough, parents of such women have been able to shift their paradigms about the perception of the familial role of their daughters while retaining older paradigms in defining their own roles. As a result, they willingly accept the stress associated with providing their daughters with a relatively liberal upbringing and nurturing their career ambitions.

It is likely that these daughters have been brought up by parents who uphold old values, but are willing to bring up female offspring in a more progressive manner. In fact, the continual exposure to this dual-value system in their formative years could be partly responsible for the ambivalence and role conflict these women experience while juggling their organizational and familial roles in adulthood.

As a consequence, daughters begin to develop a distinct self-perception. They see themselves as liberal, emancipated women who are intellectually and technically competent to take on the challenges of the organizational environment. They have a high level of determination and ambition. They have all that may be required for effective performance in an organization.

However, deep down, women's frame of reference continues to be their traditional mother's—role models they find hard not to emulate. Although the achievement motivation and ambition have been successfully inculcated, other values (e.g., the sanctity of marital relationships, *pati parameshwar* [superiority of the husband], *sati savitri* [the silently suffering wife], and *kartavya* [duty-consciousness]) toward the home, children, and spouse have been subtly reinforced at each juncture by the very same role senders.

Accordingly, women from these families experience ambivalent feelings about their professional and personal roles: They would like to fulfill the familial role expectations to the utmost, but want their career aspirations to be satisfied. Their strong achievement motivation causes them to strive for excellence on both fronts. Therefore, they become perceptually defensive against any cues that suggest that managing both roles to a great degree of perfection might be unrealistic.

Hence, before entering organizational careers, women do not perceive how their organizational roles might negatively affect their familial roles. It is only when they experience the real-life role conflict that they finally come to terms with this reality, and struggle to find ways of coping with it.

Familial role stress is particularly severe in the early years of marriage. At this time, women adjust to their new life partner, his family, and perhaps motherhood. Hence, the various role senders' expectations are in conflict again.

Attitudes of Indian Males

Indian male spouses' attitudes toward their working spouses is also a significant factor in creating familial role stress. Indian males have developed a distinct perception of their own familial role, and experience a similar ambivalence toward their familial role as do their spouses.

On the one hand, their exposure to modern ideas through education, media, Western values, and so on supports the liberal view of working women. On the other hand, their own upbringing in the conventional mold revives the views of *pati parameshwar* and *sati savitri*. These conflicting perceptions of their own and their spouse's familial roles affect their attitude toward their working spouse. Although such men would pay lip service and be seemingly "supportive" of career-conscious spouses, their actual contribution in attempting to reduce their wives' familial role stress may be limited, as reflected in the limited assistance rendered to them in childrearing, domestic chores, and so on, discussed later in this chapter.

The conventional mold in which Indian males are bred reinforces their perception of their familial role. They see themselves as the *annadaata* (breadwinner), and subconsciously attach greater importance to their own career than to their spouse's. Hence, males often expect greater compromises from their spouse about her professional role than they would be willing to make.

As a result of their early exposure to traditional role models, Indian males experience stress while performing the nontraditional role they would like to uphold. The role of the "significant others," including members of extended family or close relatives, again hinder effective performance of the familial role. Family members are likely to make male spouses feel uncomfortable about providing the working wife with the required support because this conflicts with their own ideas about males' familial role. This could partly explain why husbands in nuclear families are more supportive of working women's familial role than husbands in extended families.

A respondent in our study mentioned how the husband's family, although not physically a part of her nuclear family unit, exerted a "long-distance" pressure on her to perform her traditional familial role. This resulted in feelings of guilt for "neglecting" her home and family by being away from home. The attitudes and behavior of "significant others" become a major stressor in the Indian context.

Interestingly enough, especially in urban centers, as a result of Westernized education and English media influences, there appears to be a strange paradox within urban Indian women. On the one hand, in their early life, they experience the subservient role of women in the familial hierarchy, despite taking on the prime responsibility for the housekeeping and childrearing. On the other hand, women's parents, who are probably still set in the older mold, are willing to encourage ambitious pursuits and a quest for self-realization beyond the realms of homemaking.

Stresses of Urban Living

The lifestyle in metropolitan cities exerts its own pressures on working women, hindering the effective performance of their familial role. The time and effort spent in commuting by public transportation systems, the high cost of living, limited supply of effective domestic help, and the emergence of the nuclear family as the social unit all contribute, in some form or another, to the stress experienced by working women in highly urbanized centers. In addition, the work culture in metropolitan cities demands a higher standard of job efficiency and effectiveness.

Emergence of the Nuclear Family

The emergence of the nuclear family as the social unit has eroded the socioemotional support systems provided by the traditional extended family. In the nuclear family, household duties, problems, and anxieties (e.g., care of a sick member, financial crises) now become the sole responsibility of the working couple. In the extended family, the presence of other family members often diffuses tensions and conflicts between the spouses, whereas in the nuclear family, underlying conflicts are often overtly manifested and possibly result in a higher level of marital conflict.

Stressful Physical Environment

The physical environment, including overpopulation, level of pollution and lack of sanitation (resulting in sickness and ill health), and time and effort spent in commuting creates cumulative stress conditions. Welfare facilities such as child care are scarce and undependable. Domestic help is expensive and difficult to come by.

Cost of Living

The high cost of urban living, including housing, makes dual incomes nearly imperative. The quest for a higher standard of living and the emergence of a "consumerist culture" have added substantially to this pressure. This has led to an increasing number of educated women taking to jobs or entrepreneurial activities.

A STUDY OF WORKING WOMEN

An exploratory study of working women (N = 45) was conducted in the metropolitan city of Bombay in early 1994. Bombay is the commercial nerve center of India, and has a population of over 10 million. The city is over-populated, has a higher level of pollution, and has a phenomenally higher cost of living, especially in terms of housing. Accordingly, the pace of life is hectic, and day-to-day living for an average Bombay resident is extremely stressful. Bombay is also highly cosmopolitan and progressive in outlook, and is able to provide a highly satisfying and financially lucrative working environment for aspirants. Hence, individuals brave heavy odds to live in this city.

The purpose of this study was to identify the factors causing stress and anxiety for working women living in urban centers, who are engaged in a struggle to balance their personal and professional roles. It is surmised that family role-related stressors adversely affect mental and physical health and, in turn, result in decreased effectiveness of organizational role performance. Poorer performance of the organizational role results in lowered self-esteem, diminished confidence, and greater anxiety. These characteristics are all manifested in behavioral changes, including anger, irritability, and hysterical be-

Table 8.1 Educational and family characteristics

Characteristic	% respondents
Education	
Some college	2.2
College graduate	31.1
Postgraduate	46.8
Above postgraduate	20.0
Husband's occupation	
Government employee	11.1
Entrepreneur	8.9
Professional	28.9
Self-employed professional	31.1
Nongovernmental employee	20.0
Total monthly income (self) (rupees)	
≤ 3,000	7.9
3,001–5,000	20.2
5,001–7,000	26.1
> 7,000	45.8
Total family income (rupees)	
≥ 3,000	—
3,001–5,000	—
5,001–7,000	—
> 7,000	100.0
Family type	
Joint	44.4
Nuclear (spouse and children)	55.6

havior in the family, as well as a whole host of psychosomatic disorders. Hence, the vicious cycle continues to spin at the cost of working women's emotional well-being.

Demographics of the Sample

The target group for the present study consisted of women working full-time in organizations from both the public and private sectors, as well as those who are self-employed. They were between 25 and 40 years of age, and were married with or without children, and were thus at a "peak stage" in their life cycles. Sixty-eight percent of the women had postgraduate and doctoral qualifications, and 60% had spouses who were professionals. Fifty-one percent had incomes over 7,000 rupees (comfortable income by Indian standards). There was a fair mix of women from joint (44%) and nuclear (56%) families. Most of them were exposed to a Westernized educational system. Educational and family characteristics for the sample are reported in Table 8.1.

Reasons for Working

Table 8.2 reports on reasons for working, job satisfaction, and husbands' attitudes about working. When asked why they wanted to work, in order of

Table 8.2 Reasons for working, job satisfaction, and husbands' attitudes

Response	% Respondents
Reasons for working	
Financial	8.9
Better standard of living	22.2
To make fuller use of qualifications and capabilities	68.9
Utilization of spare time	2.2
Enjoy the challenge it offers	51.1
For financial independence	35.6
To assist spouse/family in business	4.4
Everyone at home works	—
Socializing with people	—
Other	—
Husband's feeling about the job	
Approves	93.4
Disapproves	4.4
Don't know	2.2
Satisfaction level	
Very satisfied	33.3
Reasonably satisfied	60.0
Neither satisfied nor dissatisfied	6.7
Very dissatisfied	—

priority, 69% of the women indicated that they wanted to utilize their qualifications and capabilities, 51% stated that they enjoyed the challenge it offered, 36% worked for financial independence, 22% wanted to improve their living standards, and 9% worked for financial reasons. Most women stated they were working more for higher order needs than for the remuneration. Covertly, financial reasons were predominant in their thinking.

Spouses' Attitudes

The women were questioned about their husbands' attitudes toward their careers. Ninety-three percent reported that their husbands were at least reasonably satisfied (see Table 8.2). This could be due to their own self-denial of their husbands' disapproval of their career, to legitimize their choice of lifestyle, or it could be attributed to the fact that the Indian woman's ethos of *pativrata* results in her perception of her husband as righteous, thus preventing her from showing her husband in a poor light to others.

Job Satisfaction

Ninety-three percent of the women reported a fair degree of satisfaction with their jobs (see Table 8.2). Factors of job satisfaction were: nature of work, pay, recognition, working conditions, advancement opportunities, and sense of achievement, as reported in Table 8.3. Lack of advancement opportunities rated the highest on sources of job dissatisfaction. Reasons for this dissatisfac-

Table 8.3 Factors causing job satisfaction or dissatisfaction

	% Respondents	
Factor	Satisfaction	Dissatisfaction
Type of work	86.7	11.1
Advancement opportunities	48.9	44.4
Income/salary	71.1	20.0
Sense 'of achievement	88.9	13.3
Recognition of work	68.9	15.5
Work conditions	75.6	8.9
Relations with colleagues	82.2	4.4
Relations with bosses	84.4	2.2
Working hours	68.9	26.7
Volume of work	75.6	8.9
Other factors	—	—

tion could be manifold. First, social conditioning is responsible for strong stereotypes of women. They are often perceived as being unable to give high priority to their careers—of not having the desired level of ambition and drive for career advancement as their male counterparts. This becomes a self-fulfilling prophecy; thus superiors and colleagues tend to deny women the opportunities, assuming that they are not interested.

Further, women, who are subconsciously reconciled to their subservient role, try to organize their careers within the paradigms of their perceived conventional familial role. Very often they even avoid career advancement opportunities because they are aware of the greater commitment of time and effort that is associated with it. They realize that the familial atmosphere is not conducive to happiness and emotional well-being, and failure in organizational role performance is nearly inevitable. Thus, women tend to turn into victims of fear of success.

Job Role Stress

Table 8.4 reports perceived workplace stress, coping strategies, and preferred activities. Ninety-five percent of the respondents found their jobs to be stressful. When asked about methods used to cope with work-related stress, 71% planned and prioritized, 36% delegated, 27% confronted and discussed issues with co-workers, 20% suppressed feelings, and 38% discussed with boss and family members. Forty-four percent reported a preference for home-oriented activities, whereas 56% indicated a preference for career-oriented tasks.

Family Chores and Help

Respondents were asked how they performed their household chores and responsibilities. It emerged that physical work, such as cleaning (56%) and

Table 8.4 Perceived organizational stress, workplace coping strategies, and preferred activities

Response	% Respondents
Stress level	
Very stressful	—
Rather stressful	34.0
Occasionally stressful	47.2
Moderately stressful	10.0
Not stressful	8.8
Coping strategy	
Delegate some work	35.6
Confront issues that cause conflict	26.7
Take a holiday	6.7
Plan and prioritize work	71.1
Remain patient and hope the problem will resolve itself	15.5
Get tense but suppress feelings	20.0
Get tense and express feelings	11.1
Get irritated and vent it on family	8.9
Talk it over with boss/colleagues	37.8
Discuss with family/friends	37.8
Preferred activities	
Home-oriented	44.4
Career-oriented	55.6

washing (53%), was performed by professional domestic helpers (see Table 8.5). In Bombay city, it is easier to hire part-time help for such activities than to find reliable "live-in" helpers. Jobs that were perceived as requiring greater level of personal attention, such as cooking, shopping, and care of the sick, were performed more often by women, with the help of spouses and family members in the case of an extended family.

The husbands' participation was highest in the case of shopping (60%) and care of the sick (29%) and minimal for cooking, cleaning, and washing. The activities in which husbands participated the most were those that were socially legitimate for Indian males. Although women reported that their husbands

Table 8.5 Management of household responsibilities

| Responsibility | % Respondents | | | | | |
	Alone	With spouse	Family members	Servant	Not involved	Friends/ relatives
Shopping	33.3	51.2	—	11.1	2.2	2.2
Cooking	40.0	8.9	22.2	28.9	—	—
Cleaning	13.9	13.3	17.8	50.6	2.2	2.2
Washing	22.2	8.9	8.9	53.3	6.7	—
Care of sick family member	26.7	28.8	26.7	2.2	4.4	—

were supportive, no significant contribution by them in assisting her to perform her familial role was seen. One could surmise that, although husbands would like their wives to work, they also expected their wives to shoulder the domestic responsibilities simultaneously, with only limited assistance.

In the Indian context, husbands are perceived as the *annadaata* (breadwinner), or the provider for the family. Their participation in household duties has not yet gained the desired legitimacy. Women often experience guilt feelings when husbands perform these duties. Similarly, husbands' self-perceptions of their familial role do not include these activities as an integral part, and hence they might dislike performing them or do them grudgingly.

When asked about the reasons for husbands' "supportive" attitude, 10% of the women indicated that their husbands were pleased to have additional income for the household. It is possible that husbands permitted their spouses to take up jobs for extraneous reasons, like supplementary finances and a boost to their pride, rather than to support the women's own search for higher order need satisfaction and identity.

Attitudes of Other Family Members

Women who lived in joint families ($n = 20$) were asked about other family members' attitudes toward their careers. Fifty percent reported that family members felt the women neglected their familial duties, and 40% said family members were dissatisfied with the way in which the house was run in their absence (see Table 8.6). These factors become important sources of familial role stress. In India, members of the joint family are included in the "significant others" category, or those who matter (i.e., their opinions and attitudes, apart from those of the immediate family, are important). Often husbands have a supportive attitude, but the others have their reservations and succeed in generating guilt feelings within the women. The women who participated in this study were asked about their satisfaction with various aspects of child care, including medical care, meals, disciplining, help with school work, counseling, providing recreation and vacations, and developmental inputs. The highest dissatisfaction was reported on the issue of providing recreation, that is, being able to take long vacations (13%), as may be noted in Table 8.7.

Marital Relationships

The effects on marital relations as a consequence of women's career are reported in Table 8.6. Sixty-two percent of the women reported that their husbands were "proud" of their achievements, 51% said that their working helped the spouses empathize with each other, and 44% said that husbands felt they should assist the women with their familial responsibilities. In addition, having inadequate time for each other (33%), feeling neglected (22%), and husbands' perceptions of wives being negligent about their household responsibilities (16%) were also reported.

Dissatisfaction with the manner in which children were reared or how household activities were conducted in their absence seems to be a significant source

Table 8.6 Relationships with husband, children, and other family members

Response	% Respondents
With husband	
Don't get enough time for each other	33.3
He feels neglected at times	22.2
Gives a better understanding of each other's problems	51.1
He feels professionally insecure	—
He feels proud of me	62.2
He feels domestic responsibilities are neglected	15.6
He feels he should help in household activities	44.4
With children	
Want you to spend more time with them	57.8
Dislike being looked after by someone else	13.3
Are proud to have a working mother	17.8
Feel they are being neglected	2.2
Feel women should stay home and not work	8.9
Feel envious that some of their friends' mothers are at home	15.6
With other family members	
Disapprove of your work	5.0
Feel you are neglecting them/husband/children	40.0
Feel you are neglecting household activities	50.0
Feel children are not sufficiently cared for in your absence	15.0
Feel household activities are not being taken care of	40.0
Approve; it influences positively	15.0

of stress for working women. Their values and belief systems affect their ideas about homemaking and childrearing. Being independent, they also wish to bring up their children and design their homes in a distinct manner. Differences of opinions on issues like housekeeping and childrearing could create conflict, tensions, and stressful conditions for women, especially in the case of the extended family. This stress could be overtly manifested or may be suppressed.

Table 8.7 Satisfaction level on treatment of children

Factors	% Respondents		
	Greatly	Somewhat	Little
Personal hygiene	53.3	17.8	—
Medical care when ill	51.1	20.0	—
Cooking/meals	42.2	24.4	8.9
Grooming	42.2	24.4	6.7
Disciplining	35.6	22.2	4.4
Educational help	44.4	8.9	2.2
Counseling	28.9	22.2	6.7
Providing recreation	20.0	33.3	13.3
Additional inputs	8.9	44.4	8.9
Other factors	—	—	—

Table 8.8 Profile of familial environment

	% Respondents				
Factors	Almost always	Very often	Sometimes	Seldom	Never
Insufficient time to do domestic work	13.3	31.1	35.6	8.9	4.4
Too many things are happening at once	6.7	13.3	48.9	17.8	11.1
Wish you had some help	4.4	28.9	33.3	22.2	6.7
Family expect too much from you	—	26.7	28.9	15.6	26.7
Happy that family understands	35.6	35.6	11.1	11.1	—
Housework leaves you no time	26.7	26.7	20.0	20.8	10.9

When asked about their feelings in regard to their familial roles, 13% of the women commented that they had insufficient time for their domestic chores, 7% said that they feel confused and inundated with work, and 27% said that their housework left them with little time for themselves (see Table 8.8). As reported in Table 8.9, 33% of the women experienced dissatisfaction concerning their involvement with recreational activities, including picnics, movies, social obligations, and hobbies; 24% of the women felt that their work moderately affected their family lives.

Table 8.9 Recreational activities, effect of work on family life, and domestic coping strategies

Response	% Respondents
Satisfaction with recreational activity level	
Very satisfied	8.9
Somewhat satisfied	18.0
Satisfied	40.0
Somewhat dissatisfied	27.2
Very dissatisfied	11.1
Amount that work affects family life	
Very much	—
Moderately	23.4
Somewhat	37.2
A little	17.0
Not at all	22.4
Coping strategy	
Reassure self that it will work out all right	28.9
Suppress feelings of anxiety	15.5
Discuss situation with spouse	77.8
Actively try to solve the problem	28.9
Assign duties to family members	8.8
Do something you enjoy	31.1

Table 8.10 Profile of women executive's opinions

Statements	% Respondents		
	Strongly agree	Agree	Disagree
Income is as vital as my husband's	40.0	28.9	24.4
Ours is a successful and meaningful marriage	48.9	38.2	12.9
My career has made me a better mother	31.1	26.7	11.1
I strive to be as successful in my job as my husband	51.1	48.9	—
I have the best of two worlds: employment and family life	46.7	51.1	—
I would not have been so satisfied without familial cooperation	68.9	28.9	—
I don't find as much understanding than at home	42.2	37.8	20.0
I would opt for the same type of life had I a choice	35.6	40.0	17.8
My husband is superior and I should serve his every need	8.9	8.9	77.8
Raising children is more a mother's responsibility	8.9	31.1	55.6
I would not work if my husband/family disapproved	6.7	22.2	64.4

Coping Strategies

The methods of coping with family role stress were explored. Seventy-eight percent of the women indicated that they discussed their frustrations and anxieties about their role inadequacy with their husbands, 29% reassured themselves that things would sort themselves out, 31% soothed themselves by doing something they enjoy, and 29% actively tried to sort out the problem (see Table 8.9).

Questions about the women's beliefs regarding their familial role were also included. As can be seen in Table 8.10, 40% believed that their incomes were as important to the family as their spouses'; 69% felt that, despite their busy schedules, their marriages were still meaningful; 51% responded that they strived for performance effectiveness in their jobs as much as their husbands; 47% stated that they were fortunate enough to enjoy the best of both worlds; 69% felt they would not be as satisfied if their families were opposed to their working; 78% strongly disagreed that their husbands were superior; 56% disagreed that childrearing was primarily mothers' responsibility; and 64% believed that they would have worked despite spouse and family members' disapproval.

The women's responses reflect inherent contradictions in their belief systems. For example, women placed high value on the family cooperating with the former's career. However, most women stated they would be willing to continue their career pursuits despite familial disapproval. Such reactions reflect the role ambivalence or dual-role perceptions coexisting within women in the sample selected.

CAUSES OF FAMILIAL ROLE STRESS

Causes of familial role stress, as identified through the researched sample, could be summarized as follows:

Work Overload

Excessive physical activities involved in performing both roles causes too much strain. This factor is of particular significance in metropolitan cities in India, where unique potential stressors (e.g., overpopulation, limited availability of domestic help, predominance of the nuclear family, high cost of living, etc.) play a major role.

Intersender Role Expectations Conflict

Conflicting expectations are expressed by various role senders (e.g., spouses encourage wives to work, children feel they need more time with their mothers, and the family members generate guilt feelings within women about wanting to pursue a career).

Self-Role Distance

Working women are not entirely satisfied with their quality of life because of their dual-role lifestyle. They feel unable to find adequate time for themselves for personal and social growth.

Interrole Conflict

While striving for a happy and harmonious relationship with their spouse, women's desire to be effective in their organizational role results in inadequate time devoted to nurturing their marital relationship, again creating potential stress. Working women also experience guilt, frustration, and anxiety about not being able to give adequate attention to their domestic responsibilities. As they advance in their career, they tend to be increasingly stressed in their family role, and may fall victim to the "burnout syndrome."

Role Ambiguity

Working women often experience ambiguity and ambivalence in role expectations from their spouse. On the one hand, he would like to have a working wife either for financial reasons or to satisfy his own need to have an intellectual companion. On the other hand, his deep-rooted perceptions and beliefs about the traditional familial role women should play prevents him from providing the necessary support to his working wife. Quite often, women are left confused about their familial role in times of family emergencies. When they are expected to take leave from their work by their spouses, however, they would also be expected to take care of their career interests.

CONSEQUENCES OF FAMILY ROLE STRESS

The following are some of the consequences working women feel in relation to family role stress:

1. Feelings of guilt and inadequacy as a result of work overload and personal role conflict.
2. Inadequate time for nurturing relationship with spouse, which could possibly cause marital conflict.
3. Impact on effective performance of the organizational role, as family role-related stress is likely to be carried to the workplace. Also, role overload on the family front could result in lesser time available for organizational role performance.
4. Ineffective organizational role performance results in further feelings of personal inadequacy and anxiety. These feelings further aggravate family role stress, and working women get caught in a downward spiral of performance at the workplace, which becomes rather difficult to break. This rebounds on the quality of their participation in the family life.
5. Role overload on both fronts could result in physical strain and affect women's general health, making it more difficult to handle the physical demands of their personal and professional roles. This gives rise to a "vicious emotional cycle," wherein failure to perform generates negative feelings and feelings of frustration, and low esteem affects performance and causes women to feel even more frustrated.
6. Marital conflict is likely to arise out of factors like the spouse's reluctance to participate in homemaking, perception of women being negligent of house and children, or inadequate time for spouse. Occasional cases of a spouse feeling professionally insecure and resenting his wife for having her own social circle, especially socializing with male colleagues, have been reported in the research group.

RECOMMENDATIONS FOR FAMILIAL ROLE STRESS REDUCTION

Greater participation of spouse in household duties. If husbands can resolve their ambivalence and can fully accept their working wives' contribution, their participation in the household work can help reduce the women's stress. It may even mean adjustment of work schedules between them.

Assertiveness with spouse and family members. Most barriers lie within women themselves, who are shackled by their own self-perceptions. If women undergo a paradigm shift of their own self-perceptions, they can articulate their problems and difficulties more easily. Working women can reduce their stress through greater and freer discussion of issues with spouse and family members, thus involving them in problem solving to reduce stress and anxiety.

Increasing gadgetry use and changing mind sets about "ways of doing things." More reliance on household gadgets (e.g., microwave, dishwasher, and washing machine), which are now easily available in the Indian market, can also lead to stress reduction. By conserving physical energy and reducing dependence on domestic help, spouse and family members' guilt feelings of "dumping her work on others" can be alleviated, and a greater sense of fulfillment on the family front can be achieved. Also, changing old ways of doing things (e.g., eliminating elaborate cooking and relying on healthy convenience foods and even packaged foods at times, which are making their way into the Indian market at reasonable costs) can be beneficial.

Locating family near close relatives. Planning careers in the same city as parents or in-laws can also be a way to create greater socioemotional and physical support, for the spouse as well as the children. Family members can be a great source of support (e.g., caring for the sick or young children).

Planning careers. A greater understanding is necessary between dual-career couples while planning their careers. Nature of jobs, time commitments, flexibility of hours, geographical location, and many other factors need to be looked at to weigh their effect on familial role performance as well. Also, dual-career couples must have careers that complement each other so that the stress of familial role performance can be shared by both partners.

Realistic expectations. Husbands' expectations regarding the familial role must be clarified and discussed to ensure that they are achievable and realistic. Failure to meet them may result in a great deal of stress for women.

Independence as a key value in raising children. Because the Indian family structure has been benevolently autocratic, rather than democratic, parents are conditioned to make decisions and care for the physical needs of their children well beyond the age required. Raising children to become more independent and self-reliant, keeping in mind their physical maturity levels, is important for reducing women's family role stress.

Sharing achievements with spouse and children. Involving spouse and children in their work and achievements could go a long way in giving them a sense of pride in women's work. This also creates a positive and supportive attitude to them working, which, in time, can successfully reduce stress. When the family members understand, appreciate, and take pride in women's work and achievements, they are willing to bear the inconveniences caused by their organizational role performance.

Organizational support. Because familial role stress experienced by working women affects their performance in a job, the employer cannot be a casual, disinterested, and mute witness to the "lame-duck" situation of its women employees. If the organization provides for personal growth and development of women employees, and helps them develop assertiveness and work out bilateral coping strategies through role negotiation, it will do considerable good both to itself and the women it employs. The organization could also consider introducing some measure of flexibility in its work schedules to accommodate the demands on working women's time made by the family chores and responsibilities. In fact, the sooner organizations adapt themselves to the management of gender diversity, the better off they will be in terms of enhanced contribution from the women employees.

Societal support. Given the powerful electronic media so avidly watched and heard by the general mass of people in India, there is a pressing need for devising programs aimed for ironing out the "crumpled," kinked, and inconsistent attitudes of the people at large toward women's role in society and their employment in industry. A welcome beginning in this direction has been made in India through a program entitled *"Shakti"* (The Power). The program is offered by Zee TV, which confronts issues related to women and their problems in the society upfront, and tries to reshape public opinion about women's place, roles, and contributions in Indian society.

CONCLUSIONS

The world has become an amazingly small and compact global village over the last few years. The pace of modernization in society is accelerating, causing stresses, strains, and even maladjustments in society. Women's employment can be viewed as part of this process, and it is here to stay and grow. As the number of employed women increases, society has to prepare itself for some "tectonic adjustments," which cause socioemotional tremors: women's familial role stress, organizational role stress, and ambivalence and ambiguity in the attitudes of the inherently male-dominated society toward these relatively new players in the economic field. These tremors have taken their toll: Women agonizingly adjust to the new world in the midst of an environment that has not been too friendly. The various causes of familial role stress and its emotional consequences (manifested in anger, aggression, resignation, and diminished physical and emotional well-being) need to be watched by society, which aspires to globalize itself. Innovative strategies are needed to take care of the causes and consequences of familial role stress so that working women can be equal and effective partners in the progress and prosperity of the family, and can contribute optimally to the growth of the economy and the quality of life in society.

REFERENCES

Gupta, A. (1982, February). *Stress among working women: Its effect on marital adjustment.* Paper presented at the UGC seminar on Stress in Contemporary Life: Strategies of Coping, Delhi, India.

Gupta, G. R., & Murthy, V. N. (1984). *Role conflict and coping strategies: A study on Indian women.* Unpublished manuscript, Bangalore University, Bangalore, India.

Kapur, R. (1969). Role conflict among employed housewives. *Indian Journal of Industrial Relations, 5,* 39–67.

Pestonjee, D. M. (1992). *Stress and coping: The Indian experience.* New Delhi: Sage.

Srivastava, K., & Srivastava, A. K. (1985). Job stress, marital adjustment, social relations and mental health of dual career and traditional couples. *Perspectives in Psychological Research, 8,* 28–33.

Surti, K. (1982). *Some psychological correlates of role stress and coping styles in working women.* Unpublished doctoral dissertation, Gujarat University, Ahmedabad, India.

Surti, K., & Sarupria, D. (1981, November). *Psychological factors affecting women entrepreneurs: Some findings.* Paper presented at the 2nd international conference of Women Entrepreneurs, New Delhi, India.

9

Work Stress Experienced by Persons with Severe Mental Disorders

Jeffrey R. Bedell
Mt. Sinai Medical School, Elmhurst, New York, USA

Robert Gervey and Deborah Draving
Cambridge Hospital, Harvard School of Medicine, Boston, Massachusetts, USA

Abstract   *Supported Employment (SE) is an innovative treatment designed to improve employment rates of persons with severe mental disorders. SE is characterized by the immediate placement of individuals in competitive employment without extensive preemployment training. A job coach is at the work site to teach all necessary work skills and provide psychological support. Critics of SE argue that the immediate placement of persons with severe mental disorders in competitive employment unduly subjects them to work stress, which can worsen symptoms and result in employment loss. This research evaluated a group of successful SE subjects to determine: (a) whether SE negatively affected subjects; (b) how frequently stressful events occurred on the job, how important these stressful events were, and how much stress was experienced; and (c) what methods patients used to cope with the work stresses they experienced. Results generally indicate a positive effect of SE on self-concept, as well as relations with family and friends. Ratings of the frequency and importance of various types of job stress were shown to have an interactive effect on the experience of job stress. Finally, the subjects studied used adaptive and appropriate coping skills to deal with work stress.*

Supported Employment (SE) is an innovative approach to vocational rehabilitation that has recently been applied to persons with serious psychological disorders. Although the effectiveness of SE has been demonstrated for people with handicaps who have been placed in competitive employment environments, concerns have been raised that it might be overly stressful for patients with emotional disorders.

SE follows a "place-and-train" model of rehabilitation, which involves placing the client in a competitive job and then having a job coach teach him or her the necessary work skills on site. Traditional vocational rehabilitation programs are said to follow a "train-and-place" model, which emphasizes "work-readiness" training. These programs use low-demand, "sheltered" job training to prepare the client for competitive work.

Most traditional "train-and-place" methods result in a 10% placement rate, whereas "place-and-train" SE systems report placement rates of up to 73% (Bond & Dincin, 1986; Cook, Soloman, Jonikas, & Frazier, 1990; Drake et al., in press; Fabian & Wiedefield, 1989; Gervey & Bedell, 1994; Mellen & Danley, 1987; Trotter, Minkoff, Harrison, & Hoops, 1988). Partly because of this high job-placement rate, SE programs are considered a superior treatment method. Funding for SE programs exceeded $260 million in 1993.

The high placement rate of SE has raised concerns about stress. Although SE treatment methods are effective in placing patients in competitive employment, critics suggest that the stresses of on-the-job training can overtax the coping skills of persons with mental illness (Black, 1992). This overtaxing may result in exacerbated symptoms, relapse, and loss of employment. The slow-paced and supportive "readiness-training" procedures of the more traditional "train-and-place" system protect clients from these unmanageable stresses.

This study was designed to evaluate the experiences of individuals working in a SE program. Specifically, three questions were addressed: (a) Has employment resulting from the "place-and-train" system of rehabilitation negatively affected persons with mental disorders? (b) How frequently did stressful events occur on the job, how important were these events, and how much stress was experienced? and (c) How did patients cope with the work stresses they experienced?

ABOUT THE SUBJECTS

Subjects were 13 adults who had been referred for vocational rehabilitation services at a community mental health center and were placed on a job using the "place-and-train" model. This program has been described elsewhere (Gervey & Bedell, 1994). There were eight males and five females, whose average age was 26.16 years. Subjects were diagnosed with severe mental disorders, including schizophrenia and psychotic disorder ($n = 6$), bipolar disorder ($n = 3$), major depression ($n = 1$), and others ($n = 3$). The average number of prior psychiatric hospitalizations was 1.5; the average hospitalization was 85.3 days. Subjects had an average of 2.16 prior jobs, and the average length of longest prior employment was 9.5 months. All subjects were considered to be successfully placed in their current jobs, and had maintained employment for at least 90 days.

MEASURING WORK STRESS FACTORS: THE JOB STRESS INTERVIEW

All subjects were administered the Job Stress Interview (JSI), a 24-item semistructured interview developed specifically for use in this research. Administration took approximately 60 minutes. The first 10 questions asked what the subjects liked and disliked about work, the effect work has had on their lives, how they would change their jobs if that were possible, and whether they would prefer SE or sheltered employment if given a choice. Responses to these questions were recorded in narrative form during the interview and summarized for presentation.

The other section of the JSI evaluated 14 work-stress factors that are cited in the research literature as being significantly related to psychological strain, job satisfaction, and job turnover. The work stressors evaluated included (a) concerns about adverse work conditions that might result in *physical harm* on the job (Hall & Spector, 1991; Shankar & Famuyiwa, 1991; Zautra, Elben, & Reynolds, 1986), and (b) evaluations of the *work load* (Hall & Spector, 1991; Hamel & Bracken, 1986; Zautra et al., 1986; McGee, Goodson, & Cashman, 1987; Jones-Johnson & Johnson, 1992). Subjects also rated (c) the degree to which their *psychological symptoms* were affected by work (Foss & Peterson, 1981; Wallner & Clark, 1989), (d) whether they found their work to be *challenging and interesting* (McGee et al., 1987; Zautra et al., 1986), and (e) if they thought the current job was a "dead end" or if it offered *career prospects* (Shankar & Famuyiwa, 1991). Subjects also determined (f) the degree to which their skills were *underutilized* (Hamel & Bracken, 1986) in their current employment, and (g) *interpersonal conflicts with co-workers* (Shankar & Famuyima, 1991) were assessed. Regarding job stress related to supervisors, three areas were assessed: (h) *lack of support from supervisors* (Burke, 1986; Jones-Johnson & Johnson, 1992; Turnage & Spielberger, 1991), (i) *lack of admiration and respect for supervisor* (McGee et al., 1987), and (j) *lack of positive relationship with supervisors* (Burke, 1986; Foss & Peterson, 1981; Israel, House, Schurman, Heaney, & Mero, 1989; McGee et al., 1987; Wallner & Clark, 1989). The JSI also evaluated (k) the amount of *role conflict* (i.e., experience of conflicting demands at work; Burke, 1986; Hall & Spector, 1991; Hamel & Bracken, 1986; Shankar & Famuyima, 1991; Westman, 1992), and (l) *role ambiguity* (i.e., uncertainty about job responsibilities; Burke, 1986; Hall & Spector, 1991; Hamel & Bracken, 1986; Shankar & Famuyiwa, 1991; Westman, 1992). The subjects also reported on (m) the degree to which they felt a *match between the demands of the job and their own abilities* (Westman, 1992), and (n) the degree to which they perceived *communication to be timely and useful* (McGee et al., 1987)—that is, hearing about information when it is useful as opposed to when it was too late.

Each of these 14 work stressors was evaluated using a conceptualization developed by Turnage and Spielberger (1991), whose research demonstrated that both the frequency with which a stressor occurred as well as the intensity of the stressful event played a role in the subjects' experience of strain. In the present research, intensity was evaluated by assessing the subjects' rating of the importance of the stressor when it occurred. The interview was set up to determine: (a) how frequently each stressful event occurred, (b) how important the stressful event was considered to be, and (c) how much strain was experienced due to each type of stressful event. The frequency and importance of the stressor, and the amount of strain experienced, were rated by subjects using 4-point Likert scales.

The final section of the interview was designed to assess the skills that subjects used to cope with stress on the job. During the JSI, whenever a subject indicated that he or she had experienced one of the 14 stressors being evaluated, he or she was asked: "How do you deal with or cope with . . . (insert stressor named by subject)?" The responses were recorded and summarized for presentation.

FREQUENCY, IMPORTANCE, AND STRAIN PRODUCED BY STRESSFUL EVENTS IN THE WORKPLACE

The evaluation results are presented in three sections: (a) Has employment using the "place-and-train" model had a negative effect on persons with mental disorders? (b) How frequently did stressful events occur, how important were these stressful events, and how much strain was experienced? and (c) What methods did subjects use to cope with work stresses?

Has Employment Using the "Place-and-Train" Model Had a Negative Effect on Persons with Mental Disorders?

Subjects were asked five questions to determine the effect of SE on their lives. When asked, "If you had a choice of working in either a sheltered workshop or your current job, which would you choose?", 12 of 13 subjects (92%) chose to retain their current employment. That is, they chose the employment that was based on the "place-and-train" model. Subjects' responses indicated that they preferred the pay, challenge, satisfaction, and autonomy associated with their current jobs, as compared with sheltered employment. No subject said he or she would prefer to stay on his or her present job to avoid the difficulties associated with a change in employment.

The individual who preferred a sheltered workshop environment indicated a desire for more training and a dislike for the tedium of the current job. Because neither of these goals would be better accomplished in sheltered employment than in SE, transfer to sheltered employment would not appear to be a good choice for this individual.

Part of the interview procedure included assessing the subjects' understanding of sheltered employment to ensure that they could make a rational choice. Because all subjects had been briefly involved in sheltered employment in the past, they were asked to use that experience in their decision making. The interviewer also provided them with a standard verbal description of sheltered employment.

The second question asked subjects if they were better or worse off working than doing whatever they were doing before. As with the first question, most subjects (85%) believed they were better off in their current job. Here again, they liked the income, challenge, and satisfaction of their work. Interestingly, many of those who considered themselves worse off cited salary as a reason. Some subjects indicated that the increased stress and loss of leisure time made them think they were worse off now.

The third question was composed of three parts. Subjects were asked how being employed had affected how they thought or felt about: (a) themselves, (b) their relationships with family, and (c) relationships with friends. All subjects responded that being employed affected how they felt about themselves. They most frequently (46%) indicated an increase in self-acceptance, self-esteem, pride, or motivation. Subjects also reported increased feelings of independence, strength, and contentment. They further suggested that being employed helped them to socialize better. When asked how employment affected their relationship with their families, the most frequent response (38%) was that there had been no change. Some subjects indicated that work caused them to see family members less. Thirty percent of the subjects indicated that family members had reacted with a sense of happiness and pride. As for relationships with friends, subjects stated that employment frequently had no effect (31%), although a few indicated they have developed new friends on the job (19%) and related better socially. However, some respondents indicated that friends began to resent their success, and saw the subject as a source for borrowing money or a target of negative conversation.

The next question asked, "If you had the opportunity to change your employment situation, how would you change it?" Subjects indicated a surprising degree of satisfaction with the nature of the work they performed. Generally, they wanted to earn more money and work better hours (46%), or leave their current work to attend school or get a better job (46%).

In response to the question, "What are the things that you like and dislike about your current employment situation?", almost everyone (92%) liked their co-workers, and most people (54%) liked the nature of the work they performed. Some people just liked having a job. However, many subjects (62%) complained about the conditions in which they worked, saying that they were noisy, dirty, hot, or crowded. A number of subjects (69%) disliked some of their co-workers and supervisors. Given that there were 12 positive responses and 5 negative responses regarding co-workers, some of the 13 subjects appeared to have liked certain co-workers and disliked others. Some people (38%) felt time pressures or had too much work to do.

How Frequently Did Stressful Events Occur, How Important Were the Stressful Events, and How Much Strain Was Experienced?

Subjects were asked to respond to three questions pertaining to the 14 types of stress presented earlier (see Table 9.1). Each of the three questions evaluated a different aspect of stress. One question assessed the frequency with which the stressors occurred (i.e., "How often are you in a situation at work where you might be hurt or injured?"). Response choices were: *almost never, sometimes, often,* and *almost always.* The second question asked the subject to indicate the importance of the stressor when it occurred (i.e., "How important is it that your work situation is free of danger and risk of injury?"). The response choices were: *not at all important, somewhat important, moderately important,* and *very important.* Third, subjects were asked to indicate the amount of stress (strain) they experienced due to the factor being evaluated

Table 9.1 Frequency-response table indicating how *frequently* each source of stress occurred

Item no.	Source of stress	Almost never 1	Sometimes 2	Often 3	Almost always 4
1.	Possible injury	9	3	1	0
2.	Overwork	6	6	1	0
3.	Symptoms	7	4	2	0
4.	Lack of challenge	3	3	5	2
5.	Poor career prospects	4	6	1	2
6.	Underutilization	5	6	1	1
7.	Peer conflict	8	3	1	1
8.	Lack supervisor support	5	4	0	4
9.	Lack respect for supervisor	4	2	3	4
10.	Negative relationship with supervisor	2	4	3	4
11.	Role conflict	6	5	0	2
12.	Role ambiguity	8	2	0	3
13.	Job not match skills	6	4	0	3
14.	Untimely communication	6	3	3	1

Note. $M = 1.98$.

(i.e., "How much stress do you experience because of the possibility that you might be hurt or injured on the job?"). Response choices were: *almost no stress, some stress, moderate stress,* and *very much stress*. Subjects responded to these questions by indicating their rating on a Likert scale.

To summarize these data, frequency-response tables were developed. In these tables, the frequency with which subjects chose each of the four alternatives provided on the Likert scale are recorded for each question. Tables 9.1, 9.2, and 9.3 show the ratings describing: (a) how frequently each of the types of stress occurred, (b) how important the stress was when it occurred, and (c) the amount of stress (strain) that was associated with each factor assessed. The stressors listed in these tables correspond to the 14 stress factors described earlier.

As may be seen in Table 9.1, the mean Likert scale rating of *frequency* for all 14 stressors evaluated was 1.98, indicating that stressors *sometimes* occur. Examining individual stress factors, it may be seen that the most frequent ratings were associated with *almost never* being subjected to possible injury (Item 1), peer conflict (Item 7), and role ambiguity (Item 12). In general, the responses suggest a mild to moderate amount of stress distributed across the whole range of possible stressful situations.

Table 9.2 shows the ratings of *importance* for each stressor. The average rating of importance was 3.31, indicating that the stressors were considered to be *moderately* to *very* important. Looking at individual stress factors, it appears that most important stressors were related to knowing one's job duties (Item 12), having respect for one's supervisor (Item 9), and receiving timely and useful communication (Item 14).

Table 9.2 Frequency-response table showing the *importance* of each source of stress

Item no.	Source of stress	Not very important 1	Somewhat important 2	Moderately important 3	Very important 4
1.	Possible injury	0	3	2	8
2.	Overwork	4	2	1	6
3.	Symptoms	3	1	0	9
4.	Lack of challenge	2	3	3	5
5.	Poor career prospects	1	4	1	7
6.	Underutilization	2	1	4	6
7.	Peer conflict	9	3	1	0
8.	Lack supervisor support	2	0	2	9
9.	Lack respect for supervisor	0	1	2	10
10.	Negative relationship with supervisor	1	2	3	7
11.	Role conflict	1	3	0	9
12.	Role ambiguity	1	0	1	11
13.	Job not match skills	0	2	2	9
14.	Untimely communication	1	0	1	11

Note. M = 3.31.

Table 9.3 shows the ratings of the *amount* of stress (strain) experienced due to each of the 14 factors. The average rating was 2.03, indicating *some stress.* The circumstance considered to be the most stressful by the greatest number of subjects was lack of admiration or respect for one's supervisor (Item 9). Generally, the ratings were distributed across the range of ratings for all stress factors.

Table 9.3 Frequency-response table indicating how much stress was *experienced* in each stress category

Item no.	Source of stress	Almost no stress 1	Some stress 2	Moderate stress 3	Very much stress 4
1.	Possible injury	7	4	2	0
2.	Overwork	8	2	2	1
3.	Symptoms	7	4	1	1
4.	Lack of challenge	5	5	1	2
5.	Poor career prospects	7	2	3	1
6.	Underutilization	7	2	2	2
7.	Peer conflict	7	4	1	1
8.	Lack supervisor support	1	8	0	4
9.	Lack respect for supervisor	2	3	2	7
10.	Negative relationship with supervisor	3	6	0	4
11.	Role conflict	5	5	1	2
12.	Role ambiguity	7	3	0	3
13.	Job not match skills	6	4	0	3
14.	Untimely communication	3	7	0	3

Note. M = 2.03.

The data in Tables 9.1, 9.2, and 9.3 show that no single factor was rated high or low on all three factors of frequency, importance, and amount of stress (strain). In general, it seemed that the importance of the various stressful factors was rated higher than those of either frequency of occurrence or amount of strain associated with each stressor. This observation was tested statistically using t tests to compare the average ratings of the Frequency of Stressful Events, Importance of Stressful Events, and Amount of Stress Experienced. The results of these t tests indicated that the average rating of the Importance of Stress ($\chi^2 = 3.31$, $SD = 0.59$) was significantly higher than either the average rating of Frequency of Stressful Events ($\chi^2 = 2.03$, $SD = 0.70$), t (12) $= -6.36$, $p < .001$), or the Amount of Stress Experienced ($\chi^2 = 2.03$, $SD = 0.70$), t (12) $= 6.49$, $p < .001$). There was no significant difference between ratings of the mean Frequency of Stressful Events and the mean Amount of Stress Experienced (t [12] $= -0.48$, ns).

These ratings suggest that subjects recognized a variety of stressful events as being important, but the frequency with which they occurred was significantly lower. Ratings of the Amount of Stress Experienced were the same (statistically) as ratings of the Frequency of Stressful Events, indicating a relationship between amount and frequency of stress.

To further evaluate the relationship between the frequency, importance, and experience of stress, correlations were performed on the average ratings of Frequency of Stressful Events, Importance of Stressful Events, and Amount of Stress Experienced. The correlation of .81 between the frequency of occurrence of a stressful event and the amount of stress experienced was highly significant ($p < .001$). In comparison, the correlations between the importance of the stressful event and the frequency of its occurrence ($r = .21$), and between the importance and the amount of stress experienced ($r = .41$) were not statistically significant ($p > .05$). Thus, the amount of experienced stress was strongly associated with how frequently the stressor occurred, but not with the importance of the stressful event.

To further explore the relationship between the frequency and importance of stressful events and the experience of stress, the data were reconfigured so that frequency and importance were considered independent variables, and ratings of the magnitude of experienced stress (strain) were dependent variables. Subjects were assigned to high and low stress frequency groups by a median split of subjects' frequency scores. Similarly, high- and low-importance groups were established, based on a median split of the ratings of importance.

A 2 × 2 analysis of variance (ANOVA) was performed comparing the Frequency of Stressful Events (high vs. low) and the Importance of Stressful Events (high vs. low) on ratings of the Amount of Stress Experienced. Results of this analysis indicate significant main effects of Frequency of Stressful Events (F [1,12] $= 10.34$, $p < .01$) and Importance of Stressful Events (F [1,12] $= 6.55$, $p < .05$). The interaction effect of Frequency × Importance (F [1,12] $= 7.23$, $p < .05$) was also significant.

The interaction effect was the most meaningful, and the means associated with the interaction effect are described in Fig. 9.1. This interaction effect indicated that, when the Frequency of Stressful Events was low, there was no

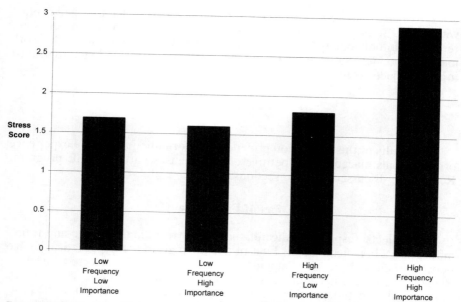

Figure 9.1   Interaction of Frequency of Stressful Events (high vs. low) and Importance of Stressful Events (high vs. low) on ratings of the Amount of Stress Experienced.

difference in the amount of stress experienced between high and low importance. Furthermore, when the Frequency of Stressful Events was high and the Importance of Stressful Events was low, the Amount of Stress Experienced remained low. However, when the Frequency of Stressful Events was high and the Importance of Stressful Events was also high, the Amount of Stress Experienced significantly increased. Thus, it appears that, in a situation where stressors important to the individual occur frequently, the experience of strain is significantly increased. Neither high frequency nor high importance alone was found to create this high level of strain on the individual.

What Methods Did Subjects Use to Cope with Work Stress?

During the JSI interview, whenever a subject indicated that he or she had experienced a stressor being evaluated, he or she was asked, "Tell me how you deal with or cope with the stress of . . . (insert stressor)." A review of the subjects' statements showed that some coping responses were applied to a variety of situations. The two most frequently mentioned coping responses were talking with another person and avoidance.

Subjects reported discussing the problem situation with another person when: their symptoms became unstable, they lacked supervisor support, they did not respect their supervisor's behavior, they had poor relations with their boss, they experienced role conflict or role ambiguity, or they experienced untimely communication. They used avoidance as a coping method when they were worried about being hurt or injured on the job, or when they had conflict with peers. Some coping methods were used frequently, whereas others were responses to only one type of stressful situation. For example, when the work load was too high, subjects suggested they would "just do it." To guard against injury, subjects would "be careful."

DISCUSSION

The results of this evaluation provide key information about the experience of individuals placed in competitive employment as part of an SE program. Results are discussed in three sections.

Effect of Employment

The subjects' responses indicated that employment in the "place-and-train" model had a beneficial effect. First of all, when given the hypothetical choice between sheltered employment and SE, 12 of the 13 subjects selected the latter. Responses to the other four questions were consistent with this decision. Almost all subjects thought they were better off than they had been in the past, citing increased income and feelings of independence and responsibility. In addition, they felt that their self-esteem had increased. When asked to describe the effect of work on self, family, and friends, the responses were nearly all positive. However, many subjects did not like the physical conditions of their workplace. Statements about having less contact with families and increased conflicts with friends might indicate a negative effect of work on the subjects. However, it is possible that contact with families was still adequate. The nature of the conflicts with friends seemed to be a sign of positive change on the part of the subjects and inappropriate behavior on the part of the friends.

Frequency, Importance, and Amount of Stress

The results of this section show that subjects were clearly able to differentially report their evaluations of Frequency of Stressful Events, Importance of Stressful Events, and Amount of Stress Experienced. In the present sample, ratings of Importance of Stressful Events were found to be significantly higher than those of either the Frequency of Stressful Events or the Amount of Stress Experienced. Apparently this interview tapped into significant dimensions of stress. It also suggested that subjects perceived their current jobs as being rather low in the Frequency of Stressful Events, and also rather low in the perceived strain. This relationship among the three variables was confirmed by multiple t tests comparing these variables.

Results also indicate that there was a significant correlation between the Amount of Stress Experienced by subjects and the Frequency of Stressful Events. However, there was no significant relationship between the Importance of Stressful Events and the Amount of Stress Experienced.

The relationship between the Frequency and Importance of Stressful Events and the Amount of Stress Experienced indicated significantly higher levels of strain when both the Frequency and Importance of Stressful Events were high. Thus, the two variables of Frequency of Stressful Events and Importance of Stressful Events interact to produce a much greater level of strain than either produces separately.

Coping

The coping responses were generally adaptive and appropriate, even if they were not extremely sophisticated. Curiously, although mental health staff were available to help subjects cope with stress, use of mental health staff was rarely mentioned. In fact, the idea of talking to a therapist was mentioned only once in response to the situation where there was a lack of admiration or respect for one's supervisor. One would expect this coping method to be utilized more frequently by persons involved in an SE program.

It was interesting to evaluate the coping strategies used by these subjects in response to the stressors evaluated. Moos and Billings (1982) developed a system for classifying coping behaviors into three major classes, each of which had several subclasses. Briefly, their system is as follows: *Appraisal-focused coping* involves an attempt to redefine a situation so that it is less stressful. Three types of appraisal-focused coping are: (a) logical analysis or attempts to define what caused the situation, (b) cognitive redefinition to restructure reality into something less threatening, and (c) cognitive avoidance including denial, suppression, and repression. *Problem-focused coping* employs specific actions designed to alleviate the stress or prevent its reoccurrence. This type of coping includes: (a) seeking information or advice, (b) direct problem solving, and (c) adapting to the stress by changing one's own behavior. Finally, *emotion-focused coping* includes attempts to manage the emotional consequences of the stressor. Included in this type of coping are: (a) the use of cognitive and behavioral methods to control an emotional reaction, (b) resigned acceptance, and (c) verbal or behavioral expression of stress-induced emotion.

Keeping these categories in mind, it is clear that a diversity of coping styles was suggested by the subjects. As stated earlier, two methods of coping were used most frequently. The first was to ignore the stressor, which suggests the use of appraisal-focused coping in the form of cognitive avoidance, or emotion-focused coping in the form of resigned acceptance. The other frequently used technique was to talk to another person about the stressful situation. This implies the use of problem-focused coping, and would be characterized as use of the information- or advice-seeking method.

It is not possible to state whether this pattern of coping is optimal. Nevertheless, it would appear that the variety of coping styles used is adaptive and positive because these subjects have successfully maintained their jobs. Also, the balance between ignoring stressors and taking action to seek advice and information may prove to be effective. That is, you take action where you can (problem-oriented coping); when that is not possible, you change your appraisal (appraisal-focused coping) or resign yourself to the stressor (emotion-focused coping).

CONCLUSIONS AND FUTURE RESEARCH

The current results are limited by the sample size. Subjects were all successfully maintaining employment, and had been on the job for at least 90 days. Thus, these results describe the experiences of successful patients. The study of individuals who did not stay on the job, but rather terminated within a month of being employed, would provide interesting comparisons with the present data. Also, an evaluation of individuals who were successfully employed in the same workplaces, but who did not have a mental illness, would provide an interesting comparison.

REFERENCES

Black, B. J. (1992). A kind word for sheltered work. *Psychosocial Rehabilitation Journal, 15,* 87–89.

Bond, G. R., & Dincin, J. (1986). Accelerating entry into transitional employment in a psychosocial rehabilitation agency. *Rehabilitation Psychology, 31,* 143–155.

Burke, R. J. (1986). The present and future status of stress research. *Journal of Organizational Behavior Management, 8,* 249–267.

Cook, J. A., Soloman, M. L., Jonikas, J. A., & Frazier, M. (1990). *Supported competitive employment program for youth with severe mental illness.* Final report to the U.S. Department of Education (Grant No. G008630404). Chicago: Thresholds.

Drake, R. E., Becker, D. R., Biensanz, J. C., Torrey, W. C., McHugo, G. J., & Wyzik, M. A. (in press). Partial hospitalization vs. supported employment: I. Vocational outcomes. *Community Mental Health Journal.*

Fabian, E., & Wiedefield. (1989). Supported employment for severely psychiatrically disabled persons: A descriptive study. *Psychosocial Rehabilitation Journal, 13,* 53–59.

Foss, G., & Peterson, S. L. (1981). Social-interpersonal skills relevant to job tenure for mentally retarded adults. *Mental Retardation, 19,* 103–106.

Gervey, R., & Bedell, J. R. (1994). Supported employment in vocational rehabilitation. In J. R. Bedell (Ed.), *Psychological assessment and treatment of persons with severe mental disorders* (pp. 151–175). Washington, DC: Taylor & Francis.

Hall, J. K., & Spector, P. E. (1991). Relationships of work stress measures for employees with the same job. *Work & Stress, 5,* 29–35.

Hamel, K., & Bracken, D. (1986). Factor structure of the job stress questionnaire (JSQ) in three occupational groups. *Educational and Psychological Measurement, 46,* 777–786.

Israel, B. A. House, J. S., Schurman, S. J., Heaney, C. A., & Mero, R. P. (1989). The relation of personal resources, participation, influence, interpersonal relationships and coping strategy to occupational stress, job strains and health: A multivariate analysis. *Work & Stress, 3,* 163–194.

Jones-Johnson, G., & Johnson, W. R. (1992). Subjective underemployment and psychosocial stress: The role of perceived social and supervisor support. *Journal of Social Psychology, 132,* 11–21.

McGee, G. W., Goodson, J. R., & Cashman, J. F. (1987). Job stress and job dissatisfaction: Influence of contextual factors. *Psychological Reports, 61,* 367–375.

Mellen, V., & Danley, K. (1987). Special issue: Supported employment for persons with severe mental illness. *Psychosocial Rehabilitation Journal, 11,* 2.

Moos, R. H., & Billings, A. G. (1982). Conceptualizing and measuring coping resources and processes. In L. Goldberg & S. Breznitz (Eds.), *Handbook of Stress: Theoretical and clinical aspects* (pp. 212–239). New York: Free Press.

Shankar, J., & Famuyiwa, O. O. (1991). Stress among factory workers in a developing country. *Journal of Psychosomatic Research, 35,* 163–171.

Trotter, S., Minkoff, K., Harrison K., & Hoops, J. (1988). Supported work: An innovative approach to the vocational rehabilitation of persons who are psychiatrically disabled. *Rehabilitation Psychology, 13,* 27–36.

Turnage, J. J., & Spielberger, C. D. (1991). Job stress in managers, professionals, and clerical workers. *Work & Stress, 5,* 165–176.

Wallner, R. J., & Clark, D. W. (1989). The functional assessment inventory and job tenure for persons with severe and persistent mental health problems. *Journal of Applied Rehabilitation Counseling, 20,* 13–15.

Westman, M. (1992). Moderating effect of decision latitude on stress-strain relationship: Does organizational level matter? *Journal of Organizational Behavior, 13,* 713–722.

Zautra, A. J., Elben, C., & Reynolds, K. D. (1986). Job stress and task interest: Two factors in work life quality. *American Journal of Community Psychology, 14,* 377–393.

III

STRESS AND EMOTION IN THE SCHOOLS

10

Changes in Anxiety and Anger for College Students Performing a Rock-Classification Task

Mary E. Westerback
Long Island University, New York, New York, USA

Louis H. Primavera
St. John's University, New York, New York, USA

Charles D. Spielberger
University of South Florida, Tampa, USA

Abstract *Changes in state (S) and trait (T) anxiety and anger were investigated for 40 university students (20 females, 20 males) taking a geology course who were required to group rocks in appropriate categories. Spielberger's State–Trait Personality Inventory (STPI) was administered on three occasions: on the first day of class (initial), after some practice with the rock-classification task (pretest), and following a laboratory practical examination (posttest). Students were divided into high- and low-achievement groups based on their lab exam. The pattern of change in S-Anxiety and S-Anger scores across the three testing periods differed for the two achievement groups. Both groups increased in S-Anxiety from initial testing to the pretest, suggesting that the students found the task more difficult than they had anticipated. From pretest to posttest, the S-Anxiety of low achievers continued to increase, whereas high achievers showed a significant decline in S-Anxiety, indicating that pretest–posttest changes in S-Anxiety were inversely related to student performance. S-Anger for low achievers also increased from initial testing to pretest, and even more from pretest to posttest; S-Anger for high achievers was essentially unchanged. Males were significantly higher in S-Anxiety and S-Anger than females. No gender differences were found in the trait measures, which were relatively stable across the three testings.*

There is substantial evidence that emotions such as anxiety influence learning and achievement in academic settings (e.g., Hembree, 1988; Sarason, 1960; Spielberger, 1966a, 1966b), but only limited research has shown the effects of anxiety and other emotions on the performance of specific academic tasks. Positive emotions are usually beneficial, whereas negative emotions can have

181

either positive or negative effects. For example, the anxiety evoked by academic failure may stimulate some students to study or seek help, whereas increased anxiety, anger, or shame may produce hopelessness accompanied by poorer performance in others (Pekrun, 1992).

Theoretical analyses and empirical research on the nature and assessment of anxiety (e.g., Spielberger, 1966a, 1979, 1985), and the effects of anxiety on learning and academic performance (e.g., Alpert & Haber, 1960; Brown, 1938; Spence, 1958; Spence & Spence, 1966; Spielberger, 1966b; Taylor, 1956), have been linked in the research literature for more than half a century. Recent reviews also indicate growing interest in the effects of anxiety on learning in science courses (Westerback & Primavera, 1988, 1992). In contrast, there is as yet relatively little research on how anger affects learning and performance in course work. According to Pekrun (1992), between 1974 and 1990, there were more than 700 studies of anxiety and achievement, but only 31 anger-achievement studies, most of which were related more to Type-A personality than to angry feelings.

Spielberger (1988) and his colleagues (Spielberger et al., 1985; Spielberger, Krasner, & Solomon, 1988) have proposed working definitions that distinguish anger as an emotional state, individual differences in anger-proneness as a personality trait, and how anger is expressed and controlled. As an emotional state, anger varies in intensity from mild irritation or annoyance to intense fury and rage. People differ in how often and under what circumstances they experience S-Anger, and in the manner in which they deal with their angry feelings. Those who outwardly express anger, directing it toward other people or objects in the environment, are high in "anger-out." Individuals who hold in or suppress their anger are high in "anger-in."

In this information age, with an ever-increasing dependence on computers and complex technology, developing appropriate models to convey an understanding of science, determining what should be learned about science, and defining how this learning can best be accomplished are matters of increasing concern (Pinet, 1989). As Watson (1988) noted:

> *Attempts to clarify the goals of general education science have focused on many issues: student-centered versus subject-centered emphasis, using subject matter to develop broad viewpoints, what different bodies of students should know, illustrating science in its historical context, science and society's impact on each other, and what curriculum requirements should be. (p. 432)*

Recognizing the critical role of teachers in science education prompted faculty at Utah State University to revise their curriculum to give greater emphasis to using "hands-on" activities as a means of demonstrating how science is actually done. Redirection of science education to focus on the interaction of students with specific science content in narrowly delineated areas is also strongly recommended (e.g., Finley, 1981; Stewart & Atkin, 1982). For example, the classification of mineral and igneous rocks is one of the most important and difficult areas in geology and earth science courses (Finley, Stewart, & Yarroch, 1982). However, how rock classification is accomplished depends on how the task is defined. One can simply learn to name the rock or mineral, or one can use a classification scheme based on the conceptual understanding of the origin and formation of rocks.

Westerback, Gonzales, and Primavera (1985) found that university students taking geology and earth science courses were able to successfully classify hand specimens of minerals and rocks using a conceptual system based on visual characteristics that reflect an understanding of how rocks are formed. They also found that achievement on a rock-classification task using this system was inversely related to the students' anxiety. Because rocks vary in composition and texture, understanding the arbitrary boundaries of the Westerback et al. well-defined conceptual classification scheme is a critical component of their system. Westerback and Azer (1991) subsequently revised and refined this classification scheme to make its use even more practical for college students in hand-specimen work.

THE ROCK-CLASSIFICATION TASK: STUDY METHODS AND PROCEDURE

The goals of this study were to examine relationships between anxiety/anger and success on a rock-classification task, using a conceptual system based on the origin of rocks developed by Westerback et al. (1985) and refined by Westerback and Azer (1991). The relationship between gender and performance on the rock-classification task was also examined.

Subjects

The participants in this study were 47 undergraduate students at an eastern U.S. university who were taking a geology course to fulfill a science requirement. The grade distribution for the 43 students who completed the course indicated a wide range of achievement. The final course grades for these students were: A = 13, B = 14, C = 6, and D = 10. In determining each student's final grade in the geology course, lecture tests counted 75% and laboratory performance counted 25%. The rock-classification task comprised 10% of the laboratory grade component. Forty students (20 males, 20 females) completed all of the requirements for this study.

Test Instruments

State–Trait Personality Inventory. The State–Trait Personality Inventory (STPI) is comprised of six 10-item subscales that assess S-Anxiety, T-Anxiety, S-Curiosity, T-Curiosity, S-Anger, and T-Anger (Spielberger, 1979). For this study, the title on the STPI test form, "Self-Analysis Questionnaire," was changed to "How Do You Feel About Identifying Rocks" for the state scales, and to "How Do You Feel in General" for the trait scales. Only the findings for the anxiety and anger scales are reported in this chapter.

In responding to each of the 30 STPI state items (e.g., "I feel tense"), subjects rated themselves on the following 4-point intensity scale: *not at all* (1), *somewhat* (2), *moderately so* (3), and *very much so.* (4). In responding to the 30 STPI trait items (e.g., "I feel nervous"), subjects indicated how they generally felt by rating themselves on the following 4-point frequency scale: *almost never* (1), *sometimes* (2), *often* (3), and *almost always* (4). The alpha reliability coefficients reported in the STPI test manual ranged from .78 to .92 for the state subscales, and from .80 to .87 for the trait subscales, indicating high levels of internal consistency for all six STPI 10-item subscales.

The laboratory practical. Twenty specimens, each with clear and unambiguous characteristics, were used in the laboratory rock-classification task. Each student was given an answer sheet, with columns listing rock textures and space to check off textures relating to the appropriate rock type. All students classified the same specimens, which were passed from one student to another (for detailed information about the rock-classification system and rock textures and types, see Westerback & Azer, 1991).

Procedure

The process of rock formation and the resulting textures were explained in lectures in the geology course, which included presentations of charts, motion pictures, and videos. The rationale for the rock-classification scheme was presented by the instructor at the beginning of the course, and was discussed and illustrated in detail. Slides were used to show hand specimens of rock types, rocks in their natural setting, initial landforms produced by rocks, and subsequent modifications by processes of erosion.

In the laboratory work, the focus was on recognition of different types of rocks. Using the conceptual schema developed by Westerback and Azer (1991), students learned to recognize textures and other distinguishing characteristics so that they could classify any rock. Students were not required to memorize technical terms. For example, *aphanitic,* a technical term for fine-grained texture in volcanic igneous rocks, was referred to simply as *fine-grained.*

The laboratory practical exams were designed to focus on classifying rocks. The students' task was to identify and check off the appropriate texture and rock group. They were informed that no samples from the regular student rock boxes would be used in the practical exams; they also were advised to "name the rock" only if they were quite sure of the relationship between texture and origin. Finally, they were informed that bonus points could be earned for each rock that was correctly named, whereas incorrect responses would result in points deducted. The students were given the opportunity to practice using the classification schema in the laboratory, and were encouraged to come to the lab for additional practice before the examination.

The STPI was administered on three occasions; (a) on the first day of class, prior to any instruction (initial testing); (b) 2 weeks later, after lectures and laboratory exercises on classifying minerals and igneous rocks (pretest); and (c) 3 weeks later (posttest), after they had completed a lecture examination on igneous, sedimentary, and metamorphic rocks, and had actual experience with the conceptual schema they had been taught to use in classifying rocks. The posttest was administered shortly after the practical examination was taken and scored, and after class discussion of correct and incorrect responses. Thus, the students knew their grades on the laboratory practical prior to the posttest.

RESULTS

The major goals of this study were to examine relationships between achievement on a scientific task (e.g., rock classification) and changes in S-Anxiety/S-Anger and T-Anxiety/T-Anger. In evaluating these relationships, the geology students were divided into two groups on the basis of their grades on the laboratory rock-classification task. The rock samples used in the examination were unambiguous; most students understood the relationship between texture and origin, and had sufficient practice in visually determining textures prior to the laboratory test. Because the lab work was designed to promote success, it was reasonable to expect grades of 80% or higher on the practical exams.

If the associations between texture and origin were not understood and/or the student had not practiced identifying rocks with actual samples, her or his grade was generally lower. However, intellectual understanding alone does not usually result in success; satisfactory performance on the rock-classification task requires actual practice with representative rock specimens.

The median grade for the students in the geology course was 80%. Those with grades below 80% were classified as *low achievement;* students who scored at or above 80% were classified as *high achievement.* As expected, this procedure resulted in a higher proportion (60%) of the students being placed in the high-achievement group.

Effects of Achievement on Anxiety and Anger

Relationships between achievement on the rock-classification task and changes in anxiety and anger for students in the high- and low-achievement groups were examined by performing two-factor, split-plots analyses of variance (ANOVAs) for each dependent variable (Maxwell & Delaney, 1990). The between-subjects variable in these analyses was Achievement, with two levels: low achievement (grades below 80%, $n = 16$) and high achievement (grades at or above 80%, $n = 24$). The within-subjects, repeated-measures variable was Testings, with three levels: initial testing, pretest, and posttest.

The level of significance was set at the .05 level for all analyses. Significant interactions were further evaluated in follow-up analyses of simple effects, using t tests of contrasts with pooled and separate error terms, as described by Maxwell and Delaney (1990). Main effects were examined only if the Testing × Achievement interaction was not significant.

The means and standard deviations for the initial, pretest, and posttest S-Anxiety/S-Anger and T-Anxiety/T-Anger scores for students in the high- and low-achievement groups are reported in Table 10.1. In the ANOVA for the

Table 10.1 Means and standard deviations for initial, pretest, and posttest STPI
S-Anxiety/S-Anger and T-Anxiety/T-Anger scores for geology students in
the high- and low-achievement groups

		Testing condition		
		Initial	Pretest	Posttest
STPI subscales	N	M (SD)	M (SD)	M (SD)
S-Anxiety				
High achievement	24	18.12	23.96	19.50
		(7.00)	(7.76)	(6.56)
Low achievement	16	18.25	23.94	27.31
		(4.11)	(6.37)	(5.15)
S-Anger				
High achievement	24	13.71	14.75	14.67
		(7.12)	(7.06)	(6.86)
Low achievement	16	13.44	17.06	22.00
		(4.88)	(8.92)	(10.34)
T-Anxiety				
High achievement	24	19.04	18.58	20.21
		(5.81)	(5.47)	(6.09)
Low achievement	16	18.19	19.44	21.25
		(4.70)	(3.78)	(4.40)
T-Anger				
High achievement	24	22.58	21.29	20.67
		(5.59)	(6.19)	(5.71)
Low achievement	16	22.12	22.06	23.00
		(6.90)	(6.08)	(7.00)

S-Anxiety scores, the highly significant Achievement × Testings interaction
effect (F [2,76] = 7.21, $p < .001$) indicated that the pattern of change in the
S-Anxiety scores across the three testing periods was different for the high-
and low-achievement groups.

Follow-up analyses revealed that the S-Anxiety scores for both achievement
groups increased significantly from initial testing to the pretest. The S-Anxiety
scores of the low-achievement group also increased significantly from pretest
to posttest, and were substantially higher at posttest than at either the initial
testing or pretest. In contrast, the high-achievement group decreased significantly in S-Anxiety from pretest to posttest, returning almost to the same level
as in the initial testing, as can be noted in Table 10.1.

The follow-up analyses also indicated that the initial testing and pretest
S-Anxiety scores for the two achievement groups were quite similar, and that
the low-achievement group was significantly higher in S-Anxiety on the posttest
than the high achievers, as can be noted in Table 10.1. These findings provide
clear evidence that S-Anxiety and science achievement were inversely related.

In the ANOVA for the S-Anger scores, the significant Achievement ×
Testings interaction (F [2,76] = 4.07, $p < .05$) indicated that the high- and

low-achievement groups showed different patterns of change in S-Anger across the three Testings periods. Follow-up analyses revealed that the S-Anger scores of the high achievers were essentially unchanged across, whereas the S-Anger scores of the low achievers increased significantly from initial testing to pretest, and increased even more from pretest to posttest, as can be noted in Table 10.1. The follow-up analyses also showed that the S-Anger scores of the two achievement groups did not differ significantly from each other at initial testing or pretest, and that the low-achievement group was significantly higher in S-Anger than the high achievers on the posttest.

The only significant finding in the ANOVAs for the T-Anxiety scores was the Testings main effect for T-Anxiety ($F[2,76] = 7.99 \ p < .001$). The results of the follow-up analyses indicated that the mean T-Anxiety score for the 40 students was essentially the same at initial testing ($M = 18.70$) and pretest ($M = 18.92$), and that the mean T-Anxiety score for the total group on the posttest ($M = 20.62$) was significantly higher than at either initial testing or pretest. As can be noted in Table 10.1, this increase in T-Anxiety was due primarily to the low-achievement group, even though the Achievement $\times$ Testings interaction was not significant. Although statistically significant, the increase in T-Anxiety from initial testing and pretest to posttest for the total group reflected a change of only 1.8 points (less than half a standard deviation), which was quite small relative to the observed changes in the S-Anxiety scores.

The mean T-Anger scores for the high- and low-achievement groups were quite similar on the initial testing. Although there was a slight tendency for the T-Anger scores of the high achievers to decrease and for scores of the low achievers to increase, as can be noted in Table 10.1, the Achievement $\times$ Testings interaction was not significant, nor were either the Achievement or the Testings main effects. Thus, it may be concluded that the T-Anger scores for both the high- and low-achievement groups were stable across the three Testing periods.

Effects of Gender on S-Anxiety/S-Anger and T-Anxiety/T-Anger

A second goal of this study was to evaluate changes in S-Anxiety/S-Anger and T-Anxiety/T-Anger as a function of gender. The means and standard deviations for the initial testing, pretest, and posttest anxiety and anger scores for males and females enrolled in the geology course are reported in Table 10.2. Changes in the anxiety and anger scores were evaluated by two-factor, split-plots ANOVAs similar to those used in the analyses for the Achievement groups (Maxwell & Delaney, 1990). Gender was the between-subjects variable, with two levels (males and females). As in the previous analyses, Testings was the within-subjects variable, with three levels (initial testing, pretest, posttest).

In the ANOVA for the S-Anxiety scores, the Gender $\times$ Testings interaction was not statistically significant, suggesting that the pattern of change across Testings periods was similar for males and females. However, significant main effects were found for both Gender ($F[1,38] = 4.77, p < .05$) and Testings ($F[2,76] = 11.87, p < .001$). The S-Anxiety means for males and females, averaged across the three Testings periods, were 23.23 and 19.93, respectively. The

Table 10.2 Means and standard deviations for initial, pretest, and posttest STPI
S-Anxiety/S-Anger and T-Anxiety/T-Anger scores for female (*N* = 20)
and male (*N* = 20) geology students

	Testing condition		
STPI subscales	Initial M (SD)	Pretest M (SD)	Posttest M (SD)
S-Anxiety			
Female	16.60 (4.51)	21.30 (6.97)	21.90 (7.03)
Male	19.75 (6.86)	26.60 (6.44)	23.35 (7.31)
S-Anger			
Female	11.05 (1.43)	11.80 (2.31)	13.60 (4.46)
Male	16.15 (8.03)	19.55 (9.43)	21.60 (10.73)
T-Anxiety			
Female	18.75 (4.56)	18.10 (4.66)	19.60 (5.06)
Male	18.65 (6.14)	19.75 (4.97)	21.65 (5.73)
T-Anger			
Female	21.80 (3.65)	19.50 (4.51)	19.90 (4.80)
Male	23.00 (7.83)	23.65 (6.83)	23.00 (7.20)

mean S-Anxiety scores of the females at each Testings period were substantially
higher than those of the males, as may be noted in Table 10.2.

Follow-up analyses of the Testings main effect indicated that mean S-Anxiety scores for the total group increased significantly from initial testing (*M* =
18.18) to pretest (*M* = 23.95), but did not change from pretest to posttest (*M*
= 22.65). Thus, both males and females became increasingly anxious before
the laboratory test, and their anxiety remained at this higher level after the
test. Because differential patterns of change in S-Anxiety were found for the
high- and low-achievement groups in the previous analyses, it seems evident
that Achievement, and not Gender, contributed to the observed changes in the
students' S-Anxiety scores over the three Testings periods.

The Gender × Testings interaction in the ANOVA for the S-Anger scores
was not significant, but significant main effects were found for both Gender
($F[1,38]$ = 20.36, $p < .001$) and Testings ($F[2,76]$ = 4.19, $p < .019$). The
highly significant Gender effect indicated that, across the three testings periods, the overall mean S-Anger score for the males (*M* = 19.10) was much
higher than the corresponding overall mean for females (*M* = 12.15). Follow-
up analyses for the total group further revealed that the small increase in

S-Anger from initial testing (M = 13.60) to pretest (M = 15.68) was not statistically significant, nor was the increase from pretest to posttest (M = 17.60); but the four-point increase in S-Anger scores from initial testing to posttest was significant.

When Gender was taken into account in the ANOVA for the T-Anxiety scores, the Testings' main effect ($F[276]$ = 7.38, p < .001) was the only statistically significant finding. Follow-up analyses for the total group indicated that the mean posttest T-Anxiety score (M = 20.62) was significantly higher than either the initial (M = 18.70) or pretest (M = 18.92) T-Anxiety mean, as was found in the Achievement × Testings analysis previously reported. In the corresponding analyses of the T-Anger scores, no statistically significant effects were found. Thus, the study procedures had relatively little impact on anger and anxiety as personality traits, except for a small, but significant, increase in T-Anxiety, which appeared to be due primarily to the higher posttest T-Anxiety scores of the low-achievement students (see Table 10.1).

DISCUSSION AND CONCLUSIONS

Most students who participated in this study had little or no previous experience in rock classification, and did not initially perceive this task as threatening. The significant increase in S-Anxiety from the initial testing baseline to the pretest indicated that a number of students found the rock-classification task to be more difficult, frustrating, and threatening than originally anticipated. In several similar studies, Westerback (1986) and her associates (Westerback, Gonzales, & Primavera, 1984; Westerback et al., 1985) also found that students' anxiety scores were relatively low before they began to study rock classification, but then increased after some experience in working on this task.

Although the classification of rock specimens may seem relatively easy at first, this task can actually be quite difficult. In classifying transitional hand specimens, recognizing characteristics such as grain size and color requires sensitive judgments based on extensive experience. For example, consider the classification of two related igneous rocks, basalt and gabbro, which have similar chemical composition, but differ in grain size. Basalts are volcanic rocks formed at the surface of the earth with fine grains as a result of rapid cooling; gabbros are plutonic rocks formed deep within the earth and are coarse grained due to slow cooling. Although classification of some basalts and gabbros may be quite obvious, transitional rocks of both types are difficult to distinguish in hand specimens.

The pattern of change in the S-Anxiety and S-Anger scores of the high- and low-achievement groups in this study differed across the three Testings periods. Both groups showed a similar increase in S-Anxiety from initial testing to pretest. Low achievers continued to increase in S-Anxiety from pretest to posttest, whereas the S-Anxiety of the high achievers declined to about the same level as in the initial testing period. These results were consistent with findings in previous research on the classification of rocks and minerals, in which higher anxiety was associated with poorer achievement (Westerback et al., 1985).

The S-Anger scores of the low achievers in this study increased significantly from initial testing to pretest, and even more from pretest to posttest, suggesting that the rock-classification task was frustrating for them. In contrast, the S-Anger of the high achievers was essentially unchanged across the three Testings periods. The S-Anxiety and S-Anger scores of the males were significantly higher than those of the females, which appeared to result from the fact that a higher proportion of the males had poor grades. In previous research on students taking required geology or earth science courses, no gender differences were found in either achievement or S-Anxiety (Westerback et al., 1984).

Although the T-Anxiety and T-Anger scores of the participants in this study were relatively stable across the three Testings periods, the T-Anxiety scores of the low-achievement group were slightly elevated on the posttest. The T-Anger scores for both the high- and low-achievement groups remained relatively constant across the three Testing's periods.

Pekrun (1992) observed that when emotions are assessed before, during, and immediately after an achievement situation, anxiety generally drops markedly following the assessment of achievement, whereas anger is only slightly reduced. In the present study, this was true only for the high achievers, whose mean S-Anxiety score was significantly lower after completion of the rock-classification task than during the pretest. The S-Anger scores of the high-achievement group remained at about the same level across the three testings periods. In contrast, the low achievers showed continuing increases in both S-Anxiety and S-Anger from the initial testing period to the posttest.

Although anxiety and anger were both related to Achievement and not related to Gender, males had significantly higher S-Anxiety and S-Anger scores than females. Examination of the individual students' grades indicated that more males than females had poor grades, with males comprising almost two thirds of the low-achievement group. Consistent with their higher S-Anger scores males expressed anger more overtly regarding disappointment about their performance; several expressed anger when filling out the forms, and a few physically slammed their books on the table. Pekrun (1992) observed that anger is associated with a pattern of cognitions indicating high difficulty and low mastery. However, anger and frustration have received scant attention in studies of learning and achievement. In the present study, the geology students who were most angry were those with low achievement.

The significant effects of emotion on learning are increasingly recognized by science educators. The availability of the STPI, which is easy to administer and can be adapted to assess anxiety, anger, and curiosity in classroom settings (see Westerback & Primavera, 1988, 1992), makes it possible for classroom teachers to investigate how different teaching strategies influence these emotions. Using the STPI in combination with standardized achievement measures can also shed light on how emotions influence learning and achievement in science courses.

REFERENCES

Alpert, R., & Haber, R. N. (1960). Anxiety in academic achievement situations. *Journal of Abnormal and Social Psychology, 61*, 207–215.

Brown, C. H. (1938). Emotional reactions before examination: III. Interrelations. *The Journal of Psychology, 5*, 27–31.

Finley, F. N. (1981). A philosophical approach to describing science content: An example from geologic classification. *Science Education, 65*, 514–519.

Finley, F. N., Stewart, J., & Yarroch, W. L. (1982). Teachers' perceptions of important and difficult science content. *Science Education, 66*, 531–538.

Hembree, R. (1988). Correlates, causes, effects, and treatment of test anxiety. *Review of Educational Research, 58*, 47–77.

Maxwell, S. E. & Delaney, H. D. (1990). *Designing experiments and analyzing data: A model comparisons approach.* Belmont, CA: Wadsworth.

Pekrun, R. (1992). The impact of emotions on learning and achievement: Towards a theory of cognitive/motivation mediators. *Applied Psychology: An International Review, 41*, 359–376.

Pinet, R. (1989). Developing models to convey understanding rather than merely knowledge of the methods of science. *Journal of Geological Education, 37*, 332–336.

Sarason, I. G. (1960). Empirical findings and theoretical problems in the use of anxiety scales. *Psychological Bulletin, 57*, 403–415.

Spence, J. T., & Spence, K. W. (1966). The motivational components of manifest anxiety: Drive and drive stimuli. In C. D. Spielberger (Ed.), *Anxiety and behavior* (pp. 291–326). New York: Academic Press.

Spence, K. W. (1958). A theory of emotionally based drive (D) and its relation to performance in simple learning situations. *American Psychologist, 13*, 131–141.

Spielberger, C. D. (1966a). Theory and research on anxiety. In C. D. Spielberger (Ed.), *Anxiety and behavior* (pp. 3–20). New York: Academic Press.

Spielberger, C. D. (1966b). The effects of anxiety on complex learning and academic achievement. In C. D. Spielberger (Ed.), *Anxiety and behavior* (pp. 361–398). New York: Academic Press.

Spielberger, C. D. (1979). *Preliminary manual for the State–Trait Personality Inventory (STPI).* Tampa, FL: Center for Research in Behavioral Medicine and Health Psychology, University of South Florida.

Spielberger, C. D. (1985). Assessment of state and trait anxiety: Conceptual and methodological issues. *The Southern Psychologist, 2*, 6–16.

Spielberger, C. D. (1988). *Professional manual for the State–Trait Anger Expression Inventory (STAXI)* (Res. ed.). Odessa, FL: Psychological Assessment Resources.

Spielberger, C. D., Johnson, E. H., Russell, S. F., Crane, R. J., Jacobs, G. A., & Worden, T. J. (1985). The experience and expression of anger: Construction and validation of an anger expression scale. In M. A. Chesney & R. H. Rosenman (Eds.), *Anger and hostility in cardiovascular and behavioral disorders* (pp. 5–30). New York: Hemisphere/McGraw Hill.

Spielberger, C. D., Krasner, S. S., & Solomon, E. P. (1988). The experience, expression and control of anger. In M. P. Janisse (Ed.), *Health psychology: Individual differences and stress* (pp. 89–108). New York: Springer-Verlag.

Stewart, J., & Atkin, J. A. (1982). Information processing psychology: A promising paradigm for research in science teaching. *Journal of Research in Science Teaching, 19,* 321–332.

Taylor, J. A. (1956). Drive theory and manifest anxiety. *Psychological Bulletin, 53,* 303–320.

Watson, F. G. (1988). General education in the sciences in transition. *Journal of College Science Teaching, 17,* 432–483.

Westerback, M. E. (1986, March). *Anxiety levels of college students taking required science courses.* Paper presented at the National Association for Research in Science Teaching, San Francisco, CA.

Westerback, M. E., & Azer, N. (1991). Realistic expectations for rock identification. *Journal of Geological Education, 39,* 53–79.

Westerback, M. E., Gonzalez, C., & Primavera, L. H. (1984). Comparison of anxiety levels of students in introductory earth science and geology courses. *Journal of Research in Science Teaching, 21,* 913–929.

Westerback, M. E., Gonzalez, C., & Primavera, L. H. (1985). Comparison of preservice elementary teachers' anxiety about teaching students to identify minerals and rocks and students' anxiety about identification of minerals and rocks. *Journal of Research in Science Teaching, 22,* 53–79.

Westerback, M. E., & Primavera, L. H. (1988). Anxiety about science and science teaching. In C. D. Spielberger, & J. N. Butcher (Eds.), *Advances in personality assessment* (pp. 173–202). Hillsdale, NJ: Lawrence Erlbaum Associates.

Westerback, M. E., & Primavera, L. H. (1992). *A science educator's and a psychologist's perspective on research about science anxiety.* Long Island University, Department of Geology. (ERIC Document Reproduction Service No. ED 357 977)

11

Relations of Anger Expression to Depression and Blood Pressure in High School Students

Frances M. Culbertson
Madison Medical Center, Madison, Wisconsin, USA

Charles D. Spielberger
University of South Florida, Tampa, USA

Abstract *This study examined relations between anger expression, anger control, and depression and blood pressure, taking gender and family constellation into account. The participants were 179 high school students in a midwestern U.S. school district. Anger and depression were assessed by Spielberger's Anger expression (AX) scale and the Reynolds Adolescent Depression Scale (RADS). Anger expression (AX/Out) scores of participants in this study were slightly higher and suppressed anger (AX/In) scores were somewhat lower than those reported for normative samples of high school students. AX/In scores were more strongly and positively related to depression than AX/Out scores; anger control (AX/Con) scores were inversely related to depression. Systolic blood pressure (SBP) was negatively related to AX/In and positively related to AX/Con. Males and females did not differ on the anger measures, but females had substantially higher RADS scores than the males. Students from single-parent families had higher AX/Out and depression scores than those from intact families. It was concluded that personality and emotional concerns should be given as much attention as academic factors in the "learning world" of high school students.*

Anger has been conceptualized in many ways: as a response to frustration, a strong feeling aroused by a real or supposed wrong, a call for help, a disruptive emotion in interpersonal relationships, and a significant determinant of delinquency, neurosis, and depressive psychopathology (Weiner, 1982). Psychoanalytic theory and case studies have also strongly supported the presence of a relationship between anger and depression (Alexander & French, 1948). Redl and Wineman (1951) considered anger and aggression to be general manifestations of intrapsychic conflict. According to Rothenberg (1971), anger

The authors gratefully acknowledge the assistance of Jayne Roth Mohoney, Ed.S. (School Psychology) for her help in collecting the data for this study. The authors are also indebted to Roger L. Brown, Ph.D., and Laura Wong, Computer Associate, for their expert contributions to the data analyses.

contributes to communication problems, disturbed interpersonal relationships, and psychosomatic disorders, and is a critical factor in motivating violent behavior.

Clinical and personality psychology have much to gain from a clearer understanding of the nature of anger and its consequences. Konecni (1975a, 1975b) conceptualized anger as an affective response to stress that is comprised of high levels of both emotional and physiological arousal. Spielberger (1988) defined *anger* as a psychobiological emotional state that varies in intensity from feelings of mild irritation and annoyance to intense fury and rage. Novaco (1975) noted that anger is a major component of aggressive behavior. In addition to its role as the motivator of aggression and violent behavior, anger directed inward (i.e., toward the self) results in low self-esteem and depression (Weiner, 1982).

Conceptualizing anger simply as an aspect of aggression overlooks the fact that, even when angry feelings do not lead to aggressive behavior or depression, such feelings may nevertheless have detrimental physical and psychosomatic effects. For example, recent research has linked anger and hostility to cardiovascular disorders (Chesney & Rosenman, 1985; Spielberger & London, 1982). Spielberger and his colleagues (Crane, 1981; Spielberger, Jacobs, Russell, & Crane, 1983; Spielberger et al., 1985; Spielberger & London, 1990) also reported that suppressed anger contributes to elevated blood pressure (BP) and hypertension.

STATE–TRAIT ANGER AND ANGER EXPRESSION

There is considerable conceptual ambiguity and overlap in the definitions of *anger, hostility,* and *aggression,* which Spielberger et al. (1983) referred to, collectively, as the *AHA! Syndrome.* Conceived as "more fundamental and less complex than hostility and aggression" (p. 166), *anger* is defined as both "an emotional state that varies in intensity, and as a relatively stable personality trait" (p. 166). State anger (S-Anger) ". . . consists of feelings that vary in intensity, from mild irritation or annoyance to intense fury and rage" (Spielberger et al., 1983, p. 160). Situations that are perceived as involving injustice, or in which one is treated badly or unfairly, typically evoke S-Anger reactions.

Trait anger (T-Anger) is defined in terms of anger-proneness (i.e., individual differences in the disposition to experience S-Anger more or less frequently over time; Spielberger, 1988). Persons high in T-Anger are more likely than those low in this trait to respond with elevations in S-Anger to a wide range of situations perceived as frustrating, irritating, or annoying. They are also more likely to experience "more intense elevations in S-Anger whenever annoying or frustrating conditions are encountered" (Spielberger et al., 1983, p. 167).

Most measures of anger tend to confound the experience of anger with aggressive behavior and anger-provoking situations, and fail to distinguish between feelings of anger as an emotional state and individual differences in anger-proneness as a personality trait. The state–trait conceptualization of anger has stimulated and guided the development of the State–Trait Anger Scale (STAS), which provides objective self-report measures of S-Anger and T-Anger (Spielberger et al., 1983). Unlike other measures of the components of the AHA! Syndrome, the STAS does not confound anger with anger-provoking situations, nor with hostility or aggressive behaviors. Normed and validated on high school and college students, naval recruits, and working adults, the STAS S-Anger and T-Anger scales have excellent internal consistency (high alpha coefficients).

Spielberger et al. (1985) noted that: "The expression of anger must be distinguished conceptually and empirically from the experience of anger as an emotional state (S-Anger) and individual differences in anger as a personality trait (T-Anger)" (p. 11). The Anger expression (AX) scale was constructed by Spielberger (1988) and his colleagues (Spielberger et al., 1985) to assess how people generally react or behave in expressing and controlling their angry feelings. When angry or furious, people differ in the extent to which they overtly and directly express their anger (e.g., "I say nasty things," "I lose my temper"), and in how often angry feelings are held in or suppressed (e.g., "I boil inside, but don't show it"). They also differ in the extent to which they endeavor to control their anger (e.g., "I keep my cool," "I control my angry feelings").

RESEARCH ON ANGER IN CHILDREN AND ADOLESCENTS

The literature on anger in children and adolescents reflects a paucity of research, which is due, in part, to the lack of adequate measures for assessing anger. As a research area, aggressive behavior has been easier to quantify. Consequently, anger is often considered as part of an aggressive reaction, culminating in impulsivity, as well as verbal and physical aggression. In studies of such aggressive behavior, anger is not generally assessed as an independent construct.

Rule and Nesdale (1976) observed that the arousal of anger in children motivates aggressive behavior toward the perceived source of provocation. Anger directed toward the self is closely associated with the suicidal acts of children, and is especially important as the motivating component of suicide for adolescents 12–20 years of age (Hussain & Vandiver, 1984). In residential facilities for children and youth, disordered and aggressive behavior, often motivated by intense anger, is one of the most common referral problems. Moreover, aggressive behavior is also cited as the most frequent reason for referral of children to outpatient mental health clinics (Patterson, 1974, 1975).

The expression of anger as an emotional response is instantly alerting and disturbing to all who spend time in school environments. When expressed in aggressive behavior, anger is frightening to students, teachers, and administrators, no matter where it occurs—be it in the classroom, the hallways, the playground, or the gymnasium (Feshbach, 1983). School personnel generally view intense anger as the most significant underlying element in inappropriate and disruptive aggressive behavior and violence (Halatyn, 1981; U.S. Department of Health, Education and Welfare, 1978).

Unfortunately, the study of anger in school-age children and adolescents has received relatively little attention. When anger has been assessed, it has usually been done with projective techniques, such as the Draw-A-Person Test (Koppitz, 1968; Machover, 1949) and the Children's Apperception Test (Bellak, 1975)—measures plagued with subjectivity, low reliability, and limited validity. Most of the available objective measures of the AHA! Syndrome are more closely associated with hostility and aggression than with anger (e.g., Cook & Medley, 1954; Siegal, 1956). Moreover, these measures are at best only marginally applicable to adolescents.

In developing the STAS and the AX scale, Spielberger et al. (1983, 1985) included junior and senior high school students in standardizing these scales. However, there are as yet relatively few studies in which these instruments have been used with school-age adolescents. In an exploratory study of S-Anger and T-Anger in midwestern high school students, Culbertson (1991) found that S-Anger was more important than T-Anger in assessing the school-related angry feelings of students assigned to regular and special education classes. It is of interest to note that Culbertson's study took place during a total school assessment period.

The items on the S-Anger scale, on which the special education students had significantly higher scores, suggested that they tended to experience more intense feelings of anger, which could lead to the expression of physically aggressive behavior directed toward other persons or objects in the environment. The T-Anger items, on which the special education students had higher scores in Culbertson's exploratory study, revealed a strong disposition to feel angry when negatively evaluated by teachers or other students. Academic assessment is no doubt frustrating and painful for special education students, and therefore more likely to provoke significant elevations in S-Anger.

This chapter reports findings from a study of anger expression in high school students. Relationships between different modes of anger expression and control with measures of depression and BP were examined. The relations of gender and family constellation to anger expression and control and depression measures were also investigated.

METHOD

The participants in this study were 179 high school students (85 males, 94 females) enrolled in regular 9th- and 11-grade classes in a midwestern U.S. public school district. Teacher cooperation for the participation of these students in the study was obtained during an inservice training program 2 weeks prior to the time the data were collected.

Personality Measures

The two personality measures used in this study were the Anger Expression (AX) scale (Spielberger et al., 1985) and the Reynolds Adolescent Depression

Scale (RADS; Reynolds, 1987). The AX scale is a 24-item self-report inventory composed of three 8-item, factorially derived subscales that assess overt expression (AX/Out), suppression (AX/In), and control (AX/Con) of angry feelings. The following standard instructions for the AX scale are printed on the test form:

> Everyone feels angry or furious from time to time, but people differ in the ways that they react when they are angry. A number of statements are listed which people have used to describe their reactions when they feel angry or furious. Read each statement and then indicate how often you generally react or behave in the manner described.

Representative examples of the items in the AX/In, AX/Out, and AX/Con scales are: "I am boiling on the inside but I don't show it," "I express my anger," and "I control my temper." All 24 AX scale items are rated on a 4-point frequency scale with the following response alternatives: *almost never, sometimes, often,* and *almost always.*

The RADS was developed by Reynolds (1987) to identify and assess clinically relevant levels of depressive symptomatology experienced in school settings by adolescents ages 13–18 years. This 30-item, self-report scale assesses how often students have depressive thoughts and feelings (e.g., a representative RADS item is "I thought about writing a will"). Students are instructed to indicate how often they have experienced a particular thought or feeling in the past month by rating themselves on a 7-point Likert-type scale, with response choices ranging from *I never had this thought* to *almost every day.*

Procedure

The AX scale and the RADS were administered with standard instructions to students in Grades 9 and 11 attending regular public school classes. The tests were given during an academic assessment period that occurred in the middle of the school year. BP was taken by the school nurse during a physical education lecture period in which there was a discussion of BP. BP was measured with an automatic monitor, similar to the one used in previous research by Spielberger et al. (1985).

STUDY RESULTS

The mean and standard deviations for the AX/In, AX/Out, and AX/Con subscales are reported in Table 11.1, in which they are compared with the normative samples of male and female high school students reported by Spielberger et al. (1985). The AX/Out scores were slightly higher for the students in the present study than in the normative samples, whereas the AX/In scores were higher than those of the students in the present study. However, most of these differences were only one point or less, except for the AX/In scores of the males in the normative sample, which were two points higher than those of the males in the present study.

Table 11.1 Means and standard deviations of scores on the Anger Expression (AX) subscales for male and female high school students

AX scale	Present study		AX scale norms	
	Males ($N = 85$)	Females ($N = 94$)	Males ($N = 635$)	Females ($N = 482$)
AX/In				
M	16.87	17.30	18.92	18.03
SD	4.68	4.33	5.92	5.25
AX/Out				
M	17.82	17.53	16.65	16.73
SD	4.25	4.54	4.17	4.34
AX/Con				
M	23.50	23.49	—	—
SD	4.42	4.78	—	—

Correlations of the AX subscales with RADS scores, and with systolic blood pressure (SBP) and diastolic blood pressure (DBP), are reported in Table 11.2. The correlations of all three AX subscales with the RADS were highly significant ($p < .001$), demonstrating a complex relationship among the various facets of anger with depression. The correlation of the AX/In subscale with the RADS ($r = .53$) was substantially higher than the correlations of the AX/In scores with the AX/Out ($r = .27$) and AX/Con ($r = .27$) subscales. These findings indicate that higher levels of depression were more strongly associated with anger-in than with anger-out. Depression was also associated with lower levels of anger control.

AX/In scores correlated negatively with both SBP ($r = -.13$) and DBP ($r = -.10$), but only the correlation with SBP was statistically significant ($p < .05$). The positive correlation of AX/Con with SBP ($r = .14$) was significant ($p < .02$); the AX/Con correlation with DBP ($r = .12$) approached significance ($p < .06$). The very small correlations of the AX/Out scores with SBP and DBP (both $r = -.07$) were not significant. The findings in this study of small negative correlations of AX/In scores with SBP differ substantially from the results reported by Spielberger et al. (1985), who found a moderate

Table 11.2 Correlations of Anger Expression (AX) subscales with the Reynolds Adolescent Depression Scale (RADS) and with SBP and DBP for high school students

AX scale	RADS	SBP	DBP
AX/In	.53***	−.13*	−.10
AX/Out	.27***	−.07	−.07
AX/Con	−.27***	.14*	.12

*$p < .05$. ***$p < .001$.

Table 11.3 Means and standard deviations of the Anger Expression (AX) subscale and RADS depression scores by gender and family constellation

	Gender			Family constellation		
Scales	M (N = 85)	F (N = 94)	t test	Intact (N = 134)	Other (N = 45)	t test
AX/In						
M	16.87	17.30	−0.66	16.96	17.38	−0.57
SD	4.68	4.33		4.31	4.85	
AX/Out						
M	17.82	17.53	0.47	17.10	18.81	−2.61*
SD	4.25	4.54		4.15	4.74	
AX/Con						
M	23.50	23.49	0.32	23.83	22.95	−1.74
SD	4.42	4.78		4.45	4.82	
Depression						
M	66.85	73.11	−3.98***	68.7	73.3	2.56**
SD	9.88	11.13		10.9	10.7	

*$p < .05$. **$p < .01$. ***$p < .001$.

positive correlation between AX/In and SBP of .50, which was highly significant ($p < .001$).

The means and standard deviations of the RADS and the AX subscale scores for males and females are reported in Table 11.3. The females had substantially higher depression scores than the males, and this difference was highly significant ($p < .001$). It can be noted in Table 11.3 that the scores on the AX subscales were quite similar for both sexes; the results of t tests confirmed that the male and female students did not differ in their anger scores.

Most of the students in this study came from intact families ($n = 134$). The 45 students with parents who were widowed, separated, or divorced, or who resided in one-parent homes, were combined to form a single group with other-than-intact families. The mean AX/Out and depression scores for students in the intact family group are compared with students in other-than-intact family arrangements in Table 11.3. The students from the nonintact families had significantly higher scores than the students from the intact families group on the AX/Out subscale ($p < .05$), and on the RADS measure of depressive symptomatology ($p < .01$). No significant differences were found in the AX/In and AX/Con scores for students from intact and nonintact families.

DISCUSSION AND CONCLUSIONS

This study investigated relations between measures of anger expression and control with depression and BP. Relations of gender and family constellation to anger and depression were also evaluated. The reliability and internal consistency of the AX subscales were quite good, with alpha coefficients of .75 or higher and no subscale item remainder correlation of less than .50.

The means and standard deviations for the AX/Out and AX/Con subscales of the midwestern high school students in the present study were quite similar to those reported by Spielberger et al. (1985) for the normative samples of high school students from the southern part of the United States. The AX/Out scores in the present study were slightly higher, whereas the AX/In scores were somewhat lower than those reported for the Spielberger et al. (1985) normative samples.

The higher AX/In scores of the students in the normative sample, especially those of the males, may be due, in part, to the fact that these students were enrolled in a noncollege-preparatory curriculum. Approximately 30% of the normative sample was composed of African-American students—a much higher proportion than in the midwestern sample of the present study. The noncollege-bound minority students in the normative sample, most from low-income families, might be expected to experience more frustration, which would result in higher AX/In scores. However, the AX/Out scores of the students in the normative sample were slightly lower, perhaps reflecting a school environment that was less accepting of the overt expression of anger.

The finding that suppressed anger was moderately related to depression was consistent with psychoanalytic theory and case studies (Alexander & French, 1948). No gender differences were found in the anger measures, but females scored substantially higher on the RADS measure of depressive symptomatology than the males, which was also consistent with the gender differences reported by Culbertson (1991) for adults. The findings that the RADS and AX/Out scores of students from nonintact families were significantly higher than those of the students from intact families were also consistent with the probability that adolescents from single-parent homes would experience more frustration and conflict. Although angry feelings can motivate a person to be assertive and push forward in overcoming obstacles, thus leading to positive outcomes, such feelings are often linked to psychopathology and aggressive acting-out behaviors. Also, as previously noted, Hussain and Vandiver (1984) listed anger and despair as affective states that were most often found in suicidal children.

The finding in this study that the female students had higher RADS scores than the males was consistent with Goleman's (1990) *New York Times* article, which concluded that: ". . . girls as young as 12 are more prone to depression than boys." Goleman reported the following symptoms to be more common for girls than boys: "body image distortion, loss of appetite and weight, and lack of satisfaction about herself, life at school and at home and social life" (p. B7). Among the more common symptoms reported for boys were irritability and social withdrawal, which appear to be consistent with the higher suppressed anger scores of the boys in the present study.

The results of this study suggest that school personnel may need to attend as closely to high school students' anger and depressive feelings as they do to their academic needs. Adolescents who are depressed, angry, and generally upset are not likely to be either attentive or receptive in learning situations.

These findings also suggest that the relationship of anger and depressive symptomatology to BP merits additional research to determine whether depression and anger in adolescents may contribute to hypertension and cardiovascular disorders in later life.

REFERENCES

Alexander, F. G., & French, T. M. (Eds.). (1948). *Studies in psychosomatic medicine. An approach to the cause and treatment of vegetative disturbances.* New York: Ronald Press.

Bellak, L. (1975). *The TAT, CAT, SAT in clinical use* (3rd ed.). New York: Grune & Stratton.

Chesney, M. A., & Rosenman, R. H. (Eds.). (1985). *Anger and hostility in cardiovascular and behavioral disorders.* New York: Hemisphere/McGraw-Hill.

Cook, W. W., & Medley, D. M. (1954). Proposed hostility and pharesaic-virtue scales for the MMPI. *The Journal of Applied Psychology, 38,* 414–418.

Crane, R. S. (1981). *The role of anger, hostility, and aggression in essential hypertension.* Unpublished doctoral dissertation, University of South Florida, Tampa, FL.

Culbertson, R. M. (1991, August). *Mental health of women: International perspectives.* Presidential Address, APA, Division 12, Section 4 (Clinical Psychology of Women). Presented at the annual meeting of the American Psychological Association, San Francisco, CA.

Feshbach, N. D. (1983). Learning to care: A positive approach to child training and discipline. *Journal of Clinical Child Psychology, 12,* 266.

Goleman, D. (1990, May 10). Why girls are prone to depression. *New York Times,* p. B7.

Halatyn, T. V. (1981, July). *Preliminary results of the statewide SB-72 survey of school crime and associated programs and strategies.* Paper presented at the Educational Leadership Seminar, San Jose, CA.

Hussain, A., & Vandiver, M. S. (1984). *Suicide in children and adolescents.* New York: S. P. Medical & Scientific Books.

Konecni, V. J. (1975a). Annoyance, type, and duration of past annoyance activity and aggression: The "cathartic effect." *Journal of Experimental Psychology, 104,* 76–102.

Konecni, V. J. (1975b). The mediation of aggressive behavior: Arousal level versus anger and cognitive labeling. *Journal of Personality and Social Psychology, 2,* 706–712.

Koppitz, E. M. (1968). *Psychological evaluation of children's human figure drawings.* New York: Grune & Stratton.

Machover, K. (1949). *Personality projection in the drawings of the human figure.* Springfield, IL: Charles C Thomas.

Novaco, R. W. (1975). *Anger control: The development and evaluation of an experimental treatment.* Lexington, MA: Lexington Books/D.C. Heath.

Patterson, G. R. (1974). Intervention for boys with conduct problems: Multiple settings, treatment and criteria. *Journal of Consulting and Clinical Psychology, 42,* 471–481.

Patterson, G. R. (1975). The coercive child: Architect or victim of a coercive system? In L. Hamerlynck, L. C. Hendy, & E. J. Mash (Eds.), *Behavior modification and families: I. Theory and research. II. Applications and developments.* New York: Brunner/Mazel.

Redl, F., & Wineman, D. (1951). *Children who hate.* New York: The Free Press.

Reynolds, W. M. (1987). *Reynolds Adolescent Depression Scale: Professional manual.* Odessa, FL: Psychological Assessment Resources.

Rothenberg, A. (1971). On anger. *American Journal of Psychiatry, 128,* 454–460.

Rule, B. G., & Nesdale, A. R. (1976). Emotional arousal and aggressive behavior. *Psychological Bulletin, 83,* 851–863.

Siegal, S. (1956). The relationship of hostility to authoritarianism. *Journal of Abnormal and Social Psychology, 52,* 368–373.

Spielberger, C. D. (1988). *Professional manual for the State–Trait Anger Expression Inventory (STAXI)* (Res. ed.). Odessa, FL: Psychological Assessment Resources.

Spielberger, C. D., Jacobs, G., Russell, S., & Crane, R. S. (1983). Assessment of anger: The State–Trait Anger Scale. In J. N. Butcher & C. D. Spielberger (Eds.), *Advances in personality assessment* (Vol. 2, pp. 161–189). Hillsdale, NJ: Lawrence Erlbaum Associates.

Spielberger, C. D., Johnson, E. H., Russell, S. F., Crane, R. S., Jacobs, G. A., & Worden, T. J. (1985). The experience and expression of anger: Construction and validation of an anger expression scale. In M. A. Chesney & R. H. Rosenman (Eds.), *Anger and hostility in cardiovascular and behavioral disorders* (pp. 5–30). New York: Hemisphere/McGraw-Hill.

Spielberger, C. D., & London, P. (1982). Rage boomerangs. *American Health, 1,* 52–56.

Spielberger, C. D., & London, P. (1990). Blood pressure and injustice. *Psychology Today,* pp. 48–52.

U.S. Department of Health, Education and Welfare (1978). *Violent schools-safe schools: The safe school study report to Congress.* Washington, DC: U.S. Government Printing Office.

Weiner, I. B. (1982). *Child and adolescent psychopathology.* New York: Wiley.

IV

STRESS, EMOTIONS, AND DISEASE

12

Anger Suppression, Cynical Distrust, and Hostility: Implications for Coronary Heart Disease

Esther R. Greenglass
York University, Toronto, Ontario, Canada

Abstract *Research findings document the role of anger and hostility as significant factors in understanding the development of coronary heart disease (CHD). Recent research has also shown that a high potential for anger and hostility, in combination with an inability to deal constructively with one's anger, may contribute to the progression of CHD. The data reported in this chapter demonstrate the psychological implications of the simultaneous experience of high hostility and distrust, and the suppression or control of such emotions. Anger may be managed by controlling anger-out, holding anger in (suppression), and through supportive relationships. When individuals are able to discuss the source of their anger with others, they appear to be more able to cope with annoying obstacles, thus lowering the intensity of their anger and hostility. However, individuals who are highly cynical and hostile generally report less familial and interpersonal support, and therefore are less likely to benefit from the health-related benefits of social support. A comprehensive theory of CHD development requires the integration of social, psychological, and physiological variables with coping theory within a dynamic framework.*

An examination of the relationship between coronary heart disease (CHD) and psychosocial factors reveals significant relationships among emotional factors, coping, and illness. Moreover, although originally researchers based their theories of the etiology of disease primarily on physiological factors, there is increasing recognition of the role of emotion and its management in the onset and progression of disease, including CHD.

ANGER, HOSTILITY, AND CHD

Previous research has shown that the Type-A Behavior Pattern (TABP) predicts CHD independently of traditional risk factors in a variety of research

Grateful acknowledgment is due to Imperial Oil Ltd. and York University for supporting this research.

settings. Moreover, the Type-A construct is composed of many components, not all of which predict CHD. There is considerable evidence for a relationship between anger/hostility and CHD incidence and mortality—findings that have been reported in several studies (Barefoot, Dahlstrom, & Williams, 1983; Barefoot, Williams, Dahlstrom, & Dodge, 1987; Shekelle, Gale, Ostfeld, & Paul, 1983). Although research has established hostility and anger as predictors of CHD, it is also important to specify the particular dimensions of the hostility and anger that relate to illness.

The type of hostility discussed by Williams et al. (1980) and others derives from the Cook–Medley Hostility (Ho) scale (Cook & Medley, 1954), which reflects an attitude characterized by suspiciousness and distrust. Originally, Cook and Medley described individuals scoring high on this scale as having chronic rage and anger, and having little confidence in others. Given the importance of Cook–Medley hostility as a predictor of CHD progression, as seen in several research studies (e.g., Barefoot et al., 1983; Blumenthal, Barefoot, Burg, & Williams, 1987; Shekelle et al., 1983; Williams et al., 1980), later research has centered around analyzing the structure of the Ho scale and establishing relationships between various aspects of hostility and CHD.

In a factor-analytic study of the structure of the Cook–Medley Ho scale with Canadian undergraduates as subjects, Greenglass and Julkunen (1989) reported results that yielded a general factor relating to the dimensions of Distrust and Cynicism. A nine-item subscale (alpha = .75), consisting of items with the highest loadings on this factor, was interpreted as a measure of Cynical Distrust. The Cynical Distrust Scale items are listed here:

1. No one cares much what happens to you.
2. It is safer to trust nobody.
3. I think most people would lie to get ahead.
4. Most people inwardly dislike putting themselves out to help other people.
5. Most people will use somewhat unfair means to gain profit or an advantage rather than lose it.
6. Most people are honest chiefly through fear of being caught.
7. I commonly wonder what hidden reason another person may have for doing something nice to me.
8. Most people make friends because friends are likely to be useful to them.
9. When a man is with a woman, he is usually thinking about things related to her sex.

Greenglass and Julkunen reported highly significant correlations between this Cynical Distrust factor, as measured by a new nine-item scale, and independent measures of Cynicism (positive) and Trust (negative). Given the highly positive and significant correlation ($r = 0.79$) between Cynical Distrust and Cook–Medley Ho scores, Greenglass and Julkunen (1991) concluded that Cynicism and Distrust are the central dimensions assessed by the Cook–Medley Ho scale. Moreover, in light of the significant negative correlations between Cynical Distrust, as measured by this new nine-item scale, and scores on the Interpersonal Relationship Scale (IRS; Schlein, Guerney, & Stover, 1977), a measure of trust or intimacy in close relationships, individuals high on Cynical Distrust are not likely to trust even someone close to them.

ANGER MANAGEMENT AND ILLNESS

Additional data based on Finnish undergraduates provide further evidence for the construct validity of the nine-item Cynical Distrust scale (Greenglass & Julkunen, 1989). Greenglass and Julkunen (1991) reported significant positive correlations between Cynical Distrust scores and scores on a Cynicism scale (Jackson & Messick, 1970), as well as negative correlations between Cynical Distrust and Trust scores (as measured by scores on the IRS). Taken together, the data suggest that cynically distrusting attitudes are associated with an interpersonal deficit that may result in these individuals being less receptive to social support.

According to Smith and Frohm (1985), individuals scoring high on the Ho scale are likely to experience anger often, to be bitter and resentful, and to view others with distrust. They also suggested that the scale should be seen as one of Cynical Hostility. Costa, Zonderman, McCrae, & Williams (1986) also argued that the primary component of the Ho scale is Cynicism.

Studies have found that cynically hostile and angry people experience greater stress and interpersonal conflict in several domains of their lives. Individuals high on hostility report greater interpersonal conflict and less social support in general, in their familial relationships, and in the workplace (Houston & Kelly, 1989; Smith, Pope, Sanders, Allred, & O'Keeffe, 1988). Cynically hostile individuals have negative interpersonal expectations that contribute to an unsupportive and stressful interpersonal environment. One hypothesis is that highly hostile individuals respond to interpersonal stressors with increased levels of physiological arousal, which, in turn, could lead to illness (Smith & Pope, 1990).

Additional data suggest that the way individuals manage their hostility and anger may mediate the relationship between anger/hostility and CHD. Although culture may evoke anger in individuals in terms of obstacles to gratification, at the same time they are taught to restrain their anger. People learn an association between anxiety and anger because aggressive behaviors are often punished. Anger can be managed in three possible ways: keeping anger in ("anger-in"), expressing anger outwardly ("anger-out"), and discussing angry feelings with others. Use of one mode in anger management does not preclude use of another. However, through controlled research design, one can delineate psychological, physiological, and health-related consequences associated with each.

Haynes, Feinleib, and Kannel (1980) investigated these three modes of anger management in relation to CHD. Results show that low anger-out was associated with greater CHD in men, especially in the 55–64 age group. Low anger-out, low scores on discussing anger, and high anger-in were associated with greater CHD among employed women under 65 years of age. Taken together, these data suggest that the inhibition of angry feelings may increase the risk for CHD.

Suppressed anger has been found to be associated with sustained blood pressure (BP) elevation and hypertension (Esler et al., 1977; Gambaro & Rabin, 1969; Hokanson & Shelter, 1961). Also, in a study comparing scores on anger measures in hypertensive versus normotensive subjects, Hartfield (1985) found that hypertensive subjects experienced longer lasting anger of greater intensity, felt more physical symptoms during anger episodes, and expressed less anger than normotensive subjects. Hypertensive subjects also used more distancing, self-control, and escape-avoidance coping than normotensive subjects, who were more likely to confront the situation and seek social support when presented with an anger-provoking situation.

Schneider, Egan, Johnson, Drobny, and Julius (1986) administered the State–Trait Personality Inventory (STPI; Spielberger et al., 1979), the State Angry Reaction Scale (Johnson, 1984), and the Anger Expression (AX) scale (Spielberger et al., 1985) to borderline hypertensive subjects who were instructed to record their own BPs for 1 week. Subjects whose BPs were elevated during the 7-day monitoring period had higher suppressed anger (AX/In) scores and were more likely to report having more intense angry reactions to time pressure and evaluative and threatening situations. In general, data suggest that hypertension is related to frequent suppression of intense anger. Not only are hypertensive individuals more likely to respond more frequently with intense anger when evaluated negatively, they are also more likely to use anger-in as a coping technique.

ANGER MANAGEMENT, HOSTILITY, AND ILLNESS

Further research suggests that a more comprehensive view of the precursors of CHD may involve the simultaneous consideration of a high degree of potential for hostility along with strategies individuals use to manage their anger. For example, Dembroski, MacDougal, Williams, Haney, and Blumenthal (1985) examined the interaction between anger-in (an unwillingness to express anger and a tendency to withhold its expression) and the potential for hostility, and their relationship to CHD severity in a group of patients with coronary atherosclerosis. Their data indicated that potential for hostility was associated with disease end points, or pathology, only for patients who were also high on the anger-in dimension. Their definition of *hostility* was that of a relatively stable predisposition to experience various combinations of anger, irritation, disgust, annoyance, contempt, and resentment, which may or may not be associated with overt behavior directed toward the source of frustration.

More recently, Julkunen, Salonen, Kaplan, & Salonen (1992), in their prospective study of middle-aged Finnish men, examined the role of different aspects of hostility as predictors of the progression of carotid atherosclerosis (PCA) during a 2-year follow-up. One of the measures of hostility employed here was the Cynical Distrust scale (Greenglass & Julkunen, 1989) discussed earlier. Anger control was simultaneously examined with various measures of hostility in relation to PCA. Anger control is characterized by an individual's efforts to strictly control angry feelings and reactions, avoiding open expression of irritation or aggression (Spielberger et al., 1985). Results show that, in addition to previously established risk factors (i.e., high serum cholesterol concentration, smoking, and age), three psychological variables—Cynical Distrust, Impatience/Irritability, and Anger Control—contributed significantly to a multiple regression that explained nearly one third of the PCA variation. Further results in the same study confirm the hypothesis that a high level of hostility in combination with high anger suppression would predict PCA.

Julkunen et al. found a fourfold accelerated PCA in groups of subjects that were high on anger control and high on any of the three measures of hostility or anger they used, including Cynical Distrust, Anger-Out, and Impatience/Irritability. Contrary to expectations, anger control seemed to be more important than anger-in as a modifier of the impact of other aspects of hostility on atherosclerosis. Thus, an individual would appear to have a greater predisposition to develop atherosclerosis when he or she is investing a great deal of energy in monitoring and preventing the experience of anger, which, at the same time, is likely driving intense feelings of cynicism, suspicion, and distrust of those around him or her.

Anger Control as a Moderator

In discussing the effects of anger control, Julkunen et al. (1992) raised the possibility that anger control could reflect repression or lack of insight in dealing with one's angry feelings. They raised the question of whether anger control in the present context represents a true capability to cope constructively with angry feelings, or is instead a function of social desirability, indicating the "expected" way to deal with anger in society.

Taken together, these data suggest that a high potential for hostility and anger, in combination with an inability to deal constructively with one's anger/hostility, may contribute to the progression of CHD. In this context, an inability to deal effectively with anger may take the form of anger-in or anger control. When individuals are able to discuss the source of their anger and frustration with others, they may be more able to modify annoying obstacles, thus potentially lowering their anger and hostility. Supportive networks may also offer individuals necessary information, practical advice, and morale boosting, all of which can be employed to modify individuals' frustrations, thus lessening their angry feelings.

MODERATING EFFECTS OF SOCIAL SUPPORT

Research evidence documents the health-damaging effects of isolation from social support. For example, Kaplan, Berkman, and Breslow (1983) followed several thousand healthy California residents for several years. Those with fewer social ties had higher death rates than those who were more closely connected to other people and to groups. Considerable research has shown that social attachments can influence well-being by serving as a buffer against stress or by directly improving well-being (Cohen & Wills, 1985; Greenglass, 1993; Hobfoll, 1986). Direct effects of social support occur when negative correlations are reported between social support and stress/strain. The buffering hypothesis states that stress may affect some people adversely, but that those with social support resources are resistant to the deleterious effects of stressful events. The evidence for the buffering or moderating effects of social support is mixed (Himle, Jayaratne, & Thyness, 1991), as reported in a number of research studies among a variety of occupations in various settings. In one review (LaRocco, House, & French, 1980), evidence was cited for a buffering effect of social support on problems created by occupational stress. However, in other studies, no buffering effects of social support on work-related stress have been found (Himle, Jayaratne, & Thyness, 1989; Shinn, Rosario, March, & Chestnut, 1984).

Increasingly, evidence is showing specific buffering effects of different types of social support. For example, in one study, which examined burnout among social workers, Himle et al. (1991) reported that informational and instrumental support provided by supervisors and co-workers had buffering effects on burnout related to work stress. It is likely that the possession of knowledge gained from informational support, and significant help to complete a task gained from instrumental support, may have resulted in social workers' perceptions that they had greater control over their job situation. As a result, they experienced less burnout. Additional data have indicated that emotional support can also buffer burnout in teachers (Greenglass, Fiksenbaum, & Burke, 1996). *Emotional support* refers to the provision of morale boosting, listening to one's problems, and being a confidant.

Social Support, Anger, and Hostility

Additional research findings have indicated that social support can function as a buffer of anger in managerial women (Greenglass, 1987). These results parallel other work that has reported higher support to be associated with lower hostility and anger (Smith & Pope, 1990; Thomas, 1989). Other findings have indicated that the higher the reported family support perceived by managers, the less they used anger-in to manage their anger (Greenglass, 1991). High Ho scores have been found to be related to low reported quality of social support (Barefoot et al., 1983).

One hypothesis advanced in this regard (the Transactional hypothesis) is that hostile or angry individuals expect the worst from others, and thus behave in an antagonistic manner, which, in turn, elicits unfriendly responses from others. This reinforces the original expectation, thus producing a pattern of escalating antagonism. Thus, the hostile individual likely elicits high levels of conflict while undermining potential sources of social support (Smith & Pope, 1990). As a result, the hostile individual is reducing the possibility of receiving information, practical assistance, and morale boosting from others. Hence, the hostile individual is less likely to have a forum available where sources of frustration and anger can be discussed and dealt with constructively and effectively. Emotional support from others can help increase a person's self-esteem. By reducing social interaction with potential support providers, the hostile individual likely suffers from reduced self-esteem because emotional support from others is not forthcoming.

THE PRESENT STUDY

The previously cited research suggests the need to examine the psychological concomitants associated with prevalent modes of anger management. In particular, research suggests that the way individuals manage their hostility and anger may have significant health-related consequences, which, to date, have not been investigated. Given the positive relationship between anxiety and anger (Greenglass, 1987; Polivy, 1981; Spielberger, Jacobs, Russell, & Crane, 1983), anxiety may function, at times, as a mediator of the relationship between anger management and CHD. There is also research evidence of a significant relationship between anxiety and CHD, as reported in a variety of settings (Coryell, Noyes, & Hause, 1986; Haines, Imeson, & Meade, 1987; Kawachi et al., 1994).

In the present study, the relationship among anger, hostility, anger-in, and anger control is investigated in a sample of male and female managers. The implications of this relationship for anxiety and social support are analyzed and reported in men and women. On the basis of the research reported earlier, it is hypothesized that individuals simultaneously obtaining high scores on Cynical Hostility and Anger-In would also obtain higher Anxiety scores, and would report lower social support from those close to them, as well as lower interpersonal trust than their low-scoring counterparts.

In this research, respondents were 252 male and 65 female first-line government supervisors in a large Canadian city. A mail-out questionnaire was used to collect data, and a 44% response rate was obtained. Respondents were in senior management, junior management, and supervisory levels.

The variables included in this study were Type-A Behavior, Social Support, Anger, and Cynical Hostility. Type-A Behavior was assessed using the Jenkins Activity Survey (Jenkins, Zyzanski, & Rosenman, 1979), the most widely used measure of Type-A behavior. In addition to a Type-A Behavior score, this scale yields scores on three subscales: Speed and Impatience, Hard-Driving and Competitive, and Job Involvement. Anxiety was assessed using the State–Trait Anxiety Inventory (STAI) A-State Anxiety measure, which is based on 20 items (Spielberger, Gorsuch, & Lushene, 1970) and is an indicator of the level of transitory anxiety. In this study, instructions were modified by asking respondents to indicate how they felt on their present job by circling a number from 1 to 4. Thus, the STAI-Anxiety measure was employed as a measure of job anxiety.

Two of the Social Support measures employed here come from Sarason, Shearin, Pierce, and Sarason (1987) and consist of 12 items. Social Support was measured using the SSQ6, a short social support assessment scale assessing perceived number of available others for support (SSQ6–N) and perceived degree of satisfaction with support (SSQ6–S). An example of an item measuring perceived number of supportive available others is: "Whom can you really count on to be dependable when you need help?" Respondents were then asked to list all of the people they know on whom they can count.

Another measure of Social Support employed in this study was the Family Support Scale (Julkunen & Greenglass, 1989), a 13-item scale that assesses perceived support by family members for home- and family-related issues. An example of an item from this measure is: "My family supports me in all my efforts." Respondents were then asked to check the appropriate alternative on a scale from *strongly disagree* (1) to *strongly agree* (5).

The Interpersonal Relationship Scale (IRS) was employed here as a measure of trust. The IRS, devised by Schlein et al. (1977), assesses the quality of interpersonal relationships, particularly trust and intimacy. This is a 52-item questionnaire with 5-point response alternatives ranging from *strongly agree* (1) to *strongly disagree* (5). Respondents were instructed to respond to the IRS items with regard to a close relationship in which they were presently involved.

The experience and expression of anger were measured by the *State–Trait Anger Expression Inventory (STAXI)* scales developed by Spielberger (1988). The STAXI is a self-report scale consisting of six scales and two subscales. State Anger (S-Anger) is a 10-item scale that measures the intensity of one's angry feelings at a particular time. Trait Anger (T-Anger), also a 10-item scale, assesses individual differences in the disposition to experience anger. Anger-In (AX/In), an eight-item scale, measures the frequency with which angry feelings are held in or suppressed. Anger-Out (AX/Out) is an eight-item scale that measures how often an individual expresses anger toward other people or objects in the environment. Anger Control (AX/Con) is an eight-item scale that assesses the frequency with which an individual attempts to control the expression of anger.

Cynical Distrust

Greenglass and Julkunen (1989) devised a nine-item measure of Cynical Distrust based on the items from the Cook–Medley Ho scale. The theme of this scale centers around cynicism and distrust. It has a reliability of .75.

In the data analyses, scores were rank ordered on the following scales: Cynical Distrust, Anger-In, Anger-Out, and Anger Control. Within each of the male and female samples, scores were divided at the median on both Cynical Distrust and Anger-In. Two groups were created: respondents above the median on both scales, and respondents below the median on both scales. The same procedure was employed to create two groups of respondents above and below the median on both Anger-In and Anger-Out scales. Using scores on Cynical Distrust and Anger Control scales, the same procedure yielded two groups of respondents above and below the median on both scales. Then *t* tests were done separately in males and females between means of scores on composite variables between respondents above and below the median on each of the previously mentioned pairs of variables.

Table 12.1 *t* tests on means of variables between respondents above and below the median on Cynical Distrust and Anger-In

Variable	Above median			Below median			
	$\overline{X}$	*n*	SD	$\overline{X}$	*n*	SD	*t*
Males[a]							
Anxiety (STAI)	42.58	79	10.12	36.40	167	8.93	−4.86***
SSQ6–N	2.88	77	2.02	3.60	156	2.29	2.34*
Family Support	48.84	74	8.20	53.17	155	7.88	3.84***
IRS	212.54	79	27.12	227.90	166	24.40	4.44***
Speed and Impatience	1.66	83	9.06	−1.34	169	9.26	−2.44*
Females[b]							
Anxiety (STAI)	46.47	19	7.11	37.77	44	8.93	−3.76***
Family Support	47.60	15	10.16	53.56	36	7.25	2.37*
IRS	205.17	18	34.73	223.80	41	28.31	2.17*

[a]$n = 252$. [b]$n = 65$.
*$p < .05$. ***$p < .001$.

Results

The *t* tests were conducted on psychological variables between groups high on Cynical Distrust and Anger-In and those low on both, separately in men and women. In all respondents, those scoring high on both scales were significantly higher on anxiety and lower on family support and interpersonal trust than those scoring low on both scales. Men scoring high on Cynical Distrust and Anger-In were significantly higher on Speed and Impatience, and also reported significantly less available others for support (see Table 12.1).

When *t* tests were conducted on psychological variables between groups high and low on Cynical Distrust and Anger Control (instead of Anger-In), in men only, one significant effect was found: Those high on both Cynical Distrust and Anger Control had significantly lower Trust scores ($t = 2.65, p < .01$). Women with high Cynical Distrust and Anger Control scores had significantly higher Type-A scores than their lower scoring counterparts ($t = −2.12$, $p < .05$).

Additional *t* tests were conducted on psychological variables between respondents scoring high on both Anger-In and Anger-Out. Results show that all respondents high on both scales reported less family support than respondents with low scores on both scales—in women ($t = 2.32, p < .05$) and in men ($t = 2.31, p < .05$). In addition, men scoring high on both Anger-In and Anger-Out had significantly higher scores on Anxiety ($t = 2.59, p < .01$), and reported significantly less available others for support ($t = 2.68, p < .01$). Table 12.2 summarizes the results of *t* tests on differences in psychological variables between groups high on Anger/Hostility measures and their low-scoring counterparts. Respondents simultaneously scoring high on Cynical Distrust and Anger-in were most likely to be significantly higher on Anxiety and lower on Social Support and Trust. Examination of high scorers on Cynical

Table 12.2 Summary of *t* tests between high and low scorers on Anger/Hostility and Anger Suppression on psychological variables

Contrast		Anxiety		SSQ6-N		Family Support		Trust		Speed and Impatience		Type A	
		M	F	M	F	M	F	M	F	M	F	M	F
High Cynical Distrust / High Anger-In	vs. Low Cynical Distrust / Low Anger-In	H>L	H>L	H<L	H=L	H<L	H<L	H<L	H<L	H>L	H=L	H=L	H=L
High Cynical Distrust / High Anger Control	vs. Low Cynical Distrust / Low Anger Control	H=L	H=L	H=L	H=L	H=L	H=L	H<L	H=L	H=L	H=L	H=L	H>L
High Anger Out / High Anger In	vs. Low Anger Out / Low Anger In	H>L	H=L	H<L	H=L	H<L	H<L	H=L	H=L	H=L	H=L	H=L	H=L

Note. H>L, Respondents scoring high on both Anger/Hostility and Anger Suppression variables have significantly higher scores on this variable than their low-scoring counterparts; H<L, Respondents scoring high on both Anger/Hostility and Anger Suppression variables have significantly lower scores on this variable than their low-scoring counterparts; H=L, There is no significant difference between high scorers on Anger/Hostility and Anger Suppression variables and their low-scoring counterparts on this variable.

Distrust and Anger Control, or on Anger-Out and Anger-In, indicated far fewer effects. However, taken together, there was some evidence of higher anxiety, lower social support, and lower trust among respondents scoring high on Anger/Hostility and Anger Suppression measures compared with lower scoring respondents.

Tables 12.3 and 12.4 report correlation matrices for the composites variables in the study for men and women, respectively. In all respondents, Anger-In correlated positively with Anxiety, Cynical Distrust, and Speed and Impatience, and negatively with Family Support . Anger-Out correlated negatively with Anger Control in all respondents. Thus, the higher the monitoring of anger, the lower the respondent's anger-out. Cynical Distrust correlated positively with Anxiety and negatively with Family Support in the total sample; in men only, Cynical Distrust was positively correlated with Anger-Out and Speed and Impatience scores, and negatively with Trust, Anger Control, and number of supportive others.

MANAGEMENT OF ANGER AND HOSTILITY: PSYCHOLOGICAL IMPLICATIONS

Data from the present study illustrate the psychological consequences of high Anger-In and high Cynical Distrust that coexist in an individual. The study was conducted to further elucidate the mediator between psychological factors and the progression of heart disease. Although previous research has suggested that hostility is the major factor predicting CHD (Dembroski & Costa, 1988; Williams & Barefoot, 1988), more recently, studies are pointing to the importance of simultaneously taking into account both high hostility/distrust, the suppression or control of such emotions, and their psychological implications (Dembroski et al., 1985; Julkenen et al., 1992).

ANGER, ANXIETY, AND ILLNESS

As predicted earlier, the study reported here indicated that higher Anxiety scores were observed in both women and men when the respondents also had high scores on both Anger-In and Cynical Distrust. Additionally, in males, higher Speed and Impatience, as measured by one of the Type-A subscales (Jenkins et al., 1979) was found when they had high scores on both Cynical Distrust and Anger-In scales. It is suggested that such an emotional configuration may be a precursor of hypertension. Previous research data have shown that a greater number of hypertensive patients have been found to have higher levels of suppressed anger while scoring higher than normal controls on scales assessing anxiety and depression (DeQuattro et al., 1981).

Traditionally, researchers have tended to focus on the study of the relationship between various illness measures and management of a single emotion. However, increasingly, studies are pointing to the importance of examining emotional configurations and their roles as precursors of CHD. As discussed

Table 12.3 Correlation matrix of all composite variables, Males

	Anxiety 1	Cynical Distrust 2	IRS 3	Anger-In 4	Anger-Out 5	Anger Control 6	Family Support 7	SSQ6-N 8	Type A 9	Speed and Impatience 10	Hard Driving 11	Job Involvement 12
1		.26***	-.16*	.32***	.12	-.16*	-.10	.01	.21**	.30***	-.04	.07
2			-.32***	.30***	.23***	-.24***	-.21**	-.15*	.07	.26***	-.11	-.11
3				-.22**	-.08	.08	.67***	.28***	.11	-.12	.12	.13*
4					.11	-.03	-.23***	-.16*	.07	.17**	-.03	-.07
5						-.39***	-.10	-.07	.21**	.20**	-.06	-.05
6							.19**	.12	-.21**	-.21**	.05	.08
7								.32***	-.21**	-.18**	-.02	.11
8									-.03	-.11	.08	.09
9										.55***	.41***	.26***
10											.02	.11
11												.14*

Note. N = 252.

*p < .05. ** p < .01. *** p < .001.

216

Table 12.4 Correlation matrix of all composite variables, Females

	Anxiety 1	Cynical Distrust 2	IRS 3	Anger-In 4	Anger-Out 5	Anger Control 6	Family Support 7	SSQ6-N 8	Type A 9	Speed and Impatience 10	Hard Driving 11	Job Involvement 12
1		.44***	−.30*	.37**	−.04	−.11	−.19	−.32*	.32*	.39**	.14	−.02
2			−.24	.44***	−.01	−.24	−.32*	−.22	.15	.22	.05	−.18
3				−.22	.00	.13	.71***	.23	−.05	−.12	.05	.17
4					−.31*	.12	−.31*	−.13	.21	.27*	.03	−.00
5						−.50***	.02	−.06	−.13	.14	−.28*	.10
6							.09	.42**	.02	−.16	.13	.21
7								.28	−.00	−.20	.16	.23
8									.03	−.24	.03	.35**
9										.55***	.46***	.07
10											.07	.01
11												.03

Note. N = 65.
*p < .05. **p < .01. ***p < .001.

by Booth-Kewley and Friedman (1987), the picture of a coronary-prone individual is one in whom there exists one or more negative emotions. These may include anger, anxiety, depression, and so on. As Groen (1975) suggested, in discussing the role of emotion in psychosomatic illness, rather than examining a single emotion, there is a need to focus on how anxiety, rage, and depression combine to contribute to psychosomatic illness.

Data support the idea of negative emotions coexisting in a configuration (e.g., as seen in studies of university students and managers). Spielberger et al. (1983) reported a positive correlation between S-Anxiety and S-Anger in college students. In other research conducted in both laboratory and natural settings, Polivy (1981) also reported that anger, depression, and anxiety tend to co-occur in university students. The coexistence of negative emotions has also been reported by Greenglass (1987), who found a positive correlation between anger, S-Anxiety, and depression in women managers.

Additional research supports the idea of the health-related implications of the interaction between emotions. For example, studies indicate that anger causes increased BP in primarily hostile, as opposed to nonhostile, individuals. In one study conducted by Suarez and Williams (1989) in a laboratory setting, subjects high and low in hostility were provoked by the experimenter's rude treatment. When highly hostile men were provoked while trying to perform a mental task, they reported much higher levels of anger and irritation afterward than their lower Hostility scoring counterparts. In addition, their BP, the blood flow to their muscles, and their stress hormones all increased more in response to the experiment's provocation. Further findings indicate that anger does not have similar effects on the BP of nonhostile individuals. In other research, similar findings were reported. For example, Jamner, Shapiro, Goldstein, and Huy (1991) studied stress reactions in ambulance workers. Workers with high Hostility scores showed larger BP increases during angry interchanges with emergency room personnel than did those with low Hostility scores. Moreover, the closer link between angry emotions and physiological hyperreactivity could contribute to the greater health problems observed among hostile persons.

SOCIAL SUPPORT, DISTRUST, AND ANGER-IN

Data from the present study also showed that respondents with high scores on Cynical Distrust and Anger-In reported receiving less support from familial members and reported less trust in their close relationships. In addition, male respondents scoring high on Cynical Distrust and Anger-In reported less people available to them for support. These data are in line with those of Greenglass (1991), who found that reported support from family members in managers was negatively correlated with scores on an Anger-In measure. Although family members are generally thought of as primary source of support, particularly in difficult times, for a cynically hostile person, this is less likely to be the case. As Smith et al. (1988) argued, the family of a cynically hostile individual would less likely be a source of support, and instead may be a source of stress. As discussed earlier, highly hostile individuals frequently view their interpersonal world, including their families, as a source of an ongoing irritating struggle that requires vigilance. Given that they rarely view others as trustworthy, these individuals may also experience more daily stressors and interpersonal conflict, as well as less satisfying social networks.

According to Hardy and Smith (1988), the antagonistic expectations and behaviors of cynically hostile individuals may elicit hostility in others. For example, in times of stress, rather than eliciting informational, practical, or emotional resources of others, hostile individuals are more likely to bring out antagonism in others, including those close to them. Hostile persons' expectations may preclude the development of the maintenance of a buffering social support network. Thus, the social orientation of cynically hostile individuals may create a stressful interpersonal environment. At the same time, this may undermine the social ties that would otherwise lessen the risk of disease. Also, given the more frequent and severe interpersonal conflicts that highly hostile individuals experience, the psychological climate that results is likely to be physiologically taxing, thus contributing to a greater susceptibility to illness. Conflict may impose increased stress, which may have harmful biological and physiological consequences. Although it remains to be shown just how social isolation and social conflict harm a person's health, another possibility is that persons lacking close social ties are less likely to have good health habits because others are less likely to be around to monitor daily routines.

What are the psychological implications of anger-in as a way of managing anger or hostility? Correlations in the present study between Anger-In and other psychological variables indicate that Anger-In is significantly related to Speed and Impatience in both men and women. Thus, individuals who suppress their anger using anger-in are more likely to experience impatience and are likely to be irritable as well. Although Anger-In did not relate significantly to Anger-Out in men, in women, the higher the Anger-In the lower their Anger-Out. Thus, the more women suppress their angry feelings, the less likely they are to express their feelings of anger in aggressive behavior directed toward others. However, in all respondents, high Anger-In was significantly related to lower Social Support. As discussed by Spielberger (1988), a person scoring high on Anger-In frequently experiences intense angry feelings. It may be that the suppression of these feelings gives rise to impatience and irritability, which may contribute to antagonistic interpersonal relationships, thus precluding the development of relationships that provide useful social resources. At the same time, individuals with high Anger-In, because of their interpersonal style, may not be able to participate in forums where obstacles and frustrations may be discussed with others.

COPING WITH AND MANAGING ANGER

The issue of how individuals manage their anger may be conceptualized as one of how individuals cope with their anger. In general, when researchers talk about coping, they refer to the processes involved in how people cope with stress, including life stress, daily hassles, and job-related strain and stress

(Carver, Weintraub, & Scheier, 1989; Folkman & Lazarus, 1985). Interest in the processes by which people cope with stress has grown considerably in recent years. For Lazarus and Folkman (1984), *coping* is defined as a person's constantly changing cognitive and behavioral efforts to manage specific external and/or internal demands that are appraised as taxing or exceeding the person's resources. For them, *coping* is defined as the person's efforts to manage demands. Coping is seen as having two widely recognized major functions: regulating stressful emotions (emotion-focused coping) and altering the person–environment relationship causing the distress (problem-focused coping; Folkman & Lazarus, 1980, 1985). Additionally, emotion-focused coping is aimed at reducing the emotional distress that is associated with the situation, and problem-focused coping is aimed at doing something to alter the source of the stress.

According to Folkman and Lazarus (1980), people tend to employ problem-focused coping when they feel that something constructive can be done, whereas emotion-focused coping tends to predominate when people feel that a stressor is something that must be endured. This conceptualization of coping may be applied to individuals' efforts in managing anger. For example, a person scoring high on Anger-In is one who frequently experiences intense angry feelings, but tends to suppress rather than express these feelings (Spielberger, 1988). Anger-in, then, may be seen as an emotion-focused coping strategy because it tends to be used to regulate one's emotional reactions or make one feel better without solving the problem.

Additional research suggests that emotion-focused strategies, such as wishful thinking and self-blame, may not be "coping" measures, in that they have been shown to be positively correlated with symptoms of distress such as depression, anxiety, somatization, and drug taking, and negatively with job satisfaction (Greenglass, 1988). Data from the present study with managers indicate significantly positive correlations between Anger-In, Anxiety, and Speed and Impatience scores, thus confirming previous suggestions that emotion-focused strategies are associated with distress. In the present context, anger-in correlated positively with Cynical Distrust. Thus, like other emotion-focused coping strategies, anger-in may be associated with psychological distress such as depression, anxiety, irritability, and impatience, thus increasing the individual's susceptibility to developing illness.

CYNICAL DISTRUST, ANGER-IN, AND SOCIAL SUPPORT: A PSYCHODYNAMIC EXPLANATION

Given the importance of social support for health, along with research findings of the deleterious effects of social isolation, it is important to discern the psychological factors linking low Social Support with high Cynical Distrust and Anger-In, as reported in the present study. In their discussion of strategies for controlling hostility that can harm one's health, Williams and Williams (1993) speculated on the dynamics involved in hostility and their psychological implications. This is particularly important when examining the role of social support and health, and the ways in which individuals are more or less receptive to support from others. Given the self-involvement of the hostile individual, he or she most often pays little attention to what others are saying or doing. The focus on self, with little attention to gathering information or seeking advice from others, may be one of the main reasons for the angry interchanges so frequent in a hostile person's life (Williams & Williams, 1993). When the cynically hostile individual also employs anger-in to control his or her angry impulses, tension develops between the simultaneous operation of opposing tendencies—thoughts of distrust/hostility along with attempts to suppress anger. With so much energy directed toward monitoring angry impulses, the individual ends up focusing almost exclusively on his or her own thoughts, feelings, and impulses. The low level of trust in others, along with a high level of self-involvement, further distances the hostile individual from others.

CONCLUSIONS

A comprehensive understanding of the development and progression of CHD requires an integration of psychological, coping, and social variables within a dynamic framework that links social-psychological constructs with physiological and biological bases of CHD.

REFERENCES

Barefoot, J. C., Dahlstrom, W. G., & Williams, R. B., Jr. (1983). Hostility, CHD incidence and total mortality. 25-year follow-up study of 255 physicians. *Psychosomatic Medicine, 45*, 59–63.

Barefoot, J. C., Williams, R. B., Dahlstrom, W. G., & Dodge, K. A. (1987). Predicting mortality from scores on the Cook–Medley scale: A follow up study of 118 lawyers. *Psychosomatic Medicine, 49*, 210.

Blumenthal, J. A., Barefoot, J. C., Burg, M. M., & Williams, R. B. (1987). Psychological correlates of hostility among patients undergoing coronary angiography. *British Journal of Medical Psychology, 60*, 349–355.

Booth-Kewley, S., & Friedman, H. S. (1987). Psychological predictors of heart disease: A quantitative review. *Psychological Bulletin, 101*, 343–362.

Carver, C. S., Weintraub, J. K., & Scheier, M. F. (1989). Assessing coping strategies: A theoretically based approach. *Journal of Personality and Social Psychology, 56*, 267–283.

Cohen, S., & Wills, T. (1985). Stress, social support and the buffering hypothesis. *Psychological Bulletin, 98*, 310–357.

Cook, W. W., & Medley, D. M. (1954). Proposed hostility and pharisaic-virtue scales for the MMPI. *Journal of Applied Psychology, 38*, 414–418.

Coryell, W., Noyes, R., & Hause, J. D. (1986). Mortality among outpatients with anxiety disorders. *American Journal of Psychiatry, 143*, 508–510.

Costa, P. T., Zonderman, A. B., McCrae, R. R., & Williams, R. B., Jr. (1986).
    Cynicism and paranoid alienation in the Cook and Medley Ho scale. *Psychosomatic Medicine, 48*, 283–285.
Dembroski, T. M., & Costa, P. T. (1988). Assessment of coronary-prone behavior: A current overview. *Annals of Behavioral Medicine, 10*, 60–63.
Dembroski, T. M., MacDougal, J. M., Williams, R. B., Haney, T. L., &
    Blumenthal, J. A. (1985). Components of Type A, hostility, and anger-in: Relationship to angiographic findings. *Psychosomatic Medicine, 47*, 219–233.
DeQuattro, V., Sullivan, P., Foti, A., Schoentgen, S., Kollock, R., Verasales,
    G., & Levine, D. (1981). Central neurogenetic mechanisms in hypertension and in postural hypotension. In G. Laragh, F. Buhler, & D. Seldin (Eds.), *Frontiers in hypertension research* (pp. 301–305). New York: Springer-Verlag.
Esler, M., Julius, S., Zwefler, A., Randall, O., Harburg, E., Gardiner, H., &
    DeQuattro, V. (1977). Mid high-renin essential hypertension. *New England Journal of Medicine, 296*, 405–411.
Folkman, S., & Lazarus, R. S. (1980). An analysis of coping in a middle-aged
    community sample. *Journal of Health and Social Behavior, 21*, 219–239.
Folkman, S., & Lazarus, R. S. (1985). If it changes it must be a process: A
    study of emotion and coping during three stages of a college examination. *Journal of Personality and Social Psychology, 48*, 150–170.
Gambaro, S., & Rabin, A. I. (1969). Diastolic blood pressure responses fol-
    lowing direct and displaced aggression after anger arousal in high and low guilt subjects. *Journal of Personality and Social Psychology, 12*, 87–94.
Greenglass, E. R. (1987). Anger in Type A women: Implications for coronary
    heart disease. *Personality and Individual Differences, 8*, 639–650.
Greenglass, E. R. (1988). Type A behaviour and coping strategies in female
    and male supervisors. *Applied Psychology: An International Review, 37*, 271–288.
Greenglass, E. R. (1991, July). *Social support, anger and the Type A behaviour
    pattern: Implications for psychological functioning*. Paper presented at the 2nd European Congress of Psychology, Budapest, Hungary.
Greenglass, E. R. (1993). Social support and coping of employed women. In
    B. C. Long & S. E. Kahn (Eds.), *Women, work and coping: A multidisciplinary approach to workplace stress* (pp. 215–239). Montreal, Quebec, Canada: McGill-Queens University Press.
Greenglass, E. R., Fiksenbaum, L., & Burke, R. J. (1996). Components of
    social support, buffering effects and burnout: Implications for psychological functioning. *Anxiety, Stress, & Coping*.
Greenglass, E. R., & Julkunen, J. (1989). Construct validity and sex differ-
    ences in Cook–Medley hostility. *Personality and Individual Differences, 10*, 209–218.
Greenglass, E. R., & Julkunen, J. (1991). Cook–Medley hostility, anger, and
    the Type A behavior pattern in Finland. *Psychological Reports, 68*, 1059–1066.

Groen, J. J. (1975). The measurement of emotion and arousal in the clinical psychological laboratory and in medical practice. In L. Levi (Ed.), *Emotions: Their parameters and measurement* (pp. 727–746). New York: Raven.

Haines, A. P., Imeson, J. D., & Meade, T. W. (1987). Phobic anxiety and ischaemic heart disease. *British Medical Journal, 295,* 297–299.

Hardy, J. D., & Smith, T. W. (1988). Cynical hostility and vulnerability to disease: Social support, life stress, and physiological response to conflict. *Health Psychology, 7,* 447–459.

Hartfield, M. T. (1985). Appraisals of anger situations and subsequent coping responses in hypertensive and normotensive adults: A comparison. *Dissertation Abstracts International, 46B,* 4452.

Haynes, S. B., Feinleib, M., & Kannel, W. B. (1980). The relationship of psychosocial factors to coronary heart disease in the Framingham Study: III. Eight-year incidence of coronary heart disease. *American Journal of Epidemiology, III,* 37–58.

Himle, D. P., Jayaratne, S., & Thyness, P. (1989). The effects of emotional support on burnout, work stress and mental health among Norwegian and American social workers. *Journal of Social Service Research, 13,* 27–45.

Himle, D. P., Jayaratne, S., & Thyness, P. (1991). Buffering effects of four social support types on burnout among social workers. *Social Work Research and Abstracts, 27,* 22–27.

Hobfoll, S. E. (1986). *Stress, social support, and women.* Washington, DC: Hemisphere.

Hokanson, J. E., & Shelter, S. (1961). The effect of overt aggression on physiological arousal level. *Journal of Abnormal and Social Psychology, 63,* 446–448.

Houston, B. K., & Kelly, K. E. (1989). Hostility in employed women: Relation to work and marital experiences, social support, stress, and anger expression. *Personality and Social Psychology Bulletin, 15,* 175–182.

Jackson, D. N., & Messick, S. (1970). *The Differential Personality Inventory.* New York: Research Psychologists Press.

Jamner, L. D., Shapiro, D., Goldstein, I. B., & Huy, R. (1991). Ambulatory blood pressure in paramedics: Effects of cynical hostility and defensiveness. *Psychosomatic Medicine, 53,* 393–406.

Jenkins, C. D., Zyzanski, S. J., & Rosenman, R. H. (1979). *Jenkins Activity Survey Manual.* New York: The Psychological Corporation.

Johnson, E. H. (1984). *Anger and anxiety as determinants of elevated blood pressure in adolescents.* Unpublished doctoral dissertation, University of South Florida, Tampa.

Julkunen, J., & Greenglass, E. R. (1989). *The Family Support Scale.* Unpublished manuscript.

Julkunen, J., Salonen, R., Kaplan, G. A. & Salonen, J. T. (1992, July). *Hostility and the progression of carotid atherosclerosis.* Paper presented at the 25th International Congress of Psychology, Brussels, Belgium.

Kaplan, G., Berkman, L. F., & Breslow, L. (1983). *Health and ways of living: The Alameda County study.* New York: Oxford University Press.

Kawachi, I., Colditz, G. A., Ascherio, A., Rimm, E. B., Giovannucci, E., Stampfer, M. J., & Willett, W. C. (1994). Prospective study of phobic anxiety and risk of coronary heart disease in men. *Circulation, 89,* 1992–1997.

LaRocco, J. M., House, J. S., & French, J. R. P., Jr. (1980). Social support, occupational stress, and health. *Journal of Health and Social Behavior, 21,* 202–218.

Lazarus, R. S., & Folkman, S. (1984). *Stress, appraisal, and the coping process.* New York: McGraw-Hill.

Polivy, J. (1981). On the introduction of emotion in the laboratory: Discrete moods or multiple affect states. *Journal of Personality and Social Psychology, 41,* 803–817.

Sarason, B. R., Shearin, E. N., Pierce, G. R., & Sarason, I. G. (1987). Interrelations of social support measures: Theoretical and practical implications. *Journal of Personality and Social Psychology, 52,* 813–832.

Schlein, S. P., Guerney, B. G., Jr., & Stover, L. (1977). The Interpersonal Relationship Scale (IRS). In B. G. Guerney, Jr. (Ed.), *Relationship enhancement* (pp. 349–354). San Francisco: Jossey-Bass.

Schneider, R., Egan, B., Johnson, E., Drobny, H., & Julius, S. (1986). Anger and anxiety in borderline hypertension. *Psychosomatic Medicine, 48,* 242–248.

Shekelle, R. B., Gale, M., Ostfeld, A. M., & Paul, O. (1983). Hostility, risk of coronary heart disease, and mortality. *Psychosomatic Medicine, 45,* 109–114.

Shinn, M., Rosario, M., March, H., & Chestnut, D. (1984). Coping with job stress and burnout in the human services. *Journal of Personality and Social Psychology, 46,* 864–876.

Smith, T. W., & Frohm, K. D. (1985). What's so unhealthy about hostility? Construct validity and psychosocial correlates of the Cook and Medley Ho scale. *Health Psychology, 4,* 503–520.

Smith, T. W., & Pope, M. K. (1990). Cynical hostility as a health risk: Current status and future directions. *Journal of Social Behavior and Personality, 5,* 77–88.

Smith, T. W., Pope, M. K., Sanders, J. D., Allred, K. D., & O'Keeffe, J. L. (1988). Cynical hostility at home and work: Psychosocial vulnerability across domains. *Journal of Research in Personality, 22,* 525–548.

Spielberger, C. D. (1988). *State–Trait Anger Expression Inventory (STAXI).* Tampa, FL: Psychological Assessment Resources.

Spielberger, C. D., Gorsuch, R. L., & Lushene, R. E. (1970). *The State–Trait Anxiety Inventory.* Palo Alto, CA: Consulting Psychologists Press.

Spielberger, C. D., Jacobs, G., Crane, R., Russell, S., Westberry, L., Barker, L., Johnson, E., Knight, J., & Marks, E. (1979). *The preliminary manual for the State–Trait Personality Inventory.* Unpublished manual, University of South Florida, Tampa.

Spielberger, C. D., Jacobs, G. A., Russell, S. F., & Crane, R. J. (1983). Assessment of anger: The State–Trait Anger Scale. In J. N. Butcher & C.

D. Spielberger (Eds.), *Advances in personality assessment* (Vol. 2, pp. 159–187). Hillsdale, NJ: Lawrence Erlbaum Associates.

Spielberger, C. D., Johnson, E. H., Russell, S., Crane, R., Jacobs, G., & Worden, T. (1985). The experience and expression of anger: Construction and validation of an anger expression scale. In M. A. Chesney & R. H. Rosenman (Eds.), *Anger and hostility in cardiovascular and behavioral disorders* (pp. 5–29). New York: Hemisphere/McGraw-Hill.

Suarez, E. C., & Williams, R. B. (1989). Situational determinants of cardiovascular and emotional reactivity in high and low hostile men. *Psychosomatic Medicine, 51,* 404–418.

Thomas, S. P. (1989). Gender differences in anger expression: Health implications. *Research in Nursing and Health, 12,* 389–398.

Williams, R. B., & Barefoot, J. C. (1988). Coronary-prone behavior: The emerging role of the hostility complex. In B. K. Houston & C. R. Snyder (Eds.), *Type A behavior: Research, theory and intervention* (pp. 189–211). New York: Wiley.

Williams, R. B., Jr., Heaney, T. L., Lee, K. L., Kong, Y.-H. Blumenthal, J. A., & Whalen, R. E. (1980). Type A behaviour, hostility and coronary atherosclerosis. *Psychosomatic Medicine, 42,* 539–549.

Williams, R. B., & Williams, V. (1993). *Anger kills: Seventeen strategies for controlling the hostility that can harm your health.* New York: Random House.

13

Suppressing Your Anger: Good Manners, Bad Health?

Juhani Julkunen
Rehabilitation Foundation, Helsinki, Finland

Abstract   *Anger and hostility are key concepts in research on the interplay of emotions, behavior, and health. As possible risk factors for coronary heart disease (CHD), they have been the subject of extensive research. Although epidemiological research has favored straightforward, single-risk factor models for psychological variables, this chapter reports empirical studies that demonstrate the usefulness of testing more complicated, interactional, and contextual models for examining the development of CHD. The results of one of the studies described here, based on 351 North Karelian women, indicate that anger-in was associated with elevated blood pressure (BP), but only if the atmosphere in the work unit was experienced as hostile and tense at the same time. In a second study of 119 men from eastern Finland, anger control, together with high levels of cynical hostility, predicted the progression of carotid atherosclerosis (PCA) during a 2-year follow-up. Accelerated PCA was also observed in subjects scoring high on both Anger Control and Anger-Out. It was concluded that these findings have significant implications for future studies of the health consequences of anger suppression and control.*

Anger and hostility have become key concepts for psychologists and other professionals who study the interplay of emotions, behavior, and health. These concepts refer to a variety of emotional and behavioral phenomena that have potentially important links to human well-being, ranging from health risks to extreme modes of violence. Although the available evidence strongly suggests that hostile persons seem to be at increased risk for coronary heart disease (CHD) and other life-threatening illnesses, critical conceptual and methodological issues need to be addressed. Especially important among the empirical issues that require more intensive scrutiny is the social context of the relationship between hostility and health (Smith, 1992).

Nobody can escape the basic human dilemma of how to deal with anger and hostility, but the guidelines that tell people how to cope with these conditions

Preparation of this chapter was supported by a grant of the Signe and Ane Gyllenberg's Foundation.

The author is grateful to Esther Greenglass for her many helpful comments on an earlier draft of this chapter and for her stylistic advice.

vary considerably from one culture to another. Yet in every society, individuals must learn, one way or another, to inhibit anger and control aggressive behavior. To function in the social world, one must learn to inhibit selfish desires and aggressive outbursts, and to behave in socially defined acceptable ways (Pennebaker, 1992).

The contradiction between individual desires and cultural norms was addressed by Freud (1920) early in this century. Currently, Freud's theorizing provides, in part, the historical background for psychosomatic research traditions that have focused on the health consequences resulting from the employment of a variety of mechanisms for the suppression of angry feelings and the inhibition of aggressive behavior (Alexander, 1950; Dunbar, 1947).

Severe criticisms were later leveled against many of the early psychodynamic arguments on methodological grounds. However, more recent epidemiological and health psychological research has produced evidence supporting some of the earlier hypotheses employing psychodynamic explanations. For example, Julius, Harburg, Cottington, and Johnson (1986) reported that subjects likely to suppress their anger had a significantly higher mortality risk than those expressing their anger. Moreover, the excess mortality rate among these subjects seemed to be mediated by elevated blood pressure (BP) in persons high on anger-in.

Dembroski, MacDougal, Williams, Haney, and Blumenthal (1985) investigated several aspects of hostility and Type-A behavior in relation to angiographic findings. These researchers concluded that hostility, in conjunction with acquired coping mechanisms such as anger suppression (anger-in), might be the core of coronary-prone behavior. This conclusion was later supported by Suarez (1986), who found a significant interaction between potential for hostility and anger-in as risk factors for more severe angiographic findings. Moreover, many authors today argue that the most important coronary-prone element in the Type-A construct would be hostility (for reviews, see Matthews, 1988; Williams & Barefoot, 1988).

Given the growing body of research evidence suggesting the potential influence of hostility on health, especially in the development of CHD, it is important to recognize the complex and multidimensional nature of the *hostility* construct (Siegman, Dembroski, & Ringel, 1987; Smith, 1992). As a psychological construct, hostility is associated with many emotional and behavioral phenomena: aggression, anger, annoyance, irritability, suspicion, and cynicism.

Hilgard (1980) proposed that three aspects of hostility in particular should be conceptually separated and assessed. First, the *cognitive* component of hostility consists of negative beliefs of others who are seen as unreliable, undeserving, immoral, and possibly threatening antagonists. Cynicism, or cynical distrust, has been proposed as the umbrella concept for this element (Greenglass & Julkunen, 1989; Julkunen, Salonen, Kaplan, Chesney, & J. Salonen, 1994; Williams, 1984). Second, the *affective* component includes several emotional states, such as anger, irritability, disgust, and contempt. The third component includes various forms of aggressive *behavior,* ranging from sulking and verbal aggression to overtly aggressive acts (Barefoot, 1992).

Spielberger, Krasner, and Solomon (1988) extensively discussed this issue using the concept of the *AHA! Syndrome* (anger–hostility–aggression) as a collective expression of this complex set of emotions and behavior. In their terms, *anger* refers to an emotional state, whereas *hostility* represents a set of attitudes and rather stable traits. *Aggression* refers to aggressive behavior, implying destructive or punitive behavior directed toward other persons or objects (Spielberger, Johnson, Russell, Crane, Jacobs, & Worden, 1985; Spielberger et al., 1988). This notion of aggression mirrors the origins of the term in Latin: *ad gredior,* meaning literally "to rush toward something."

One of the questions that could be asked has to do with the relative importance of each of these three aspects of hostility (i.e., cognitive, affective, and behavioral) regarding CHD risk. Further, one could inquire into the implications of the various combinations of the components for health—in particular, CHD. Although several authors (Barefoot, 1992; Smith & Frohm, 1985; Spielberger et al., 1985; Williams & Barefoot, 1988) have underlined the complex nature of hostility and aggressive behavior, research practice has often favored single-factor, univariate analyses. At best, results of these studies have shown statistically significant, but substantially weak, person–disease relationships, and results from different studies are often inconsistent.

At the same time, an old methodological issue has emerged. It has become increasingly evident that studies of hostility–health relationships should be based on more sophisticated interactional and contextual models that investigate the simultaneous relationships between more than one risk factor and health. This implies the need to include in our models the situational factors and the context in which the (aggressive) behavior took place (Smith, 1992). Furthermore, this same methodological principle should be applied to the assessment of individual personality, which means that a single feature (e.g., a tendency to hold anger in) may have drastically different health consequences, depending on other personality characteristics such as trait anger or self-esteem. The potential fruitfulness of this approach was well demonstrated in studies by Dembroski et al. (1985) and Suarez (1986). Their results indicate that hostility was a risk factor for coronary atherosclerosis, but only in subjects high on anger-in.

The idea of using a contextual approach to study behavior is not new: The best classic example is Field Theory (Lewin, 1952). Lewin's famous formula— "B = f (P, E),)" where B = behavior, P = person, E = perceived environment—postulated that behavior should be understood as a function of person–environment interaction (Lewin, 1952). One example of the application of Lewin's theory is his discussion of findings of different levels of aggressiveness in democratic and autocratic atmospheres, which clearly demonstrates the moderator impact of the social context on aggressive behavior (Lewin, 1952). It is proposed here that Lewin's model can be modified for health psychological studies by replacing the concept of *behavior* with that of *health.* An extended, modified model is described herein and presented in schematic form in Fig. 13.1.

In Lewin's original formulation, *environment* was explicitly defined as perceived environment. In Lewin's (1952) words: "In this equation the person (P) and his environment (E) have to be viewed as variables which are mutually dependent upon each other. In other words, to understand or to predict behavior, the person and his environment have to be considered as one constel-

1. Univariate "trait-disease" model

Person ———→ Disease

2. Kurt Lewin's (1952) Field theoretical model

B = f (P, E)

B = behavior
P = person
E = perceived environment

3. Contextual model

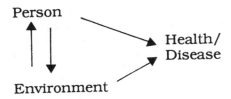

4. Extended, modified model

H = f (P, E, PhE, B)

H = health
B = biological factors
P = personality
E = perceived environment
PhE = physical environment

Figure 13.1 Univariate, contextual, and interactional models in health psychology.

lation of interdependent factors" (pp. 239–240). The relevance of this notion is well demonstrated in current discussions of social support and health (see Sarason, 1988). It was also addressed in a recent study by Christensen and Smith (1993) on hostility and blood pressure (BP) reactivity, which is discussed in more detail later.

If one is interested in health, one must also take into account the quality of the physical environment (PhE). This includes variables such as pollution, noise, temperature, and so on. For example, Anderson (1989) reported evidence from field studies showing that heat increases aggression. Therefore,

PhE is a necessary element in a general model such as the one proposed here, although assessment of physical factors usually goes beyond psychologists' expertise. In a parallel way, the vast area of biological determinants of health, including genetic factors and predispositions, as well as various mediating physiological processes, must be taken into account (as presented in Model 4 in Fig. 13.1). This model is meant to emphasize the complex interplay among personality, perceived environment, physical environment, and biological factors: Each has its own impact on human health, and probably modifies the effects of the model's other variables.

One might still ask, what is the advantage of employing such abstract models? As many authors have noted (e.g., Price, 1982; Smith, 1992), studies in health psychology and research on Type-A behavior as a risk factor for CHD have been characterized by an overly empirical and atheoretical approach. Although many basic associations have been identified between psychological traits and health, this approach has often led to fragmented, and sometimes even contradictory, results and inconsistent conclusions. Some of the previously noted problems can be overcome by applying more sophisticated models that reflect the complexity of the emotion–behavior–environment–health interrelationship. Of course, there are several implications for research strategy and statistical testing of this kind of model. These implications are beyond the scope of this chapter, but have been extensively discussed by Baron and Kenny (1986) and Cox and Ferguson (1991). This chapter attempts to highlight the usefulness of adapting the methodological principles presented earlier to some recent studies of hostility, anger suppression, and cardiovascular health.

THE ANGER-IN–BLOOD PRESSURE HYPOTHESIS: THE IMPACT OF CONTEXT

According to a classic hypothesis (Alexander, 1950), suppressed anger would be a risk for elevated BP. There is some empirical evidence for this argument, but some contradictory results have also been reported (Diamond, 1982; Schwenkmezger & Hank, chap. 14, this volume; Spielberger et al., 1985). According to the previous model, one question could be: Is the anger-in–BP relationship independent of the situational characteristics, or is it affected by characteristics of the context or other personality features?

Julkunen and Korhonen (1993) addressed this question empirically using data collected from a Health Promotion Program conducted in North Karelia. The study sample consisted of 351 women. It was hypothesized that the association between anger-in and BP would be positive and more pronounced in a setting where the workplace atmosphere was tense and hostile. The rationale behind this hypothesis was that the consequences of any mode of anger expression would be most clearly seen in a situation where this particular behavior was activated.

The measures used to empirically test this hypothesis were the Anger-In (AX/In) subscale from the 24-item State–Trait Anger Expression (AX) scale

(Spielberger, 1988) and the Tenseness of Atmosphere (TA) subscale from the Work Environment Questionnaire (WEQ-22; Julkunen & Korhonen, 1993). The TA subscale consists of four items to be answered on a 5-point Likert scale (alpha = .78). Representative items: "My work unit is tense as for its atmosphere" and "Quarrels among workers are readily aroused."

The results of a two-way analysis of covariance (ANCOVA), using AX/In (classified in quartiles) and TA (median split) as independent variables and controlling for age and body mass index (BMI), revealed that a significant and positive association between anger-in and elevated BP was found only in the group of women who experienced their work unit as hostile and tense. The zero-order, unadjusted correlations of AX/In with systolic blood pressure (SBP) and diastolic blood pressure (DBP) in the total sample were nonsignificant (0.05 and 0.00, respectively; Julkunen & Korhonen, 1993). This result offers a clear example of the impact of a contextual variable (i.e., the emotional quality of the perceived environment) on the person–health relationship. In a parallel vein, Christensen and Smith (1993) showed that hostile subjects displayed heightened BP reactivity during social interaction as compared with subjects low in hostility, but only when the interaction required self-disclosure.

In both of these studies, it appears that the perceived environment acted as a moderator, changing the relationship between personality and BP. In theory, both the personality and contextual variables acted as mediators in the sense suggested by Baron and Kenny (1986). For example, in the Julkunen–Korhonen study, it could be argued that the hostile atmosphere caused an increase of AX/In, which in turn raised the BP levels. In this case, anger-in could be mediating the environment's effect on BP. This and other theoretically interesting models of the AX/In–BP interactions could be further investigated through regression analyses (for a more detailed discussion, see Baron & Kenny, 1986; Cox & Ferguson, 1991).

To a certain extent, the results discussed herein indicate that good manners (i.e., holding one's anger in) may be harmful to one's health, but only in specific circumstances. In certain situations (e.g., when long-standing tenseness prevails in a group), it might be more beneficial to openly express one's feelings of anger than to hold them in. However, there remains a number of questions about how to constructively express anger and, at the same time, to avoid escalating conflict. This leads to the question about the meaning of different ways of suppressing anger, which also seems to be no less a multidimensional construct than hostility itself.

ANGER-IN AND ANGER CONTROL:
TWO WAYS OF SUPPRESSING ANGER

Traditionally, when anger suppression is discussed in the literature, it is understood unidimensionally as anger that is held in. There has been little discussion about possible variations in "styles of anger suppression," and even less about their differential health consequences. As demonstrated by Spielberger (1988) in the development of his State–Trait Anger Expression Inventory (STAXI), anger suppression is a multidimensional construct.

In the latest version of Spielberger's AX/scale (Spielberger, 1988), three major components were extracted by factor analysis. Anger-out (AX/Out) involves the expression of anger openly toward other people or objects, as exemplified by items such as "I argue with others" and "I do things like slam doors." Anger-in (AX/In) means anger held in, or the suppression of angry feelings. Representative items from the AX/In scale are: "I boil inside, but I don't show it" and "I am angrier than I am willing to admit." As Spielberger (1988) pointed out, this should be kept separate from the psychoanalytic term *anger turned inward against self,* which is often an unconscious process resulting in feelings of guilt or severe depression. Anger Control (AX/Con) refers to attempts to control and suppress or mitigate the expression of anger. Representative items to the AX/Con scale are: "I control my behavior" and "I try to be tolerant and understanding." The AX/In and AX/Con scales have been shown to be independent dimensions of anger control, with essentially zero correlation with each other. Thus, they reflect different types of mechanisms for controlling or suppressing anger (Spielberger, 1988).

Although a growing body of research has been reported with the AX/In scale, there is considerably less research in which AX/Con is measured. The latter is also the latest subscale added to the measure. Given research interest in both AX/In and AX/Con, as well as their theoretical importance, studies are needed to establish their impact on health. Recently, the construct validity of these two scales has been studied, using the Finnish adaptation of the AX scale with a sample of 2,682 middle-aged men (Julkunen, Kauhanen, Kaplan, & Salonen, 1994). The data are part of the baseline measurements from the Kuopio Ischaemic Heart Disease (KIHD) Risk Factor Study—a prospective study to investigate previously unestablished risk factors for CHD and extra-coronary atherosclerosis in a normal population. The design and methods of the main study have been described elsewhere (Salonen, 1988).

In general, the results (Julkunen et al., 1994) support the hypothesis that the AX/In and AX/Con scales reflect two distinct ways of dealing with anger, as proposed by the authors of the scale (Spielberger, 1988; Spielberger et al., 1988). Furthermore, inspection of the correlations of these measures with a number of other psychological measures used in the KIHD study revealed several differences in the construct validity of the AX scales. For example, the correlations indicated that AX/Con was significantly associated with several positive personality features, such as self-esteem and a strong sense of coherence. Also, subjects scoring high on AX/Con reported high levels of social support from their families, coped with losses and misfortunes in optimistic ways, and tended not to be depressed. However, they seemed to be somewhat defensive, and relied more on repression than did persons scoring high on AX/In. Significant negative correlations indicated further that men obtaining high scores on the AX/Con scale tended to score lower on Helplessness, Cynical Distrust, and Alexithymia, and were less irritable than their anger-in counterparts.

In contrast, anger-in was significantly associated with many negative coping styles, such as resignation, withdrawal, and pessimism. Persons with high AX/In scores also tended to score high on Cynicism, Irritability, Alexithymia, and Helplessness. Moreover, they had low self-esteem, along with a weak sense of coherence and less family support. In fact, the correlations reported by Julkunen et al. (1994) showed a reverse pattern of features related to anger control in contrast to anger-in.

Taken together, the results cited herein indicate that construct validity for the AX/In and AX/Con scales involves quite different psychological phenomena, although both measures reflect an attempt to suppress feelings and inhibit the expression of anger. Further, differences in the construct validity measures between AX/In and AX/Con cannot be explained by level of education or socioeconomic status (SES), both of which had essentially zero correlations with the AX measures. Given these results, it could be argued that persons relying on anger control rather than anger-in have more stable personalities with better psychological resources, and therefore are more capable of coping successfully with various life crises. These data suggest that, in comparing two modes of suppressing anger, anger control should be a healthier way of dealing with angry feelings, whereas anger-in would pose a major health risk. An alternative hypothesis, based on the general notion of the benefits of expressing feelings, would lead one to expect that, either way, anger not expressed constitutes a health risk (see e.g., Swan, Carmelli, Dame, Rosenman, & Spielberger, 1992).

HOSTILITY, ANGER-IN, AND ANGER CONTROL AS PREDICTORS OF PROGRESSION OF CAROTID ATHEROSCLEROSIS

As discussed earlier, previous research indicates that hostility, together with anger suppression, would be risk factors for coronary atherosclerosis. Dembroski et al. (1985) and Suarez (1986) showed a significant interaction between potential for hostility and anger-in, whereby highly hostile men who suppressed their anger evidenced more severe disease. These results suggest a modifying role of a person's anger expression style (anger suppression) in the hostility–health relationship. So far, little research has tested this hypothesis.

In the studies cited earlier, degree of coronary atherosclerosis was assessed by angiography results. Thus, the conclusions are limited to selected clinical samples. In the study described here, Julkunen, Salonen, Kaplan, Chesney, and Salonen (1994) investigated hostility and suppression of anger as possible predictors of 2-year progression of PCA, as measured ultrasonographically. This method allows one to study the progression of extracoronary atherosclerosis in nonclinical population samples (R. Salonen & Salonen, 1990). Furthermore, recent research, supported by earlier autopsy studies, has suggested a strong association among common carotid atherosclerosis, coronary atherosclerosis, and risk of CHD (See J. Salonen & Salonen, 1991).

To replicate the earlier results of hostility and anger suppression's impact on angiography findings, Julkunen et al. (1994) tested four variants of the

Hostility × Anger Suppression model using multiple-regression analyses. The models were based on measures of Cynical Distrust, Impatience/Irritability, Anger-In, and Anger Control. Cynical Distrust, a factor-analytically derived measure from the Cook–Medley Hostility (Ho) scale (Greenglass & Julkunen, 1989), was used as an indicator of the cognitive component of the general hostility construct. The Impatience/Irritability factor (FTA-I), derived from the Finnish Type-A scale (Järvikoski & Härkäpää, 1987), was used as an indicator of the affective component of hostility. Suppression of anger was measured by the AX/In and AX/Con subscales of the Spielberger AX scale (Spielberger, 1988), discussed earlier.

It was hypothesized that hostility would be associated with PCA. Following the results of Dembroski et al. (1985) and Suarez (1986), a synergistic interaction effect between hostility and anger suppression was expected in the prediction of PCA. The study sample was composed of a subsample ($N = 119$) drawn from the KIHD study described in the previous section. To control for previously established risk factors, age, cigarette years, serum LDL cholesterol concentration, baseline common carotid intimamedia thickness, and SES were forced into all multivariate models. For a more detailed description of the methods in this study, see Julkunen et al. (1994).

Based on the psychological measures mentioned previously, PCA was predicted using four hypothetical Hostility × Anger Suppression models: 1. CynDis and AX/In; 2. FTA-I and AX/In; 3. CynDis and AX/Con; and 4. FTA-I and AX/Con. All models were tested using both continuous and dichotomized predictors.

Two of the hypothesized predictive variables, CynDis and AX/Con, showed consistently significant residual associations with PCA. Only in Model 1 was the main effect of the continuous CynDis just short of statistical significance ($p = .07$). At the same time, the other variables, FTA-I and AX/In, did not have any statistically significant association with PCA in any of the models.

Model 3, based on dichotomous CynDis and AX/Con, was best in the amount of variance accounted for in the 2-year PCA ($Rsq = 0.37$). To illustrate this model, a 2 × 2 ANCOVA was performed, controlling for the same covariates as used in the regression analyses and using the same cut-off values for the binary predictors. The adjusted mean values indicated a twofold accelerated PCA in the group high in both predictors (CynDis and AX/Con) as compared with the low-exposure group. In contrast to the proposed hypothesis, the impact of the independent variables on PCA in all models seemed to be additive, rather than synergistic. The proposed interaction effects were nonsignificant.

In summary, these findings indicate that, in addition to the previously established risk factors (i.e., high serum LDL cholesterol concentration, smoking, and old age), two hostility-related variables—Cynical Distrust and Anger Control—significantly contributed to the regression equation, which explained more than one third of the variation of 2-year atherosclerotic progression. In contrast with previous angiographic studies by Dembroski et al. (1985) and Suarez (1986), no significant interaction effect between hostility and anger suppression was found in this study.

However, a statistically significant interaction was found in a parallel model based on AX/Out and AX/Con (see Julkunen, Salonen, & Kaplan, 1992). AX/Out in this model was used as an indicator of general hostility because it has been reported to correlate highly significantly with trait anger ($r = 0.52$ for men; Spielberger, 1988). When this model was analyzed by a 2×2 ANCOVA, there was a significant interaction effect between AX/Out and AX/Con, with the group above the median on both measures showing approximately a three-fold accelerated PCA, as compared with the rest of the sample. This result supports the proposed hypothesis of the synergistic impact of hostility and anger suppression on the progression of atherosclerosis.

How does one explain an apparently contradictive combination of characteristics such as high anger-out and anger control occurring simultaneously in the same individual? This combination is, indeed, a rare one, comprising 9.4% of the subjects in the study sample. According to C. D. Spielberger (personal communication, August, 1994), this kind of person is somewhat like a driver stepping on the gas and the brake at the same time. Presumably, such contradictive efforts at the same time would result in hormonal confusion. However, these ideas require testing on larger samples.

Anger Control and Anger-In, which were both used as indicators of anger suppression, correlated quite weakly and nonsignificantly with each other in this study sample. The same was found in the KIHD sample, discussed earlier, as well as in previous studies (Spielberger, 1988). Contrary to expectations based on the correlational patterns of these measures, Anger Control, instead of Anger-In, showed a significant impact on progression of atherosclerosis. The somewhat lower internal consistency and retest reliability of AX/In, as compared with the AX/Con scale, could partly explain the lack of results using AX/In. One important concern, of course, is the fact that these data are based on self-report measures only. There may be a strong element of denial or social desirability involved. For example, a person with a tendency to suppress feelings of anger might also be likely to favor the items on the AC/Con scale over the AX/In items because anger control seems to be more socially acceptable. For example, a statement such as, "I try to be tolerant and understanding" (AX/Con) obviously seems more socially acceptable than "I pout or sulk" (AX/In). One could also speculate about the impact of the Finnish culture and gender stereotypes, which favor a calm, controlled, nonexpressive way of dealing with emotions, especially for men (Greenglass & Julkunen, 1991; Kauhanen, 1993). This would imply that AX/Con was a more valid measure of anger suppression as compared with AX/In, at least in the present sample of Finnish men. Again, these questions can only be answered with further studies using larger samples from many countries.

At the same time, AX/Con compared with AX/In may be a more direct opposite phenomenon to being openly angry because Anger Control correlates significantly and negatively with Anger-Out and T-Anger, whereas Anger-In has essentially zero correlations with these measures (Spielberger, 1988). In this sense, Anger control may reflect a more far-reaching effort to control the emotion and its expression. Thus, assuming that the progression of atherosclerosis was a function of the simultaneous operations of two opposing or contradictory dispositions, it is reasonable to expect the effect to be found with AX/ Con, rather than AX/In, because the former construct appears to be the opposite of the open expression of anger.

There are additional reasons to expect high anger control, in and of itself, to be associated with increased health risks. Significant positive correlations have been reported in other research between AX/Con and the Rationality/ Emotional-Defensiveness (R/ED) scale, suggesting that individuals who invest a great deal of energy in controlling the expression of anger are also more likely to use overrationality, repression, and denial as defenses for controlling their emotions (Swan et al., 1992). This is also supported by the previously mentioned positive correlation of AX/Con with a repressive coping style, whereas AX/In correlated negatively with the same measure (Julkunen et al., 1994). Thus, anger suppression, also in this "overrational" form as reflected by high AX/Con scores, could be a health risk, despite the significant correlations of AX/Con with several positive personality features (Julkunen et al., 1994).

The increased risk for atherosclerosis progression was especially pronounced with the combination of Cynical Distrust and Anger Control. This might suggest that it is the frequency with which one experiences anger arousal, which may be greater in persons who are high on Cynicism, in combination with a tendency to strictly control emotions that has pathogenic effects (Julkunen et al., 1994).

CONCLUSIONS

More research into the complex interactions of various forms of anger, hostility, and anger expression is needed before their health consequences can be better understood. Furthermore, the results discussed here indicate that there are psychologically subtle, but important, differences between various aspects of anger and aggressive behavior necessitating more sophisticated and multidimensional measurements of the hostility construct.

Where do these findings lead us? Is it always harmful to suppress or control negative feelings such as anger? Are good manners doomed to result in bad health? Perhaps the crucial question here is, to what extent are any modes of anger suppression or control followed by a calming down of the "hormonal storm"? If one is seething inside, even with a calm facade it seems likely that some damage will result in the long run. Thus, good manners are not likely to prevent a stroke or heart attack. Both anger-in and anger control, as operationalized in the Spielberger scales, seem to bear some risk in certain situations and/or in combination with certain other personality characteristics. The interplay of hostile emotions, behavior, and hormonal and physiological processes are far from understood and need further research. Given the health problems associated with anger and hostility, along with the social problems resulting from the increasing expression of unbridled aggression, it seems clear that hostility and aggression must remain in the forefront of research conducted by behavioral scientists.

REFERENCES

Alexander, F. (1950). *Psychosomatic medicine*. New York: Norton.

Anderson, C. A. (1989). Temperature and aggression: Ubiquitous effects of heat on occurrence of human violence. *Psychological Bulletin, 106,* 74–96.

Barefoot, J. C. (1992). Developments in the measurement of hostility. In H. S. Friedman (Ed.), *Hostility, coping & health* (pp. 13–31). Washington, DC: American Psychological Association.

Baron, R. M., & Kenny, D. A. (1986). The moderator-mediator variable distinction in social psychological research: Conceptual, strategic, and statistical considerations. *Journal of Personality and Social Psychology, 51,* 1173–1182.

Christensen, A. J., & Smith, T. W. (1993). Cynical hostility and cardiovascular reactivity during self-disclosure. *Psychosomatic Medicine, 55,* 193–202.

Cox, T., & Ferguson, E. (1991). Individual differences, stress and coping. In C. L. Cooper & R. Payne (Eds.), *Personality and stress: Individual differences in the stress process* (pp. 7–30). Chichester, England: Wiley.

Dembroski, T. M., MacDougal, J. M., Williams, R. B., Haney, T. L., & Blumenthal, J. A. (1985). Components of Type A, hostility, and anger-in: Relationship to angiographic findings. *Psychosomatic Medicine 47,* 219–233.

Diamond, E. L. (1982). The role of anger and hostility in essential hypertension and coronary heart disease. *Psychological Bulletin, 92,* 410–433.

Dunbar, F. (1947). *Mind and body: Psychosomatic medicine*. New York: Random House.

Freud, S. (1920). Beyond the pleasure principle. *Standard Edition, 18,* 7–64.

Greenglass, E. R., & Julkunen, J. (1989). Construct validity and sex differences in Cook–Medley hostility. *Personality and Individual Differences, 10,* 209–218.

Greenglass, E. R., & Julkunen, J. (1991, July). *A cross-national comparison of Type A, anger and hostility.* Paper presented at the 2nd European Congress of Psychology, Budapest, Hungary.

Hilgard, E. R. (1980). The trilogy of mind: Cognition, affection and conation. *Journal of the History of the Behavioral Sciences, 16,* 107–117.

Järvikoski, A., & Härkäpää, K. (1987). A brief Type-A scale and the occurrence of cardiovascular symptoms. *Scandinavian Journal of Rehabilitation Medicine 19,* 115–120.

Julius, M., Harburg, E., Cottington, E. M., & Johnson, E. H. (1986). Anger-coping types, blood pressure, and all-cause mortality: A follow-up in Tecumseh, Michigan (1971–1983). *American Journal of Epidemiology, 124,* 220–233.

Julkunen, J., Kauhanen, J., Kaplan, G. A., & Salonen, J. T. (1994). *Construct validity of the Spielberger Anger Expression Scale in a population sample of middle-aged Finnish men*. Unpublished manuscript.

Julkunen, J., & Korhonen, H. J. (1993, September). *Anger expression, work stress, and blood pressure: An interactional approach.* Paper presented at the 7th European Health Psychology Society conference, Brussels, Belgium.

Julkunen, J., Salonen, J. T., & Kaplan, G. A. (1992, July). *Anger expression, cynical distrust, and biological risk factors of coronary heart disease.* Paper presented at the 25th International Congress of Psychology, Brussels, Belgium.

Julkunen, J., Salonen, R., Kaplan, G. A., Chesney, M. A., & Salonen, J. T. (1994). Hostility and the progression of carotid atherosclerosis. *Psychosomatic Medicine, 56,* 519–525.

Kauhanen, J. (1993). *Dealing with emotions and health: A population study of Alexithymia in middle-aged men.* Kuopio University Publications D. Medical Sciences 25, Kuopio.

Lewin, K. (1952). Behavior and development as a function of the total situation. In D. Cartwright (Ed.), *Field theory in social science.* London: Tavistock.

Matthews, K. A. (1988). Coronary heart disease and Type A behaviors: Update on an alternative to the Booth-Kewley and Friedman (1987) quantitative review. *Psychological Bulletin, 104,* 373–380.

Pennebaker, J. W. (1992). Inhibition as the linchpin of health. In H. S. Friedman (Ed.), *Hostility, coping & health* (pp. 127–139). Washington, DC: American Psychological Association.

Price, V. A. (1982). *Type A Behavior Pattern: A model for research and practice.* New York: Academic Press.

Salonen, J. T. (1988). Is there a continuing need for longitudinal epidemiologic research—the Kuopio Ischaemic Heart Disease Risk Factor Study. *Annals of Clinical Research, 20,* 46–50.

Salonen, J. T., & Salonen, R. (1991). Ultrasonographically assessed carotid morphology and the risk of coronary heart disease. *Arteriosclerosis and Thrombosis, 11,* 1245–1249.

Salonen, R., & Salonen, J. T. (1990). Progression of carotid atherosclerosis and its determinants: A population-based ultrasonography study. *Atherosclerosis, 81,* 33–40.

Sarason, I. G. (1988). Social support, personality, and health. In M. P. Janisse (Ed.), *Health psychology: Individual differences and stress* (pp. 109–128). New York: Springer-Verlag.

Siegman, A. W., Dembroski, T. M., & Ringel, N. (1987). Components of hostility and the severity of coronary heart disease. *Psychosomatic Medicine, 49,* 127–135.

Smith, T. W. (1992). Hostility and health: Current status of a psychosomatic hypothesis. *Health Psychology, 11,* 139–150.

Smith, T. W., & Frohm, K. D. (1985). What's so unhealthy about hostility? Construct validity and psychosocial correlates of the Cook and Medley Ho scale. *Health Psychology, 4,* 503–520.

Spielberger, C. D. (1988). State–Trait Anger Expression Inventory (Res. ed.). Odessa, FL: Psychological Assessment Resources.

Spielberger, C. D., Johnson, E. H., Russell, S. F., Crane, R. J., Jacobs, G. A., & Worden, T. J. (1985). The experience and expression of anger: Construction and validation of an Anger Expression Scale. In M. A. Chesney & R. H. Rosenman (Eds.), *Anger and hostility in cardiovascular and behavioral disorders* (pp. 5–30). Washington, DC: Hemisphere.

Spielberger, C. D., Krasner, S. S., & Solomon, E. P. (1988). The experience, expression, and control of anger. In M. P. Janisse (Ed.), *Health psychology: Individual differences and stress* (pp. 89–108). New York: Springer-Verlag.

Suarez, E. C. (1986). The relationship among components of the Type A behavior pattern, Cook-Medley hostility scores, and atherosclerosis. *Dissertation Abstracts International, 47,* 2635.

Swan, G. E., Carmelli, D., Dame, A., Rosenman, R. H., & Spielberger, C. D. (1992). The rationality/emotional defensiveness scale: II. Convergent and discriminant correlational analysis in males and females with and without cancer. *Journal of Psychosomatic Research, 36,* 349–359.

Williams, R. B. (1984). Type A behavior and coronary heart disease: Something old, something new. *Behavioral Medicine, 6,* 29–33.

Williams, R. B., & Barefoot, J. C. (1988). Coronary-prone behavior: The emerging role of the hostility complex. In B. K. Houston & C. R. Snyder (Eds.), *Type A behavior: Research, theory, and intervention* (pp. 189–211). New York: Wiley.

14

Anger Expression and Blood Pressure

Peter Schwenkmezger and Petra Hank
University of Trier, Germany

Abstract *More than a half-century ago, Franz Alexander postulated that the suppression of anger was a major contributor to the etiology of hypertension and coronary heart disease (CHD). Subsequent research has demonstrated that both suppression and overt expression of anger were related to blood pressure (BP), but the results were inconsistent. To examine this relationship, 40 healthy, normotensive students with extreme high and/or low scores on the Anger-In and Anger-Out subscales of the State–Trait Anger Expression Inventory (STAXI) were selected from a sample of 406 male students to participate in laboratory and field studies of mode of anger expression and BP. In the laboratory study, BP was recorded automatically every 2 minutes during 10-minute relaxation, stress, and anger periods. This experiment was followed by 24-hour ambulatory BP monitoring, during which students recorded—via an electronic diary—all annoying episodes they experienced. In the laboratory study, students with high Anger-Out scores showed higher BP than those low in this disposition to overtly express anger. No relationship was found between suppressed anger (Anger-In) and BP. In the field study, the results were similar, but were moderated by the students' coping capabilities. Inconsistencies between these findings and previous research on anger and BP were discussed in terms of methodological issues and the procedures employed to assess anger expression and suppression.*

Cardiovascular disorders represent the major cause of death in a great number of industrial countries. Statistics compiled by the World Health Organization (1987) showed that these disorders are responsible for almost 50% of mortalities in various European industrial nations. Nowadays, cardiovascular disorders are conceived as having multifactorial causes. Alongside biological causes, behavior-determined risk factors have been named, such as smoking, obesity, diabetes mellitus, high cholesterol, and high uric acid levels (Seipel & Jehle, 1992). High blood pressure (BP) is also a major factor. It depends not only on biological causes, as evidenced by a concentration of hypertension in the family, but also on behavior-determined risk factors, such as obesity, insufficient exercise, alcohol drinking patterns, and high salt intake.

When discussing whether psychosocial factors influence the development and course of essential hypertension and, if so, which ones, numerous publications have emphasized the role of anger, anger expression, and related concepts such as hostility and aggression (for a review, see Chesney & Rosenman, 1985). This approach can be traced back to the following three lines of research:

1. Alexander (1939, 1950) proposed that psychoneurotic conditions, which express themselves in the repression of angry, hostile, and aggressive impulses, are responsible for the genesis of essential hypertension. This psychoanalytic hypothesis has had a particularly lasting impact on research.
2. The psychophysiological approaches of Ax (1953) and Funkenstein, King, and Drolette (1954) led directly to research on what role the emotion of anger could play in cardiovascular reactivity and, thus, in the development of hypertension and, in turn, cardiovascular disorders.
3. Finally, there is research on coronary-prone (Type-A) behavior, centering on an excessive need for recognition, impatience, a sense of time urgency, and a tendency toward hostility (Dembroski, Weiss, Shields, Haynes, & Feinleib, 1978; Friedman & Rosenman, 1959).

More recent work, particularly the analyses of Booth-Kewley and Friedman (1987) and Williams (1987), has increasingly claimed that not all behavioral components of Type-A behavior are equally strong risk factors, but that subcomponents (e.g., depression, hostility, anger, and anger expression) should be viewed as relevant dimensions that exhibit a relation to the occurrence of cardiovascular disorders.

Little is known about the fundamental psychophysiological mechanisms underlying the postulated connection between anger and BP response. Explanatory approaches either (a) follow concepts based on higher psychophysiological reactivity during stress or anger exposure (for a review, see Vögele & Steptoe, 1993), (b) provide an explanation based on learning theory (Engebretson, Mathews, & Scheier, 1989), (c) postulate pathophysiological reactions as a consequence of changes in behavior following exposure to stress (increased intake of alcohol and nicotine following emotional stress; see e.g., Scherwitz & Rugulies, 1992), or (d) suspect that there are interactive relations (Krohne, 1990). One specific explanatory approach that views higher BP as a consequence of an increased secretion of renin after anger stress, particularly suppression of anger, has been presented by Esler et al. (1977) and Thailer, Friedman, Harshfield, and Pickering (1985; see also Müller, 1988). Finally, Alexander's (1939, 1950) psychoanalytical hypothesis is still under discussion.

Before reviewing findings, it is necessary to sketch the concepts of *anger* and *anger suppression* (for a detailed review, see Hodapp & Schwenkmezger, 1993; Spielberger, 1988; Spielberger, Jacobs, Russell, & Crane, 1983; Spielberger et al., 1985). *Dispositional anger* describes the tendency to evaluate situations as anger-evoking and to respond to such situations with increased state anger. *State anger,* in contrast, is an indicator for the situation-specific anger reaction. In the earlier literature, externally directed anger and internally directed anger (i.e., Anger-Out or Anger-In) were considered poles of a single dimension, whereas, more recent findings indicate that the two forms of expression are independent (see Spielberger et al., 1985). A further dimension, *Anger*

Control, has been introduced to indicate interindividual differences in how far a person tries to control anger (for a review, see Schwenkmezger & Hodapp, 1993). By modifying the instructions, anger expression scales that have been conceived as dispositional constructs can also be used to measure state anger (see Schmitt, Hoser, & Schwenkmezger, 1991).

Various approaches have been used to empirically test the relation among anger, anger expression, and BP. One approach is to relate BP levels to habitual anger reactions, and then either compare the levels of anger and anger expression between normo- and hypertensives or relate them to BP levels. However, the explanatory power of many of these studies is reduced by confounds with the consequences of disease, only occasional measurement of BP, and the neglect of covariables with an impact on BP, such as body weight, alcohol consumption, or exercise. This research has been reviewed elsewhere (see Schwenkmezger, 1990; Schwenkmezger & Lieb, 1991).

A better approach is to assess cardiovascular reactivity under stress- or anger-induction conditions. Psychophysiological studies on the impact of anger and expression are particularly promising. Such studies have been carried out on samples from the normal population and in persons already suffering from essential hypertension. Confounds with the consequences of disease or risk factors can be avoided by studying normal populations and measuring cardiovascular reactivity in persons with different levels of habitual anger expression after experimentally induced exposure to stress or anger.

The numerous findings on the relationship among anger, anger expression, and cardiovascular reactivity are summarized in several reviews. Findings up to 1980 are documented in Diamond (1982). Tavris (1984) discussed the wide range of framing conditions in which forms of anger expression lead to cardiovascular reactions. Mann (1986) was rather skeptical about the impact of anger and anger expression on the development of hypertension, whereas Sommers-Flanagan and Greenberg (1989), who reviewed findings from 1979 to 1986, concluded that the connection between high BP and anger expression was confirmed more strongly.

Vögele and Steptoe (1993) recently reviewed 13 international, well-controlled laboratory studies on normal populations published between 1985 and 1992. In nine studies, externally directed anger expression, or theoretically similar variables such as hostility, were associated with increased systolic blood pressure (SBP) and/or high diastolic blood pressure (DBP). Negative relations between open anger expression and psychophysiological reactivity were found in two studies. No significant relationship was found in one study; in the other, "anger suppressors" exhibited the strongest SBP reactions. The authors also reviewed clinical studies and studies on at-risk groups, and found similarly heterogeneous findings. However, they concluded that externally directed anger was related more strongly to BP increases than suppressed anger. Siegman (1993) came to a similar conclusion.

Vögele and Steptoe's (1993) review did not include two studies by Otten (1993) and Stemmler, Schäfer, and Marwitz (1993). In an epidemiological study of men, Otten found no general relation between anger expression and cardiovascular reactivity when controlling for the following covariates: body weight, body size, alcohol consumption, and age. However, he did find a negative relation between externally directed anger expression and SBP in a subgroup of hypertensives.

Stemmler et al. studied the concept and operationalization of the anger-processing construct, and demonstrated that the construct had only a restricted homogeneity that also influenced the suspected relations to cardiovascular reactivity. However, DBP measured on four separate days showed consistent positive correlations with retrospectively assessed anger fantasies (somewhat comparable to anger-out) after experimental anger induction.

In summary, although these studies indicate a relationship between open anger expression and high SBP and DBP, in general, findings are contradictory. Vögele and Steptoe (1993) considered that this is particularly due to the lack of standardized procedures for measuring habitual forms of anger expression and to different forms of anger induction. One central problem is that internally and externally directed anger expression are repeatedly viewed as the two poles of a bipolar dimension, although, as mentioned earlier, the dimensions are largely independent (for a review, see Schwenkmezger, Hodapp, & Spielberger, 1992). In addition, most studies have compared only anger induction and relaxation while ignoring other forms of inducting emotions.

Another critical point is that anger-evoking situations in the laboratory are not derived from theory, but are conceived on the basis of researchers' "common sense" (see Wallbott & Scherer, 1985). Anger induction is generally operationalized by the experimenters or their associates "insulting" the respondent. In light of ethical and methodological constraints, the comparability of experimentally induced anger and "real," everyday anger seems questionable. In addition, participants in the laboratory hardly have the opportunity to exhibit the form of anger processing that they favor in everyday life.

For these reasons, there is growing consensus on the need to supplement experimental studies with field studies. Schönpflug (1979) already demonstrated the improved generalizability of findings in stress research when a sequence of laboratory and field studies is used. Similar arguments have also been expressed within psychophysiological research (Fahrenberg & Myrtek, in press; Johnston, Anastasiades, & Wood, 1990; Shapiro, Jamner, & Goldstein, 1993). Nonetheless, the comparability of laboratory and field studies can be impaired by differences in the behavioral options and their consequences. Finally, a temporally extended monitoring of BP also has much higher clinical relevance because it is subject to less measurement error than occasional measurement.

In line with these considerations, Rüddel, Schächinger, Quirrenbach, and Otten (1993) studied anger, anger expression, and BP over a 24-hour period. They found no relation between occasional measurements of BP and anger expression variables, whereas aggregated 24-hour DBP scores had a significant negative correlation with externally directed anger and a significant positive correlation with suppressed anger. When the 59 normotensive men were separated into two groups on the basis of their median Anger-In or Anger-Out scores, the 24-hour course revealed that the higher Anger-In group had higher DBP over the course of the afternoon and the evening than the lower Anger-

In group. Although high Anger-Out subjects had lower DBP during the afternoon and evening than those with below-median anger scores, there was no difference during the night and the morning. This finding underlines the fact that occasional measurements of BP are not a reliable means of detecting psychological relations to emotions.

In summary, previous research has generally revealed a positive relation between open anger expression and raised SBP and DBP in most laboratory studies, whereas the well-controlled field study of Rüddel et al. (1993) revealed an effect of suppressed anger that tended toward higher DBP and an effect of open anger that tended toward lower DBP, and that both showed diurnal variations.

The initial idea behind the present study was that, although previous findings have repeatedly revealed a relation among cardiovascular reactivity, anger, and anger expression, the strength and direction of this relation is not clear. Thus, it is still uncertain whether it is suppressed or openly exhibited anger that relates to increased cardiovascular reactivity. To investigate these issues, the following hypotheses were formulated:

1. Persons with high Anger-In scores will exhibit higher BP in anger-eliciting situations than persons with low Anger-In scores.
2. Persons with high Anger-Out scores will exhibit higher BP in anger-eliciting situations than persons with low Anger-Out scores.
3. When anger-eliciting situations are compared with neutral situations, persons with high scores on anger expression scales will respond with stronger changes in BP than persons with low scores.

We tested these hypotheses on normotensive males in a combined laboratory and field study design. Subjects were selected according to the principle of extreme group formation from a larger pool of subjects according to their habitual anger expression tendencies. After a laboratory session in which both anger and a mental load (labeled *stress* in the following) were induced, BP was monitored automatically for a 24-hour period, during which all anger-triggering episodes were registered with an electronic diary. This diary also recorded situation-specific efforts to cope with anger in order to study their impact on BP. Such a combined laboratory–field study also allowed us to test whether there was a correlation between cardiovascular reactivity in the laboratory and in the field. This should provide information on the reciprocal generalizability of such findings.

METHODS AND PROCEDURES OF THE
LABORATORY AND FIELD STUDIES

Sample

In a pretest, 406 male college students ages 18–31 years ($M = 23.9$, $SD = 2.7$) were given the German adaptation of the State–Trait Anger Expression

Inventory (STAXI; Schwenkmezger et al., 1992). Scores on the Anger-In and Anger-Out dimensions were used to form four extreme 10-person groups. These 40 subjects were ages 20–28 years ($M = 22.8$, $SD = 2.2$); they reported that they had had no serious illnesses during the previous 5 years. Selected subjects' BP was within a narrowly defined normal range (occasional BP at two measurements: SBP—120 ± 5 mmHg; DBP—80 ± 3 mmHg). Additionally, all subjects had ideal to normal body weight. After the selection according to these criteria, the cutoff scores for the distribution into the extreme groups were: high Anger-In: ≥ 22 (percentile rank: 90); low Anger-In: ≤ 12 (percentile rank: 15); high Anger-Out: ≥ 16 (percentile rank: 85); and low Anger-Out: ≤ 9 (percentile rank: 10).

Body weight and alcohol/cigarette consumption (according to self-reports during a 1-week protocol) were additionally assessed as control variables. Participation in the study was voluntary. Because of the large amount of time involved, subjects were paid DM 150 (about $100) upon completion of all parts of the study.

LABORATORY EXPERIMENT: PROCEDURE AND VARIABLES

The 40 subjects were exposed to an alternating sequence of 10-minute phases of relaxation, anger, and stress in the following order: (a) relaxation, (b) stress induction/anger induction, (c) relaxation, (d) anger induction/stress induction, and (e) relaxation. The sequence of stress or anger induction was randomized so that 20 subjects were first exposed to the anger induction, and the other 20 were first exposed to the stress induction. The relaxation phase directly following each induction was also analyzed.

The verbal differentiation between anger induction and stress induction is imprecise because anger can also be viewed as a stress (in this context, Scherer, 1985, talked about anger stress, anxiety stress, etc.). However, these terms are retained as verbal labels.

The entire course of the experiment was controlled by computer. Although an experimenter was present, subjects received all instructions via a PC monitor. Throughout the experiment, subjects were seated half upright and comfortably in an isometrically designed chair.

The stress induction was operationalized with mental arithmetic tasks taken from the *Konzentrations-Leistungs-Test* (KLT; Lienert, 1959). Subjects were instructed to work as quickly as possible without making errors. The relatively mild anger induction, which had been checked previously in a pretest, was operationalized by provoking the subjects. After the beginning of the task presentation, two error announcements appeared at short intervals, accompanied by the instruction "please wait." After a short time, this information was presented: "You have pressed the wrong key, please try again." This instruction was repeated three times during the 10-minute period. After 3 minutes, this instruction appeared: "Inform the experimenter." However, the experimenter calmly pointed out that the subject must have made a mistake, and that he would have to start again. Later, there were two further instructions: "Please be patient," and "Press the return key. The return key is the large key with an arrow to the left."

A portable PAR Physioport II was used to measure SBP and DBP, as well as heart rate (HR). This is a completely automated test-values memory that performs auscultatory measurements of the previously mentioned variables at previously programmed intervals. The experiment used approximately 2-minute intervals. To avoid adjustment effects, BP was measured at random intervals of 2 minutes ± 15 seconds. In addition, each subject's activity was measured by an activity recorder carried in the trouser pocket. This used three piezoelectric crystals to measure accelerations on all three body axes, which were then aggregated and recorded as a dimension-free activity indicator.

First, the transducers (electrodes, microphone, and activity recorder) were attached to the subjects. Electrocardiograms (ECG) were measured on the chest wall. Blood pressure was taken approximately 5 cm above the elbow with a Korotkof microphone over the brachial artery. This was covered with a sphygmomanometer cuff tightly wound round the subject's upper left arm. Leads and the sphygmomanometer tube ran from the left shoulder across the back of the neck and over the right shoulder to the right-hand side of the stomach. Transducers were connected to the test-values memory and fixed to the subject's belt together with an accumulator. All this equipment weighed approximately 800 grams. In the following test phase, we checked the Physioport II by comparing readings with simultaneous manual measurements.

To mark the beginning and end of each phase exactly, subjects had to press the event key on the Physioport. In addition, subjective data were collected at the end of each of the five phases. These were: (a) the state of relaxation on a 7-point rating scale with the poles *relaxed* (0) and *tense* (6); (b) situation-related anxiety as a stress indicator using five randomly selected items from the State Anxiety (S-Anxiety) scale of the German adaptation of the State–Trait Anxiety Inventory (STAI; Laux, Glanzmann, Schaffner, & Spielberger, 1981) for each phase; and (c) state-related anger using randomly selected items from the State Anger (S-Anger) scale of the STAXI. When selecting S-Anxiety items, in each case, two or three positively poled items were combined with two or three negatively poled items. The reliabilities for these short scales (internal consistency) ranged between .65 and .79.

MONITORING BLOOD PRESSURE IN THE FIELD STUDY

Directly after the experiment, BP was monitored in the field with the previously attached measurement system. Each experimental session began in the morning (all subjects started at 8:00) and lasted approximately 2 hours, including the attachment of the measurement instruments, instructions, and so forth. This was followed by instructions regarding the field study, which continued until 8:00 on the following morning. Two measurement intervals were defined for the analysis: From 11:00 to 23:00, measurements were set at approximately 10-minute intervals. Once again, to avoid adjustment effects, measurements were made every 10 ± 1 minute (triggered by a random sequence generator). With six measurements per hour, this resulted in 72 individual measurements. From 23:00 to 8:00 on the next day, the measurement interval was set at 30 minutes to minimize disruption of sleep behavior. During this phase, 18 measurements were carried out. Thus, 90 individual measurements were made across the entire 21-hour period.

In addition to monitoring BP, anger experience and anger expression were registered in the field through systematic self-observation. A specially developed anger protocol was recorded on an accompanying pocket computer. Subjects had to note the time and location of the anger episode; the source of anger; and the identity of offenders, victims, and any third persons present. These reports were used to record external behavior-determining variables. Current anger intensity was also assessed with five items from the S-Anger scale of the STAXI. Anger expression and coping with anger were assessed with an adapted, situation-specific, four-item, short version of the anger expression scales in a dichotomous response format (Anger-Out: "I blurted out my anger so that other persons got to feel it"; "I hit the ceiling"; "I got very loud"; "I did things like slam doors." Anger-In: "I didn't show how angry I was"; "I boiled inside, but didn't show it"; "I was much more worked up than others could see"; "I felt a grudge, but I didn't talk to anybody about it." Anger Control: "On the surface, I kept my composure"; "I controlled my behavior"; "I controlled my angry feelings"; "I said to myself, 'Don't get worked up'").

The complete anger journal was documented on a pocket computer (ATARI Portfolio) that subjects carried with them throughout the study. Subjects were instructed to document, as immediately as possible, each episode in which they got angry or annoyed.

Significance levels were set at $p = .05$ for both the experiment and the field study. Because of the way in which the hypotheses were formulated, weighted tests were performed. These were based on multivariate analyses of variance (MANOVA) with repeated measures. In analyses with more than two-stage repeated-measures factors, Wilk's Δ was computed or degrees of freedom were corrected using the Huynh–Feldt procedure. The effect of the control variables—body size, body weight, alcohol and cigarette consumption, and physical activity—were partialed out with analysis of covariance (ANCOVA). Slight differences in the reported degrees of freedom were due to isolated missing data.

RESULTS OF THE LABORATORY AND FIELD STUDIES

The results of the experiment and field study are presented separately. An effect of body size or body weight could not be confirmed, probably because selected subjects had ideal or normal weight. The physical activity indicator also had no effect. Although this was to be expected in the laboratory experiment (see procedure), in the field study, subjects were asked to move as little as possible during the measurements to avoid measurement error. This may

Table 14.1 Means and standard deviations of tension ratings, S-Anxiety, and S-Anger in the five phases of the experiment

Phase	Relaxation		Anxiety		Anger	
	M	*SD*	*M*	*SD*	*M*	*SD*
Relaxation	2.36	.99	1.90	.45	1.18	.34
Stress	3.13	1.42	2.08	.42	1.14	.24
Relaxation	2.23	.93	1.92	.39	1.12	.27
Anger	2.62	1.07	2.06	.51	1.44	.51
Relaxation	2.05	.89	1.85	.47	1.29	.38

Note. Tension was rated on a 7-point scale (see text for details). S-Anxiety and S-Anger values are based on averaged item scores.

well explain the low impact of this variable. The effect of the covariate alcohol and cigarette consumption proved to be insignificant.

Apart from the comparison between waking and sleep periods, no diurnal rhythm could be ascertained. During the sleep phase (23:00 to 8:00), SBP and DBP scores were significantly lower ($p \leq .01$). Results on HR are not presented because they showed no clear effects.

Experimental Results

Before the results can be interpreted, it is necessary to determine whether the intended emotional state was induced successfully. The subjective impact of the relaxation phases and the two experimental conditions assessed with the tension/relaxation ratings and the five-item, short versions from the S-Anxiety and S-Anger questionnaires were tested with a multivariate analysis of variance (ANOVA) with repeated measures.

Table 14.1 presents the means and standard deviations. A test of the deviations of the mean of each critical phase from the mean of all phases showed that the experience of anger was significantly more intense under anger induction than under all other phases [$F(1, 39) = 18.8$, $p < .001$, Wilk's $\Delta = .61$]. An analogue test also revealed a significant effect of the stress induction [$F(1, 38) = 5.3$, $p < .03$, Wilk's $\Delta = .71$]. There was also a higher S-Anxiety score under the anger induction. As anticipated, perceived tension increased significantly under stress induction [$F(1, 38) = 14.1$, $p < .001$, Wilk's $\Delta = .64$], and dropped significantly in the subsequent relaxation phase [$F(1, 38) = 7.6$, $p < .01$]. No significant increase in tension could be observed for the transition from relaxation to anger induction.

It was predicted that persons with combined high, externally directed, and internally directed anger expression would have higher BP scores under anger or stress induction compared with the relaxation phases. The three BP scores for the individual phases of the experiment were aggregated (4th, 6th, and 8th minute). A 2 × 2 × 5 MANOVA, with the independent variables Anger-Out (high vs. low) and Anger-In (high vs. low), and the five phases of the experiment as the repeated-measures factor, produced no indications of an effect of internally directed anger on SBP or DBP [$F(1, 31) = 1.16, p = .29; F(1, 32) = 0.50, p = .49$, respectively]. Therefore, Hypothesis 1 had to be rejected. In contrast, the main effects of externally directed anger on SBP and DBP were significant [$F(1, 32) = 3.4, p < .05; F(1, 32) = 3.6, p < .05$, respectively].

In addition, ANOVAs with repeated measures were computed for the five experimental conditions (allowing for corrections to degrees of freedom), in which only the externally directed anger component (high vs. low) was included as an independent variable (Hypothesis 2). This analysis of a "reduced" design seemed appropriate because of the changes in degrees of freedom. For SBP, this produced a significant effect of Anger-Out [$F(1, 34) = 2.8, p < .05$] and the course [$F(3.22, 140) = 12.6, p < .01$], as well as a significant interaction [$F(3.22, 140) = 2.8, p < .05$]. For DBP, there were significant main effects of Anger-Out [$F(1, 34) = 5.1, p < .05$] and the course [$F(3.73, 140) = 18.3, p < .001$].

A posteriori comparisons between subjects with high versus low Anger-Out scores between the individual phases of the experiment produced significant differences for SBP in the third and fifth phase [$t(27) = -2.04, p < .05; t(37) = -2.98, p < .01$, respectively]. The remaining differences were not significant. For DBP, the differences in the first phase of relaxation and in stress induction were also not significant. In contrast, there were significant differences in the anger phase [$t(37) = -2.40, p < .05$], the middle relaxation phase [$t(37) = -2.72, p < .01$], and the final relaxation phase [$t(37) = -3.09, < .01$]. This supported Hypothesis 2.

To test Hypothesis 3, individual paired differences were tested a posteriori. For SBP, there were significant differences between the stress phase and subsequent relaxation phase [$t(36) = -2.28, p < .05$] and between the anger phase and the following relaxation phase [$t(37) = -2.30, p < .05$]. In contrast, increases between the preceding relaxation phase and the following induction phases were not significant. Therefore, it seemed as if cardiovascular reactivity to stress and anger was the same for both Anger-Out groups, but that the drop in the values in the subsequent relaxation phase was significantly stronger in the group with low Anger-Out compared with the group with high Anger-Out. Fig. 14.1 seems to indicate that this effect was particularly clear for the psychophysiological relaxation after the anger phase, but there was no significant difference when compared with relaxation scores following stress induction.

Field Results

Following the procedure reported in Rüddel et al. (1993), hourly means for the BP data obtained in the field study were computed and then analyzed in terms of the assumptions formulated in Hypotheses 1 and 2. Across all hourly means, there was no effect of the habitual anger expression styles of Anger-In and Anger-Out on BP levels. Indications for a diurnal rhythm could not be found apart from the day–night difference. Thus, the findings of Rüddel et al. (1993) were unable to be replicated.

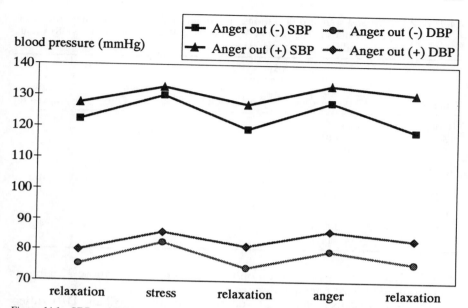

Figure 14.1 SBP and DBP as a function of externally directed anger expression (low vs. high) in the five experimental phases.

An additional analysis used the anger episodes recorded in the anger journals. Fifty-six anger episodes occurred among the 40 subjects during the period of the field study. Analyzable BP score protocols were available for 50 of these episodes. These 50 episodes were distributed across 32 different subjects. Fourteen of these subjects had a low habitual externally directed anger expression style, and the remaining 18 a high one. For Anger-In, the distribution was 17 to 15. Neither difference was significant. Two subjects reported four anger episodes, 1 subject reported three, 10 subjects reported two, and each of the remaining subjects reported one.

For the analysis, a data file containing the in situ recorded variables on anger experience and anger expressions was generated, as well as the accompanying BP levels for each of the 50 episodes treated as single cases. The phases were defined before, during, and after the anger episodes as 30 minutes before their occurrence, 30 minutes after the onset of protocols, and the following 30 minutes, respectively. As all anger episodes were reported for the time between 11:00 and 23:00, three measurements of BP at 10-minute intervals were available for each phase. The BP scores belonging to each phase were added together and averaged. These mean scores were then used as the dependent variables in the following analyses.

In the first stage of analysis, all 50 anger episodes were first treated as if they were independent. However, such an analysis is incorrect because several episodes from one subject were entered into the computations. Therefore, the

Table 14.2 Means and standard deviations of SBP and DBP before, during, and after
anger episodes in the field in 32 subjects split according to high (18) versus
low (14) habitual anger expresion

	SBP		DBP	
Time variable	High Anger-Out	Low Anger-Out	High Anger-Out	Low Anger-Out
Before				
M	140.8	135.3	85.2	80.1
SD	11.9	16.2	12.2	12.7
During				
M	152.1	144.7	85.6	80.9
SD	18.0	15.6	10.9	8.5
After				
M	141.5	137.6	85.6	84.8
SD	11.7	16.9	10.0	9.0

same analyses were carried out on only the first episodes of those 32 subjects
who reported at least one anger episode.

Table 14.2 presents means and standard deviations of SBP and DBP differentiated according to Anger-Out scores. Once again, as in the experiment,
there was no effect of Anger-In. For Anger-Out, there was only a trend toward
higher SBP in subjects with high open anger expression ($p < .10$). In contrast,
the course effect was highly significant [$F(2.00, 64) = 10.2, p < .001$]. There
was no interaction effect. Likewise, no main effects and interaction effects
were found for DBP.

To test Hypothesis 3, differences between preanger and anger phase or anger
and postanger phase were compared as in the laboratory experiment. Indications for different reactivity scores as a function of Anger-Out could not be
found.

Alongside the impact of habitual anger expression, the effectiveness of
situational anger expression was also tested using the Anger-In, Anger-Out,
and Anger Control items that subjects had to answer after each anger episode.
Subjects who gave negative answers to all items were assigned to the low anger
expression or anger control group, whereas subjects who agreed with at least
one item were assigned to the high anger expression or high Anger Control
group.

Subjects who openly exhibited their anger had higher SBP across all three
phases compared with the other groups. The course also corresponded to the
previously reported values. However, these trends were not significant. For
Anger-In, once more, no effect could be found.

Situational Anger Control had an effect on SBP insofar as the values for
subjects with high control were significantly lower [$F(1, 32) = 2.86, p < .05$].
The repeated-measures factor was also significant [$F(2.00, 64) = 8.5, p < .001$]. There were no significant differences for DBP. Results are presented in
Fig. 14.2.

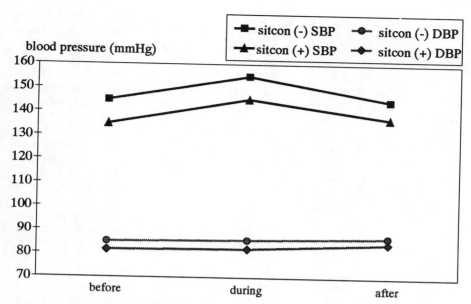

Figure 14.2 SBP and DBP before, during, and after anger episodes in the field as a function of situation-specific Anger Control (sitcon [−]: low level of Anger Control; sitcon [+]: high level of Anger Control).

Tests in line with Hypothesis 3—on the differences between preanger phase and anger phase or anger phase and postanger phase—also produced no significant differences.

GENERAL DISCUSSION AND CONCLUSIONS

When interpreting the results, it is necessary to discriminate between content-related and methodological aspects. One of the main content-related findings is that only externally directed, but not internally directed, habitual anger expression proved to have an impact on cardiovascular reactivity. This applies equally to SBP and DBP in the laboratory experiment, although a course effect is found for SBP, indicating that the normalization of BP takes longer in persons with high externally directed anger expression than in those with low scores. In the field study, an effect of habitual externally directed expression on SBP can be observed as a trend. However, differences are not significant.

Differential BP courses can only be observed in the laboratory. In subjects with high externally directed anger expression, a delayed drop in BP can be observed between the induction of stress or anger and the following period of relaxation. This indicates the diagnostic importance of the recovery rate—a finding that has also been reported in other studies. For example, Gsellhofer, Montoya, Müller, Piesbergen, and Schandry (1992) reported that an avoidant coping style is associated with delayed increases in BP.

One possible criticism of these findings has to be emphasized: For the first relaxation phases, differences in BP in the two anger groups were not anticipated, particularly because great care had been taken to select only persons with normotensive scores within a narrowly defined range in several occasional measurements. Nonetheless, even during this phase, there were already differences in BP between persons with high versus low open anger expression, although they were not significant. We consider that this may have been due to the intricate preparations for the study (e.g., fixing electrodes and introduction to the laboratory experiment and the field study) that may well have already led to a high activity level during the prestudy phase. This interpretation is also supported by the higher value on the tension-relaxation rating in the first relaxation phase compared with the two following ones (see Table 1). This difference also appears as a trend in the field study during the phases before anger provocation.

We have no explanation for the differences between our results and those reported by Rüddel et al. (1993) using similar methods. The only major difference is that Rüddel et al. used an earlier version of the STAXI that differs greatly from our version.

Beyond previously reported findings, the field study shows that the situation-specific control of externally directed anger has a moderating impact on cardiovascular reactivity. For anger situations in which anger is expressed without control, both systolic and diastolic pressure values are higher than in situations in which subjects report that they have been able to process their anger in a controlled way. However, care should be taken when interpreting these findings, because they are based on a relatively small number of anger episodes and require cross-validation.

Although the findings in the laboratory and field study were similar, inter-correlations of the reactivity scores, as reported in Schwenkmezger and Hank (1995), show that they cannot be generalized in both directions. The similarity between experimentally induced anger and anger episodes in everyday life is probably slight because behavioral options and their consequences are much more variable in field conditions, and the laboratory situation triggered only very mild anger in the sense of a general state of uncertainty. It is questionable whether structural similarity can be constructed following the proposal of Shapiro et al. (1993) because the experimental induction of anger is subject to ethical constraints. In addition, far-reaching structural similarity would make the question of generalizability redundant.

In summary, the findings show a high level of agreement with much of the more recent literature (see Siegman, 1993; Vögele & Steptoe, 1993), but they also contradict the traditionally dominant hypothesis in the psychological and psychosomatic literature on the impact of anger suppression of BP. There is increasing evidence that this hypothesis requires modification. Theoretical considerations lead to the conclusion that future studies should not negate the Anger-In components. These address both the dimensionality and functionality of anger suppression, as well as the issue of the impact of Anger Control competencies.

There is some evidence that the one-dimensional assessment of suppressed anger in the STAXI is inadequate, and that this is a multidimensional construct. Weber (1993) pointed out that behaviors such as talking oneself out of being angry, grinning and bearing it, distracting oneself by thinking about something else, calming oneself down, or withdrawing one's affections may represent very different aspects of anger suppression. The STAXI test manual (Schwenkmezger et al., 1992) also reports that anger suppression correlates with different forms of coping with stress, such as escape tendency, feeling sorry for oneself, social withdrawal, resignation, and self-blame. Hence, a differentiated, multidimensional assessment of anger suppression seems to be necessary before its health-related effects can be analyzed more exactly.

Under functional considerations, it also has to be pointed out that anger suppression does not necessarily have only a negative impact, but can also contribute to the avoidance of conflict. In everyday life, anger suppression is frequently applied in an adaptive, situation-appropriate, and goal-oriented way. It is hardly conceivable that this form of anger suppression; which can certainly represent a social regulative for living together, can cause illness. Indeed, one could even assume that it has components that protect health.

However, this situationally adaptive form of anger suppression has to be differentiated from a rigid form that is applied without considering the circumstances and that exhibits a high degree of stability in the sense of a personality disposition. It is far easier to assume an illness-related impact of this form. Although the STAXI was designed to assess this form of anger suppression, little is known about its success.

The question of the moderating impact of Anger Control expectations and competencies is also still unexplained. Here as well, the Anger Control scale of the STAXI seems to be relatively global in that it appears to tap the control of externally directed anger, but not internally directed anger. In addition, in line with the earlier considerations, there is also a need to test how far the situation-appropriate suppression of anger is a specific form of Anger Control. Indeed, the results of the field study indicate that it is possibly not dispositional, but situation-specific Anger Control that can be assigned a protective function.

In this context, it should also be pointed out that anger episodes have to be differentiated according to the way in which they are triggered (sudden and acute vs. building up slowly), their duration, and the perceived responsibility for harm (see Schmitt et al., 1991). Such differentiations of anger elicitation, as well as coping with anger, could also be involved in the cardiovascular effect (see Stemmler et al., 1993; Tavris, 1984).

Finally, it is also necessary to ask whether the findings can be generalized to other samples—above all, to clinical groups. Like Rüddel et al. (1993), this study used a very homogeneous group of subjects from the normal population whose body weight lay within the ideal to normal range and who were completely normal in terms of BP. The mechanisms for regulating anger and cardiovascular reactivity could take a different form in other samplers (e.g., in clinical samples; see Otten, 1993; Reicherts, 1993).

The chapter concludes with some methodological considerations regarding this study. In this area of research, the field approach is certainly an ideal, although unfortunately far too rarely applied, supplement to the experimental approach. Because such sequences of study call for great effort on the part of subjects, the recruitment of motivated subjects is indispensable. This does not raise any problems as long as subjects receive appropriate remuneration. In addition, the validity of such studies seems to be higher than pure questionnaire surveys or pure laboratory studies. However, the large amount of time needed makes it much more difficult to study large samples.

The description of the anger episodes can also be improved: First, episodes of anger that occur acutely and suddenly, and, second, those that accumulate silently and for which an exact onset cannot be ascertained. Both forms should also be viewed separately in terms of coping, and they may well differ in their impact on BP. The duration of anger and the drop in anger emotions as a result of control efforts or extreme changes in the situation should also be assessed more exactly.

In addition, methods could be optimized by coordinating BP measurement and the electronic journal so that either BP can be measured more frequently when anger episodes occur or protocols can be requested on the behaviors and events that accompany in situ increases in BP. The highly variable method of the electronic journal can also be used to provide better control over a host of relevant conditions—for example, risk behaviors such as cigarette smoking and alcohol consumption—but also other variables influencing BP, such as diurnal rhythms, physical activity, or nutritional factors.

REFERENCES

Alexander, F. (1939). Emotional factors in essential hypertension. *Psychosomatic Medicine, 1,* 173–179.

Alexander, F. (1950). *Psychosomatic medicine: Its principles and applications.* New York: Norton.

Ax, A. F. (1953). The physiological differentiation between fear and anger in humans. *Psychosomatic Medicine, 15,* 433–442.

Booth-Kewley, S., & Friedman, H. S. (1987). Psychological predictors of heart disease: A quantitative review. *Psychological Bulletin, 101,* 349–362.

Chesney, M. A., & Rosenman, R. H. (Eds.). (1985). *Anger and hostility in cardiovascular and behavioral disorders.* Washington, DC: Hemisphere.

Dembroski, T. M., Weiss, S. M., Shields, J. L., Haynes, S. G., & Feinleib, M. (Eds.). (1978). *Coronary-prone behavior.* New York: Springer.

Diamond, E. L. (1982). The role of anger and hostility in essential hypertension and coronary heart disease. *Psychological Bulletin, 92,* 410–433.

Engebretson, T. O., Mathews, K. A., & Scheier, M. F. (1989). Relations between anger expression and cardiovascular reactivity: Reconciling inconsistent findings through a matching hypothesis. *Journal of Personality and Social Psychology, 57,* 513–521.

Esler, M., Julius, S., Zweifler, A., Randall, O., Harburg, A., Gardener, H., & DeQuattro, V. (1977). Mild high-renin essential hypertension. *New England Journal of Medicine, 296*, 405–411.

Fahrenberg, J., & Myrtek, M. (in press). Ambulantes Monitoring und Assessment [Ambulant monitoring and assessment]. In F. Rösler (Ed.), *Enzyklopädie der Psychologie: Bereich Psychophysiologie Band I. Grundlagen und Methoden der Psychophysiologie*. Göttingen: Hogrefe.

Friedman, M., & Rosenman, R. H. (1959). Association of specific overt behavior pattern with blood and cardiovascular findings: Blood cholesterol level, blood clotting time, incidence of arcus senilis, and clinical coronary artery disease. *Journal of the American Medical Association, 169*, 1286–1296.

Funkenstein, D. H., King, S. H., & Drolette, M. E. (1954). The direction of anger during a laboratory stress-inducing situation. *Psychosomatic Medicine, 16*, 404–413.

Gsellhofer, B., Montoya, P., Müller, A., Piesbergen, C., & Schandry, R. (1992). Zum Zusammenhang zwischen Streßbewältigung und Blutdruckreaktion [The relationship between coping with stress and blood pressure]. *Zeitschrift für experimentelle und angewandte Psychologie, 39*, 419–433.

Hodapp, V., & Schwenkmezger, P. (Eds.). (1993). *Ärger und Ärgerausdruck [Anger and anger expression]*. Bern: Huber.

Johnston, D. W., Anastasiades, P., & Wood, C. (1990). The relationship between cardiovascular responses in the laboratory and in the field. *Psychophysiology, 27*, 34–44.

Krohne, H. W. (1990). Streß und Streßbewältigung [Stress and coping with stress]. In R. Schwarzer (Ed.), *Gesundheitspsychologie. Ein Lehrbuch* (pp. 263–277). Göttingen: Hogrefe.

Laux, L., Glanzmann, P., Schaffner, P., & Spielberger, C. D. (1981). *Das State-Trait-Angstinventar. Theoretische Grundlagen und Handanweisung [The State-Trait Anxiety Inventory. Theoretical bases and manual]*. Weinheim: Beltz.

Lienert, G. A. (1959). *Der Konzentrations-Leistungs-Test K-L-T [The attention test]*. Göttingen: Hogrefe.

Mann, A. H. (1986). The psychological aspects of essential hypertension. *Journal of Psychosomatic Research, 30*, 527–541.

Müller, M. M. (1988). Die Bedeutung von Ärger und Ärgerverarbeitung als ätiologisches und therapeutisches Kriterium bei essentieller Hypertonie [The importance of anger and coping with anger as etiological and therapeutic criteria for essential hypertension]. *Psychotherapie, Psychosomatik, Medizinische Psychologie, 38*, 390–393.

Otten, H. (1993). Beziehungen von Ärgerausdruck zur kardiovaskulären Reaktivität und Blutdruck bei Männern [Relationships of anger expression to cardiovascular reactivity and blood pressure in men]. In V. Hodapp & P. Schwenkmezger (Eds.), *Ärger und Ärgerausdruck* (pp. 193–215). Bern: Huber.

Reicherts, M. (1993). Solch ein Ärger—Was tun? Eine situationsorientierte Analyse der Bewältigungseffizienz bei Ärger in Alltagsbelastungen [Such an anger—what to do? A situational analysis of the efficiency of coping with daily anger]. In V. Hodapp & P. Schwenkmezger (Eds.), *Ärger und Ärgerausdruck* (pp. 227–251). Bern: Huber.

Rüddel, H., Schächinger, H., Quirrenbach, S., & Otten, H. (1993). Ärgerausdruck und Blutdruck im 24-Stunden-Verlauf [Anger expression and blood pressure in the course of 24 hours]. In V. Hodapp & P. Schwenkmezger (Eds.), *Ärger und Ärgerausdruck* (pp. 217–226). Bern: Huber.

Scherer, K. A. (1985). Streß und Emotion: Ein Ausblick [Stress and emotion: An outlook]. In K. A. Scherer, H. J. Tolkmitt, & G. Bergmann (Eds.), *Die Streßreaktion, Physiologie und Verhalten* (pp. 195–205). Göttingen: Hogrefe.

Scherwitz, L., & Rugulies, R. (1992). Life-style and hostility. In H. S. Friedman (Ed.), *Hostility, coping and health* (pp. 77–98). Washington, DC: American Psychological Association.

Schmitt, M., Hoser, K., & Schwenkmezger, P. (1991). Schadensverantwortlichkeit und Ärger [Responsibility for damage and anger]. *Zeitschrift für experimentelle und angewandte Psychologie, 38,* 634–647.

Schönpflug, W. (1979). Regulation und Fehlregulation im Verhalten [Regulation and maladaptive regulation in behavior]. *Psychologische Beiträge, 21,* 174–202.

Schwenkmezger, P. (1990). Ärger, Ärgerausdruck und Gesundheit [Anger, anger expression and health]. In R. Schwarzer (Ed.), *Gesundheitspsychologie. Ein Lehrbuch* (pp. 295–310). Göttingen: Hogrefe.

Schwenkmezger, P., & Hank, P. (1995). Ärger, Ärgerausdruck und Blutdruckverhalten: Ergebnisse einer kombinierten experimentellen und feldexperimentellen Untersuchung [Anger, anger expression, and blood pressure: Further results of a combined experimental and field study]. *Zeitschrift für Gesundheitspsychologie, 3,* 39–58.

Schwenkmezger, P., & Hodapp, V. (1993). Theorie und Messung von Ärgerausdruck [Theory and measurement of anger expression]. In V. Hodapp & P. Schwenkmezger (Eds.), *Ärger und Ärgerausdruck* (pp. 35–69). Bern: Huber.

Schwenkmezger, P., Hodapp, V., & Spielberger, C. D. (1992). *Das State–Trait-Ärgerausdrucks-Inventar (STAXI) [The State–Trait Anger Expression Inventory].* Bern: Huber.

Schwenkmezger, P., & Lieb, R. (1991). Emotionen und psychosomatische Erkrankungen: Ärger und Ärgerausdruck bei koronaren Herzerkrankungen und essentieller Hypertonie [Emotions and psychosomatic diseases: Anger and anger expression in cardiovascular diseases and essential hypertension]. In D. H. Hellhammer & U. Ehlert (Eds.), *Verhaltensmedizin: Ergebnisse und Anwendung* (pp. 21–33). Bern: Huber.

Seipel, L., & Jehle, J. (1992). Die koronare Herzkrankheit [Coronary heart disease]. In W. Siegenthaler, H. Hornbostel, & H. D. Waller (Eds.), *Lehrbuch der inneren Medizin* (3rd ed., pp. 13–24). New York: Thieme.

Shapiro, D., Jamner, L. D., & Goldstein, J. B. (1993). Ambulatory stress psychophysiology: The study of "compensatory and defensive counterforces and conflict in natural setting." *Psychosomatic Medicine, 55,* 309–323.

Siegman, A. W. (1993). Cardiovascular consequences of expressing, experiencing and repressing anger. *Journal of Behavioral Medicine, 16*, 539–569.

Sommers-Flanagan, J., & Greenberg, R. P. (1989). Psychosocial variables and hypertension: A new look at an old controversy. *Journal of Nervous and Mental Disease, 177,* 15–24.

Spielberger, C. D. (1988). *STAXI. State–Trait Anger Expression Inventory, professional manual.* Tampa, FL: Psychological Assessment Resources.

Spielberger, C. D., Jacobs, G., Russell, S., & Crane, R. J. (1983). Assessment of anger: The State–Trait Anger scale. In J. N. Butcher & C. D. Spielberger (Eds.), *Advances in personality assessment* (Vol. II, pp. 161–189). Hillsdale, NJ: Lawrence Erlbaum Associates.

Spielberger, C. D., Johnson, E. H., Russell, S. F., Crane, R. J., Jacobs, G. A., & Worden, T. J. (1985). The experience and the expression of anger: Construction and validation of an Anger Expression Scale. In M. A. Chesney & R. H. Rosenman (Eds.), *Anger and hostility in cardiovascular and behavioral disorders* (pp. 5–30). Washington, DC: Hemisphere.

Stemmler, G., Schäfer, H., & Marwitz, M. (1993). Zum Konzept und zu den Operationalisierungen von Stilen der Ärgerverarbeitung [Concept and operationalization of coping styles for anger]. In V. Hodapp & P. Schwenkmezger (Eds.), *Ärger und Ärgerausdruck* (pp. 71–111). Bern: Huber.

Tavris, C. (1984). On the wisdom on counting to ten. *Review of Personality and Social Psychology, 5,* 170–191.

Thailer, S. A., Friedman, R., Harshfield, G. A., & Pickering, T. G. (1985). Psychological differences between high-, normal-, and low-renin hypertensives. *Psychosomatic Medicine, 47,* 294–297.

Vögele, C., & Steptoe, A. (1993). Ärger, Feindseligkeit und kardiovaskuläre Reaktivität: Implikationen für essentielle Hypertonie und koronare Herzkrankheit [Anger, hostility and cardiovascular reactivity: Implications for essential hypertension and coronary heart disease]. In V. Hodapp & P. Schwenkmezger (Eds.), *Ärger und Ärgerausdruck* (pp. 169–191). Bern: Huber.

Wallbott, H. G., & Scherer, K. R. (1985). Differentielle Situations- und Reaktionscharakteristika in Emotionserinnerungen: Ein neuer Forschungsansatz [Differential characteristics of situations and reactions in remembering emotions: A new research paradigm]. *Psychologische Rundschau, 36,* 83–101.

Weber, H. (1993). *Ärger. Psychologie einer alltäglichen Emotion* [Anger. Psychology of a daily emotion]. Weinheim: Juventa.

Williams, R. B. (1987). Refining the Type A hypothesis: Emergents of the hostility complex. *American Journal of Cardiology, 60,* 27J–32J.

World Health Organization. (1987). *World health statistics manual.* Geneva: Author.

15

Anger and Anxiety in Hypertensive Patients in India

Sagar Sharma and Archna Krishna
Himachal Pradesh University, Shimla, India

Charles D. Spielberger
University of South Florida, Tampa, USA

Abstract   *The Hindi forms of Spielberger's Trait Anxiety (T-Anxiety) and Anger Expression (AX) scales were administered to hypertensive and normotensive patients being treated in the outpatient clinics of a general hospital. Systolic blood pressure (SBP) and diastolic blood pressure (DBP) were recorded on successive clinic visits over 21 days. The hypertensives had significantly higher T-Anxiety and Anger-In (AX/In) and significantly lower Anger-Out (AX/Out) scores than the normotensive patients. Correlations of AX/In with BP for the hypertensives were positive, highly significant, and stronger with SBP than with DBP. Correlations of AX/Out with BP were negative and also highly significant for the hypertensives. There was no relation between the anger measures and BP for the normotensive patients; T-Anxiety did not correlate with BP for either patient group. These findings provide further evidence of the importance of suppressed anger in the etiology of hypertension. Substantial inverse relations between AX/In and AX/Out for both hypertensives and normotensives suggested an important East–West cultural difference in regard to anger expression. Indian patients responded to the AX/In and AX/Out scales as if these scales assessed a unidimensional, bipolar continuum, rather than independent dimensions, as has been consistently observed for normal populations in the United States and other Western countries.*

Essential hypertension, defined as a sustained elevation in blood pressure (BP) of unknown cause, is a major worldwide health problem affecting 15%–20% of the adult population (Griffin & Kee, 1986). Although researchers do not agree on the significance of psychological factors in essential hypertension (see Maan, 1986), during the past two decades there has been a surge of interest in the contribution of negative emotions such as anxiety and anger to the etiology of this disorder (e.g., Crane, 1982; Hartfield, 1985; Spielberger et al., 1991).

261

Research on essential hypertension in Western countries has produced mixed results. A significant positive relationship between anxiety and BP has been observed in several studies (e.g., Schneider, Egan, Johnson, Drobny, & Julius, 1986), but not in others (e.g., Whitehead, Blackwell, DeSilva, & Robinson, 1977). In studies comparing the anxiety levels of hypertensive patients with normotensives, there were either no differences (e.g., Boutelle, Epstein, & Ruddy, 1987; Foster & Bell, 1983) or significant differences were found only for hypertensive males, who reported greater anxiety than their normotensive counterparts (e.g., van der Ploeg, Buuren, & Brummelen, 1985). With regard to anger, Boutelle et al. (1987) found that both male and female hypertensives were more anger-prone and hostile than normal controls, but only male hypertensives were more anger-prone than their normotensive counterparts in a study reported by van der Ploeg et al. (1985).

Some researchers have contended that anger suppression, rather than anger-proneness or hostility, is the critical factor in the development of essential hypertension (e.g., Schneider et al., 1986). A positive relationship between suppressed anger and systolic blood pressure (SBP) has been consistently observed for male hypertensives, but not for females, whereas suppressed anger was unrelated to diastolic blood pressure (DBP; e.g., Dimsdale et al., 1986; Gentry, Chesney, Gary, Hall, & Harburg, 1982). Suppressed anger was also found to be related to higher SBP in large samples of healthy high school students (Spielberger et al., 1985). However, suppressed anger was unrelated to BP in several recent studies (e.g., Knight, Paulin, & Wall-Manning, 1987; Mills, Schneider, & Dimsdale, 1989; Smith & Houston, 1987).

METHODS: SUBJECTS, TEST INSTRUMENTS, AND PROCEDURES

Subjects

Hypertensive patients (30 male, 30 female) with SBP of 140 mmHg or higher and DBP of 90 mmHg or higher were examined in the outpatient clinic of the Indira Gandhi Hospital at Shimla. These patients ranged in age from 44 to 50 years (M = 46.2 years) and were "aware" that they were diagnosed as hypertensives. All of the patients were middle class and had at least a high school education. None had developed any secondary complications from their hypertension, and none received medication during the 21-day period of this study. During this period, the means of the 11 SBP and DBP readings taken for the male hypertensives were 151.1 (SD = 19.4) and 106.5 (SD = 9.2), respectively. The corresponding values for the female hypertensives were 149.3 (SD = 19.9) and 101.6 (SD = 5.2), respectively.

The normotensive control group consisted of surgical outpatients (30 male, 30 female) who were being treated at the same hospital. The control patients ranged in age from 42 to 49 years (M = 44.3 years), and also had a middle-class background with at least a high school education. The means of the five SBP and DBP readings recorded for each male normotensive patient during the 21-day period were 124.9 (SD = 9.6) and 81.6 (SD = 5.4), respectively.

The corresponding values for the female normotensives were 125.8 ($SD = 9.6$) and 82.1 ($SD = 6.1$), respectively. None of the control patients had any secondary complications from their surgery.

Test Instruments

State–Trait Anxiety Inventory. Trait Anxiety (T-Anxiety) was measured with the 20-item Hindi Form (Spielberger & Sharma, 1976) of the State–Trait Anxiety Inventory (STAI; Spielberger, Gorsuch, & Lushene, 1970; Spielberger, 1983). The cross-language equivalence, internal consistency, test–retest reliability, and concurrent validity of the Hindi STAI have been consistently demonstrated in numerous studies.

Anger Expression scale. A Hindi adaptation of Spielberger's (1988) Anger Expression (AX) scale was recently developed by Sharma and his colleagues. This scale is composed of three 8-item subscales for assessing anger directed toward other people or objects in the environment (AX/Out), suppressed anger (AX/In), and anger control (AX/Con).

Procedure

The SBP and DBP readings were recorded in the clinic setting with a standard mercury sphygmomanometer. After these measures were taken, the hypertensive patients completed the Hindi STAI T-Anxiety and AX scales. Ten additional BP readings were subsequently recorded over a 21-day period. The normotensive patients also completed the Hindi STAI T-Anxiety and AX scales after their initial SBP and DBP readings were recorded; four additional BP readings were recorded over a 21-day period. The hypertensive patients were informed that the study procedures were part of their treatment, and that they were not required to take any antihypertensive medication during the study. None of the control patients received any medication during the study period.

RESULTS AND DISCUSSION

The means and standard deviations for the T-Anxiety, AX/In, AX/Out, and AX/Con scales for the hypertensive and normotensive groups are reported in Table 15.1. The hypertensive males and females scored significantly higher on T-Anxiety ($t = 4.87$ and $t = 8.34$, respectively; $p < .001$) and AX/In ($t = 15.08$ and $t = 11.38$, respectively; $p < .001$), and had significantly lower AX/Out scores ($t = 4.85$ and $t = 7.82$, respectively; $p < .001$) than their normotensive counterparts. No significant differences were found in the AX/Con scores of the hypertensive and normotensive groups for either sex.

Table 15.2 reports the correlations of the scores on the T-Anxiety and AX scales (AX/In, AX/Out, AX/Con) with SBP and DBP for the hypertensive patients (average of 11 readings for each subject), and for the normotensive control group (average of 5 readings for each subject). For the hypertensives,

Table 15.1 Means and standard deviations for the anxiety and anger scales of the hypertensive and normotensive patient groups

	Males		Females	
Scales	Normotensives ($n = 30$)	Hypertensives ($n = 30$)	Normotensives ($n = 30$)	Hypertensives ($n = 30$)
T-Anxiety				
M	27.00	35.30**	28.40	40.50**
SD	5.37	7.63	5.49	5.74
AX/In				
M	18.17	27.60**	17.90	25.90**
SD	2.75	2.04	2.65	2.51
AX/Out				
M	17.70	14.20**	17.23	13.60**
SD	2.60	2.98	1.80	1.22
AX/Con				
M	17.40	18.00	17.40	18.10
SD	2.31	8.80	2.32	9.28

**$p < .001$.

the correlations between the AX/In and BP measures were positive, highly significant, and higher with SBP than with DBP for both sexes. The correlations of AX/Out with the BP measures were negative and statistically significant for both sexes. AX/Out scores correlated more highly with SBP for males and more highly with DBP for females. The AX/Con scale did not correlate significantly with SBP or DBP for either males or females. For the normotensive control group, neither T-Anxiety nor any of the AX measures correlated significantly with SBP or DBP for either sex (see Mills et al., 1989).

Table 15.2 Correlations of the anxiety and anger measures with SBP and DBP

	Males ($n = 30$)		Females ($n = 30$)	
Scales	SBP	DBP	SBP	DBP
Hypertensives				
T-Anxiety	.05	.14	−.15	−.28
AX/In	.82**	.43*	.89**	.62**
AX/Out	−.77**	−.42*	−.59**	−.72**
AX/Con	.11	.12	.02	.03
Normotensives				
T-Anxiety	.01	−.14	−.11	−.13
AX/In	.17	.08	−.04	−.19
AX/Out	.33	.09	−.26	−.27
AX/Con	−.22	−.12	−.24	−.13

*$p < .02$. **$p < .001$.

Although the hypertensive patients of both sexes had significantly higher T-Anxiety scores than the normotensives, the correlations of the T-Anxiety scale with the BP measures were not statistically significant for either group. Although the absence of a relationship between anxiety and BP raises questions about the contribution of this negative emotion to the etiology of essential hypertension, the higher T-Anxiety scores of the hypertensives provides strong evidence that high anxiety is a concomitant of essential hypertension. It seems plausible that individual differences in T-Anxiety (anxiety-proneness) may contribute to the etiology of hypertension by enhancing anger suppression. However, an alternative interpretation is that hypertensive patients who are "aware" of their diagnosis experience anxiety more frequently because such individuals may be more concerned about, and sensitized to, the hazards of experiencing and expressing anger.

The findings of this study highlight the importance of suppressed anger in the etiology of hypertension. The correlations for the hypertensives for both anger-in and anger-out with BP were highly significant; suppressed anger was more strongly related to elevated SBP than DBP for both men and women. These findings for hypertensives in India essentially replicate, in a substantially different sociocultural milieu, the results for males in Western samples and extend them to females as well.

The results of the present study suggest that the inhibition of anger causes heightened autonomic arousal, which eventually leads to hypertension. However, given the correlational nature of this study, cause–effect generalizations cannot be confidently made because it is also plausible that reactions to the diagnosis of hypertension may evoke anxiety, which inhibits the outward expression of anger and thus heightens autonomic arousal. Another possibility is that other personality factors (e.g., gentle predisposition; see Boutelle et al., 1987) may be related to both suppressed anger and hypertension. Prospective studies of the development of hypertension, which include trait anxiety, trait anger, and anger expression, are required to rule out such alternative explanations.

Large, highly significant ($p < .001$), negative correlations ($r = -.89$ for both sexes) were found for the hypertensive patients in the present study between scores on the AX/In and AX/Out scales. The corresponding correlations for male and female normotensive patients were $-.50$ and $-.36$, respectively. The higher inverse correlations between the AX/In and AX/Out scales for the hypertensive patients, when considered along with the substantial correlations of these scales with BP, suggest that greater autonomic arousal might result from the less differentiated responses of the hypertensives to the Hindi AX scale.

Sharma and Acharya (1989) studied coping with organizational stress and anger expression for a sample of 150 engineers from Himachal Pradesh (India). A semiprojective instrument (Role Pics; Pareek, 1983) was employed to assess the dominant mode of coping for these subjects. Scores on this instrument define a bipolar continuum, with *avoidance* and *approach* as opposite poles. Lower scores on avoidance coping signify higher approach coping, and vice versa. Engineers with approach as their dominant mode of coping reported significantly less anger-in and more anger-out (as well as more anger control) than their counterparts with dysfunctional avoidance as their dominant mode of coping. The avoidance copers had significantly higher Anger-In and lower Anger-Out scores than their counterparts with approach as their dominant mode of coping.

CONCLUSIONS

Viewed as a whole, the findings for Indian hypertensive and normotensive patients in this study point to potentially important cross-cultural differences. Males and females from India seem to respond to the AX scale as if the items in the AX/In and AX/Out scales defined a unidimensional, bipolar continuum, with Anger-In and Anger-Out as opposite poles, rather than independent dimensions. The findings of a strong inverse relation between Anger-In and Anger-Out are consistent with other data from India, but contrast with the results of studies in the United States and other Western countries, in which essentially zero correlations were found between Anger-In and Anger-Out for normal populations (Spielberger et al., 1985; Spielberger, Krasner, & Solomon, 1988).

However, the samples for the Indian studies were relatively small, and the factor structure for the Hindi AX scale is yet to been determined for large samples. Nevertheless, the possibility that the AX/In and AX/Out scales define opposite poles of a unidimensional scale for populations in Eastern countries cannot be ruled out. People from these regions have been observed to be relatively less psychologically differentiated than their United States/Western counterparts (e.g., Berry, 1976; Sharma & Dogra, 1988; Sinha & Bharat, 1985; Witkin & Berry, 1975). Absence of psychological differentiation with respect to anger expression, as reflected in responses to the AX scale items in a manner that defines a bipolar continuum, would seem to have important implications for the development of tests for collaborative research across Eastern and Western countries.

REFERENCES

Berry, J. W. (1976). *Human ecology and cognitive style*. New York: Wiley.

Boutelle, R. C., Epstein, S., & Ruddy, M. C. (1987). The relation of essential hypertension to feelings of anxiety, depression and anger. *Psychiatry, 50,* 206–217.

Crane, R. S. (1982). The role of anger, hostility and aggression in essential hypertension (Doctoral dissertation, University of South Florida, 1981). *Dissertation Abstracts International, 42,* 2982B.

Dimsdale, J. E., Pierce, C., Schoenfeld, D., Brown, A., Zusman, R., & Graham, R. (1986). Suppressed anger and blood pressure: The effects of race, sex, social class, obesity, and age. *Psychosomatic Medicine, 48,* 430–436.

Foster, G. D., & Bell, S. T. (1983). Relation of state and trait anxiety to essential hypertension. *Psychological Reports, 52,* 355–358.

Gentry, W. D., Chesney, A. P., Gary, H. E., Jr., Hall, R. H., & Harburg, E. (1982). Habitual anger-coping styles: Effect on mean blood-pressure and risk for essential hypertension. *Psychosomatic Medicine, 44,* 195–202.

Griffin, L. S., & Kee, J. L. (1986). Primary hypertension: Suggestions for a preventive approach. *Family and Community Health, 8,* 59–67.

Hartfield, M. T. (1985). Appraisals of anger situations and subsequent coping responses in hypertensive and normotensive adults: A comparison (Doctoral dissertation, University of California, 1985). *Dissertation Abstracts International, 46,* 4452B.

Knight, R. G., Paulin, J. M., & Wall-Manning, H. J. (1987). Self-reported anger intensity and blood pressure. *British Journal of Clinical Psychology, 26,* 5–6.

Maan, A. H. (1986). Invited review: The psychological aspects of essential hypertension. *Journal of Psychosomatic Research, 30,* 527–541.

Mills, P. J., Schneider, R. M., & Dimsdale, J. E. (1989). Anger assessment and reactivity to stress. *Journal of Psychosomatic Research, 33,* 379–382.

Pareek, U. (1983). *Organizational role pics manual.* Ahmedabad: Navin Publications.

Schneider, R. H., Egan, B. M., Johnson, E. H., Drobny, H., & Julius, S. (1986). Anger and anxiety in borderline hypertension. *Psychosomatic Medicine, 48,* 242–259.

Sharma, S., & Acharya, T. (1989). Coping strategies and anger expression. *Journal of Personality and Clinical Studies, 5,* 15–18.

Sharma, S., & Dogra, R. (1988). A study of field dependent/independent cognitive styles in Indian and Tibetan boys and girls. *Personality Study and Group Behaviour, 8,* 1–6.

Sinha, D., & Bharat, S. (1985). Three types of family structure and psychological differentiation: A study of Jausar-Bawar Society. *International Journal of Psychology, 20,* 709–722.

Smith, M. A., & Houston, B. K. (1987). Hostility, anger expression, cardiovascular responsibility, and social support. *Biological Psychology, 24,* 39–48.

Spielberger, C. D. (1983). *Manual for the State–Trait Anxiety Inventory (Form Y).* Palo Alto, CA: Consulting Psychologists Press.

Spielberger, C. D. (1988). *Professional manual for the State–Trait Anger Expression Inventory (STAXI)* (Res. ed.). Tampa, FL: Psychological Assessment Resources.

Spielberger, C. D., Crane, R. S., Kearns, W. D., Pellegrin, K. L., Rickman, R. L., & Johnson, E. H. (1991). Anger and anxiety in essential hypertension. In C. D. Spielberger & I. G. Sarason (Eds.), *Stress and emotion* (Vol. 14, pp. 265–283). New York: Hemisphere/Taylor & Francis.

Spielberger, C. D., Gorsuch, R. L., & Lushene, R. E. (1970). *Test manual for the State–Trait Anxiety Inventory (STAI).* Palo Alto, CA: Consulting Psychologists Press.

Spielberger, C. D., Johnson, E. G., Russell, S. F., Crane, R. S., Jacobs, G. A., & Worden, T. J. (1985). The experience and expression of anger. In M.

A. Chesney & R. H. Rosenman (Eds.), *Anger and hostility in cardiovascular and behavioral disorders* (pp. 5–30). New York: Hemisphere/McGraw-Hill.

Spielberger, C. D., Krasner, S. S., & Solomon, E. P. (1988). The experience, expression and control of anger. In M. P. Janisse (Ed.), *Health psychology: Individual differences and stress* (pp. 89–108). New York: Springer-Verlag.

Spielberger, C. D., & Sharma, S. (1976). Cross-cultural measurement of anxiety. In C. D. Spielberger & R. Diaz-Guerrero (Eds.), *Cross-cultural anxiety* (pp. 13–25). Washington, DC: Hemisphere/Wiley.

van der Ploeg, H. M., Buuren, E. T., & Brummelen, P. (1985). The role of anger in hypertension. *Psychotherapy and Psychosomatics, 43,* 186–193.

Whitehead, W. E., Blackwell, B., DeSilva, H., & Robinson, A. (1977). Anxiety and anger in hypertension. *Journal of Psychosomatic Research, 21,* 383–389.

Witkin, H. A., & Berry, J. W. (1975). Psychological differentiation in cross-cultural perspective. *Journal of Cross-Cultural Psychology, 6,* 4–87.

16

Behavioral Interventions for Posttraumatic Stress Disorder

John G. Carlson
University of Hawaii, Honolulu, USA

Abstract *Behavioral and cognitive-behavioral theories and research in the area of combat-related posttraumatic stress disorder (PTSD) are selectively reviewed. Particularly emphasized are models that include mechanisms for conditioning arousal and avoidance, psychophysiological assessment methods, and treatment research focused on arousal management and exposure methods. Research at the Honolulu Veterans Administration Medical Center illustrates recent attempts to evaluate behavioral interventions with male veterans of the Vietnam combat era. Relaxation treatment in the form of muscle potential biofeedback and home practice is described. Preliminary results suggest an impact on psychophysiological and questionnaire measures of arousal, but not on reexperiencing of combat trauma. By contrast, in four case studies, exposure treatment in the form of eye movement desensitization and reprocessing appeared primarily to affect memorable aspects of trauma, but not arousal as assessed psychophysiologically. These results argue for a comprehensive PTSD treatment package that targets multiple dimensions of responding.*

This chapter provides a selective review of the current literature and research in the area of posttraumatic stress disorder (PTSD), highlighting behavioral models for understanding, assessment, and treatment of the disorder. Paralleling the bulk of the research in this area, most of the research reviewed emphasizes applications to combat veterans of the Vietnam era. An implicit assumption, as yet not thoroughly researched, is that many of the observations of this group will generalize to other trauma populations, such as survivors of natural disasters or victims of childhood abuse, rape, or violent crimes. Other, more comprehensive, reviews of the behavioral literature are included in the special miniseries on PTSD in *Behavior Therapy* (Keane, 1989).

This research was supported by grant No. 1R01NRO2855 from the NIH National Institute of Nursing Research. Additional support was provided by the Social Sciences Research Institute, University of Hawaii at Manoa, and the VA Medical Center, Honolulu. Co-investigators on this project are Drs. Claude Chemtob, VA Medical Center; and Nancy Hedlund, Cancer Research Center.

Until the 1980s and the development of explicit criteria in the *Diagnostic and Statistical Manual of Mental Disorders* (3rd ed. [*DSM–III*]), PTSD was not recognized as a distinct, diagnosable disorder—a fact that created considerable difficulties for both veterans and those responsible for their treatment. Today, however, as outlined in *DSM–IV,* the diagnostic features of PTSD are reasonably straightforward (American Psychiatric Association, 1994). On the stimulus side, the listed features of PTSD include traumatic events that are generally person- or life-threatening incidents in which the reaction is intense fear, helplessness, or horror (such as events in war and other aggressive acts, accidents, or natural disasters). On the response side, PTSD is characterized especially by (a) reexperiencing the traumatic event (e.g., in dreams or dissociative flashbacks) and intense psychological and physiological distress on exposure to related stimuli; (b) persistent avoidance of stimuli and cognitions associated with the trauma, and/or emotional "numbing" and detachment; and (c) increased arousal, involving such problems as sleep disorders, hypervigilance, startle, and/or outbursts of anger. In general, PTSD among combat veterans shows a high level of concordance among these behavioral, cognitive, and physiological indicators (Orr et al., 1990). This allows for advantageous use of multimodal approaches to both assessment and therapy, as is discussed herein.

Prevalence rates for PTSD vary greatly depending on the population studied (Barlow, 1988). The seriousness of PTSD as a disorder is mainly evidenced among war veterans, especially those of the Vietnam campaign (e.g., Helzer, Robins, & McEvoy, 1987) and women victims of assault (Kilpatrick et al., 1985). Epidemiological studies in 1988 found that, of 3.5 million Vietnam veterans in the United States, about 15%, or about one-half million, satisfy the diagnostic criteria for PTSD. About 30% of all combat veterans also continue to have various problems in social adjustment. For veterans with high exposure to combat, it is estimated that PTSD symptoms may occur in more than 38%. (For a general review of statistics relevant to PTSD in the Vietnam era veteran, see Kulka et al., 1988.)

From the standpoint of health and medical resources, PTSD is an expensive and demanding problem, especially for the Veterans Administration (VA). Perhaps 26% of all mental health outpatient visits and 19% of all inpatient discharges from VA medical centers in this country owe to patients with PTSD, despite that fewer than 20% of the veterans estimated to have PTSD seek mental health services of any kind in a given year. There also may be an increasing number of veterans seeking treatment, a hopeful sign insofar as delivering needed services is concerned, but just one more indication of the chronic seriousness of this disorder from the standpoint of demands on manpower and other health resources.

Therefore, the need for powerful conceptual models and effective treatment protocols for PTSD is a pressing one. To this end, in this chapter, behavioral and cognitive-behavioral approaches are emphasized, and the treatment modalities that follow directly from these models are described and reviewed in the context of related research in a number of laboratories, including the Honolulu VA Medical Center.

MODELS FOR BEHAVIORAL INTERVENTION

The most heuristic behavioral model to date for the study of PTSD, and the one adopted for this research, views the events of trauma as aversive stimuli underlying physiological arousal in a Pavlovian conditioning framework. In combination with a second factor, instrumental or avoidance conditioning, this model has multiple applications in the understanding of features of the PTSD profile. Together, these two learning processes underlie the general view of associative learning originally put forth by Mowrer (1947, 1960), which inspired a great deal of supportive animal research (e.g., Carlson, 1974; Carlson & Wielkiewicz, 1974) as well as theoretical controversy.

Two-Factor Learning Theory and PTSD

Aversive classical conditioning. In the application of the two-factor learning model to the development of PTSD, traumatic events are viewed as "unconditional stimuli" for emotional reactions in the traditional Pavlovian framework—a notion with origins in the early descriptions of combat-related "physioneurosis" by Kardiner (1941), and picked up by more contemporary researchers (Keane, Fairbank, Caddell, Zimering, & Bender, 1985; Kolb, 1984). In this model, it is hypothesized that life-threatening events of combat or other trauma serve as potentially powerful reinforcers for a variety of associations, allowing the establishment of conditional stimuli for the emotional reactions of fear/anxiety (e.g., autonomic distress, startle reactions, and sleep difficulties; McFall, Murburg, Roszell, & Vieth, 1989). Thus, the sights, sounds, and smells of combat, through their repeated pairings with the events of war, come to elicit powerful responses, potentially disruptive in impact and permanent in effect on the survivor. In turn, the conditioning process may imbue other stimuli with potential emotional effects through stimulus generalization. Moreover, these conditional stimuli may enter into yet other conditioning relationships through higher order conditioning, as discussed later (cf. Fairbank & Nicholson, 1987; Keane et al., 1985).

Implications of the aversive conditioning view. The implications of the Pavlovian model for conditioning of fear in humans has a checkered history, with some theorists arguing that there is little human data for fear acquisition along the lines of classical conditioning (Rachman, 1985; cited in Fairbank & Nicholson, 1987). Other theorists maintained that cognitive and biological factors must be brought to bear in the understanding of conditioning processes at both the human and animal levels (e.g., Seligman & Johnston, 1973). Another potential difficulty with the Pavlovian model is trauma disorders' apparent resistance to extinction. With numerous inevitable opportunities for the failure of avoidance and repeated reexposure to the conditional stimuli that elicit the veteran's emotional distress, why does extinction not set in that would gradually attenuate the seriousness of the disorder? In fact, in many veterans, full-blown symptoms of PTSD were delayed years after the Vietnam war, suggesting, if anything, a gradual development, rather than extinction, of the disorder outside of the combative environment.

In the particular case of PTSD, however, pertinent observations of the disorder, as well as laboratory evidence, favor the notion of a conditioning history for related arousal reactions. One of the implications of the Pavlovian model is that responses conditioned in the combat zone should generalize to stimuli outside of the context. A relatively large number of research studies, some of which are outlined later, support this possibility. Specifically, researchers have shown that Vietnam veterans react with exaggerated heart rate (HR), blood pressure (BP), electromyopotentials, and other indicators of arousal in the presence of combat-related sounds, words, visual stimuli, and verbal scripts (e.g., Blanchard, Kolb, Gerardi, Ryan, & Pallmeyer, 1986; Pitman, Orr, Forgue, de Jong, & Claiborn, 1987).

With respect to the persistence of arousal in PTSD, despite many possible opportunities for extinction, at least two possible counterarguments may be put forth. First, Solomon and his associates in classical studies using animal paradigms have shown that intense electric shocks may engender persistent avoidance responding in the absence of the shock (e.g., Solomon & Wynne, 1954). Also, Solomon's notion of anxiety conservation predicts that successful avoidance (or partial reexperiencing of conditioned anxiety) essentially protects fear reactions from extinction. To the extent that combat is one of the more intense forms of traumatic experience, and to the extent that PTSD victims are successful in avoiding full-blown emotional rearousal, persistence of conditioned hyperarousal would be possible.

Second, partial reinforcement during conditioning has long been known to be a powerful variable affecting the persistence of conditioning in animals (Pavlov, 1927). In the PTSD framework, the variety of experiences during and following the events of combat—some experiences life threatening and potentially reinforcing, many not at all threatening—could serve as a basis for partially reinforcing relationships between functional unconditional and conditional stimuli, helping to preserve conditioned reactions over time following the trauma.

Third, another learning possibility that may affect conditioned arousal in PTSD includes the presence of multiple stimuli during conditioning. Notably, Levis and his co-workers (e.g., Stampfl & Levis, 1967), as cited and used as a research model by Keane et al. (1985), have demonstrated that presentation of several conditional stimuli in a classical conditioning paradigm produces persistent responding over hundreds of trials in extinction. The implication is that repeated exposure to many kinds of stimuli in combat may enhance resistance of conditioned emotional responses to extinction. Relatedly, it has been observed that the prevalence of PTSD among Vietnam veterans is a function of the degree of exposure to combat (Kulka et al., 1988).

Finally, higher order conditioning is another process that could help explain the persistence and posttrauma development of some of the PTSD symptoms. Essentially, stimuli that have come previously to elicit emotional reactions may serve as stimuli for subsequent conditioning. Thus, internal and external cues relevant to combat experiences could serve in lieu of unconditional stimuli in repeated conditioning experiences for the combat survivor (Keane et al., 1985). Coupled with the phenomenon of stimulus generalization (i.e., the tendency for stimuli that resemble original traumatic events to evoke emotional reactions), opportunities for conditioning or reconditioning of anxiety following combat are virtually limitless. Thus, theoretically, the presence of fellow veterans, similar sights or sounds (e.g., helicopters), similar smells (e.g., gunpowder), and even similar internal states may also serve as functional unconditional stimuli in subsequent conditioning, countering the effects of extinction and permitting further acquisition of the reactions of PTSD following traumatic experiences. In the words of Keane et al.: "With the increase in stimuli conditioned to the trauma, an individual with PTSD finds it increasingly difficult to avoid cues that evoke the memory of the trauma. Moreover, other . . . stressful circumstances that evoke physiological arousal can elicit the memory of the traumatic event" (p. 264).

Instrumental (avoidance/escape) conditioning. The second of Mowrer's (1960) two factors, described by other theorists as one of "negative reinforcement," involves the strengthening of virtually any behavior that successfully reduces or eliminates the reactions of conditioned emotionality (e.g., anxiety, distress, disturbed thoughts, nightmares, and the many other symptoms of arousal).

In the case of PTSD, accordingly, the combat veteran strives to manage the residual memories and emotional vestiges of war through attempts to escape and/or avoid the stimuli and their effects. As Keane et al. (1985) stated succinctly: "This process of memory review involves recollection of stimulus cues, many of which have acquired negative emotional valence through conditioning. . . . Accordingly, the combatant attempts to avoid recollection" (p. 265). The possibilities for avoidance learning through negative reinforcement are theoretically limitless, but some results are stereotypic, to the extent of being even diagnostic of the disorder. Anything the veteran attempts in successful (or even partially successful) efforts to control his emotions—including avoiding reminders of war (films, pictures, war stories, and memorabilia), abusing substances that interfere with memory, learning ways to stay awake or sleep lightly to avoid the nightmares or night terrors of the disorder, making use of a host of defense mechanisms (e.g., repression, denial, rationalization, reaction formation), avoiding social contact—and all the variations of these and other avoidance/escape behaviors are reinforceable.

Interestingly, some of veteran's reactions that serve to attenuate anxiety may be emotional, rather than purely instrumental, in nature. Through response competition, emotions that are competitive with the anxiety of trauma, such as anger and hostility, may find ample opportunity for expression by the soldier and by the veteran, thus further insulating anxiety reactions from expression and extinction (Keane et al., 1985). Therefore, angry or hostile reactions may be characteristic of PTSD, in part, through their learned, albeit potentially maladaptive, functions in controlling the experience of emotional arousal.

Another process traditionally viewed in the context of instrumental (or operant) phenomena that may be related to some features of PTSD is behavioral contrast (Keane et al., 1985). Specifically, "the reinforcement value of current-day activities is overshadowed by the reinforcement from activities in Vietnam" (p. 267). Paradoxically, the same stimuli that control relatively low levels of activity in peacetime may, by contrast with the exciting events of combat, induce maladaptively lower activity more characteristic of depression or apathy than simple "peace." The difficulty with this analysis, not recognized in the account by Keane et al., is that behavioral contrast is understood to be a relatively time-bound process. By definition, *contrast* is a phenomenon that demands temporally contrasting events. With the passage of time, initial boredom or apathy following exposure to traumatic events would be expected to dissipate, whereas the emotional concomitants of PTSD are persistent.

More useful in accounting for depression in PTSD may be concepts of *learned helplessness* (Seligman, 1975) and cognitive variations on this theme (Abramson, Seligman, & Teasdale, 1986). Essentially, learning that reinforcers are independent of behavior may induce a condition in animals analogous to depression, low levels of behavior initiation, apathy, and withdrawal. In combat veterans, the inability to effectively control many potentially reinforcing outcomes of behavior—attaining satisfaction in permanent relationships, keeping meaningful employment, finding ways to control manifestations of arousal (including sleeplessness itself, another factor in depression)—may all contribute to the sense of helplessness and its consequences.

Related Views

Persisting difficulties and early cognitive challenges to the two-factor learning model of PTSD continue to inspire interest (e.g., Martin & Levey, 1985). For instance, Foa, Steketee, and Rothbaum (1989) challenged the ability of a strictly associative approach to account for heightened startle reactions among PTSD sufferers (but not in other anxiety disorders), some cognitive reactions (notably, intrusive thoughts and flashbacks), and sleep disturbance through trauma-related dreams. Accordingly, these commentators proposed a cognitive model for the disorder (see also Chemtob, Roitblat, Hamada, Carlson, & Twentyman, 1988). Barlow (1988) also concluded that the two-factor theory "has not fared particularly well," although he admitted to the persisting strength and strong evidence for "conditioning or emotional learning" (p. 224), especially when coupled with certain biological and cognitive factors, outlined later. Despite its detractors, the two-factor model and related learning processes, although complex in implications for PTSD, still offer the most comprehensive behavioral approach to the phenomenon of PTSD, serving as a valuable heuristic for treatment research. Refinements, variations, or parts of the model are incorporated into related behavioral approaches to the disorder, including that of Barlow (1988) and Chemtob and Carlson (1994).

Vulnerability. In Barlow's (1988) approach, anxiety in PTSD and other disorders is characterized as a cognitive-affective structure: It is one of high negative emotionality consisting of arousal, perceptions of lack of control, and attentional shifts away from the task and to the self. (In fact, in Barlow's view, what distinguishes "normal" anxiety from the disorders of anxiety is the degree to which arousal leads to lessened concentration on problems at hand and to a focus on one's own behaviors, including arousal reactions. The etiology of PTSD consists of overwhelming effects of traumatic life events in the form of intense, basic emotions (e.g., fear, anger, distress) and classically conditioned "learned alarms."

However, the experience of intense emotions in traumatic situations is not enough; the sense of "uncontrollability" of the events and/or one's emotional reactions must develop (termed *anxious apprehension*). Moreover, some individuals are said to possess an added "physiological and biological vulnerability" to the disorder. Vulnerability may include what some have termed *biological preparedness* for anxiety—a potentially heritable characteristic (Davidson, Swartz, Storck, Krishnan, & Hammett, 1985). Additionally, psychological vulnerability to learned alarms may be moderated, in part, by one's levels of social support and/or repertoire of coping skills. Together these factors may help account for observed variability in the development of PTSD among combat veterans, even those with severe combat experiences.

Adaptation. In yet another variation on a behavioral model for PTSD, efforts to integrate many of the seemingly complex and disparate phenomena of PTSD are summarized in an "adaptation" view of the disorder (Chemtob & Carlson, 1994). The essential notion is that many of the overt behaviors, bodily changes, and concomitant experiences of the PTSD victim owe to processes that are natural to the human caught in a traumatic situation, adaptive in the environment in which they developed, and disordered only to the extent that the environment changes dramatically after trauma, including the trauma of war.

To somewhat abbreviate this position, it is maintained here that PTSD arises as a consequence of an incompletely resolved challenge to a person's survival. Specifically, when a person perceives or expects an event to be threatening to survival, a number of psychobiological subsystems are activated, taken together defining what is termed the *survival system*. These are the emotional (behavioral, physiological, and cognitive, although not necessarily conscious) responses to trauma, and they have a primary and dominant quality over the other reactions in traumatic situations because they support primitive biological functions. The system is relatively nonvolitional owing to its primitive origins in the history of our species, its onset is rapid and general in effect (reflecting the underlying biology of the stress response; cf. Carlson & Hatfield, 1992), and its offset is slow in action and response specific. Moreover, as arousal increases, the survival system gains access to the control of information-processing resources that might be functional in more normal psychological environments (Chemtob et al., 1988).

Another aspect of the adaptive nature of the survival system is its conditionability, in accordance with the principles of classical and avoidance conditioning outlined earlier. Conditioning is most likely to develop over repeated exposure to traumatic events, although it may be a single-trial affair. It is influenced by such processes as stimulus generalization, partial reinforcement, and others detailed earlier in the context of two-factor learning theory.

As previously noted, a difficult problem for behavioral models of PTSD is the persistence and intensity of underlying traumatic memories. In wakeful recollection, specific events and sequences in traumatic memories often appear to be preserved in extremely vivid, intact form, sometimes described by veterans as resembling a series of slides or a videotape. Even in sleep, the "nightmares" of PTSD consist of vivid recollections of combat events (e.g., explosions, death, flights from the enemy, etc.), whereas the "normal" nightmare is more likely to be fantastical in nature and with little or no coherence of sequences of events or characters. These features of PTSD imply the development of a "core" memory of traumatic events that is never resolved or well integrated into the experiences of daily life. In an adaptational view of PTSD, the core traumatic memory, like other features of the disorder, must be understood as also functional in some sense in its original context. Perhaps a running and vivid account of recent traumatic events would be particularly advantageous for primitive social groups, particularly if such accounts promoted survival of the tribe—even at the expense of the psychological comfort of the individual. In modern warfare, vivid recollections of combat may be less obviously adaptive, but it is the mechanism that survives, just as the more general and primitive mechanism of fear conditioning survives and afflicts the modern individual with the problems of anxiety disorders in a comparatively benign environment.

Finally, the avoidant behaviors (e.g., numbing, chemical dependence, and other features of PTSD, such as dissociation) that characterize the individual's attempt to modulate his anxiety and other distress may be best understood as ultimately adaptive in origin—negative reinforcement is a profoundly functional process—but potentially painful and destructive in the posttrauma context. The "disorder" of PTSD is not a failure of processes, but a failure of regulation of behaviors (including cognitions and physiological reactions) in more normal circumstances due to learned or unlearned activities that would promote survival under extreme conditions, including defensive behaviors (aggression or withdrawal), social attachment and bonding (promoting survival in the group), and arousal modulation (inhibition and activation). In another sense, in PTSD, there is a problem of resource allocation to behaviors that continue to promote warning, defense, and arousal activation versus others that are more functional in the daily, noncombative environment, including social attachment and arousal inhibition. Veterans of combat and others who develop PTSD have continuing difficulty with the regulation of activation and inhibition, manifested in a wide range of deficits that are secondary to the disorder.

Summary

The two-factor associative model as applied to PTSD continues to offer multiple opportunities for research and innovative variations on theoretical themes to accommodate the complex phenomena of this disorder. Despite its detractors, comprehensive alternatives to this approach, with the methodological strengths of a behavioral position, have either not been forthcoming or have incorporated many of the fundamentals of arousal learning and avoidance. Nevertheless, with any theoretical framework, ultimate tests must reside in experimental evaluations, such as in the contexts of assessment and treatment.

ASSESSMENT OF PTSD

General Considerations

Assessment of PTSD in behavioral research has taken many forms, generally not driven theoretically, but rather by the tripartite criteria for the disorder. That is, assessment of PTSD focuses on the cognitive, physiological, and behavioral dimensions outlined in the *DSM* approach. Of the three classes of methods, substantially less effort has gone into the development of strictly behavioral means for assessing PTSD. Therefore, paper-and-pencil and interview methods for obtaining self-report and psychophysiological techniques are emphasized in this section. Our own research and that of others makes use of a number of standardized instruments and interview methods, which are recognized for their usefulness in assessing experiential, arousal, and behavioral components of PTSD. In addition, a wide-spectrum psychophysiological assessment procedure is employed that targets both autonomic and muscular measures of arousal. The following section selectively reviews the related instruments as generally representative of the wide array of assessment devices now available to PTSD researchers. (See Stamm & Varra, 1993, for a useful volume summarizing details of most of the relevant psychometric instruments in this area.)

Psychometric Methods

Structured clinical interviews. The Clinician Administered PTSD Survey (CAPS; Blake et al., 1990) is a structured clinical interview designed to measure the frequency and intensity of PTSD symptomatology, plus the impact of symptoms on social and occupational functioning; it also provides an overall index of symptom severity. The ratings are made on a 5-point scale, from the lowest to the highest frequency or intensity and degree of impairment. The instrument also allows for the determination of current and lifetime PTSD diagnoses. The CAPS is the only instrument in this test battery that is based explicitly on the *DSM* criteria for severe effects of trauma and that provides for direct clinical assessment of the disorder. The CAPS also goes beyond the well-known Structured Clinical Interview for DSM–III–R (SCID), in that the latter provides essentially a yes–no indication of PTSD. The CAPS also yields information on eight other features of PTSD, including guilt, anger/irritability, and depression.

Standardized instruments. The Mississippi Scale for Combat-Related PTSD is a 35-item, self-report scale using Likert-type items that sample the *DSM–IV* criteria and selected additional symptoms of PTSD. The higher the score, the more likely the diagnosis of PTSD. Studies have confirmed high

internal consistency, test–retest reliability, and sensitivity of the scale for identifying subjects with PTSD.

The Impact of Events Scale (IES; Horowitz, Wilner, & Alvarez, 1979) is
also a useful instrument in the assessment of PTSD. It is a 15-item scale, with
high internal consistency and test–retest reliability, that measures the current
subjective distress in response to a specific traumatic event. The IES is further
designed to measure the intrusive and avoidant aspects of distress.

The Beck Depression Inventory (BDI; Beck, Ward, Mendelson, Mock, &
Erbaugh, 1961) is a 21-item, multiple-choice instrument that measures the
severity of depression. Each item consists of four or five statements, listed in
order of severity, regarding mood, hopelessness, guilt, self-hate, social withdrawal, anhedonia, and sleep and appetite disturbances. The test has moderately high test–retest reliability and correlations with clinical ratings of depression.

The Spielberger State–Trait Anxiety Inventory (STAI; Spielberger, Gorsuch, & Lushene, 1970) includes a 20-item, self-report instrument consisting
of questions developed to assess transitory (state) emotional condition, and a
20-item, self-report instrument consisting of questions aimed at assessing the
relatively stable and general (trait) anxiety level of individuals.

The Minnesota Multiphasic Personality Inventory–2, (MMPI–2) and its
predecessor have been extensively documented (Butcher, Dahlstrom, Graham,
Tellegen, & Kaemmer, 1989). A subscale of the MMPI, the Keane PTSD (PK)
scale, was originally developed from a set of 49 items found to discriminate
PTSD veterans from those without the disorder (Keane, Malloy, & Fairbank,
1984), and subsequently was updated for the MMPI–2 (cf. Kulka et al., 1991).
Relatedly, Keane and others have reported a characteristic F (symptom overreporting), 8 (schizophrenia), 2 (depression) pattern among PTSD patients
(Keane, Malloy, and Fairbank, 1984).

The Stressful Scene Construction Questionnaire (SSCQ; Pitman et al.,
1987) asks subjects to provide a written account of a previously traumatic event,
including statements regarding the situation and the individuals' responses,
and a list of physiological responses that characterized responding in the situation (such as "heart races") to circle as appropriate to the episode. From this
account, a script is written in the second person by the assessor, including
physiological descriptors (usually about 30–45 sec. in duration).

Finally, for present purposes, the Dissociative Experiences Scale (DES; E.
Bernstein & Putnam, 1986) is a 28-item, self-administered questionnaire that
screens for disorders and quantifies dissociative experiences. The instrument
has been shown to correctly classify 89% of subjects into dissociative and
nondissociative disorder categories. It is recommended that therapists who use
certain exposure treatment methods exercise extreme care when treating
clients with scores in this range. In our experience, the scale has not predicted
special risks among the combat PTSD population, but is used precautionarily.

Psychophysiological Methods

In the 1980s, research was initiated in several laboratories aimed at determining the usefulness of psychophysiological measures in the assessment of

PTSD in combat veterans. The goal was an optimistic one. In the words of Pitman et al. (1987), "From a research standpoint, the presence of psycho-physiological manifestations accompanying a mental disorder [as in PTSD] offers the opportunity to obtain data that may be both more 'objective' and more readily quantifiable than self-report data" (p. 970). In short, the phys-iological arousal component of PTSD offers the opportunity for effective mea-surement and nonsubjective approaches to diagnosis and treatment that may avoid problems of reliability, quantification, clinical bias, and patient maling-ering, among other problems, that are troublesome in all areas of clinical assessment. The studies in this area have used generic and individualized combat stressors to evoke reactions in combat veterans, and have examined a range of responses, including muscle tension and a variety of autonomic reactions.

In one of the first of these studies, Blanchard, Kolb, Pallmeyer, and Gerardi (1982) investigated responding of PTSD-diagnosed veterans and a matched group of nonveterans (controls) to sounds of combat and other potentially stressful and nonstressful stimuli. Relative to the control subjects, the PTSD sufferers evidenced higher arousal in the presence of the combat sounds in terms of HR, systolic blood pressure (SBP), and forehead muscle potential (electromyographic [EMG]) levels. Interestingly, HR by itself served to dis-criminate the PTSD subjects from the nonveterans, with a 95.5% degree of accuracy.

In another study, using videotaped (including sound track) combat-related material, Malloy, Fairbank, and Keane (1983) examined psychophysiological responding (HR and skin resistance), self-reports, and a behavioral measure (stopping the video presentations) in PTSD veterans and matched control subjects who were also veterans. Relative to the two control groups, the PTSD subjects manifested significantly higher HRs and skin resistance responses. Moreover, the PTSD subjects reported significantly greater anxiety during the combat stimuli and, in a measure of behavioral avoidance, were more likely to terminate the combat scenes (most of the PTSD subjects used the opportunity to escape the combat tapes, whereas none of the control subjects did). In more recent studies, using larger and more varied samples, Blanchard et al. (1986) and Blanchard, Kolb, Taylor, and Wittrock (1989) confirmed this pattern of findings for the impact of combat sounds on HR.

In a departure from the use of muscle tension and somatic measures, McCaffrey, Lorig, Pendrey, McCutcheon, and Garrett (1993) recently reported effects of odors, in particular the simulated smell of burnt hair, on left-hemi-sphere 5–7 Hz (theta) and 8–13 Hz (alpha) brain wave activity. Levels of activity in these ranges increased in the presence of the combat-relevant stim-ulus and not other odors, consistent with previous observations of heightened left-hemisphere alpha activity to emotion-eliciting stimuli (Andreassi, 1989).

Although all of the foregoing studies utilized standardized physical stimuli, two studies in Roger Pitman's laboratory incorporated personal imagery in a study of the physiological aspects of PTSD (Pitman et al., 1987; Pitman, Orr, Forgue, Altman, de Jong, & Herz, 1990). In the first of these studies, Pitman and his co-workers developed scripts from material produced by veterans using the SSCQ method outlined earlier. Then, the scripted material was presented and the subjects were asked to vividly experience the situation. Subjects with diagnosed PTSD manifested higher HR, skin conductance, and facial EMG levels during the scripts than combat veterans with no disorders. In the Pitman et al. (1990) study, the essential results of the former research were replicated with an especially strong control group—namely, combat veterans with symptoms other than PTSD. In both studies, using discriminant analyses, the physiological data provided bases for high levels of discrimination between the groups.

The foregoing research considered overall provides strong and reasonably consistent evidence in support of the notion that there are conditioned somatic and autonomic arousal reactions in veterans with PTSD, which are especially evident in the presence of stimuli that resemble or provide reminders of combat events (and perhaps even loud stimuli generally; see Paige, Reid, Allen, & Newton, 1990). Additional, albeit modest, evidence for heightened, chronic arousal also has been demonstrated in a recent review of the cardiovascular data obtained in eight studies assessing baseline levels of HR and blood pressure (BP) in the laboratory in Vietnam era veterans with PTSD (Blanchard, 1990). Preliminary data obtained from our laboratory (Muraoka, 1994) using 24-hour ambulatory monitoring in natural work and home settings confirm the likelihood of substantially elevated HRs and somewhat elevated BPs outside the laboratory in veterans with PTSD relative to those without the disorder.

Finally, as discussed by McFall et al. (1989), in a few neuroendocrine studies of veterans with PTSD, evidence has been consistent with chronically elevated levels of epinephrine and norepinephrine (Pfeifer et al., 1984) and higher norepinephrine/cortisol ratios but, surprisingly, lower cortisol levels, suggesting a dissociation of adrenal medullary and cortical activity with this disorder (Kosten, Mason, Guiller, Ostroff, & Harkness, 1987; however, see Pitman & Orr, 1990).

Summary

As Keane and his colleagues recently observed, "the assessment of PTSD has advanced rapidly" in the 12 years since the disorder appeared in the diagnostic vocabulary (Keane, Weathers, & Kaloupek, 1992, p. 3). The power and utility of the numerous instruments and methods available in this field now greatly enhance the capabilities of behavioral researchers, especially those concerned with the effectiveness of different treatment options. The multimodal array of assessment tools also permits comprehensive analyses along the multiple dimensions of PTSD, and allows for more effective determination of the relative effects of alternative behavioral interventions.

INTERVENTIONS FOR PTSD: RELAXATION AND EXPOSURE

There have been several summaries of behavioral treatments for PTSD, primarily focused on imaginal flooding and related methods (cf. Keane, 1989).

Other behavioral methods are outlined by Keane et al. (1985) as part of their stress management package, including relaxation, cognitive restructuring, and problem solving, none of which has been thoroughly evaluated for their relative contributions to the healing process for the combat veteran. This section emphasizes relaxation and exposure treatments that have particular relevance for the theoretical focus of this chapter.

Relaxation Treatment

Theoretically, the rationale for relaxation therapy is that it will reduce the somatic and autonomic arousal that characterizes stress responding. It also provides a means for anxiety sufferers to develop control over their disorder and a means for coping in stress and anger management that may be used under a variety of stressful circumstances (e.g., Keane et al., 1985). Interest in the use of relaxation training for the treatment of stress-related disorders has a long and varied history, including the development of progressive relaxation (Jacobson, 1938), systematic desensitization (Wolpe, 1958, 1990), autogenic training (Schultz & Luthe, 1959), meditation (Benson, 1975), and frontalis (forehead) muscle action potential training (Stoyva & Budzynski, 1974), among other more recent techniques and combinations of methods (cf. Stoyva & Carlson, 1993). However, few studies have attempted to document the benefits of general relaxation training for PTSD.

Hickling, Sison, and Vanderploeg (1986) demonstrated a procedure combining progressive muscle relaxation and frontalis muscle biofeedback across 8–16 weeks in the treatment of six PTSD patients. Scores on such indicators as the STAI and a depression scale, in addition to frontalis muscle tension and self-reported tension, all decreased both within and across treatment sessions. From these measures and self-reports, it appeared that "moderate to marked" improvement in symptoms of PTSD was obtained in four of the patients and "slight" improvement in the remaining two. However, without a control group, it is not possible to evaluate the relative advantages of relaxation training in this study beyond possible placebo and attentional effects.

In the only controlled study using a relaxation procedure by itself, Brooks and Scarano (1985) assessed the effects of transcendental meditation in a group of 10 Vietnam veterans in a vet center in Denver. A second group of eight vets receiving "eclectic psychotherapy" at the center served as control subjects. The extent of PTSD in the vets was not well documented, except with an unvalidated scale ("modeled after *DSM–III* criteria"), but all vets were seeking treatment for adjustment difficulties. Transcendental meditation as used by these researchers consisted of 20-minute periods (twice daily) during which the veterans sat quietly and covertly recited a verbal mantra. The procedure was encouraged for 3 months. The meditation group showed significant improvement on all of the self-report items, and 7 of the 10 subjects felt improved enough to discontinue treatment.

Relaxation training was also used as a treatment for PTSD by Peniston (1986). It was used in the context of a form of exposure therapy—namely, systematic desensitization training—therefore effects are confounded with other procedures. Sixteen combat veterans were randomly assigned to either a biofeedback relaxation group or a control condition. Relaxation in this study was assisted with biofeedback on the frontalis area for three sessions (also including practice in rehearsing pleasant scenes). The control group was apparently given no treatment. Prior to treatment, subjects in the biofeedback-desensitization group were also involved in construction of a hierarchy of stressful scenes (e.g., morning before battle, moving out on patrol, moving through the jungle, engaging the enemy, etc.). These subjects then began a long series of desensitization training sessions (45 in all), in which they systematically rehearsed images in the hierarchy of combat scenes. EMG levels and self-reports of anxiety constituted criteria for moving through the hierarchy. There was a highly significant difference between the groups on EMG levels at posttest. More important, 24 months after treatment, the subjects were contacted by phone to determine reported instances of nightmares and flashbacks. Again, a significant advantage of the treatment was obtained in terms of minimal reported numbers of nightmares and intrusive images. By contrast, most of the control subjects were repeatedly admitted for treatment during this time and showed a high incidence of reported nightmares and flashbacks. Unfortunately, other variables were not documented in this study, including self-reports or more objective indices of PTSD during and immediately following treatment, as well as more appropriate physiological measures, including HR.

Exposure Therapies

Although the general control of arousal through relaxation in PTSD has a sound theoretical rationale, methods of intervention for alleviating situationally specific affective distress in PTSD may have particular advantages. Accordingly, several "exposure therapies" have been investigated in this context involving repeated exposure to imaginal stimuli relating to combat experiences. These methods include systematic desensitization, already discussed in the context of the Peniston (1986) study, imaginal flooding ("implosion") therapy, and, most recently, eye movement desensitization and reprocessing (EMDR). The effectiveness of exposure methods with PTSD, in terms of standardized and nonstandardized indices of cognitive and personality variables, self- and clinician-based judgments, behavioral changes, and, in a few cases, psychophysiological changes, has been investigated. Reports include case studies, single-subject designs, and a few controlled treatment-outcome studies.

Imaginal flooding. In contrast to systematic desensitization—in which efforts are made to minimize affective reactions and countercondition responses incompatible with anxiety to trauma stimuli, including graded exposure to fear-eliciting stimuli—in imaginal flooding, a subject is essentially "bathed" in memories of traumatic material with no systematic attempt to control the intensity of emotional responses. The method involves the repeated rehearsal of affectively charged material in a clinical context while maintaining high levels of anxiety. Theoretically, in the absence of the original unconditioned stimulus (UCS) or other aversive stimuli, the procedure is designed to extinguish emotional reactions to the imagined stressor (Levis, 1980).

Case studies and single-subject designs. In one early case report on the use of flooding, Keane and Kaloupek (1982) observed effects resulting from repeated presentations of war-related material in the treatment of a Vietnam veteran whose PTSD symptoms included chronic anxiety, nightmares, insomnia, flashbacks, and social anxiety. During treatment, brief periods of relaxation were followed by therapist statements with details of a traumatic combat memory, related events, and emotional state, as well as efforts to engage the client in chronological accounts of the event. The patient was encouraged to retain images accompanied by anxiety until the emotion subsided. Across 22 days, repeated rehearsal of two scenes under these conditions resulted in dramatic improvement in terms of reduced HR during the scenes, increased hours of sleep, and lowered self-reports and ratings of anxiety on the STAI (state portion). Keane and Kaloupek concluded that imaginal flooding is an effective treatment component, but that effects of relaxation, flooding, and skills training were confounded in their procedures. Black and Keane (1982) essentially replicated these results with an older World War II veteran, and demonstrated lasting improvement over a longer follow-up period (see also Fairbank, Gross, & Keane, 1983).

Fairbank and Keane (1982) reported an interesting variation on a treatment design for the use of imaginal flooding in an effort to determine the extent of generalization of extinction effects. For each of two subjects, four traumatic scenes were obtained, along with assessment of self-reported distress, to each scene on a 10-point Subjective Units of Distress (SUDS) scale (cf. Wolpe, 1990). The degree of similarity between stimulus and response events for each memory was determined. During each treatment session, one scene was presented during flooding. The context and response cues were described by the therapist, who encouraged the patient to outline the chronological sequence and continue with images that evoked high states of anxiety. The patient's subjective distress declined during flooding with each scene. For two scenes with similar traumatic memories, there was evidence of distress reduction on the SUDS ratings (generalization of extinction), but not for the other two scenes with dissimilar memories. With a second veteran treated with these procedures, reduced SUDS ratings were obtained only after flooding on each of four rather dissimilar traumatic memories. Measures of skin conductance and HR showed little or no generalization effects on two of the scenes following sessions of flooding with the other two memories; but dramatic decreases were obtained after flooding on these psychophysiological measures. The authors concluded that extinction of arousal to a memory generalized to another memory only to the extent that they shared common stimulus and response elements. However, this study lacks clear and independent methods for establishing similarity of memories. The safest overall conclusion is that separate flooding treatment for each traumatic combat memory may be necessary to produce clear evidence of clinical improvement.

Controlled studies. In the first controlled study on the use of flooding therapy with PTSD, Keane, Fairbank, Caddell, and Zimering (1989) recruited

24 male combat veterans with PTSD and assigned them either to a therapy condition or waiting-list control. (Both groups continued on pharmacotherapy in the clinic during the intervention.) Treatment began with several sessions of relaxation training (D. Bernstein & Borkovec, 1973). In subsequent sessions, the clients were allowed a short period of relaxation (10 minutes), followed by a period of flooding (45 minutes) consisting of rehearsal of individualized traumatic combat scenes. Each session concluded with a short period of relaxation (10 minutes) and an attempt to "integrate" new information or emotions from the session (10 minutes). Pre- to posttreatment improvement (including at follow-up) was apparent in a number of questionnaires and self-report indices, including the BDI, state portion of the STAI, and several scales of the MMPI, as well as on therapist ratings. However, no improvement was obtained on measures of social adjustment.

Similarly, Cooper and Clum (1989) evaluated the effects of behavioral treatment using flooding in two groups of veterans (seven veterans per group) with clearly identified PTSD. One group received an imaginal flooding treatment combined with traditional psychotherapy and drug treatment, whereas the control group received the traditional treatment and medications only. At the end of each session, if a subject was experiencing high levels of anxiety, he was switched to relaxation and positive imagery. There was a maximum of nine sessions of actual flooding treatment, plus introductory and assessment interventions. Several months after treatment, the flooding group showed greater improvement in terms of subjectively reported anxiety, nightmares, a measure of sleep disturbance, state anxiety assessed with the STAI, and other measures. Heart rate was not affected by the procedures.

Another more recent study employing flooding methods, but not confounded with a relaxation component, was reported by Boudewyns and Hyer (1990). Of the 51 combat veterans who were recruited, 38 completed treatment (19 in the experimental condition and 19 controls). The subjects were given an extensive battery of assessment instruments prior to the study, including the SSCQ. Prior to treatment, subjects were fitted with electrodes and assessed for HR, skin conductance, and frontalis EMG levels during a period of quiet (baseline) and during 5-minute presentations of the stressful scenes. Each subject was also asked to rate the scenes on a 10-point SUDS scale. (The subjects' responses were later defined as the highest level of physiological activity to each scene in a 1-minute period within the 5-minute presentation.) Subsequently, the direct therapeutic exposure (DTE) group received 10–12 flooding sessions in accordance with procedures developed by Boudewyns and Shipley (1983), using (nontaped) versions of the material that had been taped from the SSCQs. Subjects in the control condition were given 10–12 sessions of "conventional therapy or counseling" in the VA setting.

Following treatment, all subjects were again provided the recorded tapes and some psychological evaluation. In terms of the physiological measures, there were strong and highly significant responses on all measures to the combat scenes, but there were no large effects due to treatment, and both groups showed similar patterns of responding. Similarly, SUDS ratings of the tapes also did not differ between the groups. However, there were significant treatment gains on a composite score of several variables assessed 3 months after treatment (anxiety/depression, vigor, alienation, and confidence in skills). Also, there was some evidence that the veterans' gains along psychological dimensions were related to amount of physiological change irrespective of treatment group—there were some statistically significant effects here. In summary, the effects reported by Boudewyns and Hyer were generally not consistent with the conceptual bases of flooding treatment (i.e., that the procedure produces extinction of anxiety responses to trauma-related cues). However, the treatment did produce some psychological gains on the instruments that assessed change after 3 months.

Eye movement desensitization and reprocessing. A third exposure method recently applied with veterans with PTSD is eye movement desensitization and reprocessing (EMDR), first described by Shapiro (1989). The technique essentially involves having the client identify a memory and assess its level of distress with a SUDS rating. Current memory-related negative self-cognitions are identified, as well as their corresponding desired positive cognitions—the latter given a rating of believability or "validity" (a "VoC" rating). Next, sets of eye movements ("saccades") are administered, in which the client is asked to visually track the back-and-forth movements of the therapist's hand for short periods of time (about 24 back-and-forth movements) while concentrating on an image of the memory, a negative belief, and related bodily sensations. Between sets of eye movements, clients are queried on the content of thoughts, images, feelings, and sensations during the eye movements. The technique is designed to be mainly client-centered, with little analysis or interpretation. In later stages of treatment, during "reprocessing," the client is asked to focus on his positive beliefs regarding the memory during further periods of induced eye movements. As pointed out by Puk (1991), the procedure does not require many of the features of other exposure techniques, including extended exposure to fear stimuli (as in flooding) or hierarchy construction and relaxation training (as in systematic desensitization).

Evidence on the effectiveness of EMDR in applications to veterans with PTSD is mixed. The first published study of EMDR with veterans was by Shapiro (1989), in which she reported the results of a controlled study of 22 subjects, some suffering from traumatic memories of the Vietnam war (others from childhood sexual molestation, sexual or physical assault, or emotional abuse). Subjects were randomly assigned to either an EMDR treatment group and a placebo control group (in which subjects described a traumatic memory in full detail and simply were asked intermittently for SUDS and VoC ratings). In the treatment group, SUDS and VoC ratings changed significantly, often within a single treatment session. Controls were then given delayed EMDR treatment, and their posttreatment ratings changed significantly in the predicted direction as well. Gains were maintained at a 3-month follow-up.

Boudewyns, Stwertka, Hyer, Albrecht, and Sperr (1993) reported the use of EMDR in a study of 20 Vietnam war combat veterans suffering from PTSD. All subjects described their most distressing memory. From this description, an individually tailored taped "script" was prepared. All subjects listened to the tape after baseline psychophysiological measures were taken and before treatment began. Subjects were assigned to one of three groups: (a) an EMDR group, given eye movement treatment for two sessions along the lines of Shapiro's (1991) methods, (b) an exposure control group, and (c) a control group. Subjects in the exposure control group were asked to recall a traumatic memory in the same manner and for the same amount of time as subjects in the treatment group, whereas subjects in the control group received standard clinical treatment. Although client SUDS and therapist ratings reflected positive change during the scripts for subjects in the treatment group, no corresponding changes were reflected on standardized scales and the physiological measures. The authors suggested that the use of the taped script may not have been a valid method of evaluating current negative cognitions associated with the traumatic incident. It may also be observed that two sessions of treatment may be insufficient to yield effects by this or any other exposure method.

Pitman et al. (1993) reported inconsistent results from the use of an eye movement procedure with 17 Vietnam combat veterans in a design that compared treatment to an eyes-fixed procedure. Relative to the control subjects, the eye movement group showed improvement in terms of measures of intrusive memories (on both intrusion and avoidance) and psychiatric symptoms expressed on the SCL–90–R scale (Derogatis, 1977), but not on other indicators of PTSD.

Lipke and Botkin (1992) also reported mixed results for five combat PTSD cases. The authors attributed the difference between the results of their study and Shapiro's (1989) to the fact that their subjects were all inpatients with severe psychopathology. Recently, Jensen (1994) reported negative results using EMDR with Vietnam combat veterans. However, that study has a number of methodological difficulties, including a short and possibly incomplete treatment phase (two sessions) and the use of relatively inexperienced therapists.

Summary

Overall, the results of a few relaxation studies and the comparatively large number of exposure studies demonstrate a mixed variety of beneficial effects for treatment of PTSD attributable to variations on these procedures. In general, major difficulties in research to date include relatively unsystematic use of standardized assessment methods across modalities, a limited amount of research in the relaxation area, and procedural differences that may have impacted on the variable results of exposure methods. Among the latter were the inclusion of a relaxation component in flooding studies done in the Keane laboratory but not in the Boudewyns laboratory, and the use of inordinately few sessions in some of the studies using the recent EMDR technique. Clearly, more research is needed on the relative benefits and specific effects of the wide variety of relaxation and exposure methods available for PTSD treatment.

RECENT RELAXATION AND EXPOSURE TREATMENTS

Paralleling earlier efforts, our own behavioral treatment program with veterans with PTSD has focused on two types of interventions: relaxation training per se and exposure treatment, specifically EMDR. Despite the generally positive history of relaxation training with anxiety disorders, the limited use of this method as the sole intervention in the combat PTSD area leaves its potential effectiveness in this context in doubt. Also, the relative role of relaxation in other therapies is not known, such as in some applications of flooding that explicitly include relaxation as a component (e.g., Keane et al., 1989).

General Methods

The subjects in our research program are drawn from a population of male veterans seeking services at the VA Medical Center in Honolulu. They have experienced combat in Vietnam, and have a diagnosis of PTSD. They are Caucasian or Hawaiian (in lesser numbers, Asian American) in ethnic extraction, and are younger than veterans without PTSD. They are also typically unemployed and unmarried, with service-connected disabilities and a relatively high reported rate of recent hospitalization for psychiatric disorders. Finally, they are as likely as not to report a substance abuse problem. (The characteristics of this population are described in detail by Carlson, Chemtob, Hedlund, Denny, & Rusnak, 1994.) In short, this is a seriously disordered group of veterans with multiple areas of personal distress, medical difficulties, and social maladjustment characteristic of PTSD in a Vietnam veteran population.

In the laboratory, a computerized electrophysiological monitoring and feedback system consists of an analogue to digital interface for modules that measure electromyographic (EMG) responses, heart rate (HR), peripheral temperature, and skin conductance (SCL). Headphones (for auditory, pure tone, biofeedback) and a cassette tape player are also used. For the EMG measurements, frontalis (forehead), sternomastoid (neck), bilateral trapezius (upper back), and forearm flexor (underarm), in accordance with standard placements, and the equally weighted average of these sites are monitored. Using fingers on the left hand, peripheral temperature, SCL, and HR are measured (the latter with a photoplethysmograph). A blood pressure (BP) cuff is positioned on the right arm. All of the physiological data are processed with an online computer. This equipment allows for consecutive and automatic 1-minute data averaging throughout all phases of the experiments. A separate BP monitor provides for measures of diastolic blood pressure (DBP) and systolic blood pressure (SBP).

Prefacing behavioral interventions, across several 1- to 2-hour sessions, a battery of psychometric tests and interview are administered. The instruments include the Mississippi Scale for Combat-Related PTSD, the IES, the MMPI–2, the CAPS, the BDI, the Spielberger STAI, the DES, and an 11-point Likert-type scale (0–10) devised by the authors for a self-rating of overall severity of "PTSD symptoms." In addition, each subject completes an SSCQ, in which he describes memories of specific personal combat incidents considered to be particularly traumatic (cf. Pitman et al., 1987). From these accounts, two personal scenes are summarized, and each is audiotaped in a 30- to 45-second segment by a therapist for script presentation during each subject's physiological assessment at pretreatment, posttreatment, and follow-up.

Treatment with EMG Biofeedback/Relaxation

A procedure formerly developed for comprehensive muscle relaxation training is currently being investigated in the laboratory. The method combines biofeedback during 40-minute sessions in the laboratory for muscle potentials as measured and averaged across the four sites (head, neck, upper back, and forearm), combined with a home practice procedure using cassette tapes of modified progressive relaxation instructions. Earlier research determined that traditional muscle biofeedback, on the frontal area alone, was not sufficient to induce generalized relaxation in other areas (Carlson, Basilio, & Heaukulani, 1983). But biofeedback, based on averaged combinations of muscle sites, was determined to be more effective in producing relaxation in each of the sites (Diaz & Carlson, 1984; Shirley, Burish, & Rowe, 1982). Moreover, research by Stoyva and others (cf. Stoyva & Carlson, 1993) has repeatedly shown the importance of home relaxation as a component of a biofeedback relaxation program. Therefore, it was reasoned that these procedures would generally impact on relaxation in the musculature in veterans with PTSD, and potentially on other measures of arousal as well.

In the portion of the study reported here, 19 Vietnam combat veterans were included. There was typically very high agreement among the psychometric scales in terms of PTSD diagnosis of these subjects. In addition, all subjects completed the SSCQ, and two scenes were scripted for use during assessment sessions. Following pretreatment assessment, the subjects were assigned to two groups: EMG relaxation ($n = 10$) and attentional control ($n = 9$). In two baseline sessions, the subjects' physiological responses were monitored in each of the baseline sessions, with no additional stimuli presented. At the end of Session 2 of baseline, the subjects remained in the experimental room and were assessed during the taped combat scripts.

EMG relaxation group. Following pretreatment, subjects in the EMG relaxation group began multisite EMG biofeedback training. Instructions outlined the function of the feedback stimulus (i.e., that it reflected general muscle tension in the areas measured), and general suggestions for relaxation were given. At this time, subjects in the EMG relaxation condition were also given the cassette tape containing relaxation instructions plus written instructions for daily home use. There were 12 treatment sessions, approximately 1 hour per session, two sessions per week.

At the end of treatment, the psychometric assessment instruments and psychophysiological assessment were readministered. For the latter, during these sessions, subjects were seated in the experimental room, as during treatment, and given instructions to sit quietly and relax while their physiological functions were monitored. In the second half of the session, the taped scripts were again presented. The questionnaires were administered following the physiological assessment.

Attentional control group. Following the pretreatment assessment, the attentional control group was invited to attend group sessions (conducted by one of the two EMG therapists) for 6 weeks as a prelude to later treatment. During the sessions, there were discussions of the physiological bases of PTSD, as well as the opportunity to discuss traumatic combat experiences, methods of dealing with stress, and other family and social events. This group acted essentially as a control for attentional effects due to appointments in the laboratory, meetings with a therapist, and other nonspecific treatment effects. At the end of training, these subjects were given the opportunity to obtain the multisite EMG and relaxation training.

In summary, the protocol consisted of psychometric and interview assessment, two baseline psychophysiological monitoring sessions, one pretreatment session identical to baseline except for administration of the combat-related scripts, 6 weeks of treatment or group meetings, and one posttreatment session identical to the pretreatment session. (A 3-month follow-up session is still in progress and is not reported here.)

Results and Discussion

The results are expressed in terms of both psychometric measures and physiological responses. The psychophysiological data of greatest interest are those obtained during pretreatment and posttreatment, including the periods in which the combat scripts from the SSCQs were presented. Selections of the most representative of these data are shown in Fig. 16.1. Pretreatment (open bars in the figure) was the psychophysiological assessment condition, in which the subjects were administered taped combat-related material. Procedurally, posttreatment (darker bars in the figure) was the identical session following 6 weeks of treatment or control procedures. (The data are means for the entire session, including periods during the stimulus presentations.) The top three graphs in Fig. 16.1 show the effectiveness of the EMG training/relaxation procedures in terms of relaxation effects on the somatic nervous system. Relative to pretreatment, at posttreatment the overall average EMG levels (from the four combined biofeedback-trained sites) and EMG levels from the frontalis training site, most commonly used in clinical research, as well as from the forearm all showed statistically significant reductions in the EMG relaxation group, but not in the control subjects. (The other two sites yielded nonsignificant effects.) In the bottom two graphs, similarly, HR showed a significant reduction from pretreatment to posttreatment in the EMG relaxation group only. Peripheral temperature changes, although not statistically significant, were consistent with the EMG changes in showing expected increases (i.e., relaxation effects despite presentation of the stressful stimuli) in the treatment group. By contrast, decreases in temperature (possible stressful effects due to the stimuli) were obtained in the control condition. SCL and BP effects, not shown in the figure, were not significant.

Some preliminary results of the psychometric assessment, several measures from which are summarized in Fig. 16.2, also document the effectiveness of the procedures. In particular, depression in the BDI and trait anxiety in the STAI scale showed greater levels of improvement in the EMG relaxation feedback condition. Notably, the global self-rating of severity of PTSD symptoms showed significant decreases at posttreatment in both groups. This result demonstrates the importance of a control for nonspecific effects in this study. The

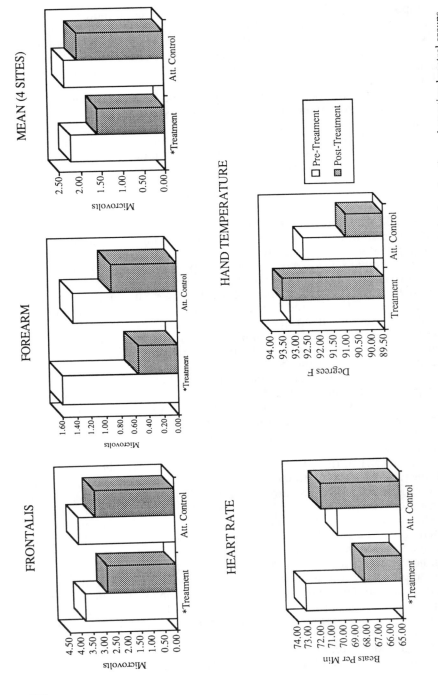

Figure 16.1 Means for psychophysiological measures during the pre- and posttreatment sessions for the relaxation and attentional control groups. Asterisk indicates $p < .05$.

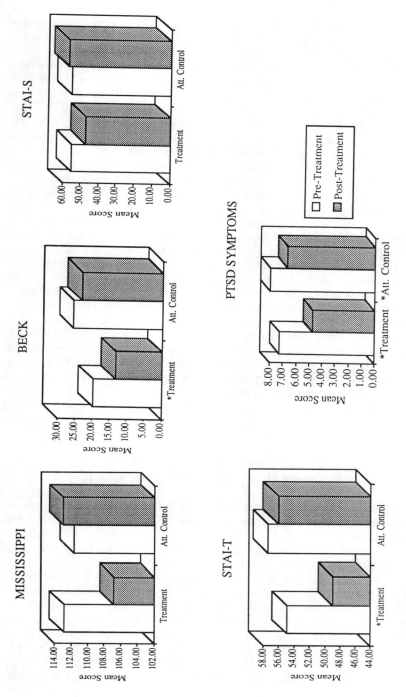

Figure 16.2 Means for the psychometric measures during the pre- and posttreatment sessions for the relaxation and attentional control groups. Asterisk indicates $p < .05$.

effects in terms of the Mississippi Scale used to provide a global assessment of PTSD were not significant, but in the expected direction. (The other scales are administered only at follow-up and are not available for analysis.)

The instrument added to assess the extent to which the subjects experienced intrusive thoughts or flashbacks related to their combat experiences (the IES) did not reflect the effects of the relaxation treatment. The apparent lack of effect on this direct measure of a cognitive class of symptoms for PTSD suggests that relaxation treatment may not impact on this dimension of the disorder, whereas selected other behavioral and somatic indices of arousal assessed by such scales as the BDI and the STAI were affected.

In summary, these results document the effectiveness of a form of arousal management (i.e., multisite EMG biofeedback and home relaxation practice) in the treatment of the arousal aspect of PTSD and some related psychometrically assessed emotional reactions. The advantages of a straightforward relaxation intervention for PTSD in combat veterans, especially with a biofeedback component, are: (a) its relative simplicity by comparison with many traditional psychotherapeutic approaches to PTSD with this population, (b) the enhanced motivation for participation of subjects observed using the biofeedback assist during relaxation training, (c) the opportunity for additional feedback for the veterans in the form of daily computer printouts of physiological responding and discussions with the therapist, and (d) the provision of an objective record of physiological change due to treatment. The generalization of treatment to at least one autonomic component—HR—considered important in the psychophysiological assessment of PTSD (e.g., Blanchard et al., 1986), and on the psychometric indices of anxiety and depression, was also encouraging. However, there is also some suggestion in the data that procedures designed to more directly affect intrusive cognitions (i.e., exposure therapies such as flooding or desensitization) may be needed to impact on this disorder along all of its dimensions.

Treatment with Exposure Therapy: Eye Movement Desensitization and Reprocessing

In contrast to the effects of relaxation training on general arousal aspects of PTSD, it is anticipated that procedures that target specific cues that evoke memories and anxiety in the disorder, such as exposure methods, should have effects on cognitive aspects, including intrusive thoughts, flashbacks, and stimulus-specific arousal (e.g., Fairbank & Nicholson, 1987).

Turning to EMDR treatment as an exposure technique, the related research reviewed earlier is at best inconclusive, especially in the context of treatment for PTSD in combat veterans, with results ranging from positive to mixed and negative. In view of the potential benefits, but the modest amount of supportive data on EMDR as a possible form of exposure treatment for PTSD in combat veterans, a second focus of research in the Hawaii PTSD laboratory has been on the application of a strict protocol for EMDR treatment to determine methods for producing reliable effects. Because this research is about midway to completion at this time, it is more illustrative to review several individual cases, rather than provide averages from small groups.

Method. Four veterans who have completed all procedures were drawn at random from the EMDR treatment condition for summary here. The subjects' ages ranged from 42 to 55 years. One subject was Asian American, and the remaining were Caucasian. Two were unemployed at the time of treatment, and three were divorced or separated. Following assessment under the general procedures outlined earlier for the relaxation study, the subjects' physiological responses were monitored during baseline and pretreatment sessions. During pretreatment, the taped combat scripts were presented. In the subsequent sessions, EMDR treatment was begun. The intervention consisted of a standardized introduction to the procedures, including a demonstration and rationale of the method. Each EMDR session was approximately 1 hour in duration, allowing for set-up time and some initial briefing in each session. The EMDR interventions consisted of a period in the first session during which each subject was asked to rate (a) the degree of emotional distress characterizing a memory using an 11-point SUDS (from *minimum* [0] to *maximum distress* [10]), and (b) the believability of a positive cognition regarding the memory (from *not at all believable* [1] to *completely true* [7]—the VoC scale). Then, approximately 3–15 times per session, each subject was asked to track the therapist's finger in 20–28 back-and-forth motions, inducing saccadic eye movements. During the eye movements, the subjects focused on related images, beginning with the memories generated for each of their two SSCQs, successively. In addition, each veteran was asked to keep in mind related negative cognitions and bodily sensations. As therapy progressed, when SUDS levels were low (in the 0–2 range), the subject was asked to focus on the positive cognition during the eye movement periods. The eye movement periods were each followed by a brief discussion period regarding material that the subject may have experienced during the eye movements. In accordance with general EMDR protocol, other material that surfaced during these periods was also dealt with in eye movement periods, as appropriate. Each session concluded with a debriefing. The general outline for EMDR treatment recommended by Shapiro (1991) was followed as closely as possible at all times. At the beginning of each treatment session, subjects were asked to rate the traumatic scene that had been reviewed during the previous session on the SUDS scale and positive cognitions on the VoC scale. Following 12 treatment sessions across 6 weeks (at posttreatment), and again after 3 months (follow-up), the cognitive-behavioral assessment instruments and psychophysiological assessment were readministered using the same format outlined for pretreatment.

Results and discussion. At pretreatment, overall the subjects manifested severe pathology on the MMPI–2. In terms of t scores (> 65), three of the subjects (AB, CD, and GH) showed elevations on the PTSD subscale and at least three of the clinical scales (the MMPI–2 scores of the fourth subject were not available). Subjects AB and CD also had high F scale scores ("overreporting" of symptoms), often seen in veterans with PTSD (Keane et al., 1984).

Table 16.1 shows results of interest in terms of the psychometric measures at pre- and posttreatment and at follow-up. Although substantial individual

Table 16.1 Scores on assessment instruments at pretreatment, posttreatment, and follow-up

				Instrument								
Subject	Miss	IES–I	IES–A	CAPS–Reexperience (Frequency/Intensity)	CAPS–Avoidance (Frequency/Intensity)	CAPS–Arousal (Frequency/Intensity)	CAPS–Overall (Frequency/Intensity)	PTSD Symptoms	BDI	STAI–S	STAI–T	DES
AB												
Pre	95	14	20	7/4	23/19	2/3	32/26	3	20	37	50	43
Post	94	3	1					0	4	27	41	
Follow-up	89	3	1	1/10	1/1	2/4	4/5	1	5	34	39	
CD												
Pre	111	23	26	8/12	19/15	21/19	48/46	8	26	54	66	17
Post	45	1	0					0	0	20	26	
Follow-up	60	1	1	0/0	0/0	0/0	0/0	0	0	34	39	
EF												
Pre	107	33	25	7/6	14/11	11/13	32/30	7	18	53	51	39
Post	67	6	1					0	1	22	25	
Follow-up	71	7	8	0/0	1/3	3/5	4/8	0	9	34	46	
GH												
Pre	116	33	23	12/12	18/13	18/19	48/44	6	15	37	40	25
Post	107	35	13					7	12	37	42	
Follow-up	105	23	14	8/12	8/7	14/12	30/31	6	16	43	41	

Note. Miss = Mississippi Scale for Combat-Related PTSD, IES = Impact of Events Scale, CAPS = Clinician Administered PTSD Survey, PTSD = Posttraumatic Stress Disorder, STAI = State–Trait Anxiety Inventory, DES = Dissociative Experiences Scale.

variation was found at pretreatment, the subjects as a group had high scores on the various measures of PTSD, including the Mississippi, the CAPS, the IES, and self-ratings of PTSD symptoms. In addition, indices of state and trait anxiety were elevated, as were the depression scores. Although DES scores were high in two cases (AB and EF), dissociation did not prove to be a problem in treatment. The physiological variables failed to show effects related to treatment, thus the data are not presented.

Subject AB. Turning to the individual subjects, AB is a combat veteran who never married, but was in a new relationship at the start of treatment. He was making efforts to reduce (but not stop) his usage of marijuana during the study, making this a difficult period of adjustment, including sleep difficulties and a chronic malaise, which the subject attributed to the change in his marijuana consumption. The problems presented by AB during pretreatment included: unemployment; situational anxiety; frequent reexperiencing of combat events; avoidance of thoughts, feelings, and situations associated with traumas; restricted affect; and social difficulties.

The subject began EMDR therapy with respect to two racially related traumatic memories described in his SSCQs—being confused with the enemy by a sentry and having a gun pushed into his chest, and being the target of verbal abuse by a group of fellow soldiers in a communications center. In the final session of treatment, the SUDS ratings of the two targeted memories had decreased and VoC ratings had increased. The subject indicated that he had virtually no other combat memories to present for therapy. Further, although he previously had thought about Vietnam at least once a day, now he indicated that he often did not have such thoughts at all. It was "easier to let go" of things in his past. As seen in Table 16.1, the subject's IES, BDI, and personal rating of PTSD symptoms were substantially lower at posttreatment and follow-up, but his Mississippi score was not. His anxiety scores were at lower, but moderate, levels both at posttreatment and follow-up. His CAPS scores at follow-up were greatly reduced.

Subject CD. This individual is a retired colonel with a history of alcohol abuse up to about 7 years prior to this study, followed by complete abstinence. He was twice divorced. In this case, EMDR treatment was focused on one memory, in which, in the middle of a bombardment, the subject was hit by a boot and a leg. A second target memory concerned his deep feeling of bitterness with regard to a young enemy soldier being treated in an American hospital, and thus taking a bed needed by Americans.

When assessed at posttreatment, this subject's SUDS dropped and his positive VoC ratings increased to a considerable degree. In addition, as shown in Table 16.1, the IES, Beck, STAI, Mississippi, and personal PTSD symptoms scores for CD were all reduced substantially. It is notable that, during the course of therapy, this subject spontaneously reconciled with three children from his first marriage, whom he had not seen for about 20 years. At 3-month follow-up, CD's CAPS scores were at 0, and his remaining scores were substantially lower than at intake (many at the 0 level), although some scores showed some partial reversal.

Subject EF. This subject was a retired Air Force Colonel, as well as a recovered alcoholic who was undergoing a divorce at the time of treatment. He had served combat flight duty in Vietnam and Laos, and military attache duty in Afghanistan. The subject had been captured and threatened by the enemy in Laos and Afghanistan, among other traumatic incidents. The subject began pretreatment with complaints of persistent reexperiencing of traumatic events, feelings of detachment, severe sleep disturbance, some anger, and other indicators of social maladjustment and avoidance.

This subject began exposure treatment with respect to memories regarding the loss of a fellow officer in another aircraft during a combat mission in Laos, and a beating and near death experience during capture at gunpoint in Afghanistan. By the final session of treatment, the SUDS ratings of the two targeted memories had declined and positive VoC ratings had increased substantially. Other decreases in EF's scores both at posttreatment and follow-up included his IES, BDI, STAI, and PTSD symptoms scores, some to 0 levels, as shown in Table 16.1. Also at follow-up, EF's CAPS scores were substantially reduced relative to pretreatment, although some increases in his STAI scores were also found, as was the case in some of the other subjects.

Subject GH. This veteran was employed but divorced, and indicated moderate use of alcohol on a daily basis. In many ways, GH was the most serious of these four subjects. He presented with several ongoing issues, most notably a serious sleep disorder and self-described anger control problems. He reported disturbing intrusive thoughts and recurrent bad dreams. He also indicated extreme attempts to avoid thoughts, feelings, and activities relevant to combat. The subject said that he was very upset with his current status, and reported a history of depression as well. The subject also had a history of physical abuse by his father and a number of other unresolved childhood issues.

Therapy was begun with respect to the memory of a sniper shooting his friend in the head while GH was standing close by. A second SSCQ memory had to do with hiding under a pile of decomposing garbage crawling with rats in order to surprise a sniper in Vietnam. GH was a cooperative subject, but he seemed to have much more difficulty working through his memories than the other subjects. He would often make efforts to avoid dealing with combat-related material, spending excessive time describing unrelated events. He complained of becoming more depressed, and maintained that reexposure to the memories of trauma was responsible. Despite offers of alternative treatments, he decided to complete EMDR training. (After follow-up, GH returned to obtain relaxation therapy, but terminated after four sessions.)

At the end of EMDR treatment, GH showed only modest signs of improvement. His SUDS ratings showed some reduction, but the ratings of his cognitions showed little change. Other test scores shown in Table 16.1 were consistent with the clinical impression that this subject's progress was somewhat less notable than that of the other subjects. In general, his scale scores at posttreatment and follow-up were mixed, with small changes in both directions and no clear pattern of improvement.

CONCLUSIONS

Although not conclusive at this stage of the research, the results of these relaxation and exposure interventions for combat PTSD are suggestive in several important respects. First, it appears that the multimodal assessment procedures yielded differential outcomes with respect to the clinical protocols. Muscle relaxation training had an effect in a therapeutic direction on the musculature and, to some extent, HR in a session following treatment that included reexposure to personal combat scripts. However, with the exception of measures of depression and anxiety, other psychometric indices were unaffected by the treatment. Second, the positive effects of the relaxation training on the physiological indices suggest that one important component of some of the exposure therapies previously studied—including systematic desensitization (Peniston, 1986) and some flooding protocols (e.g., Keane et al., 1989)—may have been physiological arousal reduction. Third, for the majority of subjects, the EMDR exposure protocol appeared to impact positively and to a large extent on a number of dimensions of PTSD assessed via standardized and interview procedures (a pattern that is being maintained as we continue to use this treatment protocol). Finally, however, the absence of any consistent physiological changes due to the EMDR exposure intervention suggests that positive effects may occur without underlying arousal reduction—a partial replication of results recently obtained in Boudewyns' laboratory (Boudewyns et al., 1993). Taken together, the outcomes of these separate manipulations imply that a more ideal protocol for treatment of PTSD may be one that takes a multimodal approach, combining arousal reduction and exposure interventions, perhaps as successive forms of treatment.

In the general behavioral approach to PTSD, these preliminary studies extend an increasing wealth of information regarding some powerful interventions for this disorder. Particular benefits to combat veterans appear to include relief from the effects of persistent reexperiencing of past trauma and possibly of at least some physiological and experiential manifestations of arousal. Continued work with behavioral models for PTSD, comprehensive assessment methods, and newly devised exposure techniques holds promise for further advances in the understanding and treatment of trauma victims.

REFERENCES

Abramson, L. Y., Seligman, M. E. P., & Teasdale, J. E. (1986). Learned helplessness in humans: Critique and reformulation. In J. C. Coyne (Ed.), *Essential papers on depression* (pp. 259–301). New York: New York University Press.

American Psychiatric Association. (1994). *Diagnostic and statistical manual of mental disorders,* (4th ed.). Washington, DC: Author.

Andreassi, J. L. (1989). *Psychophysiology: Human behavior and physiological response* (2nd ed.). Hillsdale, NJ: Lawrence Erlbaum Associates.

Barlow, D. H. (1988). *Anxiety and its disorders.* New York: Guilford.

Beck, A. T., Ward, C. H., Mendelson, M., Mock, J., & Erbaugh, J. (1961). An inventory for measuring depression. *Archives of General Psychiatry, 4,* 561–571.

Benson, H. (1975). *The relaxation response.* New York: Morrow.

Bernstein, D. A., & Borkovec, T. D. (1973). *Progressive muscle relaxation training.* Champaign, IL: Research Press.

Bernstein, E. M., & Putnam, F. W. (1986). Development, reliability, and validity of a dissociation scale. *The Journal of Nervous and Mental Disease, 174,* 727–735.

Black, J. L., & Keane, T. M. (1982). Implosive therapy in the treatment of combat-related fears in a World War II veteran. *Journal of Behavior Therapy & Experimental Psychiatry, 13,* 163.

Blake, D., Weathers, F., Nagy, L., Kaloupek, D., Klauminzer, G., Charney, D., & Keane, T. (1990, September). A clinician rating scale for assessing current and lifetime PTSD: The CAPS-1. *Behavioral Assessment Review,* pp. 187–188.

Blanchard, E. B. (1990). Elevated basal levels of cardiovascular responses in Vietnam veterans with PTSD: A health problem in the making? *Journal of Anxiety Disorders, 4,* 223–237.

Blanchard, E. B., Kolb, L. C., Gerardi, R. J., Ryan, P., & Pallmeyer, T. P. (1986). Cardiac response to relevant stimuli as an adjunctive tool for diagnosing post-traumatic stress disorder in Vietnam veterans. *Behavior Therapy, 17,* 592–606.

Blanchard, E. B., Kolb, L. C., Pallmeyer, T. P., & Gerardi, R. J. (1982). A psychophysiology study of post traumatic stress disorder in Vietnam veterans. *Psychiatric Quarterly, 54,* 220–229.

Blanchard, E. B., Kolb, L. C., Taylor, A. E., & Wittrock, D. A. (1989). Cardiac response to relevant stimuli as an adjunct in diagnosing post-traumatic stress disorder: Replication and extension. *Behavior Therapy, 20,* 535–543.

Boudewyns, P. A., & Hyer, L. (1990). Physiological response to combat memories and preliminary treatment outcome in Vietnam veteran PTSD patients treated with direct therapeutic exposure. *Behavior Therapy, 21,* 63–87.

Boudewyns, P. A., & Shipley, R. H. (1983). *Flooding and implosive therapy: Direct therapeutic exposure in clinical practice.* New York: Plenum.

Boudewyns, P. A., Stwertka, S. A., Hyer, L. A., Albrecht, J. W., & Sperr, E. V. (1993). Eye movement desensitization for PTSD of combat: A treatment outcome pilot study. *The Behavior Therapist, 16,* 29–33.

Brooks, J. S., & Scarano, T. (1985). Transcendental meditation in the treatment of post-Vietnam adjustment. *Journal of Counseling and Development, 64,* 212–215.

Butcher, J. N., Dahlstrom, W. G., Graham, J. R., Tellegen, A., & Kaemmer, B. (1989). *Manual for the restandardized Minnesota Multiphasic Personality Inventory: MMPI–2.* Minneapolis, MN: University of Minnesota Press.

Carlson, J. G. (1974). Preconditioning the effects of shock-correlated reinforcement. *Journal of Experimental Psychology, 103,* 409–413.

Carlson, J. G., Basilio, C., & Heaukulani, J. (1983). Transfer of EMG training: Another look at the generalization issue. *Psychophysiology, 20,* 530–536.

Carlson, J. G., Chemtob, C. M., Hedlund, N. L., Denny, D. R. & Rusnak, K. (1994). Characteristics of veterans in Hawaii with and without diagnoses of post-traumatic stress disorder. *Hawaii Medical Journal, 83,* 314–318.

Carlson, J. G., & Hatfield, E. (1992). *Psychology of emotion.* New York: Holt, Rinehart & Winston.

Carlson, J. G., & Wielkiewicz, R. M. (1974). Discriminative properties of shock-correlated reinforcement in an operant context. *Behavioral Research Methods and Instrumentation, 6,* 10–12.

Chemtob, C. M., & Carlson, J. G. (1994, May). *A theoretical model for the systematic treatment of PTSD.* Paper presented at the annual meeting of the Western Psychological Association, Kona, HI.

Chemtob, C. M., Roitblat, H., Hamada, R., Carlson, J., & Twentyman, C. (1988). A cognitive action theory of post-traumatic stress disorder. *Journal of Anxiety Disorders, 2,* 253–275.

Cooper, N. A., & Clum, G. A. (1989). Imaginal flooding as a supplementary treatment for PTSD in combat veterans: A controlled study. *Behavior Therapy, 20,* 381–391.

Davidson, J., Swartz, M., Storck, M., Krishnan, R. R., & Hammett, E. (1985). A diagnostic and family study of post traumatic stress disorder. *American Journal of Psychiatry, 142,* 90–93.

Derogatis, L. R. (1977). *SCL-90-R administration, scoring, and procedures manual* (Vol. 1). Baltimore: Clinical Psychometric Research.

Diaz, C., & Carlson, J. G. (1984). Single- and successive-site EMG training in responding to anticipated pain. *Journal of Behavioral Medicine, 7,* 231–246.

Fairbank, J. A., Gross, R. T., & Keane, T. M. (1983). Treatment of posttraumatic stress disorder. Evaluating outcome with a behavioral code. *Behavior Modification, 7,* 557–568.

Fairbank, J. A., & Keane, T. M. (1982). Flooding for combat-related stress disorders: Assessment of anxiety reduction across traumatic memories. *Behavior Therapy, 13,* 499–510.

Fairbank, J. A., & Nicholson, R. A. (1987). Theoretical and empirical issues in the treatment of post-traumatic stress disorder in Vietnam veterans. *Journal of Clinical Psychology, 43,* 44–55.

Foa, E. B., Steketee, G., & Rothbaum, B. O. (1989). Behavioral/cognitive conceptualizations of post-traumatic stress disorder. *Behavior Therapy, 20,* 155–176.

Helzer, J. E., Robins, L. N., & McEvoy, L. (1987). Posttraumatic stress disorder in the general population: Findings from the Epidemiologic Catchment Area survey. *New England Journal of Medicine, 317,* 1630–1634.

Hickling, E. J., Sison, G. F. P., Jr., & Vanderploeg, R. D. (1986). Treatment of posttraumatic stress disorder with relaxation and biofeedback training. *Biofeedback and Self-Regulation, 8,* 125–134.

Horowitz, M., Wilner, N., & Alvarez, W. (1979). Impact of Events Scale: A measure of subjective stress. *Psychological Medicine, 41,* 209–218.

Jacobson, E. (1938). *Progressive relaxation* (2nd ed.). Chicago: University of Chicago Press.

Jensen, J. A. (1994). An investigation of eye movement desensitization and reprocessing (EMD/R) as a treatment for posttraumatic stress disorder (PTSD) symptoms of Vietnam combat veterans. *Behavior Therapy, 25,* 311–325.

Kardiner, A. (1941). *The traumatic neuroses of war.* New York: Harper & Row.

Keane, T. M. (1989). Behavior therapy mini-series. Post-traumatic stress disorder: Current status and future directions. *Behavior Therapy, 20,* 149–153.

Keane, T. M., Fairbank, J. A., Caddell, J. M., & Zimering, R. T. (1989). Implosive (flooding) therapy reduces symptoms of PTSD in Vietnam combat veterans. *Behavior Therapy, 20,* 245–260.

Keane, T. M., Fairbank, J. A., Caddell, J. M., Zimering, R. T., & Bender, M. E. (1985). A behavioral approach to assessing and treating PTSD in Vietnam veterans. In C. R. Figley (Ed.), *Trauma and its wake* (pp. 257–294). New York: Brunner/Mazel.

Keane, T. M., & Kaloupek, D. G. (1982). Imaginal flooding in the treatment of a posttraumatic stress disorder. *Journal of Consulting and Clinical Psychology, 50,* 138–140.

Keane, T. M., Malloy, P. F., & Fairbank, J. A. (1984). The empirical development of an MMPI subscale for the assessment of combat-related post traumatic stress disorder. *Journal of Consulting and Clinical Psychology, 52,* 888–891.

Keane, T. M., Weathers, F. W., & Kaloupek, D. G. (1992). Psychological assessment of post-traumatic stress disorder. *PTSD Research Quarterly, 3,* 1–3.

Kilpatrick, D. G., Best, C. L., Veronen, L. J., Amick, A. E., Villeponteaux, L. A., & Ruff, G. A. (1985). Mental health correlates of criminal victimization: A random community survey. *Journal of Consulting and Clinical Psychology, 53,* 866–873.

Kolb, L. C. (1984). The post traumatic stress disorders of combat: A subgroup with a conditioned emotional response. *Military Medicine, 149,* 237–243.

Kosten, T. R., Mason, J. W., Guiller, E. L., Ostroff, R. B., & Harkness, L. (1987). Sustained urinary norepinephrine and epinephrine elevation in posttraumatic stress disorder. *Psychoneuroendocrinology, 12,* 13–20.

Kulka, R. A., Schlenger, W., Fairbank, J. A., Hough, R. L., Jordan, B. K., Marmar, C. R., & Weiss, D. S. (1988). *National Vietnam veterans readjustment study advance data report: Preliminary findings from the national survey of the Vietnam generation* (Executive Summary). Washington, DC: Veterans Administration.

Kulka, R. A., Schlenger, W. E., Fairbank, J. A., Hough, R. L., Jordan, B. K., Marmar, C. R., & Weiss, D. S. (1991). Assessment of posttraumatic stress disorder in the community: Prospects and pitfalls from recent studies of Vietnam veterans. *Psychological Assessment: A Journal of Consulting and Clinical Psychology, 3,* 547–560.

Levis, D. J. (1980). Implementing the technique of implosive therapy. In A. Goldstein & E. B. Foa (Eds.), *Handbook of behavioral interventions: A clinical guide* (pp. 92–151). New York: Wiley.

Lipke, H., & Botkin, A. (1992). Brief case studies of eye movement desensitization and reprocessing with chronic post-traumatic stress disorder. *Psychotherapy, 29,* 591–595.

Malloy, P. F., Fairbank, J. A., & Keane, T. M. (1983). Validation of a multimethod assessment of posttraumatic stress disorders in Vietnam veterans. *Journal of Consulting and Clinical Psychology, 51,* 488–494.

Martin, I., & Levey, A. B. (1985). Conditioning, evaluations and cognitions: An axis of integration. *Behaviour Research and Therapy, 23,* 167–175.

McCaffrey, R. J., Lorig, T. S., Pendrey, D. L., McCutcheon, N. B., & Garrett, J. C. (1993). Odor-induced EEG changes in PTSD Vietnam veterans. *Journal of Traumatic Stress, 6,* 213–224.

McFall, M. E., Murburg, M. M., Roszell, D. K., & Vieth, R. C. (1989). Psychophysiologic and neuroendocrine findings in posttraumatic stress disorder: A review of theory and research. *Journal of Anxiety Disorders, 3,* 243–257.

Mowrer, O. H. (1947). On the dual nature of learning: A reinterpretation of "conditioning" and "problem solving." *Harvard Educational Review, 17,* 102–148.

Mowrer, O. H. (1960). *Learning theory and behavior.* New York: Wiley.

Muraoka, M. (1994). *Twenty-four hour ambulatory blood pressure and heart rate monitoring in Vietnam veterans.* Unpublished doctoral dissertation, University of Hawaii, Honolulu.

Orr, S. P., Claiborn, J. M., Altman, B., Forgue, D. F., deJong, J. P., & Pitman, R. K. (1990). Psychometric profile of posttraumatic stress disorder, anxious, and healthy Vietnam veterans: Correlations with psychophysiologic responses. *Journal of Consulting and Clinical Psychology, 58,* 329–355.

Paige, S. R., Reid, G. M., Allen, M. G., & Newton, J. E. (1990). Psychophysiological correlates of posttraumatic stress disorder in Vietnam veterans. *Biological Psychiatry, 27,* 419–430.

Pavlov, I. P. (1927). *Conditioned reflexes.* London: Oxford University Press.

Peniston, E. G. (1986). EMG biofeedback-assisted desensitization treatment for Vietnam combat veterans' post-traumatic stress disorder. *Clinical Biofeedback and Health, 9,* 35–41.

Pfeifer, M. A., Ward, K., Malpass, T., Stratton, J., Halter, J., Evans, M., Beiter, L. A., Harker, L. A., & Porte, D. (1984). Variations in circulating catecholamines fail to alter human platelet alpha-e-adrenergic receptor number or affinity for yohimbe or dihydroergocryptine. *Journal of Clinical Investigation, 74,* 1063–1072.

Pitman, R. K., & Orr, S. P. (1990). Twenty-four hour urinary cortisol and catecholamine excretion in combat-related posttraumatic stress disorder. *Biological Psychiatry, 27,* 245–247.

Pitman, R. K., Orr, S. P., Altman, B., Longpre, R. E., Poire, R. E., & Lasko, N. B. (1993). *A controlled study of eye movement desensitization/reprocessing (EMDR) treatment for post-traumatic stress disorder.* Paper presented at the annual meeting of the American Psychiatric Association, Washington, DC.

Pitman, R. K., Orr, S. P., Forgue, D. F., Altman, B., de Jong, J. B., & Herz, L. R. (1990). Psychophysiologic responses to combat imagery of Vietnam veterans with posttraumatic stress disorder versus other anxiety disorders. *Journal of Abnormal Psychology, 99,* 49–54.

Pitman, R. K., Orr, S. P., Forgue, D. F., de Jong, J. B., & Claiborn, J. M. (1987). Psychophysiological assessment of posttraumatic stress disorder imagery in Vietnam combat veterans. *Archives of General Psychiatry, 44,* 970–975.

Puk, G. (1991). Treating traumatic memories: A case report on the eye movement desensitization procedure. *Journal of Behavior Therapy & Experimental Psychiatry, 22,* 149–151.

Schultz, J. H., & Luthe, W. (1959). *Autogenic training: A psychophysiological approach in psychotherapy.* New York: Grune & Stratton.

Seligman, M. E. P. (1975). *Helplessness: On depression, development, and death.* San Francisco: W. H. Freeman.

Seligman, M. E. P., & Johnston, J. (1973). A cognitive theory of avoidance learning. In F. J. McGuigan & B. Lumsden (Eds.), *Contemporary approaches to conditioning and learning.* New York: Wiley.

Shapiro, F. (1989). Eye movement desensitization: A new treatment for posttraumatic stress disorder. *Journal of Behavior Therapy & Experimental Psychiatry, 20,* 211–217.

Shapiro, F. (1991). Eye movement desensitization & reprocessing procedure: From EMD to EMD/R—A new model for anxiety and related traumata. *The Behavior Therapist, 14,* 133–135.

Shirley, M., Burish, T., & Rowe, C. (1982). Effectiveness of multiple-site EMG biofeedback in the reduction of arousal. *Biofeedback and Self-Regulation, 7,* 167–184.

Solomon, R. L., & Wynne, L. C. (1954). Traumatic avoidance learning: The principles of anxiety conservation and partial irreversibility. *Psychological Review, 61,* 353–385.

Spielberger, C. D., Gorsuch, R. L., & Lushene, R. E. (1970). *STAI manual for the State–Trait Inventory.* Palo Alto, CA: Consulting Psychologists Press.

Stamm, B. H., & Varra, E. M. (Eds.). (1993). *Instrumentation in stress, trauma and adaptation.* Oswego, NY: The International Society for Traumatic Stress Studies.

Stampfl, T. G., & Levis, D. J. (1967). Essentials of implosive therapy: A learning theory-based psychodynamic behavioral therapy. *Journal of Abnormal Psychology, 72,* 496–503.

Stoyva, J. M., & Budzynski, T. (1974). Cultivated low arousal—an anti-stress response? In L. V. DiCara (Ed.), *Recent advances in limbic and autonomic nervous system research* (pp. 369–394). New York: Plenum.

Stoyva, J. M., & Carlson, J. G. (1993). A coping/rest model of relaxation and stress management. In L. Goldberger & S. Breznitz (Eds.), *Handbook of stress: Theoretical and clinical aspects* (pp. 724–756). New York: The Free Press/Macmillan.

Wolpe, J. (1958). *Psychotherapy by reciprocal inhibition.* Palo Alto, CA: Stanford University Press.

Wolpe, J. (1990). *The practice of behavior therapy* (4th ed.). New York: Pergamon.

Author Index

Subject Index